MW00618143

THOMAS MANN'S WORLD

THOMAS MANN'S WORLD

Empire, Race, and the Jewish Question

TODD KONTJE

THE UNIVERSITY OF MICHIGAN PRESS

ANN ARBOR

2014   2013   2012   2011   4   3   2   1

A CIP catalog record for this book is available from the British Library.

Library of Congress Cataloging-in-Publication Data

Kontje, Todd Curtis, 1954–
    Thomas Mann's world : empire, race, and the Jewish question / Todd
Kontje.
        p.   cm.
    Includes bibliographical references and index.
    ISBN 978-0-472-11746-8 (acid-free paper)
    1. Mann, Thomas, 1875–1955—Criticism and interpretation.
2. Mann, Thomas, 1875–1955—Political and social views.   3. Jews in
literature.   4. Race in literature.   5. Literature and society—
Germany—History—20th century.   I. Title.

PT2625.A44Z73245   2010
833'.912—dc22   2010020150

Preface

The following study examines the interrelated themes of racial difference and the "Jewish question" in Thomas Mann's fiction. Although it focuses on Mann as the representative German writer of the early twentieth century, it touches on themes that have continuing relevance today. The effort to come to terms with the National Socialist past has arguably been the defining feature of postwar German society. As an iconic figure of this period, Thomas Mann was not only important in his time, but has inspired ongoing debates in the decades since his death. To many he remains the embodiment of the "good German," the most prominent member of the German exile community and the most outspoken opponent of Hitler and the Nazis. Increasingly, however, such a characterization of Mann and his fiction seems simplistic at best. As Mann insisted in his programmatic lecture "Germany and the Germans," delivered in the final months of the Second World War, there are not two Germanies, one bad and one good, but rather only one, in which the good and bad are intertwined. The same held true for himself, Mann continued: "I have it all within me, too; I have experienced it all myself."

Mann's conflicted response to the "Jewish question" is a case in point. Mann had close personal relations with individual Jews, wrote novels and novellas based on characters from the Old Testament, and publicly declared himself a friend of the Jews and an enemy of anti-Semitism; Mann was even suspected of being Jewish at various times in his career. At the same time, one finds occasional anti-Semitic remarks in his diaries and letters, and a steady stream of negative Jewish stereotypes in his fiction. While I do not to deny the less savory aspects of Mann and his fiction, I am also not out to issue a blanket condemnation of the man and his works. If the time for hagiography of Germany's cultural heroes is past, the time for demonization is as well. That a man of Mann's background shared some of the prejudices of his contemporaries is not admirable, but also not astonishing. That when push came to shove Mann usually said and did the right thing *is* admirable, particularly in comparison with so many of his contemporaries who did not.

My goal in this study is to broaden the scope in which we view the "Jewish question" in Mann's life and work in two ways: first, by situating it in the context of Mann's creative process, which involved a sense of being multiply stigmatized—because of his "mixed blood" from his mother's Brazilian heritage, his repressed homosexual desires, and his role as an artist in bourgeois society—but also a sense of being greatly distinguished as the patrician son of a senator and the leading representative of German culture. Writing was a delicate balancing act for Thomas Mann, as he drew inspiration from potentially destructive forces. As a result, stigmatized others in his fiction can often be inverted without notice into representations of repressed aspects of the self. Second, I consider Mann's response to the "Jewish question" and the representation of Jews in his literary works in the context of his attentiveness to race in an age of European imperialism and colonialism. "Jewishness" is one of several stigmatized categories that also include racial difference, sexual deviance, or geographical distance from northern Europe. Rather than identifying individual figures in his fiction as definitely and exclusively Jewish, I am interested in the way in which stigmatized categories seep into one another in a kind of symbolic osmosis. I thus place the representative author of the German nation into global context, while at the same time underscoring his rootedness in the local culture of Lübeck. To be a German national between 1875 and 1955 was also to be provincial and imperial.

Understood narrowly, globalization is a post–Cold War phenomenon characterized by the digital revolution, the rise of multinational corporations, ecological crisis, mass migration, and new forms of global conflict. From a longer historical perspective, however, recent developments mark only the acceleration of a process of cross-cultural contact and commercial exchange that has been under way since at least the early modern age of exploration. Current challenges to the exclusive sovereignty of the nation-state remind us that modern nationalism is of relatively recent origin and that individual nations have always existed in tension between local traditions and global concerns. Mann has traditionally been read as the representative author of the German nation at a time when German nationalism rose to catastrophic heights, but he was also a writer steeped in the local culture of Lübeck and shaped by its contacts with the larger world during the age of empire.

Today's process of globalization has opened the possibility of an unprecedented movement of peoples and exchange of ideas, but it has also provoked backlash in the form of local patriotism, religious fundamentalism, and ethnic nationalism. The Serbian campaign of "ethnic cleansing" that resulted in the genocide of untold numbers of Bosnian Muslims is only one example of a resurgent ethnic nationalism that many thought was extinct, at least in post-Holocaust Europe. Reunified Germany has been scarred by repeated outbreaks of violence against those perceived as different, by virtue of race, religion, or place of origin. One of the most appealing features of Mann's thought that emerges from this study is his consistent opposition to any form of nationalism based on ethnic "purity." He was not without prejudice, as we shall see, but he repeatedly emphasized the need for cosmopolitan openness and cultural diversity.

My effort to situate Mann's work in a worldly context reflects a broad trend in literary studies in recent decades. Beginning with the New Historicism of Steven Greenblatt and others, and particularly with Edward Said's books *Orientalism* and *Culture and Imperialism*, there has been a turn away from the formalist literary analysis that dominated postwar criticism toward an effort to view literature as a dynamic force within particular historical and cultural contexts. My goal throughout *Thomas Mann's World* is to avoid interpreting his works in terms of abstract philosophical categories, but to see how he fleshes out the recurrent structure of his imagination in terms of specific cultural content. The purpose is not, however, to deny or downplay the specifically literary, aesthetic qualities of Mann's fiction. Quite the opposite, in fact. Mann's work reveals a density of detail and a subtlety of thought that demand—and reward—close reading. His grasp of character, gift for storytelling, and sense of humor make his fiction a source of great pleasure as well as insight into the man and his times.

I would like to thank Professor Klaus R. Scherpe and the Alexander von Humboldt Foundation for supporting a three-month fellowship during the early stages of this project during the fall of 2005. Thanks also to Professors Heinrich Detering and Gerhardt Lauer for their collegiality and the invitation to present work in progress at the Georg August Universität in Göttingen. I also thank Hans Rudolf Vaget for his invitation to contribute to the Oxford University Press casebook on *The Magic Mountain* and for his many kind words of support in the course of this project. Tobias Boes extended a generous offer to present my work at the University of Notre Dame; my thanks to him and to Mark W. Roche and Robert E. Norton for their friendship and thoughtful questions during my visit. Professor Stefanie Ohnesorg and the faculty members of the Department of Germanic, Slavic, and Asian Languages at the University of Tennessee, Knoxville, invited me to present my work in the spring of 2007; I thank them for their insightful comments and generous hospitality. I am grateful for the efficient and friendly support of Ms. Gabriele

viii PREFACE

Hollender and other curators at the Thomas Mann Archives in Zurich, Switzerland. The two anonymous readers for the University of Michigan Press offered invaluable insights and caught many errors; my thanks to them for their attentive reading and perceptive comments. Professor Anthony Edwards at the University of California, San Diego, read the entire manuscript and also provided many useful suggestions. Finally, I thank Tom Dwyer at the University of Michigan Press for his initial interest in the project and his unflagging support of my work. Words are insufficient to express my gratitude for the companionship and love of Betsy, Nick, and Tim while I have been at work on the book and also when not.

Revised portions of my article "Thomas Mann's *Wälsungenblut:* The Married Artist and the 'Jewish Question,'" *PMLA* 123 (2008): 109–24, have been reprinted by permission of the copyright owner, The Modern Language Association of America. I am also grateful for permission to reprint revised portions of my "Modern Masculinities on the Magic Mountain," *Thomas Mann's The Magic Mountain: A Casebook,* ed. Hans Rudolf Vaget (Oxford: Oxford University Press, 2008), 71–93, and "Exotic Heimat: Province, Nation, and Empire in Thomas Mann's *Buddenbrooks,*" *German Studies Review* 29 (2006): 495–514.

Contents

CHAPTER ONE

Introduction

Interest in Thomas Mann has undergone a remarkable renaissance in recent decades. In reviewing the results of a widely reported survey conducted in 1975 on the one hundredth anniversary of Mann's birth, the prominent literary critic Marcel Reich-Ranicki noted that many contemporary German authors were reluctant to discuss their attitude toward the German Nobel Prize laureate: many were simply indifferent to this icon of modern German literature, while others were openly hostile.[1] Although sales of Mann's works remained strong among the general public, his perception as an old-fashioned realist and political conservative did not sit well with authors and intellectuals weaned on agitprop and student protest. Within a few years, however, that perception began to change. The gradual release of Mann's diaries, beginning in the late 1970s, afforded a look behind Mann's carefully groomed public facade, revealing carefully repressed aspects of his life, including—most sensationally—the extent of his homosexual desires. A more recent miniseries made for German television with the acclaimed actor Armin Mueller-Stahl cast as Thomas Mann has since created a sense of intimate familiarity with the author among many viewers unlikely to work their way through the ten volumes of Mann's diaries.[2]

Getting to know Mann better has not necessarily made him more likable. Marianne Krüll's muckraking portrait of the extended Mann clan cast Thomas in the role of a poisonous spider that sucked the life from his hapless family and friends.[3] Klaus Harpprecht's monumental biography of 1995 attacks Mann at every turn, accusing him of being soft on Communism, hard on his children, and wrong about nearly every decision he made in his life.[4] Most damning have been Mann's scattered comments about Jews in his diaries and previously unpublished essays that, when coupled with a number of negative Jewish stereotypes in his literary works, have created the impression that the most outspoken member of the exile community against Hitler and German National Socialism was in fact an anti-Semite.

In the following study, I examine Thomas Mann as the representative German author of the Age of Empire. I argue that his comments about Jews and the Jewish characters in his fiction must be placed in the larger context of his attentiveness to racial difference in general, both in the world at large and in himself. Mann's formative years coincided with the heyday of European imperialism, and he wrote his major works in response to the world wars unleashed by European nations eager to defend and extend their colonial possessions. I argue that Mann is a worldly author—not in the benign sense that he was an eloquent spokesman for a pan-European cosmopolitanism who had witnessed the evils of nationalism gone mad, although he was that, too—but in the sense of a writer whose personal prejudices reflected those of the world around him, a writer whose deeply autobiographical fiction not only expressed the concerns of the German nation, as he liked to claim, but also of the world in an era of imperial conquest and global conflict.

Beginning in Brazil

Johann Ludwig Hermann Bruhns, a young man from one of the most prominent families in Lübeck, set sail in 1840 to seek his fortune in Brazil.[5] Here the tall, blond, northern German, who soon began to call himself Senhor João Luiz Germano Bruhns, did well. He established a successful business in the export of coffee and sugar, and eventually became one of the leading citizens of the German-speaking community. In 1848 Bruhns married Maria da Silva, the daughter of a wealthy family of Portuguese origins that had been living in Brazil for several generations, and it was in Brazil that she gave birth to a daughter named Julia, the mother of Thomas Mann.

"It was in the jungle, not far from the Atlantic Ocean, south of the equator, where Dodo was born," recalled Julia Mann in later years, referring to herself in the third person by her childhood nickname.[6] Her youngest son Viktor, who had a flare for the melodramatic, fleshed out the scene as follows:

> On August 14th, 1851, as the married couple traveled through the jungle from one of its plantations to another near Angra—the mistress in a sedan chair, the master on horseback, slaves in front and behind—there was a sudden stop. The mistress had to be bedded quickly beneath the trees. Black women rushed in and soon presented their master with a little daughter, while up above parrots screeched, curious monkeys peered down, and tiny hummingbirds flitted like colorful rays through the shadows. The parents nicknamed the little one "Dodo," and she was baptized as Julia. Julia da Silva Bruhns: that was our mother.[7]

In Viktor Mann's rapt description, the event takes on the trappings of a jungle nativity scene: reverent slaves assist at the birth, while curious monkeys look on like wondering shepherds and tropical birds soar like exulting angels.

The story of Julia da Silva Mann's birth in Brazil and subsequent move to Lübeck reminds us how deeply Thomas Mann was rooted in the age of European imperialism and colonialism. Toward the end of his life, Mann told an audience in Chicago that he had spent the first half of his life in a political atmosphere dominated by "the continental hegemony of Germany under Bismarck and the highpoint of the British Empire under Victoria."[8] Mann was born in 1875, just four years after the founding of the German Reich, and the first four decades of his life coincided with Germany's effort to consolidate a sense of collective national identity at home and to establish an empire abroad. Mann's father was a leading citizen of a Hanseatic city-state that was the hub of a northern European trading network established in the late Middle Ages, but his mother's Brazilian origins point toward the modern development of transatlantic, and, indeed, global commerce and colonialism. The Portuguese emperor João VI had signed a decree in 1820 that welcomed Germans to Brazil, and by midcentury a considerable number of German settlements had been established.[9] At a time when Lübeck was still trying to recover from the devastating effects of the Napoleonic occupation at the beginning of the century, the colonies offered ambitious young men like Johann Bruhns a chance to get ahead. The colonies could also be used as a dumping ground for those who had caused scandal at home. Johann Bruhns was accompanied on his journey by two cousins, "black sheep" that the family banished to the New World;[10] decades later, Thomas Mann's dissolute brother-in-law Erik Pringsheim would be sent off to Argentina, where he probably committed suicide after running up gambling debts.[11] Armin Martens, the blond boy whom Thomas Mann immortalized as Hans Hansen in *Tonio Kröger,* fled Lübeck in the wake of a scandal in 1899 and died miserably several years later in German South-West Africa (Namibia).[12]

The circumstances surrounding Julia da Silva Mann's birth and early childhood underscore two paradoxically related aspects of the European mentality during the imperial era: the importance of racial distinctions and the inherent instability of precisely those distinctions. Julia's father had gone off to the New World as a quintessential European explorer and colonialist, mapping the wilderness, opening new trade routes, establishing a business, and marrying into a family of wealth and high social status. Until she was about six years old, his daughter Julia enjoyed the carefree life of a privileged child: playing on the beach at the edge of the jungle under the watchful eye of her nanny, a slave named Anna;[13] eating tropical fruits; and visiting her grandparents on their large plantation. All that changed when Julia's mother died and her father decided to send her and her brothers back to his mother's family in Lübeck, for in the new context she was the foreign girl who spoke only Portuguese and looked like an exotic import from the colonies. As Viktor Mann tells the story, there was a clear distinction in Brazil between his European grandparents and the indigenous Indians and African slaves. The ancestors of the Bruhns family had originally come to Lübeck from Scandinavia and were of "purely Nordic descent," while the da Silvas were "an old colonial family, strictly Catholic and completely 'white' and 'free.'"[14] It is probable that Johann Bruhns and Maria da Silva were given two slaves as a wedding present, and certain that they owned large numbers of slaves to work their plantations.[15] Julia later recalled that her grandmother had scolded her severely when she became too friendly with the slaves,[16] and Thomas Mann remembered his mother's stories "about the paradisiacal beauty of Rio Bay, about poisonous snakes that were killed by Negro slaves with clubs when they appeared on her father's plantation."[17] From the perspective of members of the Bruhns family who had remained in Lübeck, however, Julia and her siblings seemed almost as dark as their African nanny. "So when are Ludwig's little black ones coming?" questioned an impatient relative in the local dialect,[18] and the arrival did not disappoint: "the sight of a colorfully clad Negress with five children tanned to a dark brown wearing yellow cotton clothes and white Panama hats brought all the street urchins to their feet."[19] Within the colonies, the operative distinctions were between European and native Indian, free white and black slave; in Lübeck, however, all dark-skinned people from "over there" began to look alike.[20]

The decision of Thomas Mann's father to marry Julia da Silva Bruhns, in turn, had something dubious about it in the eyes of his fellow Hanseatic citizens. As Klaus Mann put it, "if the Senator had been entirely comme il faut, according to Lübeck traditions, he would not have fallen in love with a Brazilian beauty." The locals were never completely comfortable with Julia Mann: "She was just a trifle different—that's all."[21] While her father's experiences abroad underscored his virility, Julia's influence seemed to have had an opposite effect on the children from her mixed marriage: "The two boys, Heinrich and Thomas, would probably be more cheerful and vigorous if they had a mother of good Nordic stock, instead of the Spanish belle."[22] What enhanced a sense of masculinity in the colonies undermined that same sense of masculinity at home. The colonialists abroad remained confident in the distinction between themselves and the other; they knew that they were "white" and "free." The children of the Hanseatic senator and his Brazilian-Creole wife, however, felt that they were unmanly men suspended "between the races."

The dislocation of Julia da Silva Mann from her native Brazil to northern Germany made a lasting impression on multiple generations of the Mann family. Frido Mann, Thomas Mann's favorite grandson, published a multigenerational historical novel in 1999 based in part on the biography of his great-grandmother; he also invested considerable effort trying to establish a center for cross-cultural understanding on the site of her former estate in Paraty, Brazil.[23] More than a century earlier, Frido's great-uncle Heinrich Mann wrote his first novel about a woman born in Brazil to a German father and a Creole mother.[24] Even more closely modeled on his mother's biography is the protagonist of Heinrich's 1907 novel *Zwischen den Rassen* (Between the Races).[25] "Lola" has a blond German father and a dark Brazilian mother, and she, too, is taken at an early age from the tropics to a cold north German city. Biology is destiny, as her father tells her—"the blood that we get at birth determines what we become"[26]—but Lola's mixture of two "races . . . the Germanic and the Latin,"[27] makes it impossible for her to feel at home in either world. Small wonder that the author of *Death in Venice,* whose protagonist also inherits "exotic racial characteristics" from his mother, should have responded warmly to his brother's work.[28] In it he found a variation of a theme that was also central to his own fiction: "the blend of races—in their case, the Northern element and the Latin streak—as a stimulus and a problem."[29]

Throughout his life, Thomas Mann would attribute his particular artistic talents to the combined influence of his Hanseatic heritage and his mother's Latin–South American "blood." Mann's willingness to think in racial categories was typical of the time and informed his complex and often problematic relationship to German Jews, as we shall see, but it also informed his understanding of himself. Again and again, Mann will associate the people of southern Europe in his literary works with those from more distant lands, including northern Africa, the Middle East, and South America. They are all from "over there," "some place far down on the map," as Tonio Kröger puts it with a vague gesture to the south.[30] But they are also right here, in Mann's mixed blood, in his constant struggle with the Dionysian forces that threaten the stability of his respectable world and yet serve as the source of his creativity. When he writes about the forces of death, chaos, female sexuality, and homosexual desire, he is also exploring the "dark continent" of the imperial imagination.[31] Obviously Mann was not a writer of empire or the colonial experience in the sense of Joseph Conrad, Rudyard Kipling, or E. M. Forster, or their German counterparts Frieda von Bülow, Gustav Frenssen, or Hans Grimm.[32] His life and early works were nevertheless molded by the events and ideas of the Age of Empire to a greater extent than is generally acknowledged, influencing his ideas about the creative process, shaping his attitude toward racial difference in general and Jews in particular, and laying the foundation for his subsequent reflections on myth, national identity, and origins of German fascism.

Racial Difference and the Jews in Thomas Mann's Diaries

As a boy, Mann displayed little interest in the New World or other exotic locales. While his younger brother Viktor pretended that he was the Indian chieftain "Arrowhead" leading his tribe of local children through the streets of Munich,[33] Thomas recalled in later years that he was never interested in "Indian stories," that the *Iliad* was to him what *The Last of the Mohicans* was to many other boys his age.[34] One was more apt to find Mann listening to Wagner from his regular seat in the local opera than dreaming of expeditions to Africa or adventures in the American West. Yet Mann did not need to read about distant lands in order to experience the vicarious thrill of an encounter with alien peoples, for his mother could tell him about her adventures in paradise as a little girl, and he encountered among his schoolmates more than one Jew. There was, for instance, Ephraim Carlebach, the smart but not particularly clean son of a rabbi, whose name seemed full of "the poetry of the desert"[35] in comparison with the typical Hans or Jürgen; Franz Feher, the son of a Hungarian tailor who told stories about the circus in his strange accent; and the cheerful son of a kosher butcher who provided Mann with his first experience of "the thoroughly happy Jewish type" among a people whose experiences, Mann speculated, would seem to incline them toward melancholy.[36]

Mann's earliest memories of his Jewish classmates establish patterns that would continue throughout his life: the contradictory association of Jews with refined intelligence and loquacity but also exoticism and even barbarism; a willingness to categorize individuals as representatives of a certain type or race; and, above all, the insistence that Jews are different. In October 1945, for instance, Mann was prompted to think about the status of the Jews in the wake of the Holocaust when reading a book by Rabbi Elmer Berger titled *The Jewish Dilemma*. Berger "denies that the Jews are a '*Volk*,'" notes Mann in his diary. "'Race' is completely compromised," he continues, but then goes on with a trace of exasperation to wonder how that difference should be defined: "What should you call them? For there is something about them and not just that they are Mediterranean. Is it anti-Semitic to notice this? Heine, Kerr, Harden, Kraus up to the fascist Goldberg—it is after all a *single* race" ("*ein* Geblüt"; literally, a single blood-type or species, more broadly, a distinct ethnic or cultural group).[37]

Is it anti-Semitic to notice this? While my primary focus in this study will be on representations of racial difference and the Jews in Mann's literary works, it seems appropriate to begin with a look at the biographical evidence in response to his own question: was Thomas Mann an anti-Semite? What did he think of the Jews?[38] For an answer, we turn to the diaries written between the beginning of his exile in early 1933 until shortly before his death in August 1955. Even the most radical confession is subject to conscious or unconscious self-censorship, but Mann's diaries are certainly the closest we can get to the unvarnished truth about his opinions and beliefs.[39] While his letters are often masterpieces of diplomacy and flattery, the diaries were utterly private, written almost furtively, and, according to Mann's handwritten instructions on the sealed packages of the manuscripts, to be read by no one, including his wife and children, "before 20 years after my death."[40] "Amusing discoveries then, by God!" wrote Mann with what must have been a wry smile in 1950. "Let the world know me, but only after everyone is dead."[41]

What sort of "discoveries" do the diaries yield about Mann's relationship to Judaism and the Jews? In the first instance, they provide overwhelming evidence that Mann knew about and was revolted by the growing persecution of the Jews in Nazi Germany. On March 31, 1933, for instance, Mann notes that passports are being taken away from Jews in Breslau and that systematic boycotts of Jewish-owned businesses had begun in Munich: "It is just too unbelievably silly and insane."[42] In 1935 he recoiled in horror at news of the passage of the Nuremberg racial laws, which he dubbed "horrible, extremely horrible,"[43] "grotesque and stupid."[44] "Proclamation of a massive propaganda action against the Jews throughout Germany!" notes Mann shortly after the state-supported destruction of Jewish property and Jewish lives during the *Reichspogromnacht* of November 9, 1938: "Idiocy. Surely the people have had enough."[45] The end was nowhere near in sight, however, and by the summer of 1944, Mann sadly recorded the "horrifying acceleration of the massacres of the Jews in Europe."[46] When the concentration camps were finally opened and the German citizens forced to witness the atrocities committed in the name of the Third Reich, Mann wondered if the Germans realized "the monstrous shame,"[47] and immediately delivered a radio address condemning in the strongest possible language the perpetrators and the hypocrisy of those who pretended not to notice the stench of human flesh rising from the camps.[48]

Mann's public role as an opponent of the National Socialist regime is well known. In his radio addresses and other speeches he condemned Hitler's Germany and the persecution of the Jews in no uncertain terms. While such prominent intellectuals as Gottfried Benn, Knut Hamsun, Martin Heidegger, Ezra Pound, and Mann's former close friend Ernst Bertram sympathized with the aspirations of the Nazi regime to a greater or lesser degree, Mann never did. Although he hesitated to make a public break with Nazi Germany for nearly four long years from Hitler's seizure of power on January 30, 1933, to his open letter to the dean of Bonn University published in January 1937, the diaries make no secret of his hatred of the Nazi regime from the very first days in exile. Mann had in fact already spoken out strongly against the rising power of the Nazi Party during the years of the Weimar Republic, and he eventually became the leading figure of the German exile community in the struggle against German fascism.

Mann respected and admired Jewish artists and intellectuals such as Freud, Kafka, and Einstein, to name only a few of the most prominent, and was close personal friends with the director Bruno Walter.[49] At a time when anything vaguely associated with Judaism and the Jews was forbidden in Germany, Mann spent nearly two decades immersed in the Joseph story, reading and rereading the Old Testament, studying Torah commentaries and cultural histories of the Jews; at one point he notes with evident satisfaction that he had astonished a rabbi with his knowledge of Jewish folklore.[50] Mann received letters of gratitude from individual Jews for *Joseph and His Brothers*,[51] frequently accepted invitations to speak at Jewish organizations, supported the foundation of the state of Israel, and publicly denounced anti-Semitism.[52] Mann also married into a family of assimilated Jews and thus according to both Nazi law and Jewish tradition, his own children would have been considered Jewish.

The story of Mann's diaries and the Jews would seem to be over before it begins, reassuring us that the man who took such an admirable public stance against injustice held equally impeccable private opinions. The record is considerably more complex, however: while Mann certainly condemned anti-Semitism and the Holocaust, his views were not consistently "politically correct" in the twenty-first-century sense of the term. When confronted with ten volumes of diaries that, with commentary, extend to more than 10,000 pages, it is tempting to pick a few select quotes to make the case that Mann either was or was not an anti-Semite. A more comprehensive examination of the diaries yields a more complex and contradictory image of Mann's attitudes toward the Jews in the final decades of his life. Before passing judgment on him one way or the other, let us consider the evidence in greater detail.

Mann's effort to identify and define Jewish difference was part of his general tendency to think in racial categories, distinctions that are often linked in his mind to questions of sexual orientation and social status. Thinking about race for Mann meant in the first instance thinking about himself and his immediate family. When Frido Mann was born in 1940, Mann noted that his first grandson was "American by birth, with German, Brazilian, Jewish, and Swiss blood."[53] He later made a point of telling Frido about his own "origins and blood-mixture."[54] Mann consistently notes the ethnic background or national identity of individuals he encounters, with particular attention to attractive young men: "Handsome young shoeshine boy, Mexican type";[55] "young Eskimo hunter of childlike beauty";[56] "charming young man, probably of Filipino race";[57] "young man . . . Jewish, very refined type . . . tender and attractive."[58]

While the Eskimo, Filipino, Mexican, and Jewish youths exert an erotic appeal, black men generally leave Mann cold: "Young Negro waiter in the restaurant car . . . with exceptionally pleasant facial features, intelligent manners, slender fingers. Otherwise I never find the race attractive."[59] References to African-Americans nevertheless feature prominently in Mann's diaries. In a few instances, Mann indulges in Schadenfreude when black athletes refute Nazi racial theories: "News from the Olympics in Berlin . . . of a sensational 100-meter race won by two American *Negroes.* Nice!"[60] He is also delighted when Joe Louis, the American "Negro Champion," defeats Max Schmeling, who had been sent a congratulatory telegram in advance by Hitler.[61] For the most part, however, Mann's references to blacks are in the context of his troubling servants.

Mann lived in an era when members of his social class and economic status hired domestic help as a matter of course: "Back then we had a black couple, John and Lucie—you could do that in those days," recalled Katia Mann about their time in Princeton.[62] Already in Munich the Mann family had had servants in their large villa on Poschinger Strasse, and Klaus Mann relates a hilarious story in his autobiography about how the family was systematically robbed and publicly embarrassed by a kleptomaniacal maid.[63] Things went more smoothly as long as the Manns were in Princeton, but in Pacific Palisades the wartime draft made it increasingly difficult to staff the new house. "Twice I made a trip to the darkest negro-section of Los Angeles, sacrificing two weeks gasoline ration, and picked her up personnaly [sic]," writes an exasperated Katia Mann about the new maid; "naturally she has to be treated with the utmost regard, my personal radio . . . is on her bed table, the husband is welcome at any time . . . but anyway we are lucky to have her."[64] The husband turned out to be a problem, for Mann reports that he fought loudly with his wife, stole the Manns' car, and was promptly arrested for drunken driving.

Mann notes these incidents with the same regularity that he records progress on his latest novel or the number of sleeping pills he took the previous evening. What is revealing about his attitude toward race is the way that he almost invariably refers to his servants by their race or skin color rather than their names. "Arrival of the new Negro couple from Texas."[65] "Arrival of the new Negress."[66] "Day off for the blacks."[67] "Return of Joe. Her nigger will have to be hospitalized for a serious detoxification program."[68] The same is true for the Japanese gardeners who tend the Mann's yard in Pacific Palisades: "The yellow ones (die Gelben) have decided to stay."[69] "Said goodbye to the yellow ones who will take care of the house."[70] One could argue that turnover was high, Mann was a busy man, and if the distracted artist could not always remember the birth dates of his own children, he could not be expected to know the names of his servants. Moreover, Mann's English was never particularly good, and he may have been insensitive to the difference between the terms Negro and nigger.[71] Times were also different, with racial humor a standard feature of popular entertainment. Mann frequently listened to the Jack Benny Show on the radio and was amused by Benny's comic black valet Rochester van Jones.[72] On the other hand, Mann had been living in the United States for a decade when he made some of these comments, and he clearly did know the names of at least some of his servants, but even then, he usually identified them by their race as well as their name: "The Negress Leona is sick."[73] "The Negress Jo visits her husband in prison."[74] "Black Joe . . . is coming back."[75] Mann's condescending attitude toward his servants stems in part from the acute sensitivity to class distinctions that he absorbed in the home of his patrician family,[76] but his reduction of individuals to racial categories also reminds us that he was only two generations away from his slave-owning maternal grandparents and that his mother was born with the help of those slaves.

Black servants and racially marked young men catch Mann's eye because they look different. In the case of individuals who may be homosexual or Jewish, however, there is often room for doubt. It is actually surprising how often Mann is certain after the briefest encounter that an individual is Jewish or homosexual: "Ran into the young Jewish girl in the elevator."[77] "Our host effeminate, a young man from Cologne apparently his lover."[78] "Nice young man, whom Erika recognized as 'gay.'"[79] "Went to the theater, matinee of the mime [Marcel] Marceau . . . clearly homosexual."[80] At other times, however, Mann is drawn into a guessing game: he argues against Erika's suggestion that Frido Mann might be gay,[81] while engaging in constant speculation about the identity of his guests: "Dr. Valentiener came to dinner . . . probably homosexual."[82] "Mr. Brandt from Berlin came to tea . . . somewhat Jewish."[83] "Met our host downstairs, originally a medical doctor, now a businessman . . . probably Jewish."[84] "He doesn't seem to be a Jew."[85] In the passage about the Jews cited earlier, Mann insists that despite individual differences, Jews constitute a distinct race or ethnic group (*Geblüt*). In the absence of solid proof, however, Mann was forced to rely on circumstantial evidence. What is it about the Jews that makes them different? Or, to put it another way, what forms of behavior does Mann identify as "typically Jewish"?

We soon see that despite Thomas Mann's public support of the Jews, his respect and friendship for certain Jewish artists and intellectuals, and his private expressions of revulsion at the persecution of the Jews at the hands of the Nazis, that he was not particularly fond of the Jews per se, or at least not of what he deemed "typically Jewish" behavior. Although he did his best to help as many refugees as possible, Mann occasionally seems unmoved or even amused by their pleas for help. "Tragicomic letter from a Jew named Mayer in New York. Typical fate of a Jewish family."[86] During his first months in exile, Mann had several long conversations with the dramatist and translator Ludwig Fulda, a seventy-one-year-old Jew who saw no hope for the future and eventually did commit suicide. "Inexhaustible, never-ending discussion about the criminal and disgusting madness, the sick, sadistic character of those in power," notes Mann one evening,[87] but then a few days later he seems to have lost patience: "Fulda's complaints and Jewish despair tragicomic."[88] In the case of another Jew who committed suicide, Mann writes of "Jewish hypersensitivity" rather than "Jewish despair." Philipp Auerbach, a former Bavarian administrator, took an overdose of sleeping pills after having been convicted in a controversial trial for various unspecified crimes committed in office. Mann refers to the "highly repugnant case of Auerbach," but then considers the matter from a different angle: "on the other hand, Jewish hypersensitivity and [an effort to] mask a lack of talent with Jewishness. Not every negative critique can be blamed on anti-Semitism."[89] In other words, Mann accuses Auerbach of "playing the race card," of covering up his own ineptitude by accusing others of prejudice. Whether or not Mann's charge was justified is difficult to say, although it seems more than likely that a Jewish administrator could have been the target of a smear campaign in Nazi Germany. Mann's comment in this instance recalls his notorious exchange with Jakob Wassermann in 1921, when he confidently assured the Jewish writer that anti-Semitism could never take root in Germany.[90] In both cases, Mann tends to minimize the threat of German anti-Semitism and to blame the victims for their exaggerated complaints.

Jewish company can be unpleasant. During the early days of Swiss exile Mann complains bitterly about visits from his Jewish in-laws, "who get on my nerves as they always have."[91] Social occasions with too many Jews can be trying: "All-too exclusively Jewish group."[92] "Jewish buffet-dinner party at the Singers; horrible."[93] One of the distinguishing features of Jewish company is a certain sense of humor and a facility with language. Mann notes for instance that he and Erika had talked "about the wise-cracking Jews à la Schlamm" one evening, a reference to the exiled Viennese journalist Willi Schlamm; "brilliant, already in American slang."[94] Other passages are more critical. Mann repeatedly refers to the hated Alfred Kerr's writings on Nietzsche as his "arrogant and poisonous Nietzsche-Jewification" (*Vermauschelung*).[95] "Disgusting hate-mail in Jewish jargon (*jüdelnd*),"[96] notes Mann in another entry about someone who held him personally responsible for the British bombardment of Weimar. A card from the lunatic fringe could be shrugged off easily enough, but the perceived slights of Alfred Döblin and his Jewish friends hit home: "Wrote an energetic letter to Frank this morning about the despicable Jewish clique at the 'Tagebuch' (Kestner—Döblin)."[97] Hermann Kestner had lavished praise on Döblin for having created a new mythic epic in his latest work, without so much as mentioning Mann's *Joseph* novels—an unforgivable omission for Mann, who was acutely sensitive about his public profile. In his letter to Bruno Frank, Mann lashed out at Jewish critics who failed to appreciate his work, "while at the same time they celebrate their blood- and clique-comrade with outrageous ostentation against me, the stupid goy."[98]

Mann is slightly more generous when he does not feel directly threatened. He argues that the Jews' keen intelligence and acid wit serve as valuable, if at times unpleasant, correctives to the German tendency toward beer-soaked melancholy and a dangerous irrationalism: "It is just that the Jews have a better sense of truth; their brains are not clouded with myth."[99] At times, Mann embraces the Jewish contribution to German literature: "It is true: German literature needs the Jews!"[100] Elsewhere Mann recalls a long walk with the writer Bernard von Brentano and his "half-true, amusing monologues about the unbearable hegemony of the Jews in Germany before Hitler."[101] These entries set the context for one of the most damning passages regarding the Jews in Mann's diaries: "To a certain extent, I would have understood the revolt against the Jews, if the loss of the controlling influence of Jewish intellect on the Germans were not so disturbing, and the Germans were not so dumb as to toss me into the same pot and throw me out with them."[102]

The passage stops short of an unqualified endorsement of Nazi racial policies, but it is nevertheless alarming to read that Mann—under different circumstances and to a certain extent—could understand "the revolt against the Jews." What holds him back? First, the by-now familiar concern that the Germans will run amok without the sobering intelligence of the Jews, and second, anger and resentment that the Germans are so stupid as to lump Mann together with the Jews and expel them all from the country at the same time. To put it another way: the Jews are a bitter pill, but the Germans cannot afford throw away their medicine. I am not a Jew, but you treat me like a Jew, and this lack of subtlety is typical of a regime ruled by "the hatred of simpletons against nuance."[103] Thus the passage that begins with a qualified and hypothetical endorsement of the Nazi persecution of the Jews turns into an unqualified assault on the Nazi regime: "This revolution prides itself on its bloodlessness, but it is the most hateful and murderous [revolution] that there ever was. Its true spirit is not 'uplift,' joy, high-mindedness, love . . . but rather hatred, resentment, revenge, baseness."[104]

We are now in a better position to address the question of Thomas Mann's anti-Semitism. He was an anti-Semite in the sense that he harbored negative stereotypes of what he deemed typically Jewish behavior, even though he was quite capable of respecting and befriending individual Jews. He was not a *völkisch* nationalist in search of racial purity, however, and certainly not what Daniel Goldhagen would term an "eliminationist anti-Semite," that is, one who felt that the only solution to the Jewish "problem" was genocide.[105] In fact, Mann enlisted his anti-Semitic prejudices in his argument *against* the elimination of Jews from German society: the Jews' caustic wit and piercing intelligence may be unpleasant, but they serve as necessary correctives to the German tendency toward melancholy irrationalism. Two further points are of central importance for this study: first, the Jews are only one of several distinct and yet interrelated groups in Mann's work that are stigmatized by their place of origin, social class, race, or sexual orientation. Such categories often overlap or bleed into one another through a kind of imaginative osmosis. Second is the tendency for stigmatized others in Mann's work to reveal repressed aspects of the self. In autobiographical terms, Mann often implicates himself in the categories he would reject, most notoriously in his 1938 essay about Adolf Hitler, "That Man is My Brother."[106] As an artist in bourgeois society, a child of "mixed race" in a northern German milieu, and a man with strong homosexual desires in a strictly heterosexual society, Mann felt multiply stigmatized. Together with all those marked by physical deformity, racial difference, or sexual ambivalence, the Jews for Mann are alien others and a people with whom he clandestinely identifies. As Heinrich Detering has argued, Mann's attitude toward himself fluctuates—between self-aggrandizement and self-hatred—in tandem with his attitude toward the Jews: "the writer Thomas Mann presents himself as a philo- or anti-Semite precisely to the extent to which he is proud or ashamed of himself, to the extent that he loves or despises himself."[107]

To project unpleasant aspects of the self onto stigmatized others, be they blacks, Jews, or effeminate men, is of course a standard feature of racism, anti-Semitism, and homophobia, and at various times Mann was guilty of all of the above. These and other shortcomings in Mann's character have been exposed in recent decades with the ferocity that typically accompanies the toppling of a cultural icon from its pedestal; to claim at this late date that there is a critical conspiracy among sycophantic scholars to cover up the blemishes of their idol is hardly convincing.[108] At the risk of joining the chorus of Mann's apologists, I would venture that, on balance, Mann's role as a public intellectual was respectable and often admirable, most notably in response to National Socialism, but also in his unpopular defense of the Weimar Republic and his resistance to the excesses of the McCarthy era in his adopted country. If upon closer examination we find some "thoroughly unsavory corners of Thomas Mann's mind,"[109] that is in part because we know more about him than we do about many other writers, thanks to his decision to expose posthumously the secrets of his diaries. My primary interest in this book, however, is neither to exonerate nor to excoriate the man, but rather to explore his fiction in its dual role as a reflection of Thomas Mann's personal preoccupations and the expression of the conflicts of his time.

Thomas Mann's World

My title is deliberately ambivalent. It refers in the first instance to the historical circumstances into which Mann was born and the events that unfolded during his long life. As he recalled in 1950, he had experienced the First World War, the Russian Revolution, the rise of Italian fascism and German National Socialism, the Second World War, and the Cold War—"plenty of external drama for one lifetime."[110] Second, the title refers to the personal perspective on the world that makes Mann unique, despite historical experiences shared with his contemporaries, Finally, and most significantly, *Thomas Mann's World* reflects Mann's conviction that his life and works were *representative*, that he embodied the fate of the nation and expressed its deepest concerns and conflicts in his literary texts. One could easily dismiss such a claim as mere hubris, reflecting an audacity on par with Günter Grass's decision to title his retrospective account of the twentieth century *My Century*, and yet both writers have often been accorded just such a representative status by the German public. Let us therefore look more closely at the origins of the concept of the representative writer and consider its importance for understanding Mann's fiction in cultural and historical context.

Mann's work presents the paradoxical combination of being both intimately confessional and clinically detached. The diaries testify to his practice of daily introspection and offer even the most curious readers perhaps more than they might want to know about what he ate and how he slept, his trips to the dentist and walks with the dog, his tooth pain and hemorrhoids. Mann's correspondence is hardly less voluminous than his diaries, and here again, one finds intimate details about what he did, what he thought, and how he felt on any given day. The essays tell a similar story: in 1983 Mann's publishers assembled a 500-page volume of more or less directly autobiographical essays,[111] but even when Mann was ostensibly writing about someone else, he was usually also writing about himself. Mann's fiction, finally, contains a series of figures that even those who know very little about his life will recognize as being at least partially autobiographical: the impeccably tailored Thomas Buddenbrook, with his penchant for Schopenhauer and throbbing molars; the melancholy Tonio Kröger, who diverts his secret passion for Hans Hansen into an ascetic devotion to his art; the elderly gentleman Lord Kilmarnock of *Felix Krull,* who has a fondness for the scent of violet water and a weakness for handsome young waiters. While struggling to complete *Felix Krull* toward the end of his life, Mann claimed that its "sole appeal" lay in the opportunity it afforded him to insert his own life into the text;[112] a few years earlier he had referred to *Doctor Faustus* as a "mysterious and extremely personal work,"[113] "a radical confession."[114]

In the light of such overwhelming evidence about the confessional nature of Mann's work, readers might well be taken aback by his statement in a letter of January 19, 1952: "I tend to shy away from the directly autobiographical, which seems to me the most difficult, almost impossibly difficult task for literary tact."[115] Two years earlier, Mann had told an audience that had come to hear a talk titled "My Times" that he had "little or no inclination to present an autobiographical lecture."[116] Despite the many autobiographical elements in Mann's work, there is in fact nothing to compare with Rousseau's *Confessions*, Goethe's *Poetry and Truth*, or his beloved Tolstoy's *Childhood and Youth*.[117] Mann had a notoriously tender ego and could hold a grudge for decades against an unappreciative audience or a critic who disliked his work and yet, when it suited his purposes, Mann had what could charitably be called a very generous sense of self and intellectual property. He routinely signed letters written for him by Katia Mann, published an essay on Kafka that quoted Max Brod extensively without acknowledgment,[118] and signed off on a book review written by his son Golo.[119] In *The Story of a Novel*, Mann described what he called his "seemingly dubious montage-technique," which involved "copying factual, historical, personal, even literary events" into his text,[120] but as he confessed in a letter to Adorno, he had been practicing "a higher form of plagiarism" since the beginning of his career.[121]

One might refer to the twin poles of Mann's literary technique as Goethean, on the one hand, and Nietzschean, on the other: Goethe famously claimed that his works were all "fragments of a great confession," while Nietzsche insisted that "everything deep loves the mask."[122] *Symbolic autobiography* was one of the terms that Mann used to describe the combination of subjective confession and objective realism in his work. In his early years, Mann often complained that people read his works too literally, looking for real-life models for the characters in *Buddenbrooks* or reading *Royal Highness* as political satire, "as if I had ever dealt with any other 'material' than my own life. Who is a poet? He whose life is symbolic."[123] In writing about himself, Mann was convinced that he was also writing about his world: "I believe that I only have to tell about myself in order to loosen the tongue of the times, of the general public."[124] Symbolic autobiography elevates the merely personal into the representative and gives voice to the spirit of the age.

Mann also used the metaphor of the writer as a seismograph that intuitively sensed matters of public concern, a metaphor conceived in opposition to Heinrich Mann's overt politicizing, which he detested in the years prior to the First World War. Mann wrote of his thoughts "concerning the nature of a non-fomenting and merely seismographic-indicative sensitivity, which seems to me an alternative, quieter, and more indirect form of political knowledge."[125] Mann attributes the broad resonance of Gustav von Aschenbach's fiction to just such sensitivity, "a hidden affinity, indeed a congruence, between the personal destiny of the author and the wider destiny of his generation."[126]

Decades later, when Mann had long since established himself as a prolific political essayist, he still insisted that the proper role of the artist was to be a passive seismograph rather than a propagandist for any particular point of view: "That the writer (and the philosopher also) is a reporting instrument, seismograph, medium of sensitivity, though lacking clear knowledge of his organic function and therefore quite capable of wrong judgments also—this seems to me the only proper perspective on writing."[127] The most highly calibrated artistic instruments can even register future shocks, and, shortly before the publication of the first volumes of the Joseph novels, Mann congratulates himself for having anticipated the current interest in primitivism, the history of religion, mythology, and psychoanalysis: "Being a writer involves sensitivity and being five to ten years ahead of the times."[128]

The understanding of the artist as an exceptional individual with prophetic capabilities stretches from early romanticism to high modernism, from Shelley's claim that poets are the "unacknowledged legislators of the world," to Joyce's Stephan Dedalus, who sets forth to "forge in the smithy of my soul the uncreated conscience of my race." German Romantic literature had its own poetic visionaries in Novalis and Hölderlin, while Nietzsche took the cult of the exceptional individual to a new level. Zarathustra's disdain for the common herd and call for a new nobility driven by the will to power had a decisive impact on twentieth-century writers, including Thomas and Heinrich Mann.[129] In this spirit, Thomas Mann reassured his brother in early 1904 that any criticism he might voice of Heinrich's work presupposed the conviction "that in comparison with us, everyone else is really inferior."[130] They are not of the people and yet they are the people; as Mann wrote in response to Ernst Bertram's remarks about "Germany's fate" in 1916, "it isn't megalomania, but only a need and a habit of an intimate reflection, that I for a long time have seen this fate symbolized and personified in me and my brother."[131] From here it was a relatively short step to the identification of himself as the embodiment of the German nation: "Wherever I am, there is Germany."[132]

The Romantic understanding of the artist as a messianic visionary and a privileged representative of the people had its origins in a secularized version of Christianity and an appropriation on the part of the poets of a role previously played by the aristocracy. As Jürgen Habermas described it in his *Structural Transformation of the Public Sphere*, the burgher is defined by what he does, by a particular skill or profession that determines his function in society.[133] The aristocrat, in contrast, is defined by who he or she *is*—and the inclusion of "she" is significant, for aristocratic women had access to political power in ways that were systematically denied women in the bourgeois public sphere.[134] The king of France or the queen of England cultivated an aura of noble comportment to elevate them above the people that they also represented, and something of this same sense of distinction carried over to the senator's son in late-nineteenth-century Lübeck. "For instance, one morning I woke up and decided that I would be an eighteen-year-old prince named Karl," recalled Thomas Mann. "I dressed up in a lovable sort of majesty and walked around, proud and happy with the secret of my dignity."[135] Mann's conviction that he was not cut from common cloth certainly had its roots in his father's patrician status, but it was also a role that he actively cultivated as a young and ambitious writer. Mann's dapper style and meticulous grooming also proclaimed that he was a cut above the rest. A creative writer in Bohemian Schwabing he may have been, but he was no gypsy in a green wagon! In time, Mann would enjoy dinner at the White House and a private audience with the pope; he received accolades and awards from around the world—fitting recognition of his personal achievements, to be sure, but also the kind of tribute that the young prince might have expected as his innate privilege.

The understanding of the writer as the indirect representative of the people has still another, more sinister source in the *völkisch* thought that emerged from the conservative wing of German romanticism and continued through the racist ideology of the Third Reich.[136] In this view, the German people were bound together by their common blood and their ancient ties to the German soil. Writers such as Paul de Lagarde, Julius Langbehn, and Arthur Moeller van den Bruck scoffed at what they felt was the shallow optimism of the Enlightenment and sought instead to tap into the tragically heroic, "Faustian" soul of the German people.[137] Individuals mattered less than the group, in the eyes of these writers, and the artist was transformed from an isolated Romantic genius to a conduit that channeled the inchoate desires of the *Volk*. In the words of Paul de Lagarde, "the people (*Volk*) do not speak at all when the isolated individuals that comprise the people speak; the people speak only when the spirit of the people (*Volkheit*) finds its voice in individuals, when the collective consciousness of the clan's fundamental nature (*Grund- und Stammnatur*) awakens."[138]

In early twentieth-century Germany, Stefan George came closest to embodying this sort of charismatic figure, an austere, authoritarian leader of an esoteric yet widely influential circle of disciples. This "secret Germany" prefigured a future state "under the leadership of an all-powerful *Führer*" seen to embody "the cultural ideals and political model that all of Germany should—and would—embrace."[139] One of the leading figures of the George circle, Max Kommerell, published the ominously titled *Der Dichter als Führer in der deutschen Klassik* (The Poet as *Führer* in German Classicism, 1928),[140] and five years later the self-styled German *Führer* would seize power. As Joachim Fest has argued, Adolf Hitler had no particular genius or talent other than his uncanny ability to serve as a blank screen onto which many Germans could project their fondest hopes and darkest desires.[141] Thomas Mann derided Hitler as a charlatan and a comedian who gained power over a defeated nation by playing on their resentment with the aid of "an unspeakably inferior eloquence that was nevertheless effective with the masses."[142] Yet for all his hatred of Hitler, Mann insisted that he be viewed not as an alien representative of evil, but as a kindred, if deeply embarrassing, spirit.

Romantic artist, Nietzschean superman, representative royalty, and mystical medium of the German *Volk:* each of these concepts informs Mann's self-understanding as a writer of symbolic autobiography, as a seismographic register of the shocks that shook his world and the world around him. But what exactly was the "spirit of the age" that Mann sensed and expressed in his literary works? I will focus on a network of interrelated themes: the consolidation of German national identity in the recently united Reich; the establishment of an overseas empire; the heightened attentiveness to perceived racial differences abroad; and the increasing preoccupation with the "Jewish question" at home.

Empire, Race, and the Jewish Question

The elevation of the Prussian King Wilhelm I to German emperor on January 18, 1871, in Versailles was a defining political event in a cultural process of nation-formation that stretched back to Luther's break with Rome, Lessing's efforts to found a national theater, and Heinrich von Kleist's diatribes against Napoleonic France. Even after political unification had finally been achieved, the effort to reconcile traditional regional loyalties with a new sense of a collective national identity continued. The "nationalization of the masses" proceeded through multiple venues that included the construction of national monuments, the celebration of public festivals, and the founding of various patriotic organizations.[143] Historical fiction also played a role in the construction of the "imagined community" of the German nation.[144] Popular authors such as Gustav Freytag and Felix Dahn wrote sweeping epics that traced the origins of the German nation back to the time of the *Völkerwanderungen,* while other writers worked to transform the individuals and events of Prussian history into national heroes and a narrative of national triumph.[145] In a seeming contradiction, the period that saw the development of German nationalism also witnessed the growth of the *Heimatbewegung,* a movement dedicated to the celebration, or, if necessary, the invention of local traditions.[146] Both Celia Applegate and Alon Confino have argued that German nationalism and local patriotism were in fact not at odds with one another. Quite the contrary: cultivating regional loyalties went hand in hand with a sense of belonging to a larger whole. "Nationalism could embrace smaller worlds," writes Applegate; "Germanness could encompass their diversity."[147] Or as Confino puts it, "Germans imagined nationhood as a form of localness"; "while fatherland and nation represented Germany as the one and only, Heimat represented Germany as the one and the many."[148]

The relationship between the centralized government of imperial Prussia and its provincial periphery was nevertheless often marked by conflict rather than cooperation. In his intellectual history of nineteenth-century Basel, Lionel Gossman explains that the independent city-state belonged to a multilingual confederation of similar principalities within the Rhine basin drawn together by geography and trade, but not yet divided by the boundaries of modern nation-states. The tiny University of Basel became the site of an intellectual tradition in deliberate opposition to that of Berlin. In the words of Friedrich Meinecke, Prussian writers such as Droysen, Treitschke, Dilthey, and Ranke expressed "pride and satisfaction at the rise of Germany as a strong nation-state," while Basel intellectuals including Bachofen, Burckhardt, and Nietzsche voiced "criticism, suspicion, and anxiety in the face of that very achievement."[149]

From today's perspective, many aspects of the conservative thought emerging from these famous faculty members of the University of Basel seem harbingers of a dangerous antimodernism that led to catastrophe in twentieth-century Germany. All three writers shared a deep-seated suspicion of the modern masses and feared the rise of popular democracy and modern feminism. They rejected the Enlightenment's faith in reason and progress and were fascinated by the dark, tellurian urges of the Dionysian realm, a world more at home with Schopenhauer's blind will and Wagner's intoxicating music than Kantian antinomies or Baroque counterpoint. Still more disturbing is Burckhardt's tendency to associate the modern trend toward liberalism and democracy with the Jews, who were widely persecuted for "their alleged rootlessness, intellectualism, commercialism, and parasitism, the inability to produce an authentic, original culture."[150] Yet Gossman's nuanced account of Basel conservatism also reveals more sympathetic and less ideologically fraught aspects of their thought. Bachofen, Burckhardt, and Nietzsche shared a common commitment to the German humanist tradition, resisting nineteenth-century utilitarianism with a plea for the sort of independent thought and quiet reflection necessary for individual *Bildung* or self-cultivation. As is well known, the later Nietzsche became an outspoken opponent of German anti-Semitism, suggesting in *Beyond Good and Evil*, for example, that it might be a good idea "to expel the anti-Semitic loudmouths from the country."[151] Despite his praise of the *Übermensch*, the blond beast, and the will to power, Nietzsche had nothing but disdain for Bismarckian realpolitik, Prussian militarism, or German imperialism.[152]

When we turn from the conservative intellectuals centered in and around the nineteenth-century city of Basel to the young Thomas Mann, we find clear parallels and affinities. He, too, came from an old city-state linked to the Hanseatic League, a commercial organization based on trade within a large geographical region rather than the boundaries of a particular nation-state. Mann's chief intellectual influences included Nietzsche, Schopenhauer, and Wagner, all directly or indirectly associated with the ideas cultivated in Basel, and Mann remained at home within the ideological world of the Conservative Revolution at least until his gradual turn toward the left in the early 1920s, but in many ways beyond.[153] Looking back at his first novel in the midst of the First World War, Thomas Mann stated in his *Betrachtungen eines Unpolitischen* (Reflections of a Nonpolitical Man) that he had written "of the fall of a business establishment there [in Lübeck] midst the prosperity of victorious Germany."[154] For Mann, Lübeck represented "the age of the Hanseatic League, the age of the cities ... a purely cultural age, not a political one" (80),[155] whose citizens were loyal to the values of "German humanity, freedom, and culture" (97).[156] Bismarck's Prussia, in contrast, radiated "the triumph of '*Realpolitik*,' the tempering and hardening of Germany into a '*Reich*' ... emancipation and exploitation; power, power, power!" (98).[157]

Concomitant with the Prussian-led effort to consolidate domestic power was an aggressive drive to establish an overseas empire. While the Germans were not major players in the earlier phases of the European exploration and colonization of Africa, Asia, and the Americas, they were keenly interested in the accounts of the new worlds beyond their shores, and many of those whom Susanne Zantop termed "armchair conquistadors" harbored "pre-colonial fantasies" about the future German empire.[158] In 1884 that time had come: Bismarck reluctantly gave in to the widespread belief that it was now Germany's time to have its "place in the sun" and began an official policy of colonial expansion. By the 1890s Germany was racing to build up its navy in the effort to compete with its arch-rival Britain, and in 1914 Germany entered the First World War with the hope of securing not only hegemony within Europe, but also command of the colonies from the Middle East to India and across the width of Africa.[159]

German imperialism not only affected those who traveled abroad or settled in the colonies; it also had a decisive impact on those who remained at home. Many had relatives or friends who had immigrated to the Americas and wrote home about their experiences abroad. Even those who did not could hardly avoid contact with foreign peoples or news of distant places. Widely circulated family journals such as *Die Gartenlaube* (The Garden Bower), *Daheim* (At Home), and *Über Land und Meer* (Over Land and Sea) regularly reported on exotic cultures and the experiences of German colonialists,[160] while the popular novelist Karl May entertained millions with his tales of adventure set in the Middle East or the Wild West. Archeologists and anthropologists brought back artifacts to their rapidly expanding museums and even indigenous peoples to put on display in popular *Völkerschauen*.[161] Local grocery stores known as *Kolonialwarengeschäfte* (colonial goods stores) stocked coffee, cocoa, sugar, and cinnamon, all products of non-European origins. There were even popular board games designed as Christmas presents that allowed Germans to replay in the comfort of their home colonial conflicts between the European powers in Africa.[162]

The increased contact with the non-European world prompted new understandings of history and increased attentiveness to cultural, ethnic, and racial difference. In the eighteenth century, Georg Forster's best-selling account of his journey around the world with Captain Cook prompted lively debates about the number of human races, the distinctions between them, and the reasons for what was widely assumed to be European superiority.[163] In the course of the nineteenth century, the "Aryan myth" took on increasingly ominous overtones, as Joseph Arthur de Gobineau and Houston Stewart Chamberlain began to proclaim their theories of Aryan supremacy and to warn against the dangers of racial contamination.[164] While Edward Said's provocative declaration that "every European, in what he could say about the Orient, was consequently a racist, an imperialist, and almost totally ethnocentric" may be an overstatement,[165] the views Said identifies were certainly widespread and had a firm grasp on the popular imagination.

Increasingly intertwined with discussions of racial difference between Europeans and the peoples that they colonized (e.g., Asians), enslaved (Africans), or eradicated (Native Americans), was what came to be called the "Jewish question": to what extent, if any, could Jews be incorporated into the emerging national communities?[166] Should they convert and adapt to mainstream Christian society to the point of becoming invisible?[167] Should they retain their religion and be tolerated as one subculture among many in a pluralistic society? Should they leave Europe in search of a new Zionist homeland? Or should they be exterminated through mass genocide—the "final solution" to the Jewish question?[168]

The debate gained new urgency for a number of reasons in late nineteenth-century Germany. Pogroms in Russia and Eastern Europe drove many Jews into Germany and the Austro-Hungarian Empire, where they formed an increasingly visible minority and one that was singled out for particular prejudice, even among more assimilated western European Jews.[169] Readers of *Mein Kampf* will recall Hitler's horror when he traveled to Vienna as a young man and observed his first Jews.[170] The long-range trend toward greater democracy prompted by the Enlightenment and the French and American Revolutions encouraged many previously excluded groups to seek emancipation and enfranchisement: Mary Wollstonecraft and Theodor Gottlieb von Hippel wrote some of the first treatises in favor of women's rights, while the slaves in Haiti rose up under the leadership of Toussaint L'Ouverture against their colonial masters. German Jews demanded no less. Many had experienced a period of unprecedented freedom under the Napoleonic occupation; the Revolution of 1848 raised hopes for new gains, and in 1871 Jews were granted full legal equality in the new German nation.[171] As Till van Rahden has argued in his recent study of Jews in Breslau between the years 1860 and 1925, Jews in that city attained a high degree of integration into society without having to deny their Jewishness, a development that he views as symptomatic of larger trends in late nineteenth-century German society.[172]

Even as German Jews began to attain new freedoms, however, more virulent forms of anti-Semitism began to arise. Although Nietzsche was not an anti-Semite, his paean to the ruthlessly vital blond beast was easily appropriated by those that were, while Darwin's theories of evolution could be enlisted in pseudoscientific discussions of racial difference. The very modernism that inspired various movements toward a more inclusive society could be turned against the Jews by those fearful of change. The notoriously self-hating Jew Otto Weininger held Jews responsible for all the evils of modern times: women's emancipation, anarchy, communism, and capitalism.[173] "Real" Germans were virile men; Jews were effeminate, Semitic, Oriental, and might as well have been black.[174]

The associative link between Jewishness and blackness established a bridge between discussions of racial difference in the colonies and the Jewish question at home. "All of the discussions about race are actually encoded references to the Jewish question,"[175] argues Sander Gilman, a statement that I would modify to "discussions of race are *also* encoded references to the Jewish question." Prejudice ran rampant in late nineteenth-century Germany, and individuals and groups often shored up their own sense of identity by distinguishing themselves from stigmatized enemies. The process began at the top, with what Hans-Ulrich Wehler has defined as Bismarck's policy of "negative integration" central to his effort to establish a cohesive sense of national identity in imperial Germany.[176] During the *Kulturkampf*, German Protestants took aim at Catholics suspected of ultramontane disloyalty; the ubiquitous men in uniform in Wilhelminian Germany targeted emancipated women and effeminate men; members of the old Prussian nobility bonded with new captains of industry against the urban proletariat; colonialists like Lothar von Trotha and Carl Peters justified genocide in the name of white supremacy, and anti-Semites blamed the Jews for just about everything. Since it is the nature of language to work by suggestion and analogy, otherwise distinct, stigmatized groups could easily become associated with one another, without, however, entirely losing their independent status. In the words of Anne McClintock, the emerging categories of race, class, and gender "come into existence *in and through* relation to each other—if in contradictory and conflictual ways . . . the formative categories of imperial modernity are articulated categories in the sense that they come into being in historical relation to each other and emerge only in dynamic, shifting and intimate interdependence."[177]

The association between blacks and Jews could only go so far, for the simple reason that most German Jews looked different from the Africans put on display in the *Völkerschauen* or portrayed in the pages of the *Gartenlaube*. For proponents of Jewish assimilation, the physical similarity between European Christians and Jews gave reason for hope: if only the Jews would convert and conform to the norms of Christian society, then the problem of cultural and religious difference would disappear. But biological racism had too firm a grasp on late nineteenth-century thought to permit the unmitigated triumph of the assimilationist argument. Many believed that Jews were like colonized non-Europeans: they could learn to mimic the manners of their masters; some might even learn to pass for Christian, but deep down they remained members of an alien race.[178] The superficial physical similarity between Jews and Christians that gave hope to the assimilationists also gave rise to the fear on the part of anti-Semites that Jews could infiltrate undetected into Christian-German society.[179] Like the infectious parasites that Robert Koch was discovering under his microscope, the Jews could steal into and corrupt the body of the German nation. The Jews were thus marked by racial difference and masked by undetectability, visible and invisible, radically alien and yet eerily familiar. As we shall see, the ambivalence surrounding the Jews and their association with other forms of cultural difference and sexual deviance will play a central role in Thomas Mann's fiction.

Organization and Overview

This book is arranged chronologically. Thomas Mann's work could be reduced to a single overriding theme: the struggle of the artist to maintain a delicate equilibrium between the lure of the forbidden and the effort to keep destructive forces at bay. Mann nevertheless evolved artistically and politically in response to changing times, suggesting that we should view his works in the order in which they were written, rather than reducing them to a static grid of recurring thematic elements.[180] While I make no pretense of discussing each of Mann's works in exhaustive detail, I do examine a representative sample of his fiction from all phases of his career. In some cases, I focus on the usual suspects, major novels that have become canonical texts of modern German literature: *Buddenbrooks, The Magic Mountain,* and *Doctor Faustus.* While I make frequent passing reference to *Tonio Kröger* and *Death in Venice,* I focus more closely on other works that have not always been in the limelight of Mann scholarship: the controversial novella *Wälsungenblut,* the often neglected novel *Royal Highness;* the much maligned *Reflections of a Nonpolitical Man,* and the monumental *Joseph and His Brothers.* Together with the more familiar texts, these works shed light on the interrelated themes of empire, race, and the Jewish question in Thomas Mann's fiction. I conclude with a brief look at the *Confessions of Felix Krull* and some summarizing reflections on the ongoing meaning of Mann in the twenty-first century.

CHAPTER TWO

Buddenbrooks: Province, Nation, and Empire

Buddenbrooks is a novel about symbolic geography, about specific places in a distinct historical and geopolitical context, but also about the ideas and emotions that people project onto those places and each other. There are four major axes of tension in the novel. The first is between Lübeck and Berlin: the former, the center of a late-medieval and early-modern commercial network stretching across northern Europe, the latter, the capital of a recently unified nation-state. The second is between northern Europe and the rest of the world, represented most specifically by Valparaiso, Chile, where Christian Buddenbrook spends seven or eight years, but, more generally, anywhere associated with exoticism, eroticism, or blackness. The mentality behind this opposition could be labeled Orientalist, as long as one uncouples the concept from the representation of a specific place—the Middle East—and understands it to refer more broadly to the opposition between Europe and its colonies, the West and the rest.[1] Third is the intra-European rivalry between the German Reich and the British Empire. Fourth and finally, Mann's novel is about the local conflict between Christians and Jews, between the Buddenbrooks and the rival Hagenström family.

The multiple conflicts within the novel are drawn together by three narrative principles. The first could be dubbed the principle of symbolic overlap or contagious stigmatization, the tendency of the negative side of one opposition to be associated by analogy with that of another. The second is the principle of rivalry, which takes place between cities, nations, families, and brothers. As René Girard has argued, desire in the novel is always mediated by the desire for another: Don Quixote wants to be like Amadis of Gaul, a famous knight-errant, just as the Christian strives to imitate Christ. The more egalitarian society becomes, the closer the distance between Self and Other, and the fiercer the rivalry.[2] Freud discusses the same phenomenon under what he terms "the narcissism of minor differences."[3] This is to say that *Buddenbrooks* is about hatred, about bitter, unrelenting, all-consuming hatred. Third is the principle of reversibility: that which is deemed most foreign, most alien, turns without notice into something terribly familiar. "I have become what I am," says Thomas in his most violent argument with Christian, "because I did not want to become like you. If I have inwardly shrunk away from you, it was because I had to protect myself from you, because your nature and character are a danger to me."[4] Fear and loathing of the other is so intense because it is rooted in self-hatred.

The Buddenbrooks and the World of the Hansa

The novel begins just after the Buddenbrooks have moved into a large house on Meng Strasse, which is across the street from the main cathedral in the heart of downtown Lübeck. The Buddenbrooks are neither the oldest family in the city nor the first to occupy the house, but by the time they celebrate the one-hundred-year anniversary of the family business in 1868, they have established a long tradition of commercial success and civic leadership. Family records trace the Buddenbrooks back to Parchim, a small city in today's Mecklenburg-Vorpommern located forty kilometers south of Schwerin, or roughly halfway between Berlin and Hamburg. The son of this late sixteenth-century Buddenbrook became a prominent citizen in Grabau, a town that lies midway between Hamburg and Lübeck. Another married in the Baltic seaport of Rostock, and still another—Consul Buddenbrook's grandfather, that is, Thomas Buddenbrook's great-grandfather—moved to Lübeck and established the family business.[5] Other family members come from a broad geographical area across Germany and northern Europe: Monsieur Johann Buddenbrook's second wife Antoinette, née Duchamps, was born in Hamburg, where her family still lives; his first wife came from Bremen; a daughter lives in Frankfurt. The ever-hungry Klothilde stems from an impoverished branch of the family near Rostock. Thomas Buddenbrook marries a woman from Amsterdam, whose family is centered in Dresden, while his youngest sister Clara marries a minister from Riga, capital of today's Latvia.

The far-flung family ties match the Buddenbrooks' business connections, which unfold within the commercial zone established by the Hanseatic League. Beyond Riga to the east lie St. Petersburg and Russia, to which the Buddenbrooks export grain and from which Thomas gets the little cigarettes that he smokes with self-destructive passion. To the north is the city of Bergen in Norway, where Thomas's father served as an apprentice in his youth; the family archives also contain letters by worried mothers to their sons in Stockholm. Connections to the west include both Amsterdam and Antwerp, where Consul Buddenbrook also spent time in his youth. Between the Low Countries and Scandinavia, finally, are the British Isles. Consul Buddenbrook traveled in his youth as far north as Scotland and he still has business associates in London. In addition to these commercial ties that extend in a northern European arc from Russia to Belgium, travel for recreation and recuperation often takes the Buddenbrooks to destinations further south. The older generation vacations in Paris, Switzerland, and Marienbad, in today's Czech Republic, and when Johann Buddenbrook's health begins to fail, he visits various spas in Germany on a journey that continues through Nuremberg, Munich, Salzburg, Vienna, Prague, Dresden, and Berlin.

The Buddenbrook family is thus rooted in the city of Lübeck and connected by personal relations, commerce, and travel to a much broader European landscape. They know that they are German, but their primary allegiance is not to the modern nation-state, nor could it be, for that state did not exist until 1871, just six years before Hanno Buddenbrook's death. The older Johann Buddenbrook speaks a mixture of Low German and French, the former signaling his connection to the local community, the latter his allegiance to the enlightened philosophy of pre-Revolutionary France. His grandson Thomas will speak to his workers in a mixture of Low German and Danish. Social class matters more to both than national identity: Johann Buddenbrook admires Napoleon, but rejects his son Gotthold because he has sullied the Buddenbrook lineage by marrying a "shop" (43),[6] his disdainful metonymy for the lower-class Damoiselle Stüwing; Thomas renounces the flower-girl Anna and coerces his sister to marry the physically repulsive but seemingly respectable businessman Grünlich.

Differences between the various German-speaking principalities are in fact often greater than those between Lübeck and other northern European cities, as Tony's brief sojourn in the Kingdom of Bavaria reveals. Everything is different here, she exclaims in a letter to her mother dated April 2, 1857: the language, the food, the religion, the money, the way people act and the things that they say. It will just take time to get used to, she concludes optimistically: "it's a foreign country, after all" (303).[7] She never does get used to it, however, and as soon as she catches her husband sporting with the maid Babette, she flees back to Lübeck, refusing to be further insulted "in a drunken, illiterate dialect" (374).[8] Her first and only true love, Morten Schwarzkopf, in contrast, gets his unusual name from his half-Norwegian grandfather, which Tony thinks is "something special . . . something exotic" (126),[9] and yet there is little about him that seems foreign: they speak the same language, know many of the same people, and he—unlike the black-eyed and raven-haired Bavarian Babette—is "as blond as could be" (118).[10] What makes the relationship impossible is the social class distinction, not Morten's Norwegian relatives; what destroys the marriage with Permaneder is not his personal infidelity, as Thomas correctly observes, but the Bavarian Munich that he represents: "It isn't your husband at all. It's the place" (374).[11]

The Rise of Prussia

If Bavaria is a joke, Prussia is a threat. With his loden coat, flowered vest, elaborate watch chain, incomprehensible dialect, and enormous beer-belly, Alois Permaneder can only astonish and amuse the residents of the Hanseatic city-state, whereas Prussia can challenge its very existence. Already in 1835, when the Buddenbrooks and their friends gather in the new home on Meng Strasse, debate centers on whether or not Lübeck should enter the new Customs Union (Zollverein). While some believe that it will open up new areas of northern Germany for trade, others protest vehemently against this "Prussian invention." "And our self-sufficiency? And our independence?" (36),[12] splutters the indignant wine-merchant Köppen. In fact, Lübeck did not join the union that was an economic precursor to political unification until 1868.[13] In that same opening scene we learn that grandfather Johann Buddenbrook—otherwise a well-traveled and tolerant man—has an allergic reaction to Ida Jungmann, the orphaned daughter of a West Prussian innkeeper in Marienwerder, a town in Brandenburg northeast of Berlin. Although "the faithful Prussian" (331)[14] serves the family for decades as a governess for multiple generations of children, she always remains marked by her accent and origins, and in the end is fired by Gerda Buddenbrook and sent back to her former Prussian home.

The radical student Morten Schwarzkopf speaks with disdain of the Prussian king and denounces his draconian restrictions on the universities and the freedom of the press. Tony cannot understand why he is so upset: "What does it matter to you? You're not even a Prussian" (135).[15] As far as Morten is concerned, however, there is no essential difference between Prussia, Lübeck, or Travemünde: "Barriers, social distance, aristocracy—here as well as there" (135).[16] In terms of marital politics, the embittered Morten is certainly correct: the patrician's daughter Tony is as unobtainable to him, the son of a lowly pilot-boat captain, as if she were a real princess. The events of the revolutionary year of 1848 nevertheless suggest that there is a significant political difference between monarchal Prussia and republican Lübeck. When angry mobs take to the streets in Paris, Vienna, and Berlin, the workers in Lübeck follow suit, demanding the establishment of a republic under constitutional rule. Consul

Buddenbrook diffuses a potentially dangerous situation by reminding the workers that they already have a republic and a new constitution, to which the ringleader Carl Smolt responds: "Well, Consul, sir, then we want 'nother besides" (189).[17] Instead of storming city hall, the crowd begins to laugh, and the suddenly cheerful mob disperses peacefully. While the uprising in Berlin had caused dozens of deaths and scores of injuries, the Lübeck "revolution" goes no further than a refusal to light the streetlamps and the accidental death of the old à la mode cavalier Lebrecht Kröger.

Commercial deals or strategic alliances with Prussia are not out of the question. As we are repeatedly reminded, M. Buddenbrook had already traveled to southern Germany in 1813 to purchase grain for the Prussian troops engaged in the struggle against Napoleon. By the time of the Prussian-Danish war of 1864, the presence of the rising empire could no longer be ignored. Lübeck cast its lot with Prussia and thus preserved its independence, looking "with some satisfaction on rich Frankfurt, which was now made to pay for its faith in Austria and was no longer a free city" (428).[18] After 1871 the city retained a certain amount of autonomy, but the Prussian influence gained the upper hand. The political events that led to German unification under Prussian leadership remain in the background; we hear passing references to the "shocks and upheavals of the war just ended" (543),[19] and are told that Tony has no interest in moving to "a big city in her now united Fatherland" (620).[20] In the realm of culture, however, the new Prussian spirit has an immediate impact on the citizens of Lübeck, as we witness in the unforgettable account of Hanno's long and miserable day at school.

The old school building where his parents and grandparents were educated has been thoroughly modernized, with state-of-the-art facilities for teaching chemistry, physics, and the arts, that is, for the sciences that paved the way for industrialization during the German *Gründerzeit* and the cultural trimmings appropriate for the land of poets and thinkers (*Land der Dichter und Denker*). With the physical renovation of the building comes a new mentality, as the cosmopolitan humanism of an earlier generation yields to a roughshod Prussian nationalism: "Having grown up in the atmosphere of a bellicose, triumphant, and rejuvenated Fatherland, they had embraced the habits of crude virility" (694).[21] Surrounded by tough-talking, hard-drinking, and swaggering schoolmates, it is no wonder that the sickly and sensitive musician Hanno and his friend Kai, an aspiring writer, should be viewed "as outlaws and eccentrics" by their comrades (695).[22] Under the tyrannical rule of Director Wulicke, a former professor at a Prussian gymnasium, the school had become a "state within the state," where "the Prussian notion of rigorous service" reigned supreme. "Authority, duty, power, service, and career" had become the key virtues of a school once dedicated to the cheerful pursuit of classical education (697).[23]

Two radically different worlds confront one another in this scene: Hanno Buddenbrook, heir to a crumbling dynasty in the old city-state, marked by economic and physical degeneration, but also distinguished by a new artistic sensitivity, encounters the vitality of modern Prussia, which is urban, industrial, and imperial, bursting with virile power, but also empty, merely utilitarian, without a soul and without art. *Buddenbrooks,* from this perspective, is about the dissimultaneities (*Ungleichzeitigkeiten*) of modern Germany,[24] about the clash between Lübeck and Berlin, the independent city-state versus the unified nation-state, the artist versus the soldier, effeminate decadence versus brutal masculinity. If we look more closely at the actual Prussian characters in the novel and not the martial ethos they espouse, however, the picture becomes more complex.

Among the ministers and missionaries that haunt the Buddenbrook home of Tony's pious parents is "Pastor Trieschke from Berlin, whose nickname was Teary Trieschke" (275),[25] infamous for his ability to work up a tear at the appropriate moment each Sunday during his sermon. Although he is married with many children in Berlin, he stays for over a week at the Buddenbrook house, keeping pace with Klothilde's voracious appetite at the table and making improper advances to Tony in her bedroom. The man whose name seems to allude to the ultra-Prussian nationalist Heinrich von Treitschke is distinguished not by his martial valor, but only for his religious hypocrisy, gluttony, and lechery. The Prussian director Wulicke may demand rigid discipline from his students, but his potbelly, too-short trousers, and perpetually filthy sleeves and cuffs suggest that he does not live up to his own standards. Wulicke is on the best of terms with Dr. Marotzke, an enthusiastic officer in the reserve corps when he is not tyrannizing his students in the classroom. "Of all the teachers, he demanded the most discipline; his critical eyes would pass down the rows of students, who had to stand at attention and provide sharp, curt answers to his questions" (708).[26] Yet he, too, is lacking in personal hygiene, for his beard and hair always look greasy and it appears as though he never gets a good night's sleep. Then there is Herr Drägemüller, who normally teaches drawing but enjoys his finest hour when he has the chance as a substitute to lecture on the policies of Bismarck: "'We must stick together,' he would tell his students, grabbing one of them by the arm. 'Socialism is at the gates!'" (718).[27] Here again, the Prussian enthusiast is as physically repulsive as his colleagues: he is described as a squat man with two cheap hairpieces—a short one for when his beard has been trimmed and a longer one for when it grows out—who exudes "the oily odor of spirits, and some boys said that he drank kerosene" (717).[28]

The ethos of Bavaria versus Prussia as presented in *Buddenbrooks* could hardly be more different: there an affable but lazy environment where people are content to muddle along in their beer-drenched dialect, here a world of absolute military discipline. The characters identified as Prussian in *Buddenbrooks* are nevertheless just as much caricatures as the Bavarians. The major difference is not that the Prussians present a uniformed model of muscular efficiency in contrast with Bavarian *G'mütlichkeit,* but that they preach one thing and practice another. Permaneder knows who he is and is comfortable in his ample skin; the Prussians are hypocritical slobs and petty tyrants. The sense of duplicity associated with the Prussian figures of authority is symptomatic of more than personal shortcomings, however, for it coincides with a widespread tendency in *Buddenbrooks* for the representatives of the German Reich and the British Empire to exhibit the characteristics of those from whom they would like to distinguish themselves.

From Hamburg to Britain and Beyond

Two maps hang on the wall of the pilot-boat captain Schwarzkopf in Travemünde: a large one of Europe and a smaller one of the Baltic Sea. They sum up at a glance the geographic parameters of the older generation in *Buddenbrooks,* with their cultural roots in Europe and their commerce flowing from Lübeck down the Trave River to the Baltic Sea and on to the ports of northern Europe. In the course of the nineteenth century, trade patterns began to shift, moving instead from Hamburg down the Elbe and across the Atlantic. While Lübeck continued to grow slowly, Hamburg exploded.[29] The new gateway to the sea gave the recently united country the chance to flex its muscles in competition with other European imperial powers, in particular England. As Werner Sombart has argued, Germans were obsessed with the British and their empire during the late nineteenth and early twentieth centuries, viewing them with a mixture of envy and admiration.[30] From the time of Germany's entry into the race for overseas colonies in 1884, through the naval buildup of the 1890s, to the attempt to seize control of Europe and its colonies in the First World War, competition with Great Britain played a critical role in Germany's increasingly belligerent sense of national identity.

Given England's dual role as the dominant world power and Germany's chief rival, one might expect Mann to lend British characters in his fiction an aura of brisk efficiency or at least brute strength, and this is indeed sometimes the case in *Buddenbrooks* and other early fiction. Christian Buddenbrook's father sends him off to London, hoping that his old business associate Richardson of Threadneedle Street will set a positive example for his easily distracted son. Anton Klöterjahn of *Tristan*, Mann's "monument to testicular masculinity,"[31] is a north German businessman who wears English-style clothing, lards his speech with frequent English phrases, makes friends with the English patients at his wife's sanatorium, and displays a robust energy that contrasts with his sickly rival, Detlev Spinell. In Venice, Gustav von Aschenbach finds it impossible to get any accurate information about the extent of the plague until he goes into a British travel bureau, where a neatly groomed clerk tells him the truth that the local officials are anxious to suppress. Hans Castorp, finally, sets off for the magic mountain with an English plaid blanket and a paperback copy of *Ocean Steamships*, planning a brief vacation before he begins his career as a ship's engineer.[32]

Of course, Castorp never does begin his career; the British clerk who urges Aschenbach to leave Venice indirectly encourages him to stay, and Klöterjahn is a lecher who flirts with the nurses while his wife lies dying. In *Buddenbrooks*, Mann already suggests that there is something rotten at the core of the British Empire. Just as the Prussians fail to live up to their own standards, England more often than not is associated in *Buddenbrooks* with anything but business acumen or military prowess. Here a new alliance comes into play within the symbolic geography of the novel: while Lübeck and Berlin are defined as polar opposites, Hamburg and London become symbolic allies, with both opening the gates to the colonies, decadence, and racial difference.[33]

The initial references to Hamburg seem innocent enough. Antoinette Buddenbrook, the second wife of Johann Buddenbrook, comes from the wealthy and respected Duchamps family of Hamburg, although she has the lively black eyes of her French-Swiss grandfather, adding a touch of exoticism into the blue-eyed denizens of the northern German city. Things take a turn for the worse in the next generation. Johann Buddenbrook's son, usually referred to as Consul Buddenbrook, marries Elisabeth Kröger. Her brother, Justus Kröger, is a bad businessman, a frequent visitor to the theater, and a "suitor"—what might have been termed a "playboy" in the 1960s—who is said to make frequent business trips to Hamburg. Things unravel completely in the third generation. Justus Kröger's son Jakob lives full time in Hamburg, where he can never seem to make ends meet, until he causes a family scandal by being involved in some sort of criminal business transaction. Jakob flees to New York and is later rumored to be in Paris, London, or America. His father disowns him, but his doting mother ruins her marriage and bankrupts the family by secretly sending money to the wandering wastrel.

Bendix Grünlich is not only from Hamburg, but also occupies "a couple of rooms at the City of Hamburg Inn" (96)[34] when he comes to Lübeck in search of a wife with enough money to keep his sinking business afloat. He sports golden muttonchops in the English style, reads aloud from Scott's *Waverley* novels in perfect English, wears an ulster when it rains, and even eats a heavy English breakfast. Despite seemingly flawless business records and reports that "he lives like a gentleman" (110)—"er lebe gentleman like" (1.1: 123)—Grünlich is a manipulative liar who deceives Consul Buddenbrook, coerces Tony into marriage, and eventually goes bankrupt after all. Tony's daughter Erika from her marriage with Grünlich fares no better, for when her husband Hugo Weinschenk is released from prison, he abandons his wife and daughter and disappears in London.

The association of Great Britain and Hamburg with corruption and colonial exoticism finds its fullest expression in the figure of Christian Buddenbrook. Rather than developing better work habits under the influence of Mr. Richardson in London, Christian squanders most of his time in the theater and then sails off to Valparaiso. When he returns to Lübeck eight years later, Christian has become an anglophile colonialist. He speaks and writes fluent English and wears an English jacket and "elegant trousers of durable English wool" (435),[35] and even his neatly trimmed fingernails are said to have something vaguely British about them. In sum, Christian's "whole look was English somehow—and it suited him rather well" (255).[36] Christian has hardly become a model of British efficiency, however, but seems rather to have absorbed the spirit of the colonies. He arrives back in Lübeck carrying a walking stick with the bust of a nun carved in mahogany, a swordfish sword, and a stalk of sugarcane, while "dressed in a yellow plaid suit that certainly hinted at the tropics" (253).[37] He regales his shocked family with stories of murderous knife-fights and "exotic violence" (264);[38] he refers repeatedly to a song called "That's Maria" about someone guilty of the most disgraceful, vicious sins imaginable, and tells tales of Johnny Thunderstorm, a young man from London who is proud of the fact that he has never done an honest day's work in his life.

Christian never returns to the colonies, but he remains imaginatively and linguistically in a foreign world: "he was speaking in tongues now. He told his stories in English, Spanish, Plattdeutsch, and Hamburg dialect; he described knifings in Chile and robberies in Whitechapel" (449);[39] later in life he spends two weeks trying to learn Chinese. When his brother's attempt to reintegrate him into the family business as the chief correspondent with England fails, Christian becomes a business partner in Hamburg; when that business goes under, he moves back to London, but he soon falls ill and returns to Hamburg to marry a former prostitute. His behavior becomes ever more eccentric—one evening he rolls up his pants above his knee to show Gerda his skinny legs (clad, of course, in English socks)—until his wife commits him to a psychiatric hospital and goes back to her previous way of life.

Buddenbrooks describes two parallel developments with two equally surprising results. On the domestic front, Prussia seeks to impose a new discipline on the unified German nation, but individual Prussians display only slovenliness, stupidity, and hypocrisy. On the foreign front, Prussia looks to the rising seaport of Hamburg as its gateway to global commerce and colonial possessions to match the rival British Empire, and yet both Hamburg and London are consistently linked to corruption, theatricality, moral turpitude, and exotic violence. A look at the logic behind what Norbert Elias termed the "process of civilization" suggests an answer to this puzzling state of affairs. Elias contends that a mode of civilized comportment originated among the European aristocracy in the Middle Ages and gradually filtered its way down to the lower social classes. Civilization was by nature expansionist or imperialist; thus once the process of civilization in Europe was more or less complete, it began to expand outward to the rest of the world.[40] European imperialism may have been driven by greed and the willingness to exploit natural resources and native peoples, but it was often justified as a charitable attempt to bring the light of civilization to benighted natives. The very notion of civilization is intrinsically dualistic, for it is defined in opposition to its other: no civilization without barbarians, no proper society without savages.

The same nineteenth century that witnessed the heyday of European imperialism also produced anti-idealistic intellectuals such as Schopenhauer, Nietzsche, and Freud, however, who contended that human reason was a fragile outpost besieged by violent passions and illicit desires—what Mann would refer to as "the dogs in the basement" (*die Hunde im Souterrain*).[41] The barbaric world that had seemed safely distant was suddenly and uncomfortably close to home. Colonial literature of the time expressed the fear of "going native"—of spending so much time in the tropics that one began to forget one's innately superior European culture and to ape the customs of the local people, or, even worse, marry a local woman.[42] *Buddenbrooks* expresses these same fears in the realm of fiction. The imperial powers and the forces of European civilization become associated with their colonial opposites; they become bestial and black. "The boy's a monkey!"[43] declares Christian's grandfather as he takes a pinch from his golden snuffbox, and the seven-year-old Christian responds with an amusing imitation of his teacher scolding a naughty pupil: "Externally, my good lad, externally you are sleek and dapper, true," Herr Stengel had said with great seriousness, "but internally, my good lad, you are black" (11).[44] Bendix Grünlich associates with the strange Herr Kesselmeyer in Hamburg, whom Consul Buddenbrook characterizes as "a vicious ape gone mad" (223),[45] and while he may look like a British gentleman, Bendix, too, is "black internally, as Herr Stengel always used to say" (334).[46]

As the Buddenbrook family falls, it becomes infected with the foreign, most obviously in the case of Christian, but also in Thomas, who merely represses what his brother embraces. As Christian reminds him in one of their bitter arguments, Thomas also had his little fling with a Malaysian-looking flower girl before he settled down with Gerda Arnoldsen, a woman of an impeccable family background and great wealth who nevertheless has "something intriguing and foreign about her" (85).[47] Gerda plays "flamboyant duets" with her father, who attacks his instrument "like a gypsy, with savage passion" (290);[48] she later shares her enthusiasm for Wagner with another man who is probably Catholic and may be her lover.[49] While Tony visits Tom at home, Gerda is out listening to the Spanish violin virtuoso Tamayo; for the celebration of the one-hundredth anniversary of the Buddenbrook firm, she wears a silk Zuoave jacket (*Zuavenjäckchen*), a fashion inspired by French colonial troops from Algeria.[50] She honeymoons with Thomas in Florence, Italy; before their marriage, he spent time in Pau, a French city at the foot of the Pyrenees near Spain, and he had returned home speaking Spanish-accented French. Once established as a married couple in Lübeck, Gerda and Thomas build an ostentatious new house decorated with palm trees in the bay window, enormous Chinese vases on the mantel, and Egyptian obelisks in the garden. Thomas works at a mahogany desk; in their first house they had shared a mahogany bed. They had purchased that house from a bachelor who moved to Hamburg; later, when Thomas's penchant for fine clothing and frequent bathing has reached neurotic levels, we learn that he gets his extensive wardrobe from the most elegant tailor in Hamburg.

Taken together, the various details build a dense network of associations, linking Gerda and Thomas to southern Europe, northern Africa, people and products from the colonies (Malaysia and mahogany), gypsies, Catholics—and Hamburg. In philosophical terms, we can view Thomas Buddenbrook as one of many characters who succumb to a destructive visitation of repressed powers that break through and shatter the carefully maintained appearances of their world.[51] Too often, however, references to the philosophical underpinnings of Mann's prose result in an impoverishment of its symbolic density. One can certainly speak of the nether realms of destructive passion as manifestations of Schopenhauer's Will, Nietzsche's Dionysus, or Wagner's *Liebestod*, but one should not forget the places and peoples that Mann associates with these forces, a symbolic shorthand that links him directly to the Orientalist imagination of imperial Germany. To complete the picture of Mann's imaginary landscape, we need to add one more component, however, for the foreign lies not only in the nearby Mediterranean region or in the more distant colonies, but also in the realm of the Jews next door.

The Buddenbrooks' Jewish Rivals

The Buddenbrooks' chief rivals, and the object of Tony's undying hatred, are the members of the Hagenström family.[52] The Hagenströms are said to be relatively new in town; Hinrich Hagenström is a mover and shaker, aggressive in business and active on any number of committees, and yet he is viewed with some suspicion because of his dubious marriage to a woman from Frankfurt with jet-black hair and enormous diamonds in her ears. Although the narrator does not say it in so many words, Hinrich Hagenström is shunned because he married a Jew.[53] The various details associated with the family would have made their Jewishness obvious to Mann's contemporary readers, and any doubt is removed by Mann's early plans for the novel and his source material. On September 1, 1897, Mann's sister Julia sent him a long letter about their aunt Elisabeth, which Mann followed closely when creating Tony's character. Julia tells him that Elisabeth was taunted as a girl by the son of a man named Fehling, "who married a Jew, née Oppenheimer."[54] In Mann's early plans for the novel we find reference to "the Kohn family (Fehling),"[55] a typically Jewish name, but in the final version he changed it to the Germanic- or Nordic-sounding Hagenström and substituted Semlinger for Oppenheimer. Why did Mann only hint at the partial Jewish background of the Hagenströms rather than stating it openly, and what role do the Jews play in *Buddenbrooks*?

Tony is the only openly anti-Semitic member of the Buddenbrook family. She twice refers to the Hagenströms as "the dregs" (233, 259) (*das Geschmeiß,*

1.1: 260, 290 = trash, vermin, scum), and, most tellingly, refers to "Sarah" Semlinger, although, as her mother quickly points out, her real name is Laura
(114).[56] Given that in a few decades the Nazis would force all Jewish women to
change their name to Sarah as part of a systematic dehumanizing program designed to reduce individuals to a racial category, Tony's Freudian slip is particularly ominous.[57] That being said, the Hagenströms are the only target of
Tony's anti-Semitism. She is not associated with an anti-Semitic organization,
political party, or literary journal, as both Heinrich and Thomas Mann were in
the mid-1890s.[58] Tony's enemies are first and foremost adversaries of the family; if one of them happens to be Jewish, she does not hesitate to draw on a
reservoir of anti-Semitic slurs, but the hatred is directed primarily against
those who have done her—and thus the family—wrong, not Jews per se.
Hence she simply adds their name to the litany that she recites in never-ending
outrage: "'Teary Trieschke!' she cried, 'Grünlich! Permaneder! Tiburtius!
Weinschenk! Hagenström!'" (647–48).[59]

Both Tony's mother and her brother Thomas try to tone down her most violent outbursts against the Hagenströms. Thomas assures her that Hermann
Hagenström does not hate her, and the Consulin not only corrects Tony's comment about "Sarah" Semlinger, but also disapproves of her reference to the
family as Geschmeiß: "Assez, my dear. Such indelicate expressions" (233).[60]
Does this mean that Tony Buddenbrook is the only prejudiced character in the
novel? Hardly. The first reference to the Hagenström family makes it clear that
tolerance is not the norm, and when toward the end of the novel Sigismund
Gosch notes that the Strunck & Hagenström firm has cornered the market, the
drunken Consul Döhlmann's crass comment is "It's hard to outstink a pile of
manure" (645).[61] Thomas Buddenbrook is far more circumspect, but he delights Tony with a snide comment about how the Hagenströms may leave the
motto Dominus providebit (God will provide) above the door of the house on
Meng Strasse, but adds that the Lord had nothing to do with their rise to
power.[62] Tony offends her family members not because she harbors anti-
Semitic sentiments, but because she violates good taste in venting them so
openly. In this regard, she is similar to her brother Christian. As the narrator
comments, Lübeck "was no cradle of stainless morality. People compensated
for long days spent sitting on office stools with more than just rich wines and
rich foods" (308–9).[63] But proper citizens are discreet; they maintain appearances while committing their peccadilloes in private, whereas Christian Buddenbrook flouts custom and flaunts his sins in a way that inflames his brother's
lasting hatred because it damages the family reputation. In a similar vein, Con-

sulin Buddenbrooks chides Tony, not because she shares anti-Semitic views with other citizens of Lübeck, but because she voices them so crudely: "Such indelicate expressions."

Not explicitly identifying the Semlingers as Jewish could be viewed as stemming from a similar discretion on the part of the narrator. The hints are plain enough: the mother with black hair and big diamonds comes from Frankfurt, a financial center with a significant Jewish population, and is "née Semlinger, by the way" (58),[64] suggesting a link to Shem (*Sem* in German), one of Noah's sons and the father of the Semites.[65] She has one ruthlessly ambitious son with a prominent nose and a peculiar smell (at least to Tony), and another sickly boy who grows up to be a cunning lawyer. With such broad hints as these, there is no need to be so crude as to utter the word "Jew." In fact, as Yahya Elsaghe has argued, the very omission of the word has the insidious effect of underscoring rather than minimizing the characters' Jewishness. As in an advertising campaign in which the name of a product is elided so that the viewer or listener is manipulated into providing it, the very silence on the part of the narrator forces the reader to identify the characters as Jews.[66]

There is some truth to this argument, but it is not the whole truth. It works reductively, assuming that readers are engaged in the process of deciding who is or is not Jewish. But the Hagenströms are only *partially* Jewish, which would have been enough to condemn them in terms of Nazi racial policies, but which produces a different effect in Thomas Mann's first novel. The National Socialists sought clarity; they wanted to know who was a Jew and who was not. In *Buddenbrooks*, in contrast, Mann creates ambiguity, allowing the category of Jewishness to expand, to bleed over into other categories and individuals, including members of the Buddenbrook family. This is not to deny that anti-Semitism exists in the novel, but to note that it functions not only by identifying individuals as members of stigmatized group, but also by associating certain types of behavior as "typically Jewish"—but not limited to the Jews.

In many ways, there is little difference between the Hagenströms and the Buddenbrooks.[67] They operate similar family businesses; the men compete for the same political positions; the children attend the same schools; and the women attend the same social events. When Tony flees Grünlich and family pressure to spend the summer in Travemünde, the Hagenströms are there; when the Buddenbrooks take Permaneder on a picnic outside of town, they find the Hagenströms having their own picnic in the same place; when Thomas Buddenbrook reluctantly concludes that it is time to sell the house on Meng Strasse, Hermann Hagenström buys it. As in the relationship between

Thomas and his brother, the link between the Buddenbrooks and the Hagenströms is that of a rivalry with an alter ego rather than open conflict with a radically different foe. The Hagenströms' Jewishness serves a scapegoat function, a way of branding them as different even while the Buddenbrooks secretly suspect that they are much the same—and as the Buddenbrook fortunes begin to decline, they start acting "Jewish" as well.

When Tony's old aristocratic schoolmate Armgard is threatened with bankruptcy, Tony convinces Thomas that he should buy their grain crop in advance at half price. Armgard's dissolute husband, Ralf von Maiboom, will get a quick infusion of ready cash, and Thomas stands to double his normal profit when he sells the ripened grain a few months later. Thomas protests that the Buddenbrook family has never engaged in what he feels is a morally dubious business practice, which as far as he knows is common only in Hesse, "where quite a few of the gentry have ended up in the hands of Jews" (446).[68] Such "cutthroats" may be willing to make "a profit that is nothing but usury" at the expense of unfortunates, but not he (447).[69] Convinced that Tony's exaggerated respect for Armgard's nobility is at the heart of her desire to bail out an old friend, Thomas proudly tells her how he once won the confidence of an arrogant nobleman who had originally treated him like "a Jewish peddler" (450).[70] The point of the anecdote is clear: I may not be an aristocrat, but I can command equal respect, and I am certainly not a wandering Jew. Tony is delighted with his story, but she has already laid irresistible bait: if Thomas does not buy the grain, Hermann Hagenström will. Needless to say, Thomas accepts the challenge, makes the deal, and promptly loses everything when a hailstorm destroys the crop. The episode reveals more than his clouded business judgment, for it also exposes the self-canceling logic of his rivalry with the Hagenströms: Thomas acts like a Jew to cut off competition from his Jewish rival, while at the same time telling self-congratulatory stories about how he is not a Jew. "Jews? Cutthroats?" exclaims an astonished Tony to Tom's earlier rejections of the practice of buying grain futures. "But we're talking about you, Tom, about *you!*" (447).[71] Exactly.

Somewhat further down the road to perdition, the Buddenbrooks face new humiliation when Hugo Weinschenk, the husband of Tony's daughter Erika, stands trial for insurance fraud. The prosecuting attorney is none other than Moritz Hagenström, and Weinschenk retaliates by hiring a "Dr. Breslauer, a regular hell-raiser with a smooth tongue, a crafty virtuoso of the law with a reputation for having helped keep any number of shady bankrupts out of prison" (513).[72] Although he eventually loses the trial, even Moritz Hagenström is impressed by Breslauer's loquaciousness. Is the smart but unscrupulous lawyer from Berlin a Jew?[73] Christian's comment that they should have invited Breslauer to the family Christmas celebration, because he certainly had never seen anything like it before, may hint in this direction. The very name Breslau suggests a link to the region from which many *Ostjuden* came to Berlin, and we recall that Hugo Weinschenk "had been born in Silesia, where his aging father still lived" (432).[74] Could this fraudulent insurance agent also be a Jew? The question is deliberately left open. The point is not to produce clear-cut distinctions, but to suggest guilt by association. In order to defend himself against a person whose mother is almost certainly a Jew (Moritz Hagenström), the man who just might be an assimilated Jew from Breslau (Hugo Weinschenk) hires a lawyer from Berlin who could well be Jewish (Dr. Breslau). The question of whether these individuals actually are Jewish matters less than the hint of Jewishness that hangs over the entire scene of white-collar criminals and their tricky lawyers. Jewishness becomes associated with morally dubious modern business practices, and here again, the extended Buddenbrook family in its decline becomes slightly "Jewish."

The taint of Jewishness also extends into the realm of political radicalism. In the run-up to the Revolution of 1848, Consul Buddenbrook supports the status quo that restricts voting rights to the quasi-aristocratic burgher class (which comprised less than 6 percent of the population),[75] whereas Hinrich Hagenström sides with those willing to ease the "qualifications for citizenship, even for non-Christians" (176).[76] As Consul Buddenbrook explains to his father-in-law, "the revolution in Berlin was rehearsed at the tea tables of aesthetes" (192) and has now spread to provincial Lübeck.[77] An earlier draft of this passage added the following: "at the aesthetic tea tables of a few clever Jewish women."[78] Here again, the explicit references to Jewishness have been suppressed, yet the implication is clear: the revolution is the product of a Jewish conspiracy hatched in the salons of urban Berlin. By eliminating the explicit reference to "clever Jewish women," however, Mann expands the source of the revolution. No longer are individual Jewish women explicitly to blame; now, Berlin as a whole has been implicitly branded as "Jewish" and "female."

In a way that will be typical for Mann's subsequent fiction, Jews are simultaneously and paradoxically identified as overly refined products of modern civilization and throwbacks to an era of precivilized barbarism, decadent aesthetes who breed mob violence. After the revolution fails, the Prussian-led united Germany is distinguished by its aggressive antisocialism, resistance to women's rights, and growing anti-Semitism, and yet the Hagenström boys thrive in the Prussian atmosphere of Hanno's school. The associative links between imperial Prussia and the British Empire, Berlin, Hamburg, and London, continue in the older generation of the Hagenströms as well: Hermann Hagenström arrives to purchase the house on Meng Strasse wearing a "suit of durable English tweed" (583).[79] His brother Moritz marries a woman from Hamburg, "with butter-colored hair and an exceptionally impassive, decidedly English-looking face" (341).[80] While the male Hagenströms manage to pass as members of the power-mad society of imperial Germany, references to their sister Julchen link her to demonic violence and blackness. As a little girl, Julchen attacks Tony "like a little black devil" (60),[81] and she soon starts wearing enormous diamond earrings like her mother, a penchant for costume jewelry that she shares with the French girl at Tony's boarding school, "who looked like a Negress with her monstrous gold earrings" (84).[82] The tragicomically inept dentist Dr. Brecht, who inflicts horrible pain on Hanno and indirectly causes the death of Thomas Buddenbrook, has a sharply hooked nose and a bizarre talking parrot, implicitly linking the Schopenhauerian realm of an indiscriminate Will that causes suffering and death to both Jewishness and exoticism.

These examples point toward two general conclusions. First, Jewishness, like blackness, spreads like a symbolic contagion over the characters in the text; it cannot be identified and isolated as a distinct phenomenon, but tends rather to ooze into symbolic spaces and combine with other stigmatized categories. Hence Thomas Buddenbrook refers to his dissolute brother returned from the tropics as an infectious disease corrupting the family, a metaphor frequently used in anti-Semitic discourse: "You're an abscess, an unhealthy growth on the body of our family" (316–17).[83] Yet Thomas knows that he suffers from the same disease and, as his failed attempt to profit from grain futures proves, he is also susceptible to "Jewish" business practices. This experience is indicative of a second general tendency of Jewishness to show up on both sides of a symbolic equation: the Prussians resist effeminacy, blackness, and Jewishness, and yet are repeatedly associated with what they would suppress; the more the Buddenbrooks distance themselves from the Hagenströms, the more they resemble them. The result is a dense textual fabric of interwoven themes with a shimmering, unstable surface, like one of those trick drawings that look like one thing one second and something completely different the next, but never both at the same time.[84]

As a final example of Mann's narrative technique in *Buddenbrooks*, consider the figure of Sigismund Gosch as a minor character who draws together several thematic threads. Gosch might have been a thoroughly unremarkable individual, if it were not for his desperate desire to be otherwise. He is an unmarried real estate agent who runs a modest, respectable business and is said to be "the most honest and kindhearted man in the world" (180).[85] In his own mind, however, Gosch is a desperado, a Byronesque original, a cross between Mephistopheles and Napoleon. He speaks Spanish and Italian, affects a Jesuit-style hat, and is said to be translating Lope de Vega's complete works. Gosch is the only man from Lübeck who understands Thomas Buddenbrook's taste for modern literature; he later becomes a passionate admirer of Gerda, to whom he plans to dedicate his translations. While his fellow citizens recoil in horror at the prospect of a local revolution, Gosch wanders the streets in ecstasy, observing the mob with feverish excitement and proclaiming his readiness to be torn asunder by "the rage of unchained slaves" (188).[86] In later years, Gosch responds enthusiastically to the eloquence of Weinschenk's (Jewish) lawyer, and he also oversees the sale of the house on Meng Strasse. After sarcastically telling Thomas Buddenbrook that he can hardly expect "a nabob" from India (576)[87] to purchase the house at a fabulous price, Gosch produces the next best thing: Hermann Hagenström, fatter than ever and bearing the title of consul, or trade representative, with the royal house of Portugal. Gosch thus literally mediates between the Christian and the Jew, and suggests symbolic links between multiple disparate fields united by their opposition to the respectable burghers of Protestant Lübeck: mob violence, Catholicism, Spain, Portugal, colonial India, and the Jews.

Conclusion

Two months before his death, Mann insisted that his works could only have been written "by a German," or, more precisely, "only by a *man from Lübeck*."[88] Elsewhere, Mann writes that *Buddenbrooks* was originally received as mere *Heimatkunst*, a work steeped in local, provincial customs, while it was in fact informed by much broader European literary traditions. In Mann's view, *Buddenbrooks* signaled the breakthrough of the German novel into world literature, while at the same time retaining "the national, indeed, the regional."[89] The interplay between the local, the national, and the global in *Buddenbrooks* takes on new interest today. Globalization is often described as something new, a development of a postcolonial, post–Cold War era revolutionized by unprecedented movements of people and the instant communication of the Internet. *Buddenbrooks* reminds us, however, that nations and nationalism are of relatively recent historical origin, that they have taken different forms at different times, and that they have always had to negotiate their authority in relation to both smaller and larger spheres of interest. If in today's world the sovereignty of the nation-state would seem to be unraveling, *Buddenbrooks* depicts a period in which the nation-state was in the process of consolidation.

Attentiveness to the interplay between Lübeck, Berlin, and the places "over there" that lie "some place far down on the map" in *Buddenbrooks* suggests a way of "provincializing Europe" in a somewhat different sense than Dipesh Chakrabarty describes in his book of that name. For Chakrabarty, provincializing Europe entails thinking about the complexities that arise in non-European postcolonial subjects torn between local traditions and the allegedly universal values of the European Enlightenment. In writing about the experience of "heterotemporality" (239)[90] and hybridity in the postcolonial subject, however, Chakrabarty tends to employ "Europe" as a monolithic entity. My reading of *Buddenbrooks*, in contrast, suggests that the nineteenth-century burgher of Lübeck experienced the development of modern nationalism and imperialism in terms of a similar sense of complexity and contradiction. My point is not to criticize the shortcomings of postcolonial theory, but to use the insights of that theory to explore the dissimultaneities and hybridities that emerged within Europe itself, to provincialize Europe precisely at the moment in which it was stamping its universal authority on the rest of the world.

While *Buddenbrooks* records Mann's precise observation of external reality, it also expresses some of his deepest, most personal concerns, for Thomas Buddenbrook's struggle against the forces of chaos is one that he shares with his author. As I have stressed here, however, Mann did not represent that chaos as a void, but rather filled it with a series of stigmatized people and places. As modernist fiction, *Buddenbrooks* offers a first glimpse into the Dionysian abyss that will continue to haunt Mann throughout his career. It is a superficially realistic novel written by a modern artist weaned on Schopenhauer, Nietzsche, and Wagner; but it is also a work of German modernism that could only have been written in the age of empire.

CHAPTER THREE

The Married Artist and the Jewish Question

The immediate post-*Buddenbrooks* years that should have been a time of unmitigated triumph for Mann were in fact often marred by artistic frustration and a sense of personal crisis. The very success of *Buddenbrooks* made it a hard act to follow, and it was not until the publication of *The Magic Mountain* in 1924 that Mann would produce a sequel of suitable size and depth for a writer of his reputation and ambition. More immediate cause for concern were Mann's forbidden homosexual desires, in this case for Paul Ehrenberg.[1] "Coming out" was not an option for the successful writer and senator's son at a time when even the accusation of homosexuality spelled social ostracism and professional ruin. Mann lived in the bohemian quarter of Schwabing in Munich, which harbored the more or less open homosexuals associated with Stefan George's circle, but Mann himself was no "gypsy in a green wagon,"[2] as Tonio Kröger would put it. Nor was he a Hans Hansen, however, who could settle easily into what his alter ego imagined as a blissfully uncomplicated married life.

The trick was to find a way to look respectable and yet retain a touch of deviance, to embrace life and yet to know of "the lascivious delirium of annihilation,"[3] to be "sleek and dapper" on the outside, "but internally black."[4] As he put it nearly two decades later, "the decisive consideration and security for me remains being able to shelter myself in bourgeois life, in accordance with my nature, without actually becoming bourgeois."[5] The obvious solution to his dilemma was to get married, and in Katia Pringsheim he found someone who was attractive, intelligent, socially prominent, and fabulously wealthy. Here with one stroke Mann could refute public suspicions about his sexual orientation, repress private desires, and regain and even surpass the social status of his father. Mann's choice of marriage partner also emulated that of his father in a different, socially less acceptable way, however, for just as Senator Heinrich Mann had raised eyebrows in Lübeck with his marriage to an exotic beauty born in Brazil, Thomas Mann married a Jew.

Or did he? Katia Pringsheim was certainly Jewish in terms of Nazi racial definitions, with Jewish ancestors on both sides of the family.[6] As children, however, Katia Pringsheim and her twin brother, Klaus, had no idea that they came from a family of assimilated Jews. They had been baptized into the Lutheran church shortly before their second birthday and were surprised when they met their Jewish relatives in Berlin. Young Katia declared to her famous grandmother, Hedwig Dohm, that while she had nothing against engagements between Christian men and Jewish women, the question had nothing to do with herself: "I am quite certain that I am not a Jew."[7] Thomas Mann's mother, Julia, had her doubts, however, which came to a head when she learned that the Pringsheims planned only a civic ceremony and not a church wedding: "I think that if the Pringsheims are Protestants they should prove it at such a turning point in Katia's life."[8] Thomas Mann had clearly been aware of the Pringsheims' family background from the time he first attended their glittering salon in February 1904. "One never gives a thought to Jewishness among these people," writes Mann to his brother Heinrich; "all you sense is culture."[9] Which is to say that Mann was very much thinking about the Pringsheims' Jewishness.

Did Mann pursue and marry Katia despite or because of her Jewish background? The answer seems to be a combination of both. On the one hand, Mann viewed the Pringsheims as a successful example of the sort of complete assimilation that he touted as the ideal "solution to the Jewish question" in an essay of 1907.[10] Katia's father, Alfred Pringsheim, was a professor of mathematics at the University of Munich, an art collector, and an ardent Wagner fan, whose music turned out to be one of the few interests he shared with his future son-in-law. Perhaps in an effort to defuse the charge that his motivations for marriage into this family might include moneygrubbing or social climbing, Mann insisted proudly that he had no reason to feel ashamed of his own background: "I am a Christian, of a good family, and have earnings of the sort that these of all people know how to respect."[11] "I am a Christian"—that is, there is no stigma of Jewishness in *my* family (unlike Katia's, however assimilated the Pringsheims may be), and I have money, something that "these people" understand. The sense of pride, defensiveness, and more than a hint of anti-Semitism in these remarks suggest that Mann felt he had found a partner who was suitable in so many ways that he was willing to overlook or deny her Jewish heritage.

On the other hand, Mann seems to have also been fascinated with Katia precisely because of the touch of exoticism in her family background. In his autobiographical poem "Gesang vom Kindchen" (Song of the Little Child), Mann recalled how Katia had first appeared to him as an "Oriental princess," and their children appealed similarly to Mann's imagination. He wrote the "Song of the Little Child" to celebrate the birth of Elisabeth, his fifth child. Mann describes the baby's curious mixture of features as she slumbers in her "little Moses basket." Elisabeth has eyes as blue "as Nordic ice" and hair as blond as that of her "Hanseatic fathers," but there is something about the shape of her face and her "little Arabian nose" that make him think of desert sands in distant places.[12] Earlier Mann had been tickled by the appearance of his first daughter Erika: "Every now and then I think a see a little bit of Jewishness in her, which always puts me into a good mood."[13] A few years later, Mann remarks that the new baby Golo reminds him of Erika: "slender and a little Chinese."[14]

Mann's imaginative leap from Jewish to Arabian to Chinese demonstrates how quickly religious, ethnic, and geographic distinctions blur into a single opposition between the Hanseatic and the exotic, a conflation that points to the close proximity of European Orientalism and the language of anti-Semitism.[15] The Jews are the local version of the foreigners encountered abroad. For Mann, however, things are more complicated, for his alien wife and racially mixed children are reminders and repetitions of his mother, half Portuguese-Brazilian-Creole, and thus of the "Latin-American blood mixture" he shares with his siblings.[16] Racial difference, in turn, is associated with the maternal, feminine realm of intoxication, inspiration, and illicit homosexual desire that Mann sought to repress through marriage, but that he needed to retain and harness for the production of his art. Marriage to a "Princess from the East" was thus both a cure and poison in the sense of Derrida's reading of Plato's *pharmakon:*[17] it prevented the senator's son from succumbing entirely to "the howling triumph of the repressed instinctual world,"[18] but it also preserved enough of that world to allow him to remain an artist beneath the facade of bourgeois respectability.

In the following chapter, I discuss the psychodynamics and symbolic landscapes of Mann's early fiction. I focus in particular on the controversial novella *Wälsungenblut* (1905)[19] and Mann's frequently neglected second novel, *Königliche Hoheit* (*Royal Highness*, 1909), as responses to a period when he struggled to come to terms in his art with the repression of his homosexual desires and with his marriage to the daughter of assimilated Jews. Mann's reflections on questions of sexual and racial identity during this time were closely linked not only to his wife and her family but also to his origins as the child of a German father and of a mother of partial Portuguese Creole heritage born in Brazil. As a result, Mann's response to the intra-European Jewish question also engages questions of racial difference in the colonial world.

Mann's Earliest Fiction: Pathetic Men and Deadly Women

Thomas Mann published his first novella in a literary journal in 1894.[20] Written secretly at his desk while he was supposedly working as a volunteer in the office of a fire insurance company in Munich, *Gefallen* (*Fallen*) tells a simple story: a naive young man has finished secondary school in northern Germany and begins his studies at a university in a fairly large southern German city. There he falls in love with an actress who specializes in the role of the ingenue. With encouragement from his friend, the shy student works up his courage to visit her and is soon swept into a torrid affair. He lives in bliss for about two months until he discovers that his beloved also entertains other men for money. The discovery leaves him heartbroken, enraged, and cynical.

The story ends with the young man sitting at his desk staring mournfully at a picture of his former lover while a cello plays softly in the distance. The image evokes a mood of slightly cloying sentimentality reminiscent of Theodor Storm's popular novella *Immensee* (1850), a work that Tonio Kröger will recall as he pines for the inaccessible Ingeborg Holm. In *Fallen*, however, Mann distances himself from his fellow north-German writer by introducing a narrative frame that transforms Storm's poetic realism into a hard-edged piece of early German modernism. Four young men gather together in a Bohemian atelier crammed full of a jarring mixture of Etruscan and Japanese vases, Spanish fans and daggers, Chinese parasols, Italian mandolins, and thick Oriental rugs. One of the young men is an ardent feminist who takes every opportunity to advocate women's emancipation and to rail against the double standard that allows men to have affairs with impunity, while requiring women to remain faithful. Given the title of the novella, one might expect a reworking of Verdi's *La Traviata* (1853), a tragic opera about a prostitute with a heart of gold, or an updating of the familiar eighteenth-century theme of the innocent middle-class girl seduced and abandoned by an aristocratic rake. In Mann's world, however, it is the men who suffer. The dramatic climax of the novella occurs when the unsuspecting young man visits his beloved on a sunny summer morning, only to find her eating breakfast with a slightly disheveled, middle-aged gentleman. He is not sure what to make of the situation until he sees a stack of money on the table next to the bed. The sudden realization of his lover's infidelity has a devastating effect on the young man, as one might expect, but it also shatters the confidence of the paying customer, who trembles and falls back into his chair like a suddenly feeble old man. The woman remains unapologetic, stating baldly that morality is for the rich and that she is sick of playing the saint.

The moral of the story, at least according to the cynical doctor who tells it, is that "the woman who falls for *love* today will fall for *money* tomorrow."[21] In other words, he urges his younger companion to abandon his liberal feminism and realize that women are easily corrupted and thus not to be trusted. *Fallen* is the first of several stories that radiate fear and loathing of women as an amoral and destructive force, while introducing a series of pathetic, emasculated men who tend alternately toward self-pity and impotent rage. The young man first turns his violence against the woman, "thrusting himself upon her and covering her with insane, cruel, and punishing kisses,"[22] and then destroys the lilac bushes that give off such a deceptively sweet fragrance in front of her house. Even retelling his story brings back the same conflicting emotions, as he first inhales the aroma of the lilac blossoms that decorate the atelier and then seizes them roughly with an "embittered, sad brutality."[23] *Fallen* thus offers both an overt rejection of modern feminism and an unflinching psychological portrait of masculinity in crisis.

Patterns first introduced in *Fallen* repeat themselves, often with thinly disguised autobiographical elements, in a series of subsequent works. *Der Wille zum Glück* (*The Will to Happiness*, 1896), for instance, features a German plantation owner in South America who has married a local woman from a good family and returned to Germany. Their artistically gifted but sickly and effeminate boy, Paolo, falls in love with a young Jewish beauty, Baronesse Ada Stein. While Paolo's friend dismisses Ada's mother as "an ugly little Jewess in a tasteless gray dress,"[24] he finds the daughter dangerously beautiful, an elegant but surprisingly voluptuous young woman with dark ringlets, almond-shaped eyes, full lips, and a fleshy nose "that leave no doubt about her at least partial Semitic heritage."[25] He worries—with good reason, as it turns out—that the vibrant "young girl with her silent, volcanic, burningly sensual passion" will soon suck the life out of his sick friend.[26] Ada's father at first forbids his daughter to marry the unhealthy artist, but Paolo persists until Ada's family finally consents to the union. Unfortunately, Paolo dies "on the morning after the wedding—practically in the wedding night."[27] His friend arrives in time to see him lowered into the grave and notes a look of triumph on the young widow's face.

At first glance we might assume that Mann celebrates true, if tragic, love that has won out against parental opposition, but there is something odd about a woman who celebrates the death of the man she married just hours ago. Paolo, for his part, enters into the marriage with the same look of triumph in the face of certain death. Mann's story, in other words, is not a comic tale of young love and new life, but rather about a killer and her willing victim. The understated exoticism of *Fallen* has burst into full bloom: the duplicitous southern German actress has become a veritable Salome, a destructively seductive Jewish beauty, while the half-Latin bohemian who "feels at home in the South"[28] embodies the death drive, full of precocious sexual passion—he is caught as a schoolboy with a drawing of a naked woman hidden in his Bible—but also the seeds of a mortal illness. More precisely, the passion *is* the illness: we are in the world of the *Liebestod,* of Wagner's *Tristan und Isolde,* but transcribed into Oriental key, with Ada as a Kundry figure who lures Paolo to an early death.

Sadomasochistic relationships abound in Mann's early fiction. *Der kleine Herr Friedemann* (*Little Herr Friedemann,* 1897), the physically deformed but dapper protagonist of the novella Mann hailed as a creative breakthrough,[29] spins out of control when he falls under the spell of an officer's wife who moves to his town. Gerda von Rinnlingen is a manly woman who smokes, rides horses, and "lacks all feminine charm."[30] She is carrying a whip when Friedemann first sees her, and she pursues him apparently for the pleasure of disturbing the delicate equilibrium of his life and watching him suffer. "She wants to torment and mock me!"[31] exclaims an outraged Herr Friedemann, and yet he feels a strange shudder of delight when she provokes him into a state of "impotent, sweetly painful fury."[32] Gerda eventually allows him to confess his love to her, but she then flings him to the ground "like a dog" with a contemptuous laugh. Friedemann drags himself to the river and drowns, turning his feelings of "mad rage" and "lascivious hatred" against himself.[33] In *Gerächt* (*Revenged,* 1899), the male protagonist enjoys intellectual conversations with "a woman with a thoroughly masculine brain," but "the physical charms of a broomstick."[34] He is tactless enough to tell her how ugly he finds her after a few too many glasses of wine, but in the end she humiliates him by rejecting his sexual advances and leaving him enraged, aroused, and alone. The eponymous protagonist in *Tobias Mindernickel* (1897) vents his sense of helpless rage against a dog, rather than a woman or himself. The scene in which he first stabs and then caresses his dying pet has been aptly described as "one of the most convincingly unpleasant moments in German literature."[35]

Yet another femme fatale haunts the pages of the disturbing story *Luischen* (*Little Louise,* 1897), in which a morbidly obese lawyer named Jacoby is married to a young woman known as Amra. Her name sounds exotic, her hair is dark, her skin is yellow and covers a body whose curves "also seemed ripened by the southern sun and recalled those of a Sultana with her vegetative and indolent luxuriousness."[36] Her description anticipates that of Potiphar's Egyptian wife Mut-em-enet in *Joseph and His Brothers*, while Amra's husband Jacoby has Potiphar's small head and massive but flabby body. Both Potiphar and Jacoby are characterized as eunuchs, the latter figuratively, the former literally. In contrast with Dunja Stegemann in *Revenged*, who is smart but ugly, Mann casts Amra as beautiful but stupid, endowed with a "bird brain" and yet enough "sensuous maliciousness," "cruel lust," and "lascivious cleverness to cause trouble."[37] In a room decorated with an Oriental rug, fan palms, and a mahogany table, she and her lover plan a party designed to humiliate the husband. They hold the festivities in a hall decorated in an odd mixture of Chinese and Renaissance styles, and stage entertainment that includes a performance by students dressed up as "horrible negroes in outrageous costumes with blood red lips who bared their teeth and began howling barbarically."[38] The evening is crowned by the appearance of the husband, who sings and dances at his wife's insistence in a red silk dress, long yellow gloves, and a curly blond wig. When he finally realizes that he is the butt of the evening's joke, he collapses and is pronounced dead by a Jewish doctor.

Each of these stories was written in the decade that preceded Mann's marriage in 1905. The men are typically pathetic individuals consumed by unfulfilled desires; they often have artistic inclinations, but lack the iron discipline and burning ambition of a Tonio Kröger, Gustav von Aschenbach, or Thomas Mann that would enable them to transform their suffering into lasting works of art. The women burst with self-confidence and an almost manly swagger, and seem to enjoy nothing more than watching their would-be lovers suffer and die. While the stories can easily be seen from a biographical perspective as part of Mann's attempt to come to terms with his repressed homosexual desires, they gain broader significance as expressions of a widespread sense of masculine crisis that accompanied the advent of modernity in fin de siècle Austria and Germany.[39] Drawing on a register of language associated with European Orientalism, racism, and anti-Semitism, Mann links effeminate men who cannot hold a steady job, complete a significant work of art, or marry the woman they love to aimless travel that inevitably leads them away from northern Europe toward cities like Venice or Rome, which may seem European on the surface, "but into which the warm wind carries the sultry indolence of the Orient."[40] The women exude a dangerous power associated with animal lust, howling Negro dancers, and the sensuality of the harem.

Wälsungenblut: Marriage as Trauma

Anyone familiar with the parade of pathetic men and deadly women in Mann's early fiction might have thought him an unlikely candidate for marriage, and during the official engagement and soon after the wedding he certainly had some second thoughts. Mann had pursued Katia Pringsheim with relentless, almost desperate intensity, and now he discovered the ambiguous pleasures of having attained what he had desired. Mann's mother gradually came to terms with the marriage, but relations with his new father-in-law remained tense. "The engagement—it wasn't fun, believe me," confided Mann to his brother Heinrich, but he was trying his best "to fit into, to adjust to the new family (as best I can)."[41] Progress was apparently slow, for a year and a half later an exasperated Mann complained that his wife's family had appeared to him "yet again" as "foreign, horrible, humiliating, nerve-wracking, debilitating."[42] Worst of all, Mann was finding it difficult to write. Even on his honeymoon, Mann admitted that he could do with "a little more cloister-peace and quiet."[43] More than a year later he was still "tortured by the thought that he should not have allowed himself to be bound and tied to another person."[44]

Mann expressed these doubts about his marriage and made the devastating remarks about his new in-laws during the same period in which he wrote *Wälsungenblut,* his most notorious novella. Even before it was scheduled to be released, Mann agreed to his publisher's request that he remove the Yiddish insult mocking the "goy" who has just been cuckolded by incestuous Jewish twins. He then agreed to cancel publication entirely in an effort to avoid a scandal and to placate his outraged father-in-law.[45] More than one hundred years after its original composition and nonpublication, *Wälsungenblut* remains compelling reading: carefully conceived, brilliantly executed, and utterly scandalous. Mann portrays a wealthy family of assimilated Jews in the Tiergarten district of his contemporary Berlin. The fictional family is not identical to that of his new in-laws but close enough to invite scrutiny: the eastern European Jewish origins, the ostentatious display of wealth, the highly intellectual atmosphere, the embrace of the Wagner cult, and the twin protagonists make comparisons between the fictional Aarenholds and the Pringsheims difficult to avoid.[46] To be sure, Mann protested vigorously against efforts to read his fiction as thinly disguised reality. In the essay "Bilse und ich" (Bilse and I), written in overt defense of *Buddenbrooks* and probably also covert defense of *Wälsungenblut* in the weeks immediately after he had withdrawn the novella from publication, Mann insisted that he had done no more than Shakespeare did in breathing new life into old stories. Those immediately concerned, however, tended to see things differently: Mann's Uncle Friedel had been furious to discover himself portrayed as Christian Buddenbrook, and now Alfred Pringsheim seethed at the public ridicule of his family that might result from the publication of *Wälsungenblut*.

Individuals come and go, and in time possible links between reality and fiction fade into the footnotes of critical editions. When Viktor Mann visited Lübeck in 1917, he discovered that *Buddenbrooks*, which had once provoked such indignation, had long since become a source of civic pride.[47] *Wälsungenblut*, in contrast, has remained a "hot potato"[48] because it deals directly and controversially with the Jewish question. *Wälsungenblut* is neither the first nor the last time that Mann portrayed Jewish characters in his fiction: the Hagenströms in *Buddenbrooks*, Leo Naphta in *The Magic Mountain*, and Saul Fitelberg in *Doctor Faustus* belong to a steady stream of figures in Mann's fiction either directly identified as Jews or coded in a way that makes them immediately recognizable as such. In these and many other examples, however, Jews tend to play minor, supporting roles. The obvious exceptions are the patriarchs of the Joseph novels, but these figures function on multiple symbolic and mythical levels in a world that is long ago and far away. The Tiergarten milieu of *Wälsungenblut*, by contrast, is right here and right now, and the novella's Jewish characters are cast in the leading roles, while its pathetic Christian is a ridiculed outsider.

This is not to say that the members of the Aarenhold family appear in any sort of heroic light. In fact, it is difficult to imagine a less savory cast of characters: the father, an eastern European Jew who began his career as "a worm, a louse if you like" and still feels vaguely guilty about the "machinations" that have led to his newfound wealth;[49] the "impossible" mother, "small, ugly, prematurely aged" (289–90);[50] the older brother, a caricature of a Wilhelminian *Untertan* with his decorated military uniform and deep dueling scars; the older sister, "an ashen, austere blonde of twenty-eight, with a hooked nose, grey eyes like a falcon's, and a bitter, contemptuous mouth" (290);[51] and above all the twins, Siegmund and Sieglinde: self-indulgent, nasty, incestuous little beasts.[52] Mann's decision to portray unusual and unpleasant characters is hardly unique to *Wälsungenblut;* his early fiction contains a menagerie of such characters, like Little Herr Friedemann, Tobias Mindernickel, Raoul Überbein, and Lobgott Piepsam. What makes *Wälsungenblut* different and dangerous is not that the characters are unappealing and happen to be Jewish but that they are unappealing *because* they are Jewish. Even worse: there is nothing they can do about it. Jewishness lies in the blood. No matter how many times Siegmund bathes or shaves in the course of the day, his physical, racial characteristics keep coming back. Thus the story, often read as a commentary on the problems of Jewish cultural assimilation to mainstream Christian German society, contains a sinister element of biological racism, implying that assimilation is ultimately impossible.

Given what we know about Mann's repressed homosexuality and his initial ambivalence about his marriage, it is certainly plausible to read the novella—on one level—as Mann's way of coming to terms with his new life as a married artist, an identity that the author of such aggressively chaste figures as Tonio Kröger, Savonarola in *Fiorenza,* and the fanatical monk Hieronymus of *Gladius Dei* must have experienced initially as self-contradictory. This is not to say that Mann wrote the story as an act of calculated revenge against his in-laws, as rumor would have it, for otherwise he would not have read it aloud to Katia, Klaus, and Hedwig Pringsheim, seeking and winning their approval before he sent it to his editor. Nor is it to suggest that *Wälsungenblut* contains a strictly realistic portrait of either the Pringsheim family or their Berlin relatives, for too many details have been changed, and, more important, its source material has been transformed and uplifted (*aufgehoben*) into a tightly crafted work of art. *Wälsungenblut* is rather a kind of nightmare image of Mann's new reality, distorted by fears and resentment and condensed into chiseled prose. And here we return to the question of Mann's anti-Semitism, for the more "foreign, horrible, humiliating, nerve-wracking, and debilitating" the fictional family becomes, the more Jewish they seem.

Jewishness for Thomas Mann is thus a biological fact rooted in the blood and a relational category determined by cultural context. As Yahya Elsaghe has observed of *Buddenbrooks,* the rival Hagenströms' stereotypically Jewish traits emerge most strongly in those moments when the Buddenbrooks feel most threatened.[53] At the opposite end of the spectrum from this characterization lies the version of the Pringsheim family that Mann sees when he begins to woo Katia: all culture and not a trace of Jewishness. The apparent contradiction is consistent with the logic of assimilation that Mann defends in response to the Jewish question: he is not against Jews per se but only against Jews who act "Jewish." However odious and self-contradictory such an attitude may seem today, it was a common view at the time and one shared by many assimilated Jews, including the Pringsheims. Katia Mann's comment about a new wave of visitors during the years of Swiss exile is typical in this regard: "Tenni, Lion, and Therese, that is too much, and, frankly, also too Jewish."[54] Such an attitude toward Jewishness is hardly a model of multicultural tolerance, yet neither is it the same as the "eliminationist anti-Semitism" that motivated the Nazi campaign to exterminate all Jews, whether assimilated or not.[55] Thomas Mann's questionable distinction between being Jewish and acting Jewish enabled him to befriend and defend assimilated Jews while remaining indifferent to their supposed racial difference, and yet to disparage those who *acted* Jewish as also *being* Jewish in a biological sense: the Aarenhold twins are "of a hopelessly different breed and kind" (306).[56] But so was Thomas Mann, at least in his self-understanding, and viewed from this perspective *Wälsungenblut* is not about the Jews at all, but about the modern, homosexual, racially mixed artist.

A reading of *Wälsungenblut* as distorted autobiography suggests that Mann identified to at least a limited extent with Beckerath, the Christian interloper who remains "hopelessly different" from the all-too-Jewish milieu of his fiancée's family. As more than one reader has noticed, however, Mann's real interest lies in Siegmund.[57] The narrator observes with homoerotic fascination as Siegmund washes and perfumes his slender, boyish body, and then dons his elaborate outfit, piece by piece, while standing on a polar-bear rug. Like the bear, Siegmund has coarse hair that covers his body, a detail that gestures toward the primordial passion pervading the novella from "the brazen din, savage and primitive" (289)[58] of the gong that signals dinner in the Aarenhold house, through the "wild pulsating notes" (304)[59] of Wagner's music, to the twins' incestuous coupling on the bearskin rug. Herr Aarenhold had grown up "in a remote village in East Prussia" (293),[60] but several details point in a different direction: the mother looks "shriveled as though by tropic suns" (289–90);[61] Sieglinde and Beckerath plan to spend their honeymoon in Spain; the butler Wendelin looms like "a gigantic slave" above "the two dark, slender, fur-mantled, exotic creatures" (311).[62]

Even Baal and Zampa, the matched pair of horses that draws Siegmund and Sieglinde's carriage to the opera, hint at a realm of atavistic religion and racial difference evoking both the ancient Middle East and the contemporary colonial world. Baal was an ancient Middle Eastern fertility god associated with idol worship, frenzied dances, unbridled lust, self-mutilation, and even human sacrifice who tempted the Old Testament Hebrews to abandon the austere monotheism of Mosaic religion and revert to more primitive rites. But why would Mann name the other horse Zampa? According to Gerhard Wahrig's *Deutsches Wörterbuch, Zamba* is a term for a female child of a black and an Indian parent in Brazil (masculine *Zambo*), that is, a child of mixed race in the European colonies. Given that Mann made careful notes on the meaning of the terms *Mestize, Kreole,* and *Farbige* ("colored") while preparing to write *Royal Highness,* and that he even delved into esoteric racial distinctions between *Terzerones, Quarterones,* and *Quinterones,*[63] it is tempting to speculate that he chose the horses' names to underscore the imaginative association of Jewishness with primitivism and with racial mixtures in the colonial world.

Wälsungenblut's double subtext of homoeroticism and colonial exoticism simultaneously underscores the imagined difference between Christians and Jews in Mann's society and strengthens the link between Mann and his Jewish protagonist. The association of Jewishness with effeminacy and blackness belonged to the standard repertoire of anti-Semitic discourse around 1900. Yet Mann also had the drop of foreign "blood" and the homosexual desires that made him feel different from his companions and that were essential to his identity as an artist. Like Mann, Siegmund is an artist, or at least a dilettante and an aesthete. He takes expensive lessons in drawing and painting from a famous artist, even though he is well aware that he has no talent; he buys all the latest journals and books, but he only reads a few pages here and there; he is excited by the opera, but talks loudly during the performance and criticizes the orchestra during the intermission. Even the seemingly spontaneous desire for his sister has an element of artifice, since he is merely reenacting what he just watched on stage. In this regard, Siegmund is closely related to several other figures in Mann's early fiction, including the protagonist of *Der Bajazzo* (The Dilettante), a young man who gets up late, plays a little piano, reads a little, attends the theater or the opera, but feels bored and sorry for himself; Paolo Hoffmann of *The Will to Happiness,* who displays artistic talent as a boy, but matures into a sickly fop and dies on his wedding night; Detlev Spinell, the "writer" and poseur in *Tristan;* and the protagonist of *Das Wunderkind,* who entertains his audience with a mixture of virtuosity and calculated kitsch. Like Siegmund, each of these characters tends toward androgyny, effeminacy, or homosexuality, and they are almost all coded as racially different: Paolo has the yellow skin and dark ringlets of his South American mother, the Wunderkind is a long-haired, dark-skinned child prodigy from Greece who travels with an "Oriental" impresario (2.1: 399), and Detlev Spinell is coded in ways that suggest he is a Jew.[64]

The positive counterparts to these dilettantes include Mann's fictional portrait of Schiller in *Schwere Stunde* (Difficult Hour), Tonio Kröger, and Gustav von Aschenbach. They, too, lack the heterosexual vitality of such figures as the robust businessman Anton Klöterjahn in *Tristan* or the muscular trouble-maker Jappe in *Wie Jappe und Do Escobar sich prügelten* (How Jappe and Do Escobar Fought), and both Tonio Kröger and Gustav von Aschenbach have "exotic racial characteristics"[65] that set them apart from their more typically German counterparts. Yet each of these characters manages to overcome his weakness and to produce high-quality literature. The recipe for success seems clear: the great artist needs a touch of physical illness, homosexuality, or racial difference, but not too much. Without any stigmata, one remains normal and boring; too much difference renders one either artistically impotent or sends one careening into an abyss of destructive passion. Like his fictional counterparts, Thomas Mann had to calm his fluttering stomach, curb his illicit sexual desires, and force himself to sit and try to write a page or two of carefully conceived prose each morning. Even the productive artist walks a fine line: at his best—and the artist is always "he" for Mann[66]—the artist can sublimate Dionysian passion into Apollonian prose, as when Aschenbach observes and writes about Tadzio on the beach. There is always the danger, however, that the artist is the kind of charlatan that the later Nietzsche saw in Wagner, whose music was calculated to produce the effect of inspiration among the masses, but not truly inspired.[67] By an extension of the same logic, *Wälsungenblut* reflects not only Mann's lifelong ambivalence toward Wagner's music and the cult that surrounded it in his contemporary Germany,[68] but also his nagging doubts about the validity of his own work: he holds Wagner's Germanic heroes up to the mirror of their decadent Jewish imitators to unsettle the distinction between the genius and the dilettante and thus to call into question his own creative practice.

Royal Highness: Marriage as Fantasy

Royal Highness is the comic counterpart of the doubly nightmarish world of *Wälsungenblut:* nightmarish in its monstrous, anti-Semitic caricatures of Mann's new in-laws and in its distorted image of Mann as a sexually deviant dilettante. Like *Wälsungenblut, Royal Highness* received its decisive conceptual form in 1904–5, during the period of Mann's courtship of and marriage to Katia Pringsheim.[69] As was the case in *Wälsungenblut,* the novel contains recognizable portraits of Mann's acquaintances and family members, ranging from the dog Percival (Mann's Scottish collie Motz) to the protagonist's brother Albrecht (Heinrich Mann) and his father-in-law Samuel N. Spoelmann (Alfred Pringsheim).[70] Most obvious and important are Mann's portrait

of himself as a prince and of Katia Pringsheim as his spunky, hoydenish, alge-
bra-loving princess; Mann even incorporated some of his own love letters to
Katia into the novel. Clearly, then, *Royal Highness* is as much about Mann's
marriage as was *Wälsungenblut,* yet the contrast between the two works could
hardly be greater: in one an alien world of incest set to the dark strains of Wagner's *Ring* cycle, and in the other wedding bells chiming in tune with the triumphant chorus of the *Meistersinger.*[71] What has happened? How does Mann
turn tragedy to comedy in the fictional representation of his marriage, and
how does it reflect his response to the Jewish question?

Thomas Mann offered the reader a precisely drawn map of Lübeck and
surroundings in *Buddenbrooks,* providing every detail except the name of the
city. In his second novel, he shifted the setting to a clearly fictitious residency
that could have been almost anywhere in Wilhelminian Germany. In the place
of patrician burghers competing in business and politics, he depicted a family
of idle and idiosyncratic aristocrats. The Buddenbrooks and the Hagenströms
were defined by what they did: they ran the family businesses and participated
in the city government. The protagonists of *Royal Highness* are defined by who
they are; the function of Grand Duke Johann Albrecht and his sons Albrecht II
and Klaus Heinrich is purely representative. They live like old-fashioned aristocrats, but their way of life has become an anachronism in a society that is no
longer economically viable. As the minister of state Dr. Baron Knobelsdorff explains, the former princes were essentially peasants: "the ruling dynasty are
farmers; their capital consists in land and soil, their income in agricultural
profits."[72] Such an agrarian subsistence economy has become outmoded in the
early twentieth century, but the nobles have refused to become modern "in-
dustrialists and financiers" (8),[73] and the people are busy squandering what is
left of the natural resources that once provided the basis of their wealth. The
forests have been plundered for immediate use without a thought for future
generations, the silver mines are in disrepair, and a poorly conceived plan on
the part of the dairy farmers to make a quick profit by skimming the fat off
their milk has left the rest of the population undernourished.

The political atmosphere would seem ripe for revolution, but this is hardly
the case: "The people were pious and loyal, they loved their princes as themselves, they were permeated with the sublimity of the monarchical idea, they
saw in it a reflexion of the Deity" (30).[74] Despite the people's loyalty, neither
Grand Duke Albrecht nor his sons take any active measures to improve the
financial situation; they do not even try to understand it. As the various
palaces on their estate gradually crumble into ruins, they continue to go

through the motions of their exalted existence. Commoners who seek an audience with Klaus Heinrich know in advance that he neither grasps their problems nor is in any position to do anything about them, and yet they love their prince and seem satisfied with what is clearly a meaningless charade. Albrecht II, who is both physically weaker and sharper witted than his younger brother, has no stomach for the "hocus pocus of majesty" (134)[75] and gladly cedes his ceremonial roles to Klaus Heinrich. He performs the duties with great dignity, but only when his would-be fiancée Imma Spoelmann chides him for his detachment does he make an effort to understand the dismal financial situation of his land. He wins the favor of his reluctant bride by engrossing himself in the study of economic theory, but all the goodwill and financial acumen in the world would not improve the disastrous local economy. In the end, Klaus Heinrich makes his fortune the old-fashioned way: he marries into money. The traditional method comes with a modern twist, however, for he marries the millionaire daughter of an American industrialist and financial tycoon.

Imma's paternal grandfather was a German who immigrated to America in search of fortune. Setting off with only a pic-ax, shovel, and tin pan, he joined the Gold Rush, and, as luck would have it, found a giant nugget on a claim that he had bought with his last dollar. With a combination of continuing good fortune and shrewd business sense, Spoelmann soon became fabulously wealthy. He invested the profits in railroads, steel, and various other trusts, as well as in "the famous Blockhead Farm . . . the property which, with its petroleum wells, in a short time increased in value to a hundred times its purchase price" (173).[76] The interest from his investments soon began to snowball, and by the time that his son, Samuel Spoelmann, inherited the family business, there was little more to do "but to collect the princely dividends and keep growing richer and richer till he beat all records" (140).[77] Personally unsuited to his role as a captain of industry and of delicate health, Samuel Spoelmann seeks out the healing waters of Klaus Heinrich's duchy. Here he finds a retirement home, and his daughter Imma finds a husband. The new wealth props up the old regime as a kind of conservative theme park, a prerevolutionary social structure funded by modern industrial capital.

Taken at face value, *Royal Highness* could be read as a reactionary glorification of the monarchy in Wilhelminian Germany, but since both the people and at least Albrecht II see through the charade, it could just as easily be understood as a comic send-up of a monarchy that stages itself as an empty ritual.[78] While Mann's depiction of the aristocracy may be ambivalent, his lack of interest in the plight of the common man is clear. The people in *Royal High-*

ness are distinguished more by their foolishness than their revolutionary zeal: they revere princes that they know are impotent and ignorant, while ravishing the natural resources that once served as the foundation for the local economy. "But I have no interest at all in political freedom," declared Mann in a letter of 1904 in response to Heinrich's apparent turn toward political liberalism—the same letter that goes on to describe with a certain smug satisfaction Mann's successful entry into high society in the Pringsheim mansion: "I do have a certain princely talent for representation."[79] *Die Hungernden* (*The Hungry*, 1903), a slightly earlier sketch written in preparation for themes treated at length in *Tonio Kröger*, underscores Mann's lack of concern for the less fortunate. Mann depicts a tormented artist driven by jealousy out of a party and into the streets after observing the woman he loves flirting with another man. Here he nearly bumps into a disheveled street person, who regards the artist—with his fur coat, lorgnette, and patent leather shoes—with a mixture of envy and disdain. Does the elegantly dressed artist experience an epiphany of social consciousness in which he realizes that his own problems pale in the light of real poverty? Not at all; in fact, he aggressively rejects the very suggestion: "your image of misery is not a frightening and shaming warning from a foreign world. We are brothers, after all!"[80] Solidarity with the social outcast contributes to the self-understanding of the self-pitying artist, not to a heightened sense of compassion for the hungry and poor.

Royal Highness can also be read as an allegory of the artist, who remains detached from the people he purports to represent. Like Tonio Kröger, Klaus Heinrich is stigmatized by physical difference: he has a withered hand; Tonio has his mother's southern blood. Both characters learn to overcome their complete separation from the society they can never join. Tonio confesses in his final letter to Lisaweta Iwanowna that his love for the simple burgher is the distinguishing feature of his art, as opposed to "those proud, cold spirits who venture out along the paths of grandiose, demonic beauty and despise 'humanity.'"[81] Klaus Heinrich's devotion to the study of economics signals a similar turn toward active concern for the people he represents. As noted, however, what saves the crumbling local economy is not his sudden interest in financial theory, but an infusion of American monopoly capital. The allegory of the artist unfolds against a very worldly background.

The positive role granted the Spoelmann fortune in *Royal Highness* is surprising, given the elements of antimodernism and anti-Semitism in Mann's earlier fiction. In *Buddenbrooks*, Mann drew merciless caricatures of Prussian teachers who espoused the swaggering ethos of the modern military-industrial *Machtstaat*. While the decadent Buddenbrooks decline into sickness and artistic sensibility, the children of the partially Jewish Hagenström family thrive in the brutally robust climate of the new empire. Berlin is the home of fast-talking (Jewish) lawyers and (Jewish) women who hatch revolutionary plots around their tea tables. In *Wälsungenblut,* the wealth of the (Jewish) Aarenhold family flows from coal mines that Herr Aarenhold had acquired through dubious machinations in Eastern Europe. But surely Samuel Spoelmann is not a Jew—or is he? The Old Testament name Samuel hints in a direction that would seem to be confirmed by Mann's early drafts of the novel, in which the family name was to have been Davis or Davidsohn.

> Davis' parents were German (actually Davidsohn or Davids) and immigrated to America as small-time trades-people. Samuel D. is born in Milwaukee . . . and marries the daughter of a plantation owner near Bahia [Brazil] with a German father and a Portuguese mother.[82]

Peter de Mendelssohn concludes that "the parents of the millionaire Samuel Davis were therefore poor Jewish immigrants from Germany named Davidson, and thus Imma would have been an American who was one-quarter Jewish (*Vierteljüdin*) with German and Portuguese ancestors."[83] He speculates that Mann changed Imma's family heritage because it would have been implausible for a German crown prince to marry a woman of even partial Jewish descent at the time the novel was written, which is no doubt true, but does not account for the delicate balancing act that Mann performed in crafting the identity of Imma's family background in the final version of the novel.

Although a character named Samuel Davidsohn would almost certainly have been understood to be Jewish, Mann never explicitly identified him as such. In fact, in the very note in which he suggests Davidsohn as a possible name, Mann states directly that "he is a Protestant."[84] So was the baptized Jew Alfred Pringsheim, however, who, according to Katia Pringsheim-Mann, was clearly the model for Davidsohn/Spoelmann and would have easily been recognized as such by early readers of the novel familiar with Munich society.[85] The shift in name from Davis or Davidsohn to Spoelmann is not a switch from a character that is definitely Jewish to one that is definitely not Jewish, but from one who is very probably Jewish to one who might be Jewish or might have been Jewish before conversion. Whereas in *Wälsungenblut* Mann had exaggerated the racial distinction between Christians and Jews—a hopelessly different breed and kind—here he works in shades of gray, toning down the former Jewish caricatures into figures that are at most subliminally Jewish.

As a result of changes in the novel's conception, Samuel Spoelmann's daughter Imma inherits a particularly elaborate family heritage. In the early fragment cited previously, Mann notes that her mother was supposed to have been the daughter of Brazilian plantation owners with a German father and a Portuguese mother—a background that would have moved the fictional portrait of Katia Pringsheim closer to that of Mann's mother, Julia da Silva Bruhns-Mann.[86] The completed novel modifies this identity in an initially ambiguous way. After Imma's German grandfather found his giant gold nugget and made his fortune, he is said to have married a "woman from the South— Creole blood, the daughter of a German father and an indigenous mother [eingeborener Mutter]" (140).[87] Creole typically refers to a person of European ancestry born in the Americas, as opposed to a Native American, as Mann was well aware: "Creole in the former French, Spanish, and Portuguese colonies of America or Africa are the people born locally [die Eingeborenen] of purely European blood," notes Mann in preparation for the novel. "Mestize (literally a half-breed [Mischling]) refers to mixtures of whites and Indians," he adds, whereas "colored people [Farbige] is a general term for indigenous Indians and Negroes, who—unlike (locally born) Europeans and Creoles—are half-breeds as a result of marriage among themselves or with the whites; more specifically, only those half-breeds that are distinct from the pure-blooded Whites, Negroes, and Indians."[88]

The initial reference to Imma's South American mother could be interpreted as consistent with the earlier drafts: his mother is a Creole of purely European extraction born in South America, just like Mann's mother Julia, who, to recall Viktor Mann's words, knew that she was "white" and "free" when growing up among the slaves on the Brazilian plantation. Subsequent references to Imma Spoelmann's heritage make it clear that a shift has occurred, however, for we learn that Imma's grandfather married "a woman of Indian blood," and she is therefore technically "a quintroon" or, more simply, "a colored girl" (245)."[89] Her father, Samuel Spoelmann, married "a German-American of half-English blood, and their daughter is now Miss Spoelmann" (140).[90] As Herr von Knobelsdorff summarizes, Imma Spoelmann has a "fourfold blood mixture ... for besides the Anglo-Saxon, Portuguese and German, some drops of ancient noble Indian blood were said to flow in her veins" (316).[91]

The figure of Imma Spoelmann in Royal Highness thus draws on and significantly modifies two biographical sources. By conflating the fictional portrait of Katia Pringsheim with that of his mother, Mann transforms a potentially frightening and alien figure into someone familiar and maternal—thus anticipating Mut-em-Enet's proto-Freudian comment in *Joseph and His Brothers:* "Every man sleeps with his mother—did you not know that?"[92] Yet Mann's mother was not a "quintroon" or "colored girl" as Mann defines the term; she only looked black to her relatives when she and her deeply tanned siblings arrived in Lübeck with their African nanny. Katia Pringsheim, on the other hand, was marked as a Jew in Christian Germany. In portraying her as Imma Spoelmann, Mann minimizes her Jewishness and transforms her perceived racial difference into Indian blood. In the Americas, the "colored girl" becomes the target of racial prejudice, but in Europe she finds acceptance as a noble savage. Thus Mann transforms anti-Semitic Germany into a safe haven for the persecuted "half-breeds" of the New World!

In an effort to render Imma Spoelmann less threatening and more appealing, Mann also limits the percentage of alien blood, diluting the straight spirits of the Aarenhold family into an exotic cocktail with just a drop of Native American essence. At the same time, Mann adds a dash of Anglo-Saxon to the mix—Samuel Spoelmann's wife is half English—perhaps in an effort to further bleach out the ethnic heritage of his otherwise all-too-swarthy heroine, but perhaps also to hint at the uncanny proximity of colonizer and colonized, Christian and Jew, free white and black slave already suggested in *Buddenbrooks.* Mann also infantilizes and desexualizes Imma Spoelmann: her head and hands are often described with diminutives and "there was something childish in her manner of speech" (202).[93] "Little sister" is his term of affection for her when he finally proposes, in what the narrator dryly describes as "a peculiar plighting of troth" (313).[94] Imma is rendered still more appealing by her frequent association with Orientalist motifs: she owns an Arabian horse named Fatme and is described alternately as a "Fairy-child from Fableland" (273) or the "Queen of Sheba" (307).[95] Her father is identified as "Vogel Roch," a giant, mythical bird in *1001 Nights,* and he transforms the rundown ducal palace *Delphinenort* into something of an Oriental mansion: he fills his winter garden with palm trees of all varieties, wraps himself in a green silk robe decorated with colorful parrots, and stations two grinning black lackeys in red velvet livery before the gates.

Taken together, these changes allow Mann to transform the potentially debilitating poison of his marriage into an inoculation of exoticism—just enough racial difference, but not too much—that will grant him the "austere happiness" appropriate for the living oxymoron of the married artist.[96] In the process, he launders the filthy (Jewish) lucre of modern industrial capitalism into the fabled riches of Araby; not coincidentally, the theme of the sermon at Klaus Heinrich's wedding is based on "the passage of the Psalms which runs: 'he shall live, and unto him shall be given of the gold of Arabia'" (337).[97]

Heinrich Detering has argued that *Royal Highness* is about the mutual emancipation of a group of social outcasts, who learn to love each other and to accept themselves.[98] But not everyone is allowed to enjoy the operatic ending of Mann's romantic comedy. Just as Wagner's Beckmesser—arguably a coded Jew[99]—limps from the stage, bloodied and humiliated at the otherwise triumphant conclusion to the *Meistersinger,* so, too, *Royal Highness* ends with a suicide as well as a marriage. Raoul Überbein, Klaus Heinrich's ambitious mentor, kills himself when school administrators refuse to appoint him as the permanent teacher of group of students whom he had taught for several months as a substitute. Thwarted professional ambition is the obvious motivation for his suicide, but there may also be an element of repressed homosexual jealousy at work, as his former ward decides to marry.[100] Klaus Heinrich's withered hand can be read both as a historical allusion to Kaiser Wilhelm II's physical deformity and as a coded autobiographical reference to Mann's homosexuality and sense of racial difference. Like his Jewish friend Dr. Sammet, Überbein is also stigmatized by his "misfortunate birth":[101] his mother was an actress, his father unknown, but possibly named Raoul; Überbein refers to himself as "a born gypsy" (75).[102] Other characters in *Royal Highness* do manage to attain happiness despite their handicaps: the one-armed artist qua prince marries; Dr. Sammet overcomes the blemish of his birth (Jewishness) and assimilates to Christian society; the "colored girl" becomes the belle of the ball. Überbein's suicide serves as a reminder of the debilitating forces that Klaus Heinrich manages to keep at bay, but which will return with a vengeance to destroy Gustav von Aschenbach and Adrian Leverkühn. In *Royal Highness,* Mann allowed his protagonists the luxury of a happy ending—a decision that raised the suspicion that he was pandering to the masses and left him with mixed feelings, even though the happiness is muted and not shared by all.[103] Not until the conclusion of *Joseph and His Brothers* would Mann orchestrate a similarly upbeat finale to his fiction.

CHAPTER FOUR

Reflections of a Nonpolitical Man: Conservative Anti-imperialism

If *Wälsungenblut* is Thomas Mann's most notorious work of fiction, then the *Reflections of a Nonpolitical Man* is its essayistic equivalent, the work that critics most love to hate.[1] While Mann's fiction displays an almost uncanny sense of detail and structural precision, *Reflections* is a baggy monster, a sprawling work that often gives the impression that Mann was making it up as he went along.[2] On the level of content, Mann's repetitious tirade against democracy and the Enlightenment seems calculated to offend anyone with respect for the values of Western civilization. As a deeply personal work, moreover, *Reflections* reveals Mann at his least appealing: the work radiates hatred for his brother Heinrich and often seems to have been written with barely contained rage. The essay combines boundless self-pity with a callous disregard for the sufferings of others.[3] Mann, who sat out the war in the comfort of his villa, has the audacity to refer to himself as "a war casualty" (*Kriegbeschädigter*),[4] while convincing himself that those maimed and crippled by the war did not suffer long or unduly. In one of the strangest passages in the book, Mann reports that he has heard that those blinded in battle are actually among the most cheerful of patients, and that they often pelt each other with their new glass eyes out of a sense of playful exuberance.[5] Thus Mann's longest essay is often dismissed as compositionally flawed, politically dangerous, and personally repellent.

Reflections is nevertheless a pivotal work in Mann's career and also marks a turning point in German intellectual history. At its most disturbing, *Reflections* embraces elements of conservative thought that would soon inform the National Socialist movement.[6] That Mann's closest friend and intellectual companion of the war years, Ernst Bertram, was to emerge as a staunch supporter of the Third Reich indicates Mann's own proximity to certain ominous thought patterns at this time. Unlike Bertram, however, Mann did not allow himself to be deceived by what he very early denounced as "the swastika nonsense" (*der Hakenkreuz Unfug*),[7] and if we look more closely, we see that *Reflections* is as much a part of Goethe's and Wieland's humanistic legacy as it is an offspring of the more troubling aspects of German romanticism.[8] If nothing else, *Reflections* serves as a cautionary tale for those who would depict the intellectual origins of the National Socialist movement as a clear path that led inevitably from the *völkisch* thought of certain German Romantics to the fascist ideology of the Third Reich. Mann could easily have followed that path, but he did not; alternatives were possible even for a self-proclaimed "nonpolitical" conservative steeped in a German intellectual tradition that contained the potential for redemption as well as disaster.

Reflections also gives Mann the opportunity to look back over the first decades of his career and to reflect on the set of beliefs and—yes—*political* opinions that informed this nonpolitical writer. As Ernst Bertram aptly put it in his advertising blurb for Mann's work, "you could call the book the *intellectual Buddenbrooks*."[9] Looking forward, *Reflections* serves as a benchmark against which we can measure Mann's movement toward support of the Weimar Republic; it also marks the beginning of his subsequent role as a prolific cultural and political essayist. These essays, in turn, would leave an indelible imprint on his later fiction, transforming the realism of his first novel into the intellectual tours de force of *The Magic Mountain, Joseph and His Brothers,* and *Doctor Faustus.* Above all, *Reflections* served as a private forum in which Mann pondered his origins as a burgher of the Hanseatic city-state of Lübeck and his development as an artist in, if not quite of, the bohemian world of Munich, at a time when the centralized Prussian nation-state was consolidating its authority at home and aggressively expanding its overseas empire.

Reflections not only contains an intimate account of Mann's feud with his brother under the thinly disguised veil of "civilization's literary man" (*Zivilisationsliterat*), but also a sustained public indictment of what he terms "the empire of human civilization" (23),[10] or the "*imperialism of civilization*" (33).[11] By *imperialism,* Mann means both the political practice that had led European nations to control the vast majority of the world's territory by 1914 and the mentality that made such practice seem justified and inevitable. From Mann's perspective, the missionary zeal that inspired western European nations to export their version of civilization to the rest of the world was a form of masked aggression that had its historical roots in the French Revolution and Napoleonic Wars: rather than keeping "this specifically French concept of 'human rights' and of historical stability" to themselves, the French felt compelled "to spread them over the world, to fill the world and *all* other nations with them" (131–32).[12] Mann makes repeated references to France, or, more broadly, the West, as heirs to the Roman Empire that have now joined forces in the struggle against Germany. Looking to the future, Mann envisions a world controlled by "a few gigantic world empires, which—whether Germany is one of them or not—will have divided the administration of the globe among themselves" (258).[13]

Mann levels two particular charges against the "empire of civilization" that have their intellectual-historical roots in eighteenth- and nineteenth-century German thought, but which continue to resonate in today's postcolonial era of globalization. One is that the triumph "of the world Imperium of civilization" will lead to "a development that is leveling all national culture into a homogeneous civilization" (174–75).[14] While Mann's fear of "a complete leveling, of a journalistic-rhetorical stultification and vulgarization" (187)[15] echoes Nietzsche's disdain for the common herd and his fear that democratization will debase culture to the lowest common denominator, it also anticipates today's jeremiads about globalization's tendency to blanch out local color and leave only a drab "McWorld" behind, united by multinational corporations and fueled by franchise food.[16] Mann's second goal is to expose the hypocrisy of a civilization that preaches human rights but practices violent conquest, exploitation, and racism. Theodore Roosevelt brags about the American abolishment of slavery, when, according to Mann, he should have been ashamed that it existed in the first place (129; 13.1: 197). The British conquer India, the Italians invade Libya, the French take over Morocco, and yet civilization's literary man "has nothing but excuses . . . after all, we are dealing here with Asia, with 'dark masses,' with niggers" (259–60).[17]

Mann was not the first German intellectual to condemn abuses perpetrated in the name of Western civilization. In the eighteenth century, for instance, Johann Gottfried Herder had spoken out eloquently against cultures that sought to impose their will on others, including the ancient Romans, medieval crusaders, and modern imperialists.[18] More surprisingly, the conservative Thomas Mann of the *Reflections* also articulates ideas that anticipate the anti-imperialist critique of today's postcolonial theorists.[19] And although Mann would have been loath to admit it at the time, these passages in the *Reflections* find direct parallels in the novel that made his brother and archenemy into a European celebrity of the Left, just as Mann was publishing the essay that established his right-wing credentials.[20] Heinrich Mann's *Der Untertan* (Man of Straw) (completed 1914, but withheld from widespread distribution until 1918) paints the portrait of the typical Wilhelminian subject,

Diederich Hessling, a sadomasochistic, anti-Semitic anti-Socialist who is also a sycophantic admirer of the kaiser. In terms of both style and content, Heinrich's assault on the German *Obrigskeitsstaat* embodied the worst tendencies of what Thomas Mann rather vaguely termed "Expressionist" literature,[21] and yet Heinrich shares with his brother a fellow Lübecker's distrust of imperial Prussia. "The student corporation, armed service, and the air of imperialism had educated him and made him fit,"[22] writes Heinrich of his young protagonist, a hard-drinking fraternity boy and hypocritical draft-dodger. Hessling soon sets out to expand the family business in the spirit of the new age: "One had to become competitive. Our place in the sun!"[23] "Do you want your kaiser to give you colonies?" Hessling questions his fellow conservatives, "then you had better sharpen his sword!"[24] *Der Untertan* culminates in a patriotic celebration in which Hessling delivers a speech denouncing Great Britain and declaring support for Germany's naval buildup—"the ocean is indispensable for Germany's grandeur . . . because the business of the world is the most important business today"[25]—but a cloudburst of apocalyptic proportions drowns out his speech and signals the bankruptcy of his imperial ambitions.

My point is not to deny the opposition between Thomas and Heinrich Mann during the First World War, but to suggest how two individuals from opposite ends of the political spectrum could arrive at similarly critical assessments of German imperialism. German attitudes toward imperialism varied widely around 1900, from enthusiastic support to complete rejection.[26] After a period of youthful conservatism and anti-Semitism, Heinrich Mann developed toward an anticolonial stance typical of the left-wing Social Democratic Party. In 1889, for instance, SPD representative August Bebel delivered a speech in the Reichstag condemning colonialism, equating the practice with the violent oppression, exploitation, and extermination of foreign peoples;[27] in 1904, Bebel and Karl Liebknecht denounced Lothar von Trotha's crimes against humanity in the wake of the notorious Herero massacre.[28] The political positions of the "nonpolitical" Thomas Mann, in contrast, emerged out of the tradition of conservative thought that included Goethe, Nietzsche, and Burckhardt, and yet Goethe also resisted militant nationalism, while Nietzsche and Burckhardt opposed Prussian imperialism.[29] Mann was also influenced by Paul de Lagarde, Julius Langbehn, and Arthur Moeller van den Bruck, all of whom rejected Germany's quest for overseas colonies in favor of acquiring more Lebensraum in Eastern Europe—ideas that Hitler would reiterate in *Mein Kampf.*[30]

German National Identity and the Jewish Question

As Thomas Mann argues in the *Reflections,* imperialism takes place within Europe as well as overseas. The British had set their sights on Ireland long before they sailed for India (260; 13.1: 389) and now the Entente was threatening to overrun Germany. The German tendency to view themselves as victims of foreign aggression has a long history that extends back to Luther's invectives against Rome and eighteenth-century polemics against the cultural hegemony of the French.[31] Continuing this tradition, Mann concedes that the military invasion of Germany has stalled, but argues that the allies have set their hopes on "the intellectual invasion that is possibly by far the strongest and most overpowering *political* invasion by the West that has ever become German destiny" (19).[32] In a sense, however, the battle against Western influence has already been lost, for the unification of Germany through Prussian imperialism under Bismarck has rendered it no better than England or France. The glorification of "militarism, lordliness and power" (171)[33] has led to "a new epoch of German civilization and imperialism . . . Germany's development to *democracy*" (174).[34] In the prewar years, the "Americanization of the German lifestyle" had already begun to infect even provincial Munich, while in Berlin one was exposed to nothing but "the sharp air of the Prussian-American metropolis" (100).[35]

What, then, does Thomas Mann mean with his repeated tautological assertions that Germany must remain German? What is Germany's "natural," indigenous way of life and form of government? In simplest terms, the real Germany for Mann is the Germany of his father and his Hanseatic home. Lübeck belonged to a loose confederation of semiautonomous city-states and provinces, not to the tight administrative network of the modern, centralized nation-state. In this world, class distinctions were still clear and accepted; at least in theory, workers respected their superiors, who in turn cared for them with paternal benevolence. The burghers were happy to leave the business of government to others and to concentrate instead on their own inner development or *Bildung.* Mann's nostalgic image of the past can easily be condemned as being at best naive; his portrayal of loyal subjects in a fictive German duchy in *Royal Highness* rings false in comparison with Heinrich Mann's bitingly satirical portrait of his hometown in *Professor Unrat.* In principle, however, Thomas Mann's early political views participate in an outmoded and idealized but still respectable tradition of German humanism, in agreement with Wilhelm von Humboldt's argument that the best form of government is one that interferes least in the lives of its citizens and with Goethe's preference for organic social evolution over violent political revolution.[36]

Thomas Mann is not only a belated child of the "Age of Goethe," however, but also an autodidact influenced, however haphazardly, by the ideas of his contemporaries, and it is his occasional appropriation of *völkisch* thought that renders the *Reflections* most disturbing. One of Mann's chief sources in this regard was Paul de Lagarde (1827–91), an antidemocratic, antiliberal, antimodern, and anti-Semitic writer whom Thomas Mann embraces as a "*praeceptor Germaniae*" (199; 13.1: 301). Like Mann, Lagarde supported the monarchy and spoke of *Kultur* and *Bildung* as the highest values of his "Faustian" nation.[37] As noted, Lagarde was indifferent to Germany's overseas colonies, but only because he was obsessed with the idea that the Germans needed to expand their Lebensraum into an Eastern Europe "cleansed of its Jews."[38] Germany should be a place for Germans only, decreed Lagarde, defined in the same sort of tautological logic that Mann will adopt: "the entirety of all those who feel German, think German, and desire in a German way."[39] Following in the path of his dubious mentor, Mann calls for an almost mystical rejuvenation of the German *Volk*. "It is true," he writes, "to regard nations as mythical individuals is a primitive-popular way of regarding things, and patriotism itself may signify an emotion of more mythical-primitive than political-intellectual nature" (108).[40] The true artist must be able to tap this primitive spirit, and even if he is a respectable burgher in daily life, "he is still perhaps only an artist and poet as far as he is national and has not completely forgotten how to observe and feel in a nationally (*volkhaft*) primitive way" (108).[41] Citing Lagarde, Mann agrees that isolated individuals do not speak for the people, but that the "people (*Volk*) only speak when national character (*die Volkheit*) . . . becomes vocal in the individuals" (108).[42]

The understanding of the artist as a medium for the collective expression of the people corresponded with Mann's favorite metaphor of himself as a cultural seismograph, "because I only had to listen to my own inner voice to hear the voice of the times as well" (15).[43] Whether or not the patrician's son and artist qua political essayist was really in touch with the mystical spirit of the German *Volk* in the midst of the First World War is at best questionable;[44] more fundamentally problematic is Mann's willingness to think in such categories at all. When he writes in the *Reflections* of the "Nationalkultur" as something that emerges "out of the organic depth of national life" (179),[45] when he dabbles in the idea that the nation needs a new, Germanic religion, and when he envisions a Germanic "*Volksstaat* . . . under a leader (*Führer*) who has the characteristics of a great man of German stamp" (267),[46] Mann is moving within a realm of ideas that would soon become a terrible reality in the Third Reich. Once one begins to think of the nation as a biotic community, it is all too easy to turn on those deemed *artfremd*, racially marked others that must be excised from the body politic. According to Lagarde, there are only two conceivable solutions to the Jewish question: the Jews must either assimilate to the point of becoming invisible within Germany, or they must go somewhere else. "But for God's sake, either bring them entirely in, or [throw them] entirely out."[47] For a writer who believes that nationality lies in the "descent from a common ancestor,"[48] however, it is difficult to imagine that the Jews will ever be able to assimilate to the German people: "the Jews remain Jews."[49]

At this point Mann's critics often breathe a sigh of relief, pointing out that while Mann may have counted such writers as Lagarde, Houston Stewart Chamberlain, and Dostoyevsky among his influences, he pointedly avoids their overt anti-Semitism. "For all the criticism that can be leveled at the *Reflections*," Hermann Kurzke reassures us, "they are not anti-Semitic."[50] In his opinion, Mann was so caught up in his hatred of "civilization's literary man" that his work left no room for anti-Semitic remarks, even if Mann had wanted to make them, which he did not. Upon closer reading, however, Mann's text is considerably more complex and less unambiguously devoid of anti-Semitism than his apologists are willing to acknowledge.[51] As even Kurzke concedes, the characterization of the *Zivilisationsliterat* coincides closely with stereotypes of the modern Jewish intellectual.[52] Does Mann really exclude anti-Semitism entirely, or does he once again include it as a subliminal presence in the text? In order to address this question, we need to take a brief detour through the fragments that Mann drafted in preparation for an essay that would have been titled "Intellect and Art." As in the case of *Wälsungenblut*, which Mann withdrew at the last minute from publication, the unpublished essay fragments afford insights into aspects of Mann's treatment of the Jewish question that lie just beneath the surface of other published works.

"Intellect and Art"

Mann began "Intellect and Art" in the spring of 1909, just after completing *Royal Highness*. He worked on it throughout the year and took it up again in 1911 and 1912. Although he was unable to complete it, he drew on the fragments in several of his subsequently published essays, including the *Reflections*, while attributing the authorship of a fictitious essay of the same name to Gustav von Aschenbach in *Death in Venice*.[53] Mann's primary goal in the fragmentary essay is to defend himself against the charge that he was a mere *Schriftsteller* (writer) and not a *Dichter* (poet), that is, that he was a coldly calculating intellectual and not an inspired artist. The prejudice against the *Schriftsteller* had its origins in eighteenth-century autonomy aesthetics and the cult of the Romantic genius; it was also linked throughout the nineteenth century to the problematic status of the modern novel as a genre that had no clear classical precedent.[54] More immediate motivation for Mann's essay came from his reaction against what he felt was a general anti-intellectual tendency in Munich, exemplified by a "chauvinistic fashion in literature" that encouraged writers to proclaim the Germanness of their art,[55] and above all, his conflicted response to Wagner's music and the cult that surrounded it.

Mann begins with a direct defense of the *Schriftsteller* and the corresponding genre of *Litteratur,* the old-fashioned spelling for literature as opposed to *Dichtung* or poetry. Literature is said to come from books rather than life, he argues, and yet how can one begin to write without having read first? "Original genius without reading is a superstition."[56] The modern artist has to be an intellectual, and today's novelists write the appropriate genre for the times. Those who would elevate poets and artists above writers and critics are simply wrong. Literature is said to be out of touch with the people, but did anthologies of supposedly popular Romantic poetry ever gain a wide reading audience? The early Romantics were brilliant intellectuals who wrote for a handful of initiates, not oracles in mystic communion with the *Volk*. And yet, Mann notes with disdain, no one wants to be a good novelist these days; everyone wants to write epics. "Being able to write is considered worthless, whereas what bubbles up from Orphic depths—or pretends to—is highly valued."[57]

Other passages in "Intellect and Art" complicate Mann's defense of the *Schriftsteller* or *Litterat,* however, in ways that are often linked to the Jewish question. In one of the early fragments, Mann notes that "hostility toward literature is more or less innate to the Germans," particularly in Munich. "Berlin is better off, because of brilliance, wit. . . . Besides, Jewish intellect. People of the book."[58] In this passage, Mann praises Jewish intelligence and affinity for literature as an antidote to the Wagner-loving anti-intellectuals in Munich. Thus the next entry initially comes as a surprise: "Praise God that I am not a Jew!" Is this an example of Mann's undiluted anti-Semitism? Not exactly. The entry continues: "Otherwise people would immediately say: of course, that's another reason! But I do have a little Latin blood that protests against the antiliterary idiocy."[59] The logic behind this cryptic passage is as follows: I am already exposed to prejudice as a *Schriftsteller* or *Litterat,* and literature has close affinities with Jewish intellect. Actually being Jewish in addition to writing "Jewish" literature would hand more ammunition to my critics. In fact, as Mann notes in a later fragment, the conservative critic Adolf Bartels claimed that while both Thomas and Heinrich Mann insisted that they were not Jews, their art was "essentially Jewish."[60] In a series of vicious attacks, Bartels also cited Mann's "proximity to and dependence on Jews," called attention to the fact that he had married "the daughter of the Jewish mathematics professor Pringsheim," and noted that Mann's mother was "Portuguese, and thus perhaps not without Jewish and Negro blood."[61] Thus when Mann utters a sigh of relief that he is not a Jew, while at the same time introducing his Latin blood as a factor "that protests against the anti-literary idiocy," he combines racialist biology with literary categories in a typically convoluted way: I write literature like a Jew, even though I am not a Jew, but perhaps the reason that I can write literature is that I have a drop of Latin blood. Mann first separates ethnic or racial identity from aesthetic practice, only to reintroduce it in a new form, resulting in two distinct arguments: (*a*) I write like a Jewish intellectual because I am an intellectual, not because I am a Jew; and (*b*) I write like a Jewish intellectual because I am part Portuguese-Brazilian. Race matters after all, as long as it is the right kind of race, as the shift from Sieglind Aarenhold to Imma Spoelmann has already made clear.

While this fragment introduces the Jews as somewhat uncomfortable allies, others place Jews squarely among the enemies. In the defense of literature previously cited, Mann essentially argues that literature is the only game in town: he dismisses the notion of original genius and heaps scorn on those who babble in pseudo-profundity. We have only two different kinds of artists: those who are honest about the fact that they are modern intellectuals and those who pretend to be what they are not. Wagner is the worst offender in this regard, Mann contends, in an argument that echoes Nietzsche's critique in *The Case of Wagner.* While the early Nietzsche had hailed Wagner as a genius who could restore mythic profundity to prosaic nineteenth-century society, he later accused him of being a mere charlatan, who enraptures the masses and inspires an ill-fated turn toward a chauvinistic German nationalism in the arts. "No, one cannot admire Wagner,"[62] Mann concludes, but he is not the only example of a dissembling artist in "Intellect and Art," for Mann also singles out a certain type of Jewish writer for harsh criticism.

"The *Litterat* in a negative sense seems to me a writer who affects . . . a taste that is not really his," writes Mann, like "certain Jewish Romantics."[63] While Mann concedes that it is not inconceivable that a Jew might honestly endorse certain aristocratic and reactionary tendencies, he clearly finds it unlikely, a phenomenon that might be interesting only because of its "sublime perverseness." He concludes the fragment with a stern warning: "you should know who you are ... otherwise you will not be convincing. ... What you will produce is *Litteratur.*"[64] Still worse would be a Jew who embraces German nationalism under false pretenses: "a smart Jew ... who in his heart disdains narrow nationalism yet nevertheless makes use of it to convince the public that they are getting something robustly warm-hearted and innocently rooted in the soil ... is a repulsive example of something 'literary' in the lowest sense."[65] Mann simultaneously condemns national chauvinism in literature and internationally oriented Jews for adopting nationalist pathos as a false pose. The passage thus mounts an attack on excessive German nationalism on the back of an assault against certain shifty and rootless Jewish intellectuals.

The Jewish Question in the *Reflections*

If we return to the *Reflections,* we see that the initially positive connotation of the *Litterat* in "Intellect and Art" has turned into the negative portrait of "civilization's literary man," who has also inherited the charges of inauthenticity attributed to certain Jewish writers in "Intellect and Art." Mann explains that Nietzsche, despite being one of his firmest allies in the conservative cause, nevertheless displayed such rhetorical brilliance that he provided weapons for his enemies: "all of our civilization writers have learned how to write from him" (60).[66] Nietzsche's stylistic influence on subsequent writers resembles that of "Heinrich Heine, the Jew who adapted himself to Paris" (61).[67] The otherwise superfluous reminder of Heine's Jewishness in this context suggests a close affinity between the alleged verbal prolixity of both "civilization's literary man" and the Jew. In another passage, Mann contrasts the noble enthusiasm of the German people as they prepared for war in August 1914, with the frantic gestures and idiotic babble of a political activist whom he happened to witness in a streetcar in Munich: "He is going full steam, in a political rage ... he sticks his thumbs in his vest and with vulgar humor imitates a Jew" (79).[68] Still later Mann ridicules the "wild rhetoric" of a French general who claimed that he would wash his hands in a bucket of excrement if he happened to touch someone he considered to be subhuman. A German would never sink to such crass prejudice, Mann contends, but the French have no such qualms. Even worse, this particular Frenchman is also a Jew—"he signs his name Lévy, moreover" (332)[69]—implying that this is a case of the kettle calling the pot black, that is, a person already stigmatized by his Jewishness has no right to harbor racial prejudices of his own.

Such direct references to Jews in the *Reflections* are admittedly rare, but they underscore the associative link between Jews and *Zivilisationsliteraten*. The distinction between Thomas Mann and his blatantly anti-Semitic allies is a matter of degree rather than absolute difference; the operative distinction in the *Reflections* is not between philo- and anti-Semitism, but between overt and covert prejudice. While Mann will occasionally lapse into openly anti-Semitic stereotypes in his early essays and fiction—most notoriously in *Wälsungenblut*—he more typically codes characters with a wink and a nudge to those in the know: the Hagenström's noses, the officious salesman in *Gladius Dei*, the dilettante Detlev Spinell, the semiconcealed background of Samuel (Davidson) Spoelmann.

What most clearly distinguishes Mann from the self-righteous rhetoric of openly anti-Semitic ideologues like Lagarde, Langbehn, and Chamberlain is his willingness to indict himself as well as his enemies. Mann's early fiction depicts characters marked by physical, ethnic, sexual, or religious difference in a way that hovers between revulsion and identification, hatred and self-hatred.[70] Mann began "Intellect and Art," with its blistering critique of Wagner's theatricality and tendency to pander to the masses, immediately after he completed *Royal Highness,* a novel that he admitted had been written under the influence of Wagner's *Meistersinger* and with an eye toward pleasing the multitudes as well as the cultural elite. The same tendency toward self-criticism recurs in the *Reflections.* If "civilization's literary man" honed his rhetorical skills on Nietzsche, so, too, did Thomas Mann. Despite his contention that Germans lack words, Mann knows that he does not suffer from the same problem. Instead, he contends that he makes use of the enemy's weapon: "it seemed to me that on the contrary, I had usurped the most characteristic means of the others and used it against them" (117).[71] "I was witty and antithetical—where Germany was concerned, I was *French*" (124).[72] As Mann is well aware, there is a fine line between acting like "civilization's literary man" and being one, or at least being mistaken for one, and Mann even refers to himself ironically as "a half-Westerner" (65).[73] In the context of the passage about the affinity between Nietzsche's style and that of the Jew Heinrich Heine, Mann concedes that his own literary practice had evolved under the same influences and that critics had drawn logical, if inaccurate conclusions: "My own literary attitude corresponded only too closely to such influences, needs, and susceptibilities: so much so that people . . . wanted to make a Jew of me" (61).[74] As Mann points out in the final lines of his preface, the entire project of the *Reflections* is not only a defensive retreat in what he knows is a losing cause, but a battle fought with the intrinsically democratic and civilizing weapon of language and literature, and thus paradoxically aiding the very cause that he would defeat.[75]

As soon as Mann stigmatizes himself as an "improper" German, he alters course and declares that in Germany, the abnormal is the norm. Each of his three chief mentors shares a similarly conflicted sense of being German: as we have seen, Nietzsche, Mann's closest ally in the battle against democracy and mass culture, has also taught his opponents how to write. Schopenhauer's pessimistic philosophy was of central importance to all European intellectuals, Mann observes, and not just Germans. Even Wagner's music is not really German, but a theatrical performance of Germanness to the point of parody (53; 13.1: 85). Mann concludes that it is in fact typically German to present oneself as un-German or even anti-German, and speculates in quasi-biblical tones "that one must possibly lose one's German character to find it" (48).[76]

Mann's about-face has profound consequences for the arguments that he simultaneously sets out and takes back in the *Reflections*. When speaking as the ventriloquist of the German *Volk*, Mann is quick to point the finger at Germany's "domestic [enemies]"[77] and to accuse those of a "political esthetic character"—Heinrich Mann—of an evil "*exoticism* that consists of a real physical disgust for close, native reality (408),[78] that is, an unnatural hatred of his own people. When he styles himself as the typically atypical German, however, Mann insists "that perhaps, without some foreign admixture, no higher German character is possible; that precisely the exemplary Germans were Europeans who would have regarded every limitation to the nothing-but-German as barbaric" (48).[79] In this vein, Mann produces statements that would have been anathema in the *gleichgeschaltete* Third Reich: "Evolution, development, originality, manifoldness, and richness of individuality have always been the basic law of German life. This life has always resisted centralization, has never received its customs from a principal, central point" (202).[80] Mann will follow precisely this line of argument in his subsequent critique of National Socialism and his public condemnation of anti-Semitism. "To be merely German is to be German on a small scale (*klein-deutsch*), not German in a cosmopolitan sense (*welt-deutsch*)," writes Mann in 1931; "it is Germanness of a minor and atrophied sort."[81] Jews are not the same as Germans, Mann will contend in "The Problem of Anti-Semitism" (1937), but good Germans should be willing to tolerate difference, whereas those who cling to the notion of an "ethnically pure German *Volk*" are guilty of a "relapse into barbarism." Indeed, Mann continues, the periodic outbreaks of German anti-Semitism arise from a mistaken belief that the Jews represent something "dark and alien" to the German *Volk,* whereas in fact they contribute a spirit of intellectual enlightenment, "without which Germanness would not be Germanness."[82]

The same argument that allows Mann to conceive of Germany as united in its inner heterogeneity also provides him with a conceptual alternative to Western imperialism. While the powers of the Entente seek the violent imposition of a one-size-fits-all form of civilization onto the rest of the world, true Germans—as opposed to the Westernized representatives of the Prussian-American *Machtstaat*—display a cosmopolitan openness toward the foreign. To the long series of oppositions that structure the dialectical arguments of the *Reflections,* Mann adds the distinction between "cosmopolitan and international" (17),[83] or, in another variant, "not . . . international, but supranational" (149).[84] The Western citizen is a belligerent imperialist; the German *Bürger* is a peaceful *Weltbürger* (81; 13.1: 126). The burgher is both rooted in the local community and open to travel around the world: "Were not my ancestors Nuremberger craftsmen of the type that Germany sent out to the whole world, even into the Far East, as a sign that she was a country of cities?" (81).[85] Travel to new places produces a corresponding willingness to import new ideas and absorb foreign influence. Mann stressed elsewhere that his primary influences for *Buddenbrooks* were French, Scandinavian, and Russian authors, and yet the resulting novel was deeply German precisely because of its openness to non-German influences.[86] The cosmopolitan Schopenhauer not only transcended Germany as a European intellectual, "he was, of course, not only supranational, but also supra-European, an Asian, the first great admirer of Asia in Europe." As Mann argues, Schopenhauer's "supra-Germanness" should be viewed "as an intensification, not a blurring and abrogation, of German nationality" (96).[87] Again, to be merely German, exclusively German, is not to be German at all.

The Gender of Germanness

Mann's conception of Germany as inwardly diverse and outwardly cosmopolitan carries over in his wartime journalism into questions of gender roles and sexual politics in their relation to German national identity. As several of Mann's critics and biographers have argued, the war allowed Mann to cast off doubts about his troubled sexuality and to embrace a less complicated form of masculine strength and national pride.[88] A closer look at the *Reflections* suggests that this argument oversimplifies Mann's position, particularly after the initial euphoria at the outbreak of war had passed. Limiting as well is the tendency to reduce Mann's essays of the period to their biographical source, for Mann's efforts to come to terms with his troubled sexuality were symptomatic of a widespread sense of masculine crisis in early twentieth-century Germany. Within the space of little more than a single generation, the nation had moved from a predominantly agrarian culture to a modern industrial society. The sort of stable patriarchy idealized in popular nineteenth-century family magazines like *Die Gartenlaube* soon began to seem a thing of the past.[89] The woman's movement had begun to organize in Germany and elsewhere by the 1860s, and by the end of the century homosexual subcultures became increasingly visible in the larger cities.[90] Such cultural turmoil prompted debates about changing gender roles in German society, both in the private realm and in the public sphere. Relations between nations within Europe and between European nations and their colonies were described in gendered terms, while essays about the proper organization of society often focused on the nature of masculinity and the importance of bonds between men within the state. Mann read such literature closely in the decade between the outbreak of the First World War and the completion of *The Magic Mountain*, and his essays and fiction of the period are in constant dialogue with ongoing debates about the gender of Germanness.

Central to the arguments were the works of Friedrich Nietzsche. Although largely ignored during his lifetime, by the turn of the century Nietzsche's works began to exert a decisive, if ambivalent, influence on German intellectuals in their response to the forces that seemed to be dissolving traditional social bonds and inverting conventional gender roles.[91] There were many who heeded Zarathustra's call for a new cult of masculine strength: "This new tablet I place above you, oh my brothers: *become hard!*"[92] Such a "hard" masculinity seemed in keeping with the spirit of the nation that Bismarck had united through "blood and iron" and in which martial valor was a cardinal virtue. Men in military uniforms were ubiquitous in the Reich, while the cult of honor led officers and gentlemen to challenge one another to deadly duels with disturbing regularity.[93] Resentment and fear of emancipated women provoked misogynist tirades from Nietzsche to Otto Weininger, while biological racism gave new virulence to an anti-Semitic movement that blamed everything that seemed wrong with modern culture on degenerate and effeminate Jews. Prejudice against women and Jews could be extended by analogy to the teeming masses of the urban proletariat and the hordes of colonized peoples who allegedly posed a threat of racial contamination to those within the sanctuary of Fortress Europe. Yet Nietzsche also inspired avant-garde intellectuals from Otto Gross to Ludwig Klages to downplay "the 'masculine' imperative of dynamic and sovereign self-creation" in favor of "the more 'feminine' submersion into a transindividual Dionysian whole."[94] Drawing on an intellectual lineage that led back through *The Birth of Tragedy* to Johann Jacob Bachofen's fascination with the ancient matriarchy and the Heidelberg Romantics' exploration of the irrational aspects of Greek myth and religion, the modern thinkers sought to disrupt the staid conventions of bourgeois morality with a rejuvenating plunge into a "chthonic" world of elemental passions.

Although seemingly diametrically opposed, discourses of hard masculinity and Dionysian ecstasy found a curious fusion in writings inspired by the outbreak of the First World War. In many ways, the war represented the logical culmination of the Nietzschean machismo that dominated Wilhelminian society: as if to prove the nation's virility, Germany had flung itself into the race to colonize the few parts of the globe that had not already been claimed by other European nations, and was soon engaged in a bitter rivalry with Great Britain that spurred a naval buildup and eventually provoked the war. Soldiers set off for the battlefields with *Zarathustra* in their backpacks and a sense of camaraderie with their fellow men.[95] Yet going to war also promised to release men from the strictures of everyday life, and the battlefield experience itself offered tightly wrapped "soldier males" the chance to explode in streams of violence against the enemy.[96] Ernst Jünger described the "inner experience" of war as a weird ecstasy of destruction that contained within it the potential for "rebirth and renewal,"[97] thus voicing a widely held view that the war marked a definitive turning point in world history that would sweep away the stagnant culture of the past and usher in something radically new. "But there will be war," prophesizes Hermann Hesse's Demian. "People will love it. Even now they can hardly wait for the killing to begin—their lives are that dull. . . . But that, too, will only be the beginning. The new world has begun and the new world will be terrible for those clinging to the old."[98]

"War! It was purification, liberation, that we experienced, and a monstrous hope."[99] Mann wrote these "Thoughts in War" in August and September 1914. Drawing on ideas that he had first jotted down in preparation for the essay "Intellect and Art," Mann introduced an argument that would also be of central importance for the *Reflections:* "Civilization and culture are not only not the

same thing, but rather opposites." Culture is "stylized wildness . . . but civilization is reason, enlightenment, moderation."[100] Behind Mann's distinction between culture and civilization lies Nietzsche's differentiation in *The Birth of
Tragedy* between Apollonian art that gives adequate form to the inchoate
Dionysian realm and mere Socratic reason. "Intellect is civil," continues Mann,
"it is the sworn enemy of drives, passions; it is antidemonic, antiheroic,"
whereas genius flows from "a deeper, darker, and hotter world, whose
transfiguration and stylistic subjugation we call culture."[101] Needless to say,
Germans possess true culture, whereas the French have only civilization, and
while Germany will defend itself like a lion, the French fight like sissies. Mann
likens the French to suffragettes who toss bombs and then cry foul in their
falsetto voices when the enemy retaliates: "This nation is claiming the privi-
leges of a lady, there is no doubt."[102]

Mann's militancy continues in "Frederick and the Great Coalition," written
between September and December 1914. Although he stops short of revealing
the open secret of the Prussian king's homosexuality, Mann does place repeated emphasis on Frederick's extreme misogyny.[103] He speculates that Frederick's hostility toward women may have been caused by the fact that he spent
so much of his time in the army, surrounded only by men—and this in the
century of France, "a real woman's century, which was completely filled and
saturated with the 'perfume of the eternal feminine.'"[104] Frederick dedicates
himself entirely to the service of his country, and demands the same commitment on the part of his officers, whom he expects to be unmarried monks of
war—*Kriegsmönche*—who find their pleasure in the sword, not the sheath
(i.e., vagina).[105] The key distinction is not between homo- and heterosexuality,
but between effeminate, self-indulgent voluptuousness and masculine asceti-
cism and dedication to a cause.

In constructing his image of Frederick, Mann follows Nietzsche's comments in *Beyond Good and Evil*. According to Nietzsche, Frederick's father had
been concerned that his young son could not provide what the country
needed: "*There were not enough men;* and he suspected to his bitter annoyance
that his son was not man enough."[106] Such concern was unfounded: once in
power, Frederick soon displayed a bold masculinity based on courage, tough-
ness, and an indomitable will. Again following Nietzsche, Mann makes no attempt to depict Frederick as an appealing individual who elicits the reader's
sympathy.[107] On the contrary, he goes out of his way to portray him as an evil,
even repulsive character, full of hatred and violence, whose taste for point-
blank salvos and cold steel "has something wild, radical, evil, absolute, danger-

ous" about it.[108] And yet, Mann concludes, this "evil Troll"[109] was an instrument of fate, a victim of the spirit of history that used him "to enable a great people to fulfill its destiny on earth."[110]

In the course of writing the *Reflections,* another, less belligerent aspect of Mann's thought began to emerge. While he readily admits in the *Reflections* that the events of 1914 had initially inspired him to believe that the Germans possessed "a great right to rule, a valid claim to participation in the government of the earth, in brief, to political power," he now has "moments, at least, when this belief wavers and almost dies" (147).[111] The Germans are certainly an educated people and a just people. "But a *commanding* nation? I doubt it. I doubt it to the point of *despair* every few days" (148).[112] In the place of an aggressive support for a German military victory came a melancholy resignation in the conviction that he was fighting a lost cause, "hopelessly on the defensive, as it [Germany] well knows" (45).[113] As Mann clarified in the preface to the *Reflections,* he was neither a "power-proud Junker nor a shareholder in heavy industry, nor even a social imperialist with capitalist connections," and he had his "doubts about Germany's calling to grand politics and to an imperial existence." As a result, he did not view Germany as "competing with England in power politics, but as far as she opposes her intellectually" (19).[114] Violent confrontation yields to ideological difference in which Germany is distinguished by its nonbelligerence.

In the *Reflections,* Mann adapts the metaphor of giving birth to a subtler and less bellicose understanding of German identity. To a certain extent, Mann continues his distinction between German masculinity and French effeminacy in this work. He derides French civilization as superficial, soft, sentimental, "feminine and deceitful,"[115] while praising Nietzsche as the embodiment of German virtue. "The colossal manliness of his soul, his antifeminism, his opposition to democracy—what could be more German?" (57).[116] In other passages, however, Mann switches Germany's gender from male to female: "In Germany's soul, *Europe's* intellectual antitheses are carried to the end (*ausgetragen*), 'carried to the end' in a maternal and in a warlike sense" (36).[117] Germany becomes the pregnant mother of Europe, a site of intellectual and spiritual gestation for European conflicts. When defined as a man, Germany's identity is based on the relatively simple fact that it is not Britain or France; when viewed as a woman, German identity becomes more complex, for in this case, the essence of being German is being not exclusively German, but inclusively European.

Thus Mann counters his otherwise positive response to Nietzsche's call for a new, "hard" masculinity of martial strength with an interest in Nietzsche as the greatest "psychologist of *decadence*" and not "the prophet of some kind of vague 'superman'" (54–55).[118] With a thinly veiled reference to the works of his brother Heinrich, Thomas Mann denounced the ruthless Renaissance aestheticism affected by some of Nietzsche's more literal-minded misreaders (13; 13.1: 29). As early as 1903, in fact, Mann had voiced a self-deprecating defense of writers like himself "who honor a feminine cultural and artistic ideal under the scornful smiles of the Renaissance men."[119] In the *Reflections,* Mann used the term *erotic irony* to characterize the principles behind his own artistic production: he is erotically attracted to "life"—most typically in the form of blond boys like Hans Hansen of *Tonio Kröger*—but remains an intellectually detached observer who sublimates homoerotic passion into art.[120] In August 1914, "life" erupted in the form of war. For a brief period, Mann hoped to channel this new, masculine life force into a celebration of Germany's martial valor, but as the evidence of the *Reflections* reveals, Mann soon realized that a simple affirmation of German machismo was out of character because it did not accurately reflect the complexities of his political thought. To be sure, Mann published a long essay in praise of Frederick's iron discipline and repeatedly chastised France for acting like a woman. Yet he also described Germany as the cosmopolitan mother of Europe, as an unpolitical space that should be reserved for the quiet *Bildung* of artists and intellectuals who were most typically German when they were most European. Mann feels the erotic pull of war, but retains an ironic detachment from his own enthusiasm, knowing that someone who has long espoused a "feminine cultural and artistic ideal" cannot, and ultimately does not want to, transform himself into a Nietzschean superman. With characteristic hubris, Mann then elevates his self-analysis into a diagnosis of the German nation: however much the Germans may welcome the war as a chance to prove their manhood, they remain a nation of thinkers and poets at the cosmopolitan center of Europe. The erotic attraction to blond boys and blond beasts remains essential to Mann's creative and political thought, but so does the ironic self-awareness that prohibits complete identification with either, and, indeed, transforms this apparent necessity into an artistic and cosmopolitan virtue.

In sum, Thomas Mann's *Reflections of a Nonpolitical Man* presents its readers with a series of often contradictory arguments. In many passages, Mann anoints himself as the spokesman for a manly nation locked in mortal combat with external and internal foes. In this mode, Mann is at his least tolerant, bitterly condemning his renegade brother and everything that he represents: a shallow optimism born of an overly refined, effeminate French civilization of the eighteenth century that lives on in the self-righteous rhetoric of the modern political pamphleteer and urban (Jewish) intellectual. The true Germanic artist must be capable of "'relapsing' into the primitive" (108),[121] plunging back into the chthonic forces of Schopenhauer's Will or Nietzsche's Dionysian realm, in order to move beyond the superficiality of mere civilization toward a more profound culture. As soon as he perceives the primitive in others, however, Mann recoils in horror. "Civilization's literary man" as an effete dandy morphs into an "Expressionist" with an inclination toward "lascivious estheticism and exoticism . . . anthropophagic sculpture . . . negrolike craving for pleasure" (359–60)[122]—an oscillation that recalls the alternating associations of Siegfried Aarenhold with decadent dandyism and savage primitivism. Mann was outraged that the French would guard German prisoners of war with black troops from Senegal, "an animal with lips as thick as pillows."[123] On May 5, 1919, Mann records in his diary a conversation with Ernst Bertram about saving "the West . . . from the horrors of a migration of peoples from below (*Völkerwanderung von unten*),"[124] a nicely ambivalent phrase in which "below" can refer simultaneously to the lower classes, places "far down on the map," or desires from below the belt (*die Hunde im Souterrain*). In other passages in the *Reflections*, however, we find Mann condemning British and French racism, chastising the arrogance and hypocrisy of imperial civilization, and presenting an image of Germany based on tolerance of internal diversity and cosmopolitan receptivity to foreign influence.

Which is the true Mann? The overt racist and covert anti-Semite, or the philo-Semitic cosmopolitan? The *völkisch* warmonger or the melancholy ironist? The answer is both: the inner consistency underlying the external contradictions lies in Mann's ambivalent attitude toward himself as both princely representative of the nation and its multiply stigmatized outcast. Mann projects his personal ambivalence onto his image of the nation, which is, on the one hand, a powerful physical presence at the heart of Europe, the masculine counterpart to the effeminate French, and, on the other hand, a womb, a hollow space that gives birth to the ideological conflicts of Europe, a place for the dialectical dance of theses and antitheses that can be endlessly inverted but never resolved. In keeping with the self-undermining logic of a polemic that he knew was doomed to failure, Mann signals his awareness that *Reflections* is a self-consciously eloquent indictment of rhetoric. Looking back at the completed essay, Mann concludes his subsequently composed prologue by stating that *Reflections* is "the detailed product of an ambivalence, the presentation of an inner-personal discord and conflict. It is this that makes this book, which is no book and no work of art, almost into something else: almost into poetry (*Dichtung*)" (24).[125] As a nonpolitical-political polemic, Mann's work is hopelessly confused and inherently contradictory, but as an encapsulation of the conflicting forces in his early career, an anticipation of the tensions that will play out in *The Magic Mountain,* and an obsessively self-absorbed argument intermittently illuminated by self-awareness, *Reflections of a Nonpolitical Man* forms an integral part of Mann's oeuvre and even occasionally—almost—rises to the level of art.

CHAPTER FIVE

Empires of Air: The Hermetic World of *The Magic Mountain*

In the preface to *The Magic Mountain,* Mann writes that the story he is about to tell took place shortly before the Great War, a time that was not long ago in terms of actual years, but one that stood irrevocably cut off from the present, *"before* a certain turning point, on the far side of a rift that has cut deeply through our lives and consciousness" (xi).[1] Mann had begun what he thought would be a short, comic counterpart to *Death in Venice* in the fall of 1912, a few months after he had visited Katia for three weeks in Davos, where she was undergoing treatment for suspected tuberculosis. Work on the project continued over the next few years, interrupted first by *Felix Krull* in early 1913, again by Mann's wartime journalism in the fall of 1914, and yet again in December 1915, when Mann embarked on the seemingly endless *Reflections of a Nonpolitical Man.* Even after the war had ended, Mann did not return immediately to *The Magic Mountain,* writing instead a story about his dog and a poem in honor of his daughter Elisabeth. Only then, in the spring of 1919, did Mann return to the unfinished project from what now seemed the distant past.[2]

Times had changed indeed. In 1912 Germany had been at the height of its powers, a modern, military-industrial nation-state in Central Europe with colonies in Africa, China, and the Pacific, and the ambition to acquire more. Germany had provoked the war at least in part because it hoped to establish a "large and continuous colonial empire" that would expand into Eastern Europe, down through Turkey to the oilfields of Iraq, and across the continent of Africa.[3] As late as 1918, Germany still harbored dreams of establishing "an *imperium* of grandiose dimensions" that would elevate it into "a colonial and economic power of world status."[4] Subsequent events served as a rude awakening: Germany lost the war, the kaiser abdicated, and the punitive Treaty of Versailles stripped Germany of all its overseas colonies. For the many who believed that the German army had been "stabbed in the back" by domestic traitors and thus denied its inevitable victory, the slap in the face from the victorious allies was a further blow, contributing to the resentment and sense of victimization that would poison the atmosphere of the Weimar Republic. Meanwhile, Germany had descended into chaos. Physically and psychologically scarred soldiers returned to malnourished families who were easy targets for the Spanish influenza epidemic that broke out in the final months of the war and soon killed tens of thousands. Within a few years, galloping inflation would wipe out the life savings of many and further destabilize the political landscape. In the spring of 1919 a revolutionary government led by radical intellectuals established itself in Munich, prompting the intervention of the reactionary German *Freikorps*, whose members brutalized victims with impunity.

Thomas Mann resumed work on *The Magic Mountain* in the midst of these tumultuous events. According to his diary, Mann picked up his notes and the unfinished manuscript from the Pringsheim home on Arcis Strasse on April 8, 1919. As he began to read the materials critically over the next few days, it became clear that substantial revisions would be necessary: "In any case, the whole thing has to be clearly designated as a 'story from the distant past.'"[5] Events of the present could hardly have been more urgent: on Palm Sunday, April 13, Mann was interrupted by a telephone call incorrectly reporting the collapse of the Communist government; the next day Erika returned from the city with reports of "armed workers and automobiles with soldiers" on the streets of downtown Munich.[6] Mann concluded that conflict was imminent and on several occasions he noted in his diaries the sound of gunfire in the distance. To add to the tension, Katia was in the final stages of pregnancy and expected to go into labor at any moment. As in the years of exile to come, Mann nevertheless displayed an almost uncanny ability to maintain focus on his literary work, and by Easter Sunday, the long wait was over: "*I began writing the 'Magic Mountain' again, after a four-year interruption.*"[7] The following day, Katia gave birth to Michael Mann, their sixth and final child.

By the time *The Magic Mountain* was completed and published in 1924, the originally planned short story had expanded into a novel that provides a panoramic view of European society at the height of the Age of Empire. Drawing on the literary archetype of the descent to the underworld previously explored by Virgil, Dante, Goethe, and Wagner, and informed by Romantic ideas about the proximity of sexuality and death, genius and disease, *The Magic Mountain* also portrays the world as Mann knew it between 1907 and 1914.

I begin this chapter with a focus on the relationship between Hans Castorp and Clavdia Chauchat as an implicit commentary on the sexual politics of empire. Castorp alternates between competition with his rivals Hofrat Behrens and Mynheer Peeperkorn for possession of a woman with ties to the oil-producing region of Daghestan, and a tendency to sink into the seductive world of "Asiatic" indolence that Chauchat also represents. I turn next to the debates between Settembrini and Naphta, suggesting that the latter undermines the seemingly clear opposition between his own views and those of his enlightened opponent. Mann's polemic against the "empire of civilization" in the *Reflections* lives on in Naphta's critique of Settembrini's liberal nationalism. As their arguments often turn on the political implications of male-only organizations, I pause for an excursus on some of the thinkers that influenced Mann while writing *The Magic Mountain* before turning to debates about the Jesuits and Freemasons in the novel. Here again, seemingly diametrical opposites turn out to have more in common than expected. The more critically the Freemasons are portrayed, the more "Jewish" they seem, both in their overtly liberal ideology and in their clandestine association with irrational violence and sexually charged mysticism. The implicit link between the forces of darkness, Jewishness, and either ancient or non-European primitivism recurs in Castorp's Nietzschean vision in the snow and the séance staged between Dr. Krokowski and his medium, Ellen Brand. Whereas Mann's political essays argue unequivocally for the need for reason to prevail over irrationality, he undermines his arguments in *The Magic Mountain* to the point that he can conclude only with a tenuous hope for love that may emerge out of the chaos of war.

The Magic Mountain is an empire in the air, cut off from direct contact with the flatlands below and viewed from the infinitely distant perspective of the postwar period, but a site that enacts in displaced form the ideological conflicts and geopolitical struggles of Europe at the height of the Age of Empire and on the brink of world war. Like a snow-dome, those landscapes in glass containers filled with liquid and artificial snow, *The Magic Mountain* is a hermetically sealed world unto itself, but one whose walls are transparent and invite the gaze of curious onlookers. And thus with a metaphorical shake of the dome, Mann's narrator stirs up the snow and invites us to peer into the past. "And with that, we begin" (xii).[8]

Reading for the Plot: Interracial Romance on the Magic Mountain

The Magic Mountain is a landmark in the history of the modern essayistic novel, consisting, for significant stretches, of philosophical reflections about the nature of time and debates about the meaning of life and the fate of reason. At its core, however, Mann tells a simple story: a young man who has just completed his formal education and is about to begin his career takes a three-week vacation to visit his cousin, who is being treated for tuberculosis in an alpine sanatorium. Soon after his arrival, Hans Castorp is diagnosed with a touch of the disease and thus his visit is extended indefinitely. Seven years pass. Castorp gradually loses touch with his remaining family in the flatlands and forgets his career plans, while developing new intellectual interests. Finally, the outbreak of the First World War brings his protracted visit and the long novel to an abrupt end.

Like a good, old-fashioned book, *The Magic Mountain* is also a love story. Castorp finds himself mysteriously drawn to a woman who at first merely irritates him. Too shy to approach Clavdia Chauchat directly, Castorp pumps his tablemates in the dining room for information about her, ogles the chief doctor's crude painting of her in a deep décolleté, and performs little acts of gallantry for her that amuse his fellow patients and readers alike. He finally breaks the ice during a Mardi Gras party and speaks to Chauchat at length, albeit through the dreamlike distance of a conversation that takes place largely in French. Although the narrator discreetly pulls back at the end of this scene, we later learn that Castorp enjoyed a night of riotous pleasure with Chauchat before she embarked the next morning on her scheduled departure.

Up to this point, about halfway through the novel, *The Magic Mountain* follows the pattern of the German *Bildungs-* or *Entwicklungsroman*, in which a young man typically has a romantic adventure or two on his way to marriage and integration into society, and Thomas Mann repeatedly underscored the links between his novel and what he felt was the peculiarly German genre of the *Bildungsroman*.[9] If *The Magic Mountain* is indeed a *Bildungsroman*, as Mann would have us believe, then it is a most unusual one. It does not portray a heterosexual romance leading to marriage. Chauchat is already married to another man when she spends the night with Castorp; she returns to the sanatorium only briefly with a different lover, and Castorp is drawn to her in the first place largely because she reminds him of a boy he was once attracted to in school. Nor does Castorp become a productive member of society. While he develops desultory interests in biology, astronomy, mythology, and history, he drifts away from any professional activity and is only reintegrated into German society when he joins thousands of recruits charging toward probable death on the battlefield. Castorp's affair with Chauchat is nevertheless of central thematic importance, for it engages on the level of character and plot questions surrounding sexual politics in global context that are discussed at length in the theoretical portions of the novel. To get a better idea of the issues at stake, we turn first to the flashback about Castorp's childhood and youth in chapter 2 of *The Magic Mountain,* before considering the implications of his interracial romance on the mountain.

In *Buddenbrooks,* Mann opposed Hanseatic Lübeck with imperial Berlin, the increasingly decadent, but intellectually and artistically sensitized Buddenbrook family with the ruthless Hagenströms and Hanno's Prussian teachers. In *The Magic Mountain,* Mann condenses the opposition between Lübeck and Berlin into the single location of Hamburg, another Hanseatic city-state with traditions extending back into the Middle Ages, but one that had also grown into the second largest city in the German Reich and a leading European port for global commerce.[10] Both the city's past tradition and its present industry leave their mark on Hans Castorp.

In many ways, Castorp is a typical representative of the new, imperial Germany. He has grown up in the midst of an international shipping port with "the pungent odors of the world's produce piled high" and images of "the towering, mammoth cadavers of ships that had sailed to Asia and Africa" before his eyes.[11] His grandfather's apartment is furnished with tropical hardwoods, including mahogany and rosewood, and Castorp arrives at the sanatorium with a crocodile-skin briefcase and a taste for Russian cigarettes and imported cigars made of Sumatra-Havana tobacco, all reminders of Hamburg's trading links to distant parts of the globe. Like previous characters in Mann's early fiction with a worldly flair for modern progress, Castorp is an anglophile.[12] His uncle, Consul Tienappel, enjoys a daily breakfast and supper buffet that includes "roast beef with tomato ketchup" (28),[13] and his cousin sprinkles the occasional English phrase into their conversation. Castorp is about to begin his career as a ship's engineer when he sets off to visit Joachim Ziemssen, and during his first evening in the sanatorium, Castorp finds himself speaking giddily about the "epoch-making development for our maritime commerce" that the "plans for making the Elbe more navigable" will produce (14).[14] Months later, Clavdia Chauchat predicts that he "*will soon return to the flatlands . . . to help repay his great and powerful fatherland with honest labor on the wharves*" (335).[15] His companions in Hamburg had already speculated that this engineer, "a shipbuilder in the making, a man of global commerce and technology," might well turn out to be a radical advocate of modern progress, "a go-getter, a profane destroyer of old buildings and beautiful landscapes, as footloose as a Jew, as irreverent as an American" (34).[16]

Other experiences in Castorp's childhood incline him away from modern progress and toward the medieval roots of his Hanseatic city. His mother, father, and grandfather all die in quick succession, prompting a tendency to ponder the mysteries of life that saps his energy for the working world. Castorp inherits a sense of privilege and class consciousness from his grandfather, Hans Lorenz Castorp, but one that has been reduced to mere form: rubbing one's hands together before meals as a vestige of times when they were folded in prayer; cultivating impeccable table manners and the art of dinner conversation; expecting one's butter to be sculpted into fluted balls. Castorp's grandfather also initiates him into a world of timeless tradition, symbolized by the family baptismal bowl. Seven generations have been baptized by water from that bowl, and in listening dreamily to the sounds of the "great-great-great-great—that somber sound of the crypt and buried time" (21),[17] Castorp is transported into the "moldy, cool air of Saint Catherine's Church or the crypt in Saint Michael's" (21),[18] into "a kind of fluctuating permanence, that meant both a return to something and a dizzying, everlasting sameness" (22).[19] Hans Lorenz Castorp actively resists any form of political change or technical progress and is said to be so out of touch with modern times that it seems "as if he were living in the fourteenth century" (23).[20] He is most comfortable in the elaborate, old-fashioned costume in the style of the Spanish Netherlands that he wears in his formal portrait, and when he dies, his body is displayed in full regalia in a silver-lined coffin, with an ivory cross forced into his rigid hands and a palm frond lying on the shrouded lower body. In light of these influences and also Hans Castorp's physical resemblance to his grandfather, his Hamburg acquaintances speculate that he might not be a ruthless advocate of modern progress after all: "he looked exactly like someone democrats would *not* be able to count on"; like his grandfather, Castorp might well "become a conservative, a brake on other elements" (34).[21]

The contrasting influences of Hanseatic Hamburg continue to surround Castorp on the magic mountain, but they are elevated into an abstract play of ideas and ideologies removed from any immediate, practical consequences. The Prussian spirit of military efficiency lives on in Joachim Ziemssen, but his sense of duty has been displaced from the battlefield into the punctilious fulfillment of his medical regime in the futile effort to regain his health. Settembrini speaks eloquently and "plastically" for the values of the Renaissance, Enlightenment, and French Revolution, but he, too, is chronically ill and knows that he will never be allowed to return to practical activity in the flatlands. The daily routine in the sanatorium soon draws Castorp away from his half-hearted interest in modern progress and back into the preoccupations of his earlier years. The mountain is a place of death and disease, and from the beginning Castorp exhibits a morbid curiosity about stories of corpses spirited away on bobsleds in the night and the sickening sounds of terminally ill patients coughing themselves to death. The timelessness of the tomb that Castorp had sensed in the baptismal bowl returns in a place where seasons refuse to obey their normal succession and patients measure their "sentences" in an ever-receding series of months and years rather than the minutes and hours of the business day. The seven generations of Castorp's ancestors turn into the seven years on the mountain, the seven tables in the dining hall, the seven minutes required to measure one's temperature, and the alluring woman who inhabits room number 7. The lavish meals cater to Castorp's taste for fine food and refined manners, while the enforced periods of semiconscious dozing are well suited to a young man who spent an indolent childhood drifting through porter-induced daydreams. The "medieval" atmosphere that surrounded his grandfather lives on in the head nurse Adriatica von Mylendonk, whose ancestors include a thirteenth-century abbess and whose very name "has an absolutely medieval ring" (59).[22] Castorp's latent artistic talent, evident in his carefully shaded technical drawings and his painting of a ship that hangs in his grandfather's study, blossoms into intellectual activity far removed from the practical concerns of an apprentice ship's engineer. Castorp is soon devouring works on medicine and philosophy while engaging in feverish speculations about time and eternity. The magic mountain also triggers memories and awakens desires: the desire for Chauchat reactivates repressed memories of Pribislav Hippe, and both fuel his fascination with the body and the subconscious mind.

The reminders of Germany's foreign colonies and global trade that crop up periodically in the Hamburg of Castorp's youth—the giant ships, Castorp's cigars and his crocodile-skin bag, his grandfather's gold-inlayed tortoise-shell snuff box and the tropical hardwoods that furnish his apartment, the old servant Fiete, who wears multiple earrings like an old pirate—expand into a virtual catalog of places and peoples defined by their difference from Europe in general and northern Germany in particular. Silent movies entertain patients with images of Oriental despots, caged geishas, naked natives, dancing girls, cockfights, and elephant hunts. The streets of Davos bustle with patients from all over the world, many of whom will find their final resting place in the local cemetery, whose gravestones bear "names from every corner of the earth . . . written in English, Russian or other Slavic languages, in German, Portuguese, and many more tongues" (315).[23]

An ambivalence surrounds the people and products of the colonial world assembled in *The Magic Mountain*, as it does in Mann's earlier fiction: on the one hand, an Egyptian cigarette, a pair of alligator-skin shoes, or cup of Javanese coffee can serve as a trophy of imperial conquest, underscoring the difference between the exotic colonies and the Europeans who exploit them. The "beautiful enameled boxes with gilt depictions of a globe, lots of medallions, and an exposition hall with banners flying" (248)[24] that contain Castorp's favorite cigars sum up at a glance the relations between triumphant European nations and their colonial commodities.[25] On the other hand, protracted exposure to the colonies can undermine the distinction between Europeans and their others, with potentially debilitating results. One thinks of Christian Buddenbrook returning to Lübeck with his mahogany walking stick and sugarcane, but infected with the indolence of his life in Chile; of Gustav von Aschenbach, who succumbs to the cholera born in the jungles of India; and of Mynheer Peeperkorn, who will commit suicide by injecting himself with Malaysian cobra venom. Sensing danger, Joachim and Settembrini distance themselves from the "motley set of adventurers" assembled at the sanatorium, but Hans Castorp has "a certain weakness" (310) for beer, tobacco, music, and the seductive presence of Clavdia Chauchat.[26]

Like Imma Spoelmann, whose ancestors include Native Americans, possibly Jewish Germans, and an English woman, Clavdia Chauchat has an unusual background with multiple and contradictory symbolic associations. On the one hand, she is a cultivated member of modern European society: Chauchat speaks at least three languages, including fluent French and some German in addition to her native Russian. As a married woman who smokes, travels alone, and entertains other men behind closed doors, Chauchat fits the profile of a modern, emancipated woman.[27] Unlike the other patients, who are confined to the sanatorium indefinitely, Chauchat moves from one sanatorium to another and has the leisure and means to travel from Russia to Spain. Her husband is French, not Russian, and as Kenneth Weisinger shrewdly surmises, he is in Daghestan almost certainly because of its oil reserves.[28] Russia, which struggled to control the rich natural resources of the predominantly Islamic territory of Daghestan during the late nineteenth century, entered into a military alliance with the French in 1894. England joined the alliance to form the Triple Entente in 1907—the same year in which Hans Castorp travels to Switzerland. Thus Castorp's affair with a cosmopolitan Russian woman married to a Frenchman working in Daghestan introduces him to a nexus of intra-European alliances and rivalries for the resources of an otherwise remote, mountainous region in the Caucasus.

On the other hand, Chauchat is also identified as the antithesis of a western European. Her chewed fingernails, lack of punctuality, and careless door-slamming suggest that she has not yet undergone the "civilizing process" that results in Castorp's fastidious grooming and impeccable table manners. Even her "soft, rather boneless language" (113)[29] suggests a lack of discipline and moral fiber. Chauchat's apparent sexual promiscuity associates her with the uncouth manners of both the lower classes and foreign "barbarians," those "bad Russians" who have sex before breakfast behind the thin walls that separate their room from that of Hans Castorp; even the silent young teacher who sits at the Good Russian table collapses in an embarrassingly public epileptic fit or "orgasm of the brain" (294).[30] Most important, Chauchat is marked by racial difference. In the fall of 1918, Mann read "the very interesting introduction" to Dostoyevsky's work by Arthur Moeller van den Bruck, whose comments concerning "the Slavic race" Mann found suggestive for Clavdia Chauchat's character.[31] Moeller van den Bruck argues that the Slavic race originally consisted of both Asiatic and Aryan-Germanic elements. In time, however, the more active Germanic race pursued a separate course of development, leaving the Slavs to regress toward their Asiatic roots; hence their lack of willpower and tendency toward mysticism.[32] Chauchat's high cheekbones and Kirghiz eyes mark her as just such an Asiatic Russian; thus Settembrini urges Castorp to side with Western humanism and the Enlightenment and to resist her Oriental charms. Chauchat's reddish-blond hair and French last name suggest that she is not a full-blooded Asian, however, but something of a mix, just as her previous incarnation as Pribislav Hippe is described as "the product of an ancient mixing of races, the blending of Germanic blood with Slavic-Wendish, or vice versa" (118).[33]

Chauchat's racial mixture and her association with both France and Daghestan link Castorp's romantic adventure in the sanatorium to the global context of European imperialism in two different ways: by portraying relations between Europe and its colonies in terms of heterosexual relations, and by depicting intra-European competition for extra-European territories in terms of male-male rivalries. As has often been noted, relations between European nations and their colonies were frequently imagined in terms of rape or romance.[34] The male adventurer either penetrates and conquers virgin lands or woos the indigenous maiden. Both paradigms associate heterosexual masculinity with colonial conquest, although in different ways: the imperialist-rapist simply seizes what he wants and what the civilizing process tells him he is destined to have, whereas the romantic model makes the conquered woman complicit in her seduction. The woman's spontaneous affection for her European lover provides indirect proof of his benevolent intentions and allays possible European guilt about the takeover of foreign lands.[35] At the same time, such stories could also serve as vehicles for European self-scrutiny and at least implicit critique. In the widely circulated eighteenth-century tale of the Native American Yarico's love for the shipwrecked British sailor Inkle, for instance, Inkle not only abandons his pregnant lover when he is rescued by a passing ship, but even sells her and her unborn child into slavery. Puccini's Madame Butterfly commits suicide when she learns of Pinkerton's duplicity and the protagonist of Heinrich von Kleist's *Betrothal in St. Domingo* shoots and kills the woman that turns out to be his loyal lover.

Neither pattern fits the relationship between Castorp and Chauchat. Castorp is more of a milquetoast than a rapist, and if Chauchat allows him to seduce her for one evening, she does so with a deprecatory smirk and the knowledge that she is leaving in the morning, that she is already married, and that she is free at any time to return to the sanatorium with another lover—which is precisely what she does. Although she does display a certain fondness for Castorp, it seems safe to say that the relationship means considerably more to him than it does to her. Castorp's love for Chauchat actually fits more closely into a third model of interracial romance, in which the man forgets his duties in the working world and "goes native," surrendering entirely to the charms of the foreign woman. In German literature the plot is as old as Wolfram von Eschenbach's *Parzival*, which begins when the hero's father, Gahmuret, falls in love with a black African queen and has to sneak away in the night to escape a lifetime of marital bliss. Wolfram's romance reworks Virgil's tale of Aeneas and Dido, and both anticipate the model most directly influential for Mann's *Magic Mountain:* Wagner's *Tannhäuser,* the opera about a man who loses all sense of time and purpose in life while under the spell of Venus in the Hörselberg.

In psychological terms, as Frederick Lubich has argued, Castorp regresses to the uterine realm of the mother on the mountain.[36] Castorp turns away from the stabilization of his heterosexual identity more typical of a *Bildungsroman* and surrenders to the charms of an androgynous woman with slender hips who reminds him of a boy. This is not to say that Castorp's affair with Chauchat is an expression of his essentially homosexual desires, or that it marks a movement away from youthful homoeroticism toward mature heterosexuality, but rather that his passion for Chauchat is neatly suspended between the two, that it is simultaneously hetero- and homosexual in a highly charged but undifferentiated eroticism.[37] Castorp also drifts out of the linear time of progress and goals characteristic of the engineer and soldier and back into the infinitely receding "great-great-great-great" of his family's baptismal bowl, into the mystical *nunc stans* of simultaneity rather than succession. Finally, Castorp embraces the "Asiatic" realm defined by its opposition to Western civilization, specifically in terms of racial difference. It is perhaps for this reason that he responds so strongly to the recording of *Aida* that he plays on the gramophone, for Verdi's opera tells the story of an Egyptian officer who chooses love for an Ethiopian queen over duty to his country; it ends with both buried alive and yet still singing with transcendent beauty.[38]

Castorp is also not the only man interested in Chauchat, and, as Kenneth Weisinger suggests, male-male rivalries counteract the pull of the uterine realm on the magic mountain and enact in displaced form the intra-European national conflicts over colonial possessions.[39] He focuses closely on the chapter titled "*Humaniora*," in which Behrens invites Castorp and Joachim into his apartment and shows them his painting of Chauchat. The scene in which Castorp and Behrens admire the image of the absent woman encapsulates the sort of homoerotic bonding between men theorized by Eve Sedgwick as intrinsic to patriarchal society and immortalized in Edouard Manet's iconic painting *Dejeuner sur l'herbe*, which portrays two fully clothed men having a picnic with a naked woman.[40] The pseudo-Oriental trappings of Behrens's smoking alcove remind us of the political background, as Germany and England competed together with France and Russia for control of places like the Balkans, the Ottoman Empire, and Daghestan. From this perspective, Castorp is a masculine rival for heterosexual love and a coded imperialist, not an androgynous mystic seeking union with the Magna Mater. Thus he responds with equal enthusiasm to the recording of Bizet's *Carmen*, in which another soldier abandons his duty for the love of a racially marked woman. In this case, however, the fickle gypsy Carmen betrays Don José for another man, only to be murdered by her former lover in a fit of jealous rage.

Castorp's subsequent relationship with Mynheer Peeperkorn reenacts the erotic triangle between himself, Behrens, and Chauchat, albeit with significant modifications. In some ways, the rivalry is more open, for Castorp could only guess that Behrens might have had sexual relations with Chauchat, whereas now Castorp's former lover appears with a traveling companion with whom she is clearly involved. The association of this "colonial Dutchman, a man from Java, a coffee-planter" (538)[41] with European imperialism also makes obvious what was only implicit in the earlier male rivalry. Yet Castorp's interaction with Peeperkorn deviates markedly from the open competition one might expect: unlike his literary predecessor Parzival, who defeats a series of rivals while entranced by drops of blood on the snow, Castorp seals a bond of friendship with Peeperkorn while staring at drops of red wine on the white sheets of the bed, just after confessing that he had had an affair with the older man's lover. Peeperkorn, in turn, hints that he is impotent, whereupon Castorp goes so far as to deny his own masculinity, at least in a certain sense: "I am not at all manly in the sense that I regard other men as my rivals in courting—perhaps I am not masculine at all, but most certainly not in the sense that I automatically termed 'social,' although I don't really know why" (576).[42]

In sum, Castorp's attraction to Chauchat pulls him in two different directions that coincide with the conflicting impulses of his youth in Hamburg: toward the dissolution of identity, sexual ambiguity, and timelessness, on the one hand, and toward the firming up of a sense of self, heterosexuality, and purposeful striving, on the other; between the temptation to sink into an Asiatic realm of racial difference, and the urge to fight with other Western men for its possession. Largely due to circumstances beyond his control, Castorp does not lose himself in his love for Chauchat, but neither does he become a dueling cock of the walk determined to defend himself at all costs against his rivals. Instead, he opts for a kinder and gentler understanding of masculinity that was already evident in certain passages of the *Reflections*, as Mann distanced himself from the militant rhetoric he had employed during the first months of the war. Castorp's renunciation of Chauchat is also in keeping with the "message" of *The Magic Mountain* that Mann italicized in the chapter describing Castorp's vision in the snow: "*For the sake of goodness and love, man shall grant death no dominion over his thoughts*" (487).[43] In other words, one must acknowledge the nether world—figured variously as sexuality, places "far down on the map," or racial difference—but neither bog down in it nor ride roughshod over it, neither go native nor become a militant nationalist and rampaging imperialist. Thus we are squarely within the logic that informed Mann's early fiction about the artist's effort to tap into the creative force of chthonic urges without becoming overwhelmed by them. The resolution proposed at that time involved the sublimation of physical desire into artistic creativity. But here we have a crucial difference: Castorp is not an iron-willed artist like Schiller, Tonio Kröger, or Gustav von Aschenbach; he is more of a vapid mimic in the mold of Tony Buddenbrook or Felix Krull. In renouncing sexual desire and professional ambition, Castorp becomes a passive cipher, the fictional counterpart to the image of the empty womb that Mann used to describe German cosmopolitanism in the *Reflections*. And thus the novel of individual development turns into a novel of ideas; instead of reading for the plot, we follow the twists and turns of an intellectual debate.

Negative Dialectics: Settembrini, Naphta, and the Brotherhood of Man

The debates between Settembrini and Naphta represent the intellectual core of *The Magic Mountain*. Here questions regarding the legacy of the French Revolution and the politics of the nation-state are most openly discussed. Mann structures the conflict dialectically, introducing Settembrini as Hans Castorp's principal mentor in the first half of the novel and adding Naphta only after Castorp has rejected Settembrini's advice and tasted the forbidden fruit or "pomegranate" in the night after the Mardi Gras festivities (349).[44] The arguments continue almost to the end of the novel, but no synthesis is reached. Naphta and Settembrini become only more deeply entrenched in their own positions and more openly hostile toward one another, until something snaps and the verbal sparring ends in an abortive duel and Naphta's suicide.

When first introduced, Settembrini's significance seems as clear as the light he turns on when he enters Castorp's room: he stands for the principles of the Enlightenment and the French Revolution, defending hard work for the good cause of humanity, progress, and civilization. In other words, he is what Mann until only recently had branded as "civilization's literary man." It would seem that Mann has reversed his previous position, however, for the author of the *Reflections* had nothing but scorn for the champions of civilization, while the "organ grinder" Settembrini is at worst the target of mild irony and remains a largely sympathetic figure throughout the novel. If we look more closely, however, we find that some of the negative traits of the *Zivilisationsliterat* continue to cling to Settembrini. He and his grandfather believe in a single universal truth appropriate for all humanity. Thus Settembrini's grandfather fights not only for Italian unification against the reactionary rule of Metternich's Austro-Hungarian Empire, but also goes abroad to fight for freedom in Spain and Greece. In the process he becomes entangled in what Adorno and Horkheimer would term the "dialectic of Enlightenment," or what Mann had already condemned as the hubris and hypocrisy of the "imperium of civilization." The grandfather sets out to spread world peace by fomenting violent revolution, proclaiming "that liberated peoples must unite and forge their universal happiness . . . with passionate autocratic élan" (151).[45] In the same spirit, Settembrini praises the Germans for inventing the gunpowder that serves the liberating armies. He is an Orientalist in Edward Said's sense of the word, dividing the world neatly between Western civilization and Oriental indolence, and convinced of the inevitable triumph of the West: "Because human progress was always gathering up new nations in the course of its brilliant advance, conquering new continents—indeed all of Europe itself—and had even started to press on into Asia" (154).[46] Settembrini's definition of "Asia" is both broad and narrow: broad in the sense that it refers not only to Russia but even to Vienna, narrow in that it is simply shorthand for anyone or any place that fails to share his beliefs.

Naphta serves a double function in his debates with Settembrini: the one is to serve as a representative of everything Settembrini rejects; the other is to bring out the latent contradictions of Settembrini's positions. As a Jewish-Jesuit reactionary revolutionary, Naphta has more than his share of ideological contradictions, and yet the conflicting impulses of his character correspond precisely to the traits that Mann considered typically Jewish. As the quick-witted son of a kosher butcher, Naphta has the intelligence and ability to use language as a weapon that Mann always associated with the Jews, but his father's profession also links Jewishness with something ancient and barbaric. Witnessing ritual slaughter since early childhood has taught him to associate piety with horror: "the sight and sound of spurting blood was bound up in his mind with the idea of what is holy and spiritual" (433).[47] Like Siegfried Aarenhold, Naphta's Jewishness is linked alternately with exoticism and primitivism, on the one hand, and effeminate decadence, on the other; that is, with either a deficit or a surfeit of the qualities associated with Western civilization. Not coincidentally, Naphta comes from Eastern Europe, following a pattern in Mann's fiction established by the Aarenhold family and Detlev Spinell. Naphta's schoolmates among the Jesuits include other "young foreigners (*Exoten*)—Portuguese South Americans, who looked more 'Jewish' than he," as well as an "Ethiopian prince . . . a very elegant-looking Moor with woolly hair" (437).[48] The Gothic pietà in his room is described as "a profoundly terrifying work," with Mary's face distorted in agony and the body of Christ on her lap, crowned in thorns and drenched in blood, "a primitive figure, badly out of scale, the crudely fashioned body revealing an ignorance of anatomy" (385)[49]—an accurate description of a late medieval sculpture, but one that cannot help but remind readers of the Expressionist "anthropophagic sculpture" that Mann had rejected in the *Reflections* as evidence of a barbaric reversion toward a "negrolike craving for pleasure" (359–60).[50] Naphta's puniness and pugnacity associate him with the ancient Chaldeans, "who had also waged war and conquered Babylon, although they were Semites, and so practically Jews" (365).[51] At the same time, Naphta lives above a ladies' tailor and his room is adorned with so much purple silk and fancy decorations that it "did not have much of a masculine look" (385).[52] In short, Naphta combines verbosity with violence, primitivism with decadence, effeminacy with masculinity, reason with mysticism, and voluptuousness with chastity—embodying thus overtly the latent contradictions in Settembrini's superficial optimism and associating Enlightened rationality with primitive violence and Jewishness.

The very physical appearance of the two men suggests that they are closer to one another then they might want to believe: Settembrini is "delicate" (54),[53] dapper if threadbare, flirtatious if prudish, and loquacious to a fault; Naphta is "puny" (379),[54] handsomely tailored, a spokesman for voluptuousness if personally chaste, and equally given to verbosity. A similar combination of open contrast and clandestine affinity marks the relationship between the grandfathers of Settembrini and Castorp: both men wear black in opposition to the times, but the one looks forward to a better world wrought by modern progress, while the other looks back in regret at a rapidly disappearing world of the past. By structuring polar opposites as mirror images, Mann suggests that the difference between the figures and the ideologies they represent may not be as absolute as they seem. As in the case of Thomas and Christian Buddenbrook, Settembrini and Naphta are united in their rivalry, deadly enemies in conflict with themselves as much as each other.

The initial debate between Naphta and Settembrini begins on a theological-philosophical plane: is God imminent or transcendent, to be found in nature or beyond? Did modern Europe emerge out of the Middle Ages because rational individuals worked toward a better future, or were the accomplishments of medieval monks only accidental by-products of their effort to mortify the flesh through hard labor? The abstract arguments soon turn political. About a year has passed since Castorp arrived on the mountain, meaning it is now 1908. The German colonial empire is expanding across the globe, construction of the Berlin to Baghdad railway has begun, and the German rivalry with Great Britain is at its height. All of this is lost on Hans Castorp, who proclaims with a laugh, "I've never once glanced at a newspaper since I've been here" (373),[55] but Settembrini and Naphta are well aware of what is going on in the world beneath the mountain. Settembrini moves directly from his theoretical defense of human progress to practical examples. Freedom is on the march, democracy is about to triumph everywhere, even in Turkey, where the

Young Turks are on the verge of seizing power. Naphta responds with a dismissive snort, equating the preposterous notion of the "liberalization of Islam" with "enlightened fanaticism" (373),[56] and proceeds to give Settembrini and his pupils a quick lesson in realpolitik. If the Young Turks depose Abdul Hamid II, Germany will lose its influence in Turkey and Great Britain will move in to fill the void. Russia, still reeling from its recent war with Japan, will contest British efforts to secure border states around India. Tension with Great Britain will deflect Russian attention toward Europe, provoking a possible clash with the Austro-Hungarian Empire, and so on and so forth.[57]

The details come and go too quickly for Hans Castorp to follow, but a few larger points stand out clearly. With the benefit of hindsight, we know that Naphta's prediction of imminent catastrophe is correct: the First World War will break out in less than a decade. Settembrini is a liberal in the spirit of the French Revolution, who champions the democratic nation-state as a progressive alternative to aristocratic rule. His prediction of the worldwide victory of democracy anticipates the argument of Francis Fukuyama, who grabbed headlines in the early 1990s by triumphantly proclaiming the "end of history" after the fall of the Berlin Wall and the collapse of the Soviet Union.[58] Naphta contends that the development of the nation-state has only produced international strife and capitalist exploitation. He declares the end of Renaissance humanism and the modern individual, and offers instead a harsh vision of society forged together by "absolute authority and an ironclad bond—discipline and sacrifice, renunciation of the ego and coercion of the personality" (393).[59] Looking again to the near future, Naphta's rhetoric is disturbingly proto-fascist, voicing a reactionary philosophy against which Settembrini's liberal humanism stands out in a flattering light. At the same time, however, Naphta brings out the negative implications of Settembrini's liberal convictions, demonstrating that revolutionary struggles for democracy have often produced only domestic tyranny and foreign aggression.

Excursus: Sexual Politics and the Weimar Republic

The arguments turn on questions of sexuality in relation to politics that were fiercely debated in the aftermath of Germany's defeat in the First World War, and which Mann followed closely.[60] As we recall, Mann had proclaimed a bold new German masculinity in his initial wartime journalism in the fall of 1914, but soon complicated his argument by introducing an alternative understanding of Germany as the cosmopolitan mother or womb of Europe, rather than a stalwart masculine power out to confront the duplicitous maneuvers of the effeminate French. Mann never entirely abandoned his earlier position, however, and as the war was drawing to a close and in the immediate postwar years, he read with approval works by fellow conservatives that called for a new masculine strength and a society held together by close bonds between elite men. Chief among these was that of his closest intellectual companion during the war years: Ernst Bertram's *Nietzsche: Attempt at a Mythology* (1918). The two men read aloud sections of their works in progress to one another, Bertram provided many Nietzsche quotations for Mann's use in the *Reflections,* and Mann flattered himself to think that Bertram's book would not have been possible without the influence of *Tonio Kröger* and *Death in Venice.*[61] Hence it is not surprising that Mann felt as proud of Bertram's work as if he had written it himself.[62] Mann was particularly impressed by the way in which Bertram had revealed Nietzsche's "Germanness."[63] Setting the tone for what Steven E. Aschheim has described as "the *völkisch* appropriation of Nietzsche and his transfiguration into a Germanic right-wing prophet,"[64] Bertram celebrates Nietzsche's cardinal virtues of "hardness, boldness, courage, and the joy of discovery."[65] He views Nietzsche as a kindred spirit of Albrecht Dürer, whose famous etching of a knight with Death and the devil captures a mood of darkly tragic Nordic heroism. Like the Renaissance artist before him, Nietzsche proclaimed a new concept of the German man: "Nietzsche's ideal was also a reformatory masculine one: more masculine values, more masculine virtues, more masculine ideals—like Dürer, Nietzsche could only see and present his highest ideals in masculine characters."[66]

Mann found a similarly melodramatic embrace of Western man's tragic fate in Oswald Spengler's *Decline of the West* (1918). Spengler identifies Faustian man as the driving force of Western civilization. In striving ever forward, Western man creates history in a way that passive women and static Asians cannot. Yet these vital forces of Western culture inevitably and tragically decline into modern civilization, characterized by rootless intellectuals in the modern metropolis and imperial aggression that is a sign of the end. Although Mann would soon reject Spengler's fatalism, he embraced it enthusiastically at first and even expressed admiration for the "masculine" virtues of Spengler's next work, *Preussentum und Sozialismus* (1920).[67] Spengler's concept of socialism has little or nothing to do with the nineteenth-century movement for workers' rights and social reform. He ridicules the notion of a "dictatorship of the proletariat" as symptomatic of Karl Marx's "Jewish instinct," to which he opposes Prussian culture as the purest embodiment of the will to power.[68] Spengler embraces an irrational vitalism based on instinct and destiny, and celebrates the Prussian willingness to subordinate individual desires completely to the collective will. In passages dripping with scorn, Spengler rejects Western democracy and the Weimar Republic. What Germany needs, in his view, is respect for social hierarchy in a government ruled by a handful of elite men "with dictatorial powers."[69] Spengler's ominous paean to Prussian socialism culminates in a call for a new German masculinity: "Become men! We need hardness, we need a bold skepticism, we need a class of socialist supermen."[70]

Hans Blüher completes the dubious trinity of conservative thinkers that influenced Mann in the immediate postwar years.[71] In *The Role of Eroticism in Male Society* (1917–19), Blüher identifies the basis of the state in homoerotic bonds between strong men, while denigrating heterosexual family life as something for inferior weaklings and Jews. There is always something noble about male society, contends Blüher, whereas women are a constant source of danger.[72] Blüher continued his antiliberal and anti-Semitic celebration of homosocial bonding in February, 1919, with a lecture titled "The German Reich, Jewry, and Socialism." Again he proclaimed that the Jews' dedication to family made them incapable of the male bonding of a true *Volk*, while rejecting political socialism as "the product of Jewish thought."[73] Thomas Mann sat front row center as guest of honor while Blüher delivered his tirade and responded enthusiastically: "An excellent lecture, spoken almost word for word from the bottom of my heart."[74]

These antidemocratic, anti-Semitic, and misogynist thinkers articulate ideas that Klaus Theweleit found realized in the proto-fascist members of the German *Freikorps,* a group of what he terms "soldier males" united by their bonds to one another and their fear and loathing of anything or anyone that might dissolve their impenetrable emotional armor, including women, Jews, blacks, or homosexuals.[75] Yet there is also an alternative tradition that views bonds between men as intrinsic to democracy, beginning with the revolt against aristocratic privilege in the name of liberty, fraternity, and equality during the French Revolution and continuing in Walt Whitman's homoerotically charged poems in celebration of American democracy.[76] Mann turns to this tradition when he comes out in support of the Weimar Republic. "The German Republic" (1922) enlists the intellectual support of both the German Romantic writer Novalis, generally considered to be a reactionary monarchist but hailed by Mann as a Jacobin republican, and Whitman, whose song of the "body electric" celebrates "an erotic, all-embracing democracy" based on homoerotic bonds between men.[77] Rather than simply rejecting the masculine model of the state that he had encountered in the work of Spengler and Blüher, Mann adapted it to his new ends: Frederick's belligerent and sexually abstinent soldiers, whom Mann had once praised as a typically German, antidemocratic alternative to the effeminate intellectuals of Western civilization, yield to the argument that the intense and exclusively male camaraderie among German soldiers on the battlefield in the First World War had powerfully strengthened the erotic bonds between men that are central to democracy.[78]

Oddly, Mann insisted in his preface to the essay that his thought had not undergone a fundamental change, even though the shift from a nonpolitical enemy of democracy to its political advocate seems clear enough; it was also perceived as such by Mann's contemporary conservatives, who felt betrayed by his unexpected support of the Weimar Republic.[79] Why would Mann deny the seemingly self-evident change in his thought? A partial answer lies in Mann's unwillingness to repudiate the *Reflections* that had taken him years to write and that had been published just four years earlier; in fact, he never distanced himself entirely from the *Reflections,* always viewing them as an intrinsic part of his overall development.[80] Of more immediate concern was Mann's desire to convince his audience of predominantly right-wing students in Berlin that although his thought had evolved in response to recent events—most notably the assassination of Walther Rathenau—he had remained consistent in his fundamental beliefs. And it is in this context that we need to view Mann's repeated reassurances to his audience that his new embrace of the republic was compatible with the German character and not "something for smart Jewish boys."[81]

We recall that Mann had begun the fragmentary essay "Intellect and Art" in defense of "literature" and that he had aligned himself with the Jewish intellectuals of Berlin, although substituting his mother's Portuguese-Brazilian blood for the racial difference of the Jews. As that essay developed, however, Mann distinguished between authentic and inauthentic literature in passages that alternately targeted Wagner's mendacious theatricality and dissembling Jewish intellectuals. In the *Reflections,* Mann shifted his indictment of "civilization's literary man" to a barely masked attack on his brother Heinrich, although traces of anti-Semitism and self-critique are still present. "The German Republic" offers a new reversal and a new splitting of a term into positive and negative aspects: Mann now defends the republic as consistent with the German ideals of humanity and community, which he claims are "equally distinct from Slavic political mysticism and the anarchic, radical individualism of a certain Western kind."[82] German democracy arises from the stable center; Western democracy is a product of anarchism and radicalism, defined as the mirror image of Eastern mysticism and directly linked to "smart Jewish boys." Mann thus defends the German Republic while condemning Jewish republicans, reinscribing the ambivalence surrounding the *Litterat* into a new political context, and, for the moment at least, forgetting the argument that Germanness in a higher sense has to include Jewishness.

Jesuits, Freemasons, and Jews

If we return to the debates about the Freemasons and the Jesuits on the magic mountain, we find continuing reflections on the ambivalent sexual politics of democracy that preoccupied Mann and his contemporaries in the postwar period. Naphta has been educated by the Jesuits, a group that was founded in opposition to the Protestant Reformation and associated in the popular imagination with twisted logic and the horrors of the Inquisition. Settembrini is a Freemason, an eighteenth-century organization dedicated to principles of the Enlightenment and democracy. Together with coffeehouses and literary salons, the lodges of the Freemasons comprised what Jürgen Habermas has described as the "institutions of the public sphere," in which the rigid social hierarchies of pre-Revolutionary Europe were at least temporarily suspended.[83] The opposition between the Jesuits and Freemasons seems clear: a male-only social organization that stands for reaction, obfuscation, and violence, versus another associated with progress, reason, and the spread of world peace.

In typical fashion, Naphta undermines this distinction from within, suggesting that the Freemasons are far closer to the dark side than they are willing to admit. "I detect something downright military, Jesuitical, about this Freemasonry" (499),[84] speculates his pupil Hans Castorp, and Naphta emphatically agrees. The mysticism and male bonding of the Lodge are actually antiliberal and terrorist, he contends, and points out that Adam Weishaupt, the founder of the Illuminati, was a former Jesuit, and that there was once a flourishing Freemasons' lodge in Clermont, France, the site of a Jesuit order as well.[85] The trivialized version of the organization that Settembrini knows may seem rational on the surface, but it has "a curious affinity for the occult sciences of the East, for Indian and Arabic wisdom and magical knowledge of nature" (500).[86] Their precursors were the military religious orders that took vows of poverty, chastity, and obedience in the holy war against the Muslim infidels. The arcane titles of the Freemason organization have their origins in "Oriental mysticism" (500),[87] and the high priests of the organization were initiated in the secrets of alchemy and the "*lapis philosophorum*, which is the male-female product of sulfur and mercury—the *res bina*, the bisexual *prima material*' (501)[88] employed in the mystic ceremonies of transmutation. The rites of the Freemasons are linked to the Eleusinian mysteries, with "elements of orgiastic primal religion, with unbridled nocturnal sacrifices in honor of dying and ripening, of death, transformation, and resurrection" (503).[89] In short, according to Naphta, the Freemasons are directly implicated in everything they reject, or, to put it another way, in everything that the hermetically sealed society of the magic mountain represents: the loss of time, mysticism, primitivism, exoticism, sex, death, and transubstantiation.

Mann drew his information about Freemasonry from two primary sources. One was Marianne Thalmann's *Der Trivialroman des 18. Jahrhunderts* (The Popular Novel of the Eighteenth Century, 1923), an encyclopedic survey of late eighteenth-century popular fiction in its relation to the German Romantic novel. She argues that popular novels reflected a new interest in magic, alchemy, and gloomy castles on dark and stormy nights, all symptomatic of a general turning away from the Enlightenment and toward the sort of motifs that would concern the German Romantics. Secret societies feature prominently in both popular fiction and Romantic novels, she observes, associating Freemasonry with irrationalism rather than the Enlightenment, and Mann drew on Thalmann's work for the arguments that Naphta uses to undermine Settembrini's defense of Freemasonry.[90] Thalmann's pioneering work of literary scholarship was important enough to have been reprinted in 1978,[91] and Mann's other main source on Freemasonry was also reprinted—in 1936 and 1938 in Nazi Germany. In his preface to the revised and expanded edition of Friedrich Wichtl's *Weltfreimaurerei, Weltrevolution, Weltrepublik* (World Freemasonry, World Revolution, World Republic, 1919), Robert Schneider noted in 1938 that Germans who had recently had the opportunity to travel abroad were often shocked, shocked at the nasty things people were saying about National Socialism, but he assured his readers that such rumors were merely lies spread by Freemasons and Jews.[92] If we look at the edition of 1919 that Mann read in preparation for *The Magic Mountain*, we find that Schneider's anti-Semitic remarks are in keeping with the spirit of Wichtl's original publication. In his sweeping survey of Freemasonry's history and current role in world affairs, Wichtl makes four broad arguments: first, that Freemasonry is a revolutionary order that always seeks to overthrow existing governments and set up a new world order; second, that the assassination of Archduke Ferdinand that sparked the First World War was planned, funded, and committed by Freemasons; third, that Freemasons had conspired to stab what would oth-

erwise have been a victorious German army in the back and were thus responsible for their defeat in the war; and fourth, that Freemasonry was under the
overwhelming influence of the Jews.

The dialectical reversals in the evaluation of the Freemasons in *The Magic
Mountain* underscore my larger argument concerning the role of the Jewish
question in Mann's fiction, which turns less on the identification and evaluation of characters who either are or are not Jewish, and more on the somewhat
amorphous category of Jewishness that can infiltrate individuals and organizations that would seem to have nothing to do with it and mix and blend into
other stigmatized categories of religious, racial, geographical, or sexual difference. Granted, Mann never explicitly identifies the Freemasons as Jews in *The
Magic Mountain,* nor is Settembrini Jewish, but by suggesting similarities between Naphta and Settembrini, between ancient rituals and modern Masonic
rites, and between the world-revolutionary orders of the Jesuits and Freemasons, Mann raises implicit associations that undermine seemingly clear-cut
distinctions. *The Magic Mountain* thus continues to engage with questions
surrounding German masculinity and the politics of male-only organizations
that Mann had discussed in his postwar essays, although in a substantially different way. As noted, a state based on fraternal bonding is neither intrinsically
egalitarian nor intrinsically authoritarian for Thomas Mann: with the aid of
Walt Whitman, he was able to transform Blüher's misogynist and anti-Semitic
conception of a state forged by bonds between elite men into a homoerotic celebration of an all-embracing democracy. A similar dialectical reversal concerning the status of the Freemasons takes place in *The Magic Mountain,* although with diametrically opposed results. In "The German Republic," Mann
sought clarity, arguing in favor of democracy by inverting the arguments of his
enemies. In *The Magic Mountain,* Mann produces ambiguity, first introducing
the Freemasons as an enlightened, democratic organization and then suggesting that they are in fact just the opposite. He does this by drawing arguments
from a book that claims that Germany's defeat in the First World War and the
abdication of the kaiser were all part of a larger Jewish conspiracy to conquer
the world, and places the arguments into the mouth of an Eastern European
Jew raised by Jesuits. As a result, the progressive, secular organization devoted
to democracy becomes associated with reactionary irrationalism, religious
mysticism, the Catholic Counter-Reformation, and the Jews.

The instability surrounding the evaluation of the Freemasons within the
fictional universe of *The Magic Mountain* takes on additional ambivalence
when we view the arguments in the context of Mann's earlier career. Mann's

work develops as something of a palimpsest, in which seemingly clear categories and characters carry with them faint traces of previous formulations and incarnations. Settembrini's defense of Freemasonry as an enlightened organization is in line with Mann's defense of democracy in "The German Republic," but just a few years earlier he had denounced such ideas as the anti-German opinions of "civilization's literary man," a character type most obviously identified with Heinrich Mann, but which contains subliminal ties to Jewish intellectuals. Still earlier, however, Mann had defended himself in "Intellect and Art" as a literary man and aligned himself favorably with Jewish intellectuals—only to turn on a certain type of Jewish intellectual as mendacious and opportunistic. Thus those familiar with the evolution of Mann's thought should already be on their guard when he introduces Settembrini as the seemingly uncomplicated advocate of secular humanism, and Naphta's Jesuitical logic soon exposes the latent Jewishness of the Freemasons: "Jewish" in their adherence to the optimism of civilization's literary man, and "Jewish" in their ties to primitivism, violence, and sexually charged mysticism.

Jewish Psychoanalysis and the Undead Soldier

Joachim Ziemssen, Hans Castorp's likable cousin, wants nothing more than to get well and return to his regiment. He fights against his disease with soldierly discipline; he resists his love for Marusja, the pretty but also tubercular young Russian woman; he disapproves of Krokowski's lectures on human sexuality; and he does not like Naphta, whom he regards with suspicion in part because he looks like a Jew. He even flees the mountain against doctor's orders, "deserting" his duty as a patient to rejoin his fellow soldiers, but all to no avail: Joachim returns to the mountain and even speaks with Marusja before succumbing to his illness in one of the most moving scenes in Thomas Mann's fiction. Joachim dies—but not for good, for a "highly questionable" séance brings him back, if not exactly to life, then at least as an eerie apparition returned from the grave, wearing the uniform of the soldiers who will soon take to the battlefields of the First World War. The episode reworks the theme of interracial love that played an important role in Castorp's affair with Chauchat, although in this case as the threat of miscegenation, of the symbolic rape of an innocent white virgin by a character who is an eastern European Jew in all but name, and it also revisits questions of homoeroticism and male-only societies that sets the scene for the concluding chapter of the novel.

As a soldier, Joachim is a member of yet another of the bands of brothers that play such an important role in *The Magic Mountain*. As we recall, soldiers featured prominently in Mann's earlier essays, although in different ways. In "Frederick and the Great Coalition," Mann had distinguished between the Prussian soldiers, characterized by their sexual abstinence and dedication to a common cause, and the effeminate armies of the French. "The German Republic," in contrast, argued that homoerotic bonds between soldiers served as the model for democracy in Mann's defense of the Weimar Republic. In *The Magic Mountain*, it would seem at first glance that the military would stand with the Freemasons on the side of rationality and discipline, if not necessarily in its dedication to democracy, then at least in its resistance to the debilitating forces of sickness and sexuality that pervade the sanatorium. Here again, however, seemingly clear-cut distinctions soon begin to blur, largely due to Naphta's insidious influence, for the Prussians join the Freemasons in their surprising similarity to the Spanish Jesuits. According to Naphta, the rules of the Jesuit order, originally written in Spanish, are "in some sense the equivalent of those that Frederick the Great later promulgated for his Prussian infantry" (439).[93] Loyola and Frederick share the same philosophy in battle: never retreat, always press forward, "Attaquez donc toujours!" (440; 5.1: 676). Castorp further complicates matters by viewing Spanish discipline as the inverted image of Russian indolence and formlessness. When Joachim returns with his mother to the sanatorium, they mention a chance encounter with Clavdia Chauchat in Munich and pass on the news that she had considered traveling on to Spain in the fall. By this time Castorp has lost all sense of flatland propriety and startles Frau Ziemssen by speculating out loud about the Spanish national character and the effect it might have on Chauchat: "Hmm. Spain— it lay equally as far from the humanistic middle, not toward the soft side, but the hard. Spain was not a lack of form, but an excess of form, death as form, so to speak" (495).[94] Would Spanish rigidity correct Chauchat's tendency toward slovenliness and pull her toward a humanistic center? Or would the two extremes have a synergistic effect that would throw her completely off balance? "But then, too, something very nasty and terroristic might come of the East's going off to Spain" (495).[95]

The Prussian discipline that Joachim exerts to fight his illness gradually splits into two mirroring extremes that flank what Castorp terms "the humanistic middle" on either side: slackness and rigidity, voluptuousness and violence, Russian sex and Spanish death. Just this combination of sexuality and violence repulsed Mann when he traveled to Spain in May 1923, shortly before writing the chapter about Joachim's death.[96] "A horrible people, horrible," he complained to Bertram, "all the supra-personal, mythic antipathy that I can muster, a really visceral revulsion, is directed toward the mixture of infamous, undoubtedly sexually tinged cruelty and sentimentally humanitarian rhetoric that they parade before Europe's gaze."[97] One can certainly question the validity of Mann's speculations about the Spanish national character, but within the fictional world of *The Magic Mountain* they serve to confuse neat distinctions between rationality and irrationality, men who bond together to spread democracy and equality, and those who link arms in totalitarian violence. The Prussian soldiers are like the Spanish Jesuits, but the sexually accented Spanish violence also suggests a secret affinity of both Prussia and Spain with Russia, just as the Freemasons and the Jesuits are both diametrically opposed and secretly aligned. It is thus sadly logical that Joachim should finally abandon his self-control and enter into conversation with Marusja, for, as Castorp correctly senses, speaking with the Russian woman is the equivalent of admitting that he is about to die: "Yes, he is lost" (523).[98]

Joachim is soon lost indeed, but not for good, for the Danish medium Ellen or Elly Brand summons his ghost in what the narrator speculates may well be the strangest experience in Castorp's life. His fellow participants in the séances are some of the most disreputable patients and are generally associated with irrationalism, exoticism, or eroticism. These include Frau Stöhr, notorious for her stupidity; the doltish, disheveled Hermine Kleefeld and her skinny companion Fräulein Levi, with her suspiciously Jewish-sounding name and ivory-colored skin, whose main talent is being able to whistle through her ribs; Herr Albin, a man with a knife from Calcutta who titillates women with threats of suicide; Anton Karlowitsch Ferge, the traveling salesman with stories of the Asian and Mongolian influences in Russia; the Czech Wenzel, another eastern European; Dr. Ting-Fu, a Chinese man who tends to giggle hysterically during the séances; and Wehsal, Castorp's pathetic rival for Chauchat whose primary interest is torture. Master of ceremonies is Dr. Edhin Krokowski, the psychologist whose weekly lectures on sexuality have taken a recent turn toward magic and the occult.

Krokowski is one of many characters in Mann's fiction who might well be Jewish, but is never explicitly identified as such. He is a short man who comes from Eastern Europe, speaks with a curious accent, and practices psychoanalysis, all of which suggest his Jewishness.[99] Krokowski's forked beard has something diabolical about it, and his melodramatic *ecce homo* stance at the conclusion of one of his weekly lectures gives him the aura of a false prophet, a Jew who mimics Jesus and lures good goys like Hans Castorp and Joachim

Ziemssen into a murky world of psychoanalysis and sexual obsession. Again, there is no way of knowing for certain whether or not Krokowski is a Jew, but there is also no need: Mann often works through innuendo and allusion rather than cut-and-dried distinctions; in the case of Krokowski, he drops enough clues to raise the question in the mind of the reader, and that is enough. For this reason, incidentally, I would not place too much stress on the explicitly anti-Semitic minor character Wiedemann who is satirized in the novel's penultimate chapter as a symptom of the general sense of decadence that grips the sanatorium in the final days before the war. Wiedemann is in fact something of a red herring, a blatant satire of an anti-Semitic character that can be safely written off as an aberration; the more sinister anti-Semitism works in conjunction with other forms of difference in more insidious ways.

While the motley crew of sanatorium patients is content to exploit Ellen Brand's psychic talents as a welcome diversion from their daily routine, Dr. Krokowski has more serious designs, for he wants to subject her curious gifts to a rigorous scientific investigation. He forbids the patients to conduct their own lay experiments with the Danish medium—an interdiction that they disobey like guilty children—and subjects her to private sessions with selected guests in his analytical basement. When she rings bells, stops clocks, and levitates a trash can to the ceiling, Krokowski supplies scientific names for her seemingly miraculous feats. Castorp only reluctantly joins the final séance, but Krokowski assures him that he has nothing to fear, for he can look forward only to "the manly cheerfulness of unbiased research!" (661).[100] In keeping with the scientific atmosphere, Krokowski wears a doctor's smock, and the room is decorated with a bust of Hippocrates and a copy of Rembrandt's *Anatomy Lesson* on the wall.

From the beginning, however, there is something suspect about Krokowski's interest in Ellen Brand, for he is less a scientist than a hypnotist engaged in a doctor-patient relationship with strong erotic and racial undertones. The medium Ellen Brand is a blue-eyed, nineteen-year-old Danish blonde who radiates "Nordic coolness . . . a glasslike chasteness, a virginal, childish quality" (645–46).[101] Their first encounter amounts to something of a sexually charged stare-down, as Krokowski speaks to her in his "exotic, drawling accent" (644)[102] and then bores "his exotic brown eyes" into "her bright blue ones" until she is not only forced to lower her gaze, but even slips into a trance (647).[103] Again, during the final séance when distressed by the effort of her "labor," Ellen calls on the doctor to lay his hands on her, which seems to help: "This magnetization, if that is what is was, gave her strength for further struggles" (669).[104] With the introduction of the term *magnetization* we have left the realm of twentieth-century psychology and moved back to eighteenth- and early nineteenth-century mesmerism. Franz Anton Mesmer, born in 1734 near Lake Constance, believed that there was a hidden rapport between bodies and that psychic events were in fact based on the exchange of invisible fluids.[105] He was fascinated by the idea that this "animal magnetism" could be used for medicinal purposes. A strong, charismatic healer could impart strength into a passive, weak patient through the laying on of hands—an idea with roots as old as Gospel accounts of Christ's healing miracles, but which in the late eighteenth and early nineteenth centuries marked a new, Romantic interest in phenomena that escaped the control of enlightened rationality and thus promised to reveal the living, spiritual unity of the seemingly inanimate world.[106]

By its very nature, mesmerism had the potential for abuse, as miracle-working has always had an uncomfortably close proximity to charlatanism. It was a short step from psychic healing through the charismatic laying on of hands to seduction, both on the individual level and in the political realm. According to Rüdiger Safranski, E. T. A. Hoffmann wrote *Der Magnitiseur,* a novella about a man who seeks power over his potentially unfaithful fiancée through hypnosis, in the immediate aftermath of an encounter with Napoleon. As Safranski describes it, there is an essential difference between "magnetization" and psychoanalysis, for the psychoanalyst seeks to liberate the patient from previous trauma, whereas the mesmerist in Hoffmann's tale seeks only to enthrall. "It is a matter of power," Safranski concludes, and "the victim of magnetism experiences a loss of self under the psychodynamic violence of a totalitarian force."[107]

Just five years after completing *The Magic Mountain,* Thomas Mann would write *Mario and the Magician* (1930), a story that implicitly links charlatanism with Italian fascism. The magician Cipolla gives a performance that essentially consists of breaking the audience's will and forcing them to do his bidding. He begins by forcing a young man to stick out his tongue, then compels another to bend down to the floor, and later makes the entire audience dance. Mann's narrator, who is attending the performance with his family while on holiday from Germany, feels compelled to stay even though he really wants to leave. The evening entertainment culminates when Cipolla calls a young waiter named Mario onto the stage. Cipolla insists that Mario is suffering in his love for a certain Silvestra, and then entrances Mario into thinking that he, the aging, chain-smoking charlatan, is the girl. Like a sleepwalker, Mario is drawn to the magician and gives him/her a kiss on the lips, whereupon he comes to his senses and takes revenge on the man who has publicly humiliated him, pulling out a pistol and shooting him dead.

With this story in mind and the issues of sexual and political seduction that it raises, let us return to the final séance in *The Magic Mountain*. Ellen Brand appears "in a kind of séance costume," a white crepe outfit that exposes her arms and the soft outlines of her "her virginal breasts" so clearly that it is evident that "she was apparently wearing little else" (662–63).[108] Despite Krokowski's reassurances that their "research" will be conducted solely in the name of science, Castorp finds himself thinking about his first visit to a brothel with a group of tipsy friends in the notorious Sankt Pauli district of Hamburg, and the red lampshades in Krokowski's dimly lit office are more in keeping with the atmosphere of a bordello than a laboratory.[109] Krokowski then demonstrates for Castorp the position he is to assume during the séance, sitting down on a chair directly in front of Ellen Brand, clasping her hands in his and clenching her knees between his legs. Castorp obediently follows Krokowski's lead and, after taking his place on the chair, stares "into the face of the virginal child prodigy" just as Krokowski had done in his first encounter with the medium. She meets his gaze briefly but then lowers her eyes "in token of a modesty that was quite understandable given the situation" (663).[110] Before long, however, the entranced medium is panting and groaning and whispering "a fervent 'Yes!'" (665)[111] into Castorp's ear in a simulation of sex that gives him goose bumps; she then goes into protracted "labor" and gives birth to the vision of Joachim Ziemssen.

Castorp has gotten just what he wanted, for it was he who requested that Ellen Brand bring back his cousin from the dead. Why, then, is he so upset when Ziemssen appears? The initial reaction is one of shock: it is one thing to miss your cousin and another to see a ghost. Shock immediately gives way to remorse: Castorp feels guilty about having let himself be drawn into something that he feels is wrong. Joachim was a noble young man who died with dignity against his will; Castorp should have let him rest in peace, rather than summoning him from the grave. Clearly there is an element of embarrassment as well, for the young man who was once mortified simply because Joachim called him by his first name is now simulating sex in public with a girl he barely knows. Compounding the embarrassment is the fact that Castorp interacts not with Ellen but with her male alter-ego Holger during a séance designed to resurrect his beloved cousin, which is to say that his latent but repressed homosexual desires are exposed to public view in a way that anticipates Mario kissing Cipolla.[112] But Castorp's overwhelming emotion when he breaks off the séance is anger at the doctor who has manipulated him into this compromising position and used him as a pawn in his pseudoscientific experiment. Unlike Mario, Castorp does not actually murder Krokowski, but he threatens him in a silent fury that stops just short of physical violence.

On the level of individual psychology, it is easy enough to say that Castorp has redirected his self-recriminations onto a scapegoat, blaming Krokowski for his own decision to take part in this highly questionable affair. More is at stake, however, if we look at the larger context of the incident. The sexually charged exchange between Castorp and Ellen Brand qua Holger does reveal certain repressed desires on Castorp's part, but it is also part of a public surrogate seduction of Ellen Brand by Edhin Krokowski through the medium of Hans Castorp. As noted, Castorp assumes the sexually suggestive position with Brand only after Krokowski demonstrates it for him. While Krokowski's public treatment of Brand is more paternal or avuncular than openly sexual, Castorp senses immediately that there is something suspicious about his desire to have a private "chat" with her in his office (647),[113] and, to put it colloquially, there is something creepy about the unctuous attention of this dirty old man toward the virginal medium—long ago, Settembrini had warned Castorp that Krokowski "has but one thought in his head, and it is a filthy one" (61).[114] Mann compounds the uneasiness created by their difference in age by repeatedly underscoring their racial difference: Brand is always described as white, blond, and blue-eyed; Krokowski has an exotic drawling accent and dark eyes that penetrate and enthrall. Mann is tapping into the fear of miscegenation that played such a prominent role in the early twentieth-century imagination, as captured in anti-French propaganda posters depicting black soldiers stationed along the Rhine raping German women, anti-Semitic caricatures of Jewish men molesting innocent gentiles, or, for that matter, of Fay Wray in the clutches of King Kong.[115]

Krokowski's designs on Ellen Brand go beyond the merely individual. As the narrator explains in the beginning of the chapter, Krokowski's recent turn to the occult represents a logical extension of his interest in the individual subconscious mind toward group psychology, speculating "that there may be connections and associations between the bottommost unlighted tracts of the individual soul and an omniscient universal soul" (644).[116] The séance by its nature is not individual analysis or hypnosis, but a group experience in which the medium literally mediates between the collective unconscious of those present, channeling the psychic energy within the room until it is manifested in a single vision. As in the case of the Freemasons and the Jesuits, we are again dealing with a collective rather than an individual, a group of patients that is for once not male-only, but united in their penchant for titillating experiments, their shared illness, and their association with Eastern Europe, Asia, racial difference or Jewishness. The interaction between Castorp and Ellen Brand takes place under Krokowski's supervision within this circle, and it is a closed circle that must not be broken—hence Krokowski forbids Castorp to leave the room to seek the recording of Valentin's aria from Gounod's *Faust*. In the end, Castorp liberates himself violently from this group by turning on the light, disobeying Krokowski's commands, and stalking out of the room.

The collective experience of the séance recalls the vision that Castorp had earlier in the snow, in which he believes that he has tapped into a universal truth and not just experienced a private fantasy: "We dream anonymously and communally, though each in his own way. The great soul, of which we are just a little piece, dreams through us so to speak" (485).[117] In that dream, Castorp witnesses what amounts to a visual representation of the basic concepts in Nietzsche's *Birth of Tragedy:* here the Dionysian realm, represented by hideous hags dismembering and devouring a baby, there the Apollonian domain of handsome people bathed in golden sunshine, aware of the violence opposite them but undeterred by it, in keeping with the mantra that you have to be aware of the destructive forces and yet refuse them dominion over your thoughts. In this scene, terrifying harpies stand at the gates of hell; in other passages of *The Magic Mountain,* that realm is represented by ancient Eleusinian mysteries, the orgiastic rites attributed to the original Freemasons, the terroristic violence of the Jesuits and the Prussian soldiers, the formless voluptuousness of the Russians, deadly Javanese cobra venom, or the ritual slaughter of the Jews. The point again is that Mann does not offer us an abstract Nietzschean allegory of "the Dionysian," but projects that conceptual realm into the world of prewar Europe in a global context, creating imaginative associations between seemingly disparate realms of difference and inverting seemingly clear distinctions into their opposites.

In the end, Castorp joins one more group, the soldiers who fight on the battlefields of the First World War. Does he experience battle as a regressive, Dionysian ecstasy, a step back into the world of "oracles, magic, pederasty, Vitzli-Putzli, human sacrifice, orgiastic cults, Inquisition, auto-da-fés, Saint Vitus' dance, witch trials, the efflorescence of murderous poison, and the most vivid horrors," as Mann had described the forces underlying German *Kultur* shortly after the outbreak of the First World War,[118] a rejection of all that Settembrini has tried to teach him and a refutation of his vision in the snow? Or does he experience the homoerotic camaraderie that Mann hailed in support of democracy in "The German Republic"? Not surprisingly, the answer is ambiguous. Although the actual battlefield remains anonymous in *The Magic Mountain,* it is described in ways that recall the battle of Langemarck on November 10, 1914.[119] On that day, a group of idealistic young German soldiers charged to their deaths, supposedly singing "Deutschland, Deutschland über alles" as they were cut down by enemy fire. Whether or not they were actually singing the German national anthem while slogging through mud under a hail of bullets is difficult to say, but the story was taken up by the jingoistic press and circulated as an example of heroic German resolution in the face of death. But there is nothing heroic about Mann's representation of this event. The exhausted young men run through muck so deep that it threatens to tear off their shoes at every step, across a battlefield illuminated by intermittent explosions, and filled with the sounds of whining bullets, shattering detonations, and the screams of the wounded and dying. And yet others keep coming, charging on until, they, too, "are hit, they fall, flailing their arms, shot in the head, the heart, the gut" (704).[120] The narrator does maintain that the recruits plunge into battle with joy as well as fear, but ultimately questions the entire endeavor: there is "surely no reason to bring them here to this" (705).[121]

In their midst is Hans Castorp, singing, not "Deutschland, Deutschland über alles," but Schubert's song of the Lindenbaum, "Am Brunnen vor dem Tor" (At the Well before the Gate). The melancholy song of a young man beneath a linden tree is clearly not the sort of anthem designed to inspire martial valor. Castorp is physically part of the men in arms, but psychologically detached from them—and yet spiritually in tune with them after all, for the song he sings is about death, about a young man who has lost his love and is promised eternal rest beneath the tree. Or at least so we are told in the concluding segment of "Fullness of Harmony." Castorp listens to Schubert's song as the last of the records that keep him awake nights in the sanatorium in a scene that inspires a particularly dense narrative commentary worth following in some detail. What stands behind the world of the song that so entrances Hans Castorp? "It was death" (641).[122] The peace and quiet that the tree promises the young man is the eternal rest of the grave, and thus the melancholy song epitomizes the "sympathy with death" (642)[123] characteristic of German romanticism, a sympathy that Settembrini had long ago rejected as "politically suspect." What does Castorp associate with this sympathy with death? "The workings of darkness. Dark working. Torturers at work, misanthropy dressed in Spanish black with a starched ruff and with lust in place of love" (642).[124] In symbolic shorthand, the narrator alludes here to both Castorp's dead grandfather and Naphta's advocacy of the sexually charged violence of the Spanish Jesuits. By implication, however, he also refers to the hidden parallels between the Jesuits and the Freemasons and thus to the dialectic of Enlightenment that makes "civilization's literary man" into an advocate of the "imperialism of civilization."[125] Thus the regressive rapture that can be inspired by the Romantic song of death can inspire aggression as well as quiescence. Under its influence, contends Mann's narrator, a man of talent could become "an enchanter of souls, who would then give the song such vast dimensions that it would subjugate the world. One might even found whole empires upon it, earthly, all-too-earthy empires, very coarse, very progressive, and not in the least nostalgic" (643).[126]

It is the love for the seductively sweet poison of Schubert's song that Castorp must learn to overcome: "Yes, triumph over self, that may well have been the essence of his triumph over this love—over this enchantment of the soul with dark consequences" (643).[127] If enjoyed at precisely the right moment, the "fruit" of the Romantic song can grant exquisite pleasure, but it is a fruit that quickly rots and becomes deadly if consumed too late. As Hans Rudolf Vaget interprets this passage, Mann now realizes that the time is no longer right for politically suspect romanticism; just as Nietzsche overcame his initial infatuation with Wagner's seductive music, so Mann overcame his fatal attraction to the outbreak of war and learned to embrace democracy and the Weimar Republic.[128] Is Settembrini right after all? Again, the answer is both yes and no: yes, in the sense of Mann's political essays from "The German Republic" to "An Appeal to Reason" (1930). Here Mann used all of his eloquence to shore up support for the fragile German republic and to resist the rising tide of German fascism. But no within the context of *The Magic Mountain,* or at least not entirely yes, for Naphta has effectively subverted Settembrini's loquacious defense of the Enlightenment into its opposite. The rhetoric in support of reason and democracy that Mann employs strategically in his political essays is suspended in his fiction into an endlessly mirroring series of dialectical reversals. As a result, he offers Castorp not the language of truth, but the hope for a truth beyond language: the young man who overcomes his love for Schubert's song dies with "a new word on his lips, the word of love, which he did not yet know how to speak" (643).[129] Nor does the narrator quite know how to formulate the promise that may or may not lie beyond the chaos of the battlefield, but can only wonder if "love [will] someday rise up out of this, too?" (706).[130] What remains is neither Settembrini nor Naphta, but the tender gaze of the undead soldier, "directed in friendly silence at Hans Castorp, at him alone" (671).[131] His unfamiliar uniform heralds the coming war with all its attendant horrors, but his visage radiates an austere serenity, and his eyes speak silently of a boundless love from beyond the grave.

CHAPTER SIX

Joseph and His Brothers: Fascism, Orientalism, and Ancient Cosmopolitanism

In early March 1925, little more than three months after the publication of *The Magic Mountain,* Thomas Mann traveled to Egypt.[1] The owners of a steamship line had invited the increasingly famous author on a three-week Mediterranean cruise in the hope that he would write a few lines about his experience, and, upon his return, Mann dutifully published a lively account of his journey in the *Vossische Zeitung* of Berlin. "Underway" reads like the account of an entrenched European intellectual on his first "Oriental" adventure. Mann embarked from Venice with emotional memories of his last visit to the city thirteen years earlier, a reference to the events that inspired *Death in Venice.* Once on board the luxury liner, Mann experienced an opulent ambiance that was clearly to his taste. Well-heeled passengers dressed for dinner at seven, where they were attended by smartly dressed crew members who would later strew the deck with talcum powder for after-dinner dancing. As Mann admits with mildly self-deprecating irony, unsympathetic readers could easily dismiss his description as a "social provocation, as an approving account of an orgy of postwar capitalism with *nouveaux riches* in gleaming luxurious staterooms."[2] Nevertheless, he continues, "it is after all a German ship that flies our flag on the high seas and in foreign harbors." The captain and crew exude an air of serious competence and sober cleanliness "that feels very good after the exotic bizarreness into which it has taken you."[3]

Mann disembarked from this floating island of German efficiency in Port Said, traveled by special train to Cairo and the Suez Canal, and continued the whirlwind tour with stops in Luxor and Karnak. Along the way he found time to admire the pyramids and the Sphinx, to catch glimpses of the Nile and the surrounding countryside, and to marvel at the recently excavated tomb of King Tutankhamen that was causing such a stir back home. The living Egyptians left him less than excited. While noting that many were physically attractive ("in an African sort of way"), with teeth "like I've never seen in my life," he also complained bitterly about the aggressive swarms of beggars and would-be tour guides, "a pack of rabble that makes the beggars of Southern Italy look like pure British aristocracy in comparison."[4] The only way to keep them at bay was to use the fly-swatters purchased upon arrival in port, "but they are worse than the real ones [flies]."[5] The return journey brought Mann back to Athens via Constantinople (Istanbul), and once in Greece he breathed an audible sigh of relief. "We cast aside the oppressive Orient, our souls became light and cheerful." Here in "Hellas" Mann is proud to be the European heir to ancient Greek culture. "Here you think fervently: let the Persians come again, in whatever form, and may they be defeated again and again."[6]

Readers of his jaunty travelogue would have found their curiosity piqued and their prejudices confirmed, but would hardly have suspected that Mann was contemplating a new literary project set in the ancient Middle East. Yet a month before his departure, Mann had already hinted to Ernst Bertram that there were ulterior motives behind his sightseeing tour: "it may be useful for certain somewhat vague, secret plans."[7] What he had in mind was nothing more than a novella on the theme of religious history that would take its place with companion pieces on Germany and Spain. "The same old story!"[8] As so often in the past, the project of modest scope soon began to expand: the novella grew to a novel, the novel swelled to a four-volume opus, and it was not until January 4, 1943, that Mann wrote "the last lines of *Joseph the Provider* and thus of *Joseph and His Brothers*."[9]

Cataclysmic events had shaken the world since Mann first began work on his project. The Weimar Republic had fallen, together with the stock market in New York; Hitler had risen to power; and by the time Mann wrote the final sentences, the world was once again in the grips of global conflict. Changes had come to Thomas Mann as well: he began writing in the comfort of his villa on the outskirts of Munich, where he no doubt assumed he would spend the rest of his career. Instead, he found himself continuing the novel in exile, as he moved from southern France to Switzerland, Princeton, and finally Los Angeles. The forty-nine-year-old author who made his first journey to Egypt in the spring of 1925 was sixty-seven when he completed *Joseph and His Brothers* in early 1943. Small wonder that he should have been filled with mixed emotions as he concluded *Joseph the Provider*. The sense of sadness and loss hit him hardest two months later, when he had completed the spin-off novella about Moses, *The Tables of the Law*, and packed away all his materials for posterity. "Only now do I realize what it means to be without the Joseph project, the task that for an entire decade was always at my side, before me."[10] Mann worried that he might not find the energy for a new novel, and yet he was also filled with an overwhelming sense of pride that he had completed his challenging task under the most difficult of circumstances: "I see it much more as a monument of my life than one of art and intellect, a monument of *perserverance*."[11]

Cruel fate would have it that unsympathetic readers have often rejected Mann's monumental accomplishment as a monumental bore. The sheer size of a novel cycle that stretches well over two thousand pages in some editions is daunting enough. The Wagnerian pace of the narration serves as a further deterrent, as the terse narrative of *Genesis* expands into an elaborate Alexandrine world in which conversations whose content can be summarized in a few short sentences continue for dozens of pages. The subject matter serves as a teasing enticement that soon disappoints, for readers expecting a straightforward retelling of the familiar Joseph story soon find themselves in an arcane world of ancient mythology and politico-theological debates in ancient Egypt about which they know little and care less. Despite John E. Woods' heroic retranslation of "what is actually Mann's major work,"[12] one wonders if *Joseph and His Brothers* is soon likely to regain the widespread popular appeal and euphoric critical acclaim that greeted the first translation of the work into English.[13]

The fortunate few who have the weeks and months required for sustained reading and rereading of the Joseph novels experience the literary equivalent of the Stockholm Syndrome, as they begin to fall in love with the book that holds them hostage. One gradually discovers a work of immense psychological subtlety and intellectual profundity written by a major author at the height of his powers. Yet the sense remains that *Joseph and His Brothers* is something of an anomaly in Thomas Mann's work. His best-known works of fiction—*Buddenbrooks, Death in Venice, The Magic Mountain, Doctor Faustus, Felix Krull*—all take place in or close to the historical present. To be sure, *Lotte in Weimar* is set in the early nineteenth century and *The Holy Sinner* in a fanciful Middle Ages, but *Joseph and His Brothers* takes place some three thousand years ago; it is also the only novel set outside Europe and the only one in which the protagonist is a Jew. As a result, themes of exoticism and the Jewish question that typically hover in the margins of Mann's fiction are placed firmly in the foreground. Here again, however, *Joseph and His Brothers* seems to break the mold: for once, "Jews become representative of mankind and are no longer freaks, fanatics, and clever fools," as Ruth Angress-Klüger puts it in an influential essay that otherwise pulls no punches in its critical assessment of Jewish characters in Mann's fiction.[14] While she hails *Joseph and His Brothers* as "the most inspired tribute that has ever been paid to the Jewish tradition by a non-Jew,"[15] Yahya Elsaghe scornfully rejects the notion that there might be anything redemptive about Mann's positive depiction of the patriarchs. They are simply the exception that proves the rule, he contends, the ancient standard against which the degeneracy of modern Jews can be measured. Having thus dismissed critics who complained that he had ignored the Joseph tetralogy in his first book, Elsaghe turns his attention to other works and ignores it again.[16]

Joseph and His Brothers remains as the elephant in the room of Mann's fiction, a hulking presence that is seemingly so at odds with the rest of his work that it is easier to pretend it is not there.[17] It is tempting to think of Joseph's biblical world as a counterreality, a place of refuge to which Mann could flee from overwhelming demands in terrible times, and it certainly did fulfill this role for its author during the long years of exile.[18] A closer look at the work in biographical context nevertheless reveals that it was in fact intimately linked to Mann's central concerns of the time. As Mann explained in an essay written as he was nearing completion of the tetralogy, he sought in *Joseph and His Brothers* to "wrest myth from the hands of fascism," to "narrate the birth of the individual out of the mythic collective" at a time when Germans had cast reason aside in favor of a fanatical devotion to a German *Volk* purged of Jews and other foreign elements.[19] As early as 1926 Mann had distanced himself in his "Parisian Account" (Pariser Rechenschaft)[20] from what he felt were the dangerous political implications of the irrationalism expressed in Alfred Baeumler's new edition of the works of Johann Jakob Bachofen.[21] In his extensive introduction, Baeumler places Bachofen's theory of an ancient matriarchy that preceded modern patriarchy into the context of German intellectual history, viewing it as part of "the German-Romantic revolution of the nineteenth century against the Enlightenment, Idealism, and classicism of the eighteenth."[22] While Mann notes that Baeumler's introduction makes for fascinating reading, he wonders if it is a good idea in the present political climate to reintroduce Germans to "the whole Joseph Görres complex of earth, *Volk*, nature, past, and death, a revolutionary obscurantism, to put it crudely,"[23] with the implication that now is once again the time for such a reactionary ideology. In keeping with arguments introduced in "The German Republic," Mann distinguishes between the progressive early Romantics Friedrich Schlegel and Novalis, whose work was still in the spirit of eighteenth-century Enlightenment, and irrational Romantics of a more sinister bent, including Ernst Moritz Arndt, Joseph Görres, the brothers Grimm, and Bachofen.

The fleeting remarks about Baeumler and Bachofen in "Parisian Account" set the tone for a defense of the Enlightenment that would remain central to Mann's rejection of German National Socialism over the coming years and decades. Essays on Lessing, Freud, and Goethe stress their cosmopolitanism and belief in the supremacy of human reason over instinct, progress over reaction.[24] Overtly political speeches such as the "Appeal to Reason" (1930) and "Achtung, Europa!" (1935) pleaded with the German people to overcome their addiction to the "mass opiate of the Third Reich," to snap out of their "epileptic ecstasy" and return to rationality, spiritual dignity, and social democracy.[25] *Lotte in Weimar* juxtaposed Goethe's sovereign cosmopolitanism to the potentially disastrous nationalism of a younger generation swept up in the enthusiasm of the wars of liberation against Napoleon. *Joseph and His Brothers*, finally, portrays the triumph of reason over irrationalism, the individual over the collective, and thus, by association, of male over female, patriarchy over matriarchy, the Occident over the Orient.

Generations of critics have essentially paraphrased Mann's assertion that he sought to defend humanism and the values of Western civilization against fascist barbarism in *Joseph and His Brothers*, thus placing this text squarely in the context of Mann's other fictional and nonfictional works of the period.[26] The tetralogy is deemed particularly laudable because it traces the origins of human dignity and enlightened progress back to the Jewish patriarchs at a time of an unprecedented campaign of state-supported anti-Semitism. There have nevertheless been a few dissonant voices against the chorus of praise for Mann's biblical work. Jacques Darmaun notes that Jacob's trickiness, sentimentality, and theatricality correspond to anti-Semitic stereotypes, as does Mann's stress on the ethnic or racial features of Joseph's brothers.[27] Ritchie Robertson argues that Mann's representation of the Jews as an unruly mob in *The Tables of the Law*, together with his depiction of Moses as the tyrannical and hypocritical bastard son of Pharaoh's daughter and a Jewish slave, seem more calculated to insult rather than exalt Jewish tradition;[28] in fact, one early Jewish reader saw in the novella "outbreak of hatred" against the Jews.[29] Franka Marquardt, finally, claims that there is an anti-Semitic subtext in a novel that transforms a specifically Jewish text into a mere precursor of the Christian New Testament and a paradigm for humanity as a whole.[30]

In the following chapter, I will argue that previous readings of *Joseph and His Brothers* have been either too broad or too narrow: too broad among those who celebrate Mann's universal humanism and too narrow among those who denigrate his implicit anti-Semitism. Mann's representation of the Jewish patriarchs must be viewed in the larger context of his views on race and in the context of his fictional evocation of the Egyptian empire. Mann's depiction of ancient Jews at a time of modern fascism rests on a double paradox: he defends the Jews with an argument drawn from the language of anti-Semitism, and he condemns the Nazis in the language of European Orientalism.

Fascism, Orientalism, and the Jewish Question

Mann traveled to Paris in early 1926, approximately ten months after he had returned from his first visit to Egypt. By this time he was in the midst of his preparations for *Joseph and His Brothers* and took every opportunity to expand his knowledge of Egypt and the Middle East. On one evening he renewed his acquaintance with the noted Africanist Leo Frobenius; he spent another chatting with an Egyptologist about possible names he might use for Potiphar's wife, and still another "under the sign of Orientalism"[31] discussing the recent discovery of King Tut's tomb.[32] As always, Mann's antennae were up for racial differences among the many individuals he met in Paris: he marvels at the "monumental childishness and cheerfulness, the victorious racial vitality" (*sieghafter Rassenfrische*) of an American reporter, is captivated by a handsome half-Japanese man with a "classic and immutable Asiatic smile," and observes with interest a district of Paris renowned for its male prostitution, a phenomenon that Mann had thought was restricted to southern Europe, the Orient, and parts of Great Britain and Berlin.[33] In typical fashion, Mann reminds readers of his own mixed heritage, stating once again that his mother was from Brazil (15.1: 1166); he also makes a self-deprecating reference to his "Negroid French" (*Negerfranzösisch*) (15.1: 1123).

Mann makes his comments about the reactionary obscurantism of Baeumler and Bachofen while thinking about Egypt and noting individuals marked by racial difference or sexual deviance. The common thread that pulls together these desultory remarks is a concern for rationality over irrationalism, ascetic discipline over sexual indulgence, and the victory of light over the forces of darkness. More specifically, Mann links the German fascination with fascism to historical regression and racial degradation. Of central importance to the first aspect of Mann's critique was Freud's late work on the origins of human culture, beginning with *Totem and Taboo*.[34] In an essay of 1932 Mann describes a visit to Vienna, where he had the opportunity for a long conversation with Freud in his office. Freud showed him "his collection of archaeological oddities" that included "Indian woodcuts, ancient relics from Egyptian tombs," and "small Greek sculptures of a most remarkable sort."[35] As Freud explained, these remains of ancient cultures demonstrated that the roots of the modern psychiatric movement extended deep into the past, "into knowledge about the primitive, about prehistoric man."[36] Modern neurotics are like an-cient savages, and thus one gains insight into present pathology by revisiting the past.[37] From this perspective, the German turn to National Socialism is a symptom of a collective mental illness that amounts to a throwback to ancient times, a regression to precivilized behavior. For both Mann and Freud, how-ever, the historical distance between ancient and modern can also be described in terms of the geographical distance between Europe and its colonies, or, in racial terms, between Caucasians and everyone else. Thus in "Brother Hitler" Mann compares the mass political rallies in modern Europe with a film that he had recently seen about a religious ritual in Bali "that ended in the complete trance and terrible convulsions of the exhausted youths";[38] in his radio address of September 1942, Mann contrasts "the screams and prayers of the victims" of the Nazi campaign of terror against the Jews with the "cheerful laughter of the SS-Hottentots."[39]

Mann's critique of German fascism reveals the usual pattern of continuity and reversal in his thought. Individuals and peoples marked by sexual de-viance, geographical distance, or racial difference had always been a source of fear and fascination for Thomas Mann. In the novellas written prior to the First World War, Mann had suggested that a certain amount of exoticism was essential for the modern artist, but only if kept under strict control. The forces of destruction were always lurking, whether in the form of cholera coming from the swamps of India, the deadly embrace of a Jewish femme fatale, the forces unleashed by the wild, cannibal gong that summons the Aarenhold fam-ily to dinner, or the Wagnerian music that inspires Siegfried and Sieglinde to commit incest on their bearskin rug. In the early fiction, Jewish characters are often aligned with other forms of exoticism as a potential threat to the precar-ious balance of the artistic psyche; in the essays of the 1930s, in contrast, Jews become the necessary antidote to the collective mental illness that has over-come the Germans. That illness takes the form of "the absurd idea of the racial purity of the German people."[40] Anti-Semitism arises from the barbaric belief that Germans must cleanse themselves of any non-Germanic elements, forget-ting that Germanness in a higher sense has always been based on inclusiveness and diversity. As we have seen, Mann had made this argument already in the *Reflections* and repeats it in his 1937 essay "The Problem of Anti-Semitism."[41] The desire for racial purity is in fact a sign of corruption. "People talk a lot about 'totality' these days," commented Mann in an address at Yale University in 1938, but "to the extent that this concept is applied to the state, it is some-thing terrible, monstrous, and inhuman."[42]

Mann rejects anti-Semitism, but he does not reject the idea that Jews are different from Germans, nor does he reject the concept of race. Just the opposite, in fact: he bases his argument against the anti-Semitism of *völkisch* nationalism on the need for cultural and racial diversity. People are different, difference is beneficial and necessary, and thus Germans bereft of their Jews would be impoverished. Mann uses the term *German* in a double sense: real Germans are not Jews, but real Germans without Jews would be mere Germans, not Germans in the higher sense of a people that finds room for its others. He defines the Jews with an almost oxymoronic combination of cultural and biological difference: "but the Jews in a German context represent the intellectual element physically, by virtue of their blood and race (*blut- und rassenmäßig*)."[43] Mann shares a willingness to think in racial categories with the Nazis, but he comes to diametrically opposed conclusions: for Mann, racial purity is always the problem, not the solution. This was true early on, in the distinction between, for example, the hopelessly different Siegfried Aarenhold versus the only partially stigmatized Tonio Kröger, but also between Tonio Kröger and the hopelessly blond and bland Hans Hansen. The Nazis wanted to reduce Germany to a nation of Hans Hansens, throwing out the "Portuguese" Thomas Mann together with the Jews—a lack of subtlety that Mann noted with outrage in one of the more offensive passages of his diary of 1933.[44] Difference may be good, but some kinds of difference are better than others; Mann may be like a Jew—in his stigmatization by the Nazis, his admixture of Brazilian-Portuguese blood, his repressed homosexual desires, his affinity for *Litteratur*—but he is not a Jew, and in his more sensitive moments he is keen to underscore the difference, particularly in his private diaries. In public, however, Mann stressed the unambiguous badness of totalitarianism and the murderous stupidity of a desire for national unity based on racial purity.

These comments add nuance to the Orientalist paradigm that informs Mann's critique of German fascism.[45] In broad terms, Mann links Hebrew progress over a static and indolent Egypt to the victory of Hellas over Persia and Western democracy over German fascism: here monotheism, progress, enlightenment, tolerance, and individualism; there idolatry, regression, obfuscation, bigotry, and the masses. *Joseph and His Brothers* complicates the Manichaean opposition between the Hebrews and Egyptians in three distinct ways, however: first, the Hebrew patriarchs of *Joseph and His Brothers* are not Hebrew, or at least not exclusively so. While Mann acknowledged that his choice of subject matter in *Joseph and His Brothers* was in opposition to the "racial madness" of the "fascist rabble-myth" (*Pöbel-Mythos*), he insisted that it was not a "Jewish novel" (*Juden-Roman*), that is, a novel about Jews intended primarily for Jews.[46] Its syncretic mixture of disparate religious traditions and mythologies was rather intended for humanity in its diversity, not Jews in their particularity. Second, Mann does not portray the Jews as a Chosen People defined by their untrammeled lineage or racial purity, but stresses instead their internal diversity and proximity through intermarriage to other peoples of the Middle East. Third, the Egypt of *Joseph and His Brothers* is not a monolithically primitive and ancient culture, but one that is simultaneously and paradoxically ancient and modern, primitive and decadent. The blurring of the boundaries between seemingly distinct groups permits measured criticism of the Hebrews and a qualified appreciation of the Egyptians in a novel that stresses the need for tolerance in the face of prejudice, judicious action rather than mystical daydreaming or religious ecstasy, and realpolitik rather than appeasement.

Prelude: Temporality in *Joseph and His Brothers*

Joseph and His Brothers begins with a substantial prelude on the nature of time and the meaning of myth. The narrator looks into the depths of the past, only to discover that each seemingly originary event was only a provisional beginning, a signpost on a journey that recedes, if not into infinity, then at least further and deeper than we expected and to the limit of what we can comprehend. The domestication of animals, the invention of writing, the origins of language, even the creation of the world as recorded in the opening verses of Genesis marked "only a conditional, particular beginning of things" (10).[47] "Deep is the well of the past" (3).[48] At the bottom of the well, at the end of the descent to hell, at the moment of death we are thrown out of time into timelessness, or rather, we "gain eternity and a timeless present, and thus, for the first time, real life" (39).[49] The esoteric truth grasped only by initiates is that the world is a place of simultaneous presence. But how does one render this insight visible to the masses? To put it another way, narration necessarily unfolds in time; how does one convey the truth of simultaneity in a successive medium? The answer lies in myth, repetitive, cyclical stories that have their nonverbal counterpart in rituals. "For the essence of life is presentness, and only by means of myth does it represent its mystery in past and future tenses" (39).[50] Myths and rituals tell a story that unfolds in time, but one that is essentially the same over and over again: each year nature dies in the fall, lies dormant over winter, and bursts back to life in the spring; each year the god is buried and mourned, each year he is resurrected and celebrated. Any given

moment in the eternal cycle repeats the events of previous years and anticipates those of years to come, thus suspending the linear flow of time into an
infinitely receding series of repetitions and anticipations that gesture toward
the eternal present of a single, all-encompassing *nunc stans.*

Of special significance within any given cycle is the moment of descent to
the underworld, a place of death and destruction, but also resurrection to new
life. Mann draws on Goethe's *Faust,* in which the effort to resurrect Helen of
Troy begins with a descent to the realm of "formation, transformation" represented by the dreaded "Mothers."[51] "The idea of rendering visible (*Sichtbarmachung*) the one who went down to the Mothers in the smoke of the tripod
highly relevant to *Joseph,*" noted Mann in his diary in December 1935.[52] Also
influential for Mann was Alfred Jeremias's "Pan-Babylonian" school of biblical
interpretation, which claimed that Judaism emerged out of Babylon and that
the stories of the Old Testament should be viewed in a larger network of Babylonian, Egyptian, Greek, and early Christian myth and symbolism.[53] The religious model recurs in what Northrop Frye termed the "secular scripture" of
Western literature: Goethe's Faust follows a trail to the underworld already
blazed by Odysseus, Aeneas, and Dante.[54] Interest in the mythic pattern of the
god's or hero's descent to and return from the underworld was widespread
among Mann's contemporaries, inspiring both Carl Gustav Jung's *Symbols of
Transformation* and Joseph Campbell's *Hero with a Thousand Faces.*[55] As always, Mann's most important sources for what he terms "Hell" in the prelude
to *Joseph and His Brothers* go back to the triumvirate of influences that he had
already identified in the *Reflections of a Nonpolitical Man:* the Dionysian realm
of Nietzsche's *Birth of Tragedy,* the chthonic passions of Schopenhauer's Will,
and the rippling chords that rise from the Rhine in the prelude to Wagner's
Ring.

By the time he began writing the Joseph novels, Mann was acutely aware
that descending to "hell" could be tantamount to the abrogation of reason and
thus, to quote Settembrini, politically suspect. The plot of *Joseph and His
Brothers* nevertheless turns on repeated descents to the underworld, while the
ideas of mythic repetition and eternal recurrence feature prominently in the
preface and throughout the work. How, then, can Mann avoid implicating
himself in the same sort of politically suspect ideas that he rejects in others?
The answer lay in the grafting of a second model of temporality onto the pattern of mythic repetition that allowed for progress as well as circularity.[56]
Joseph "dies" several ritual deaths in the course of the novel, but rises each time
to greater glory. His personal fate is inscribed in a larger plan that might be

termed a secularized version of Christian salvation history. The notion of repetition was also central to the premodern thinkers of the Middle Ages, but as a
form of repetition that included a promise of redemption and not the eternal
recurrence of the same.[57] Just as Jonas was swallowed up for three days and
three nights in the belly of the whale before being vomited out upon the dry
land, so, too, Jesus Christ would descend into hell and yet rise again on the
third day, and those who shared the faith could look forward to the resurrection of the dead and the life of the world to come. In the Gospel according to
Thomas Mann, the Jewish patriarchs and God coexist in an ongoing process of
mutual development, "because one served a God whose nature was not rest
and comfortable repose, a God of future plans" (38).[58] Thus when old Jacob
meets the Egyptian pharaoh Akhnaton, the two confirmed monotheists are
nevertheless described as worlds apart: Pharaoh represents the last gasp of a
dying civilization, whereas Jacob stands "at the source of far-reaching forces in
the process of becoming" (1436).[59]

In spiritual terms, Jacob and the other Hebrew patriarchs focus on the
blessing passed on from one generation to the next in anticipation of the Messiah. The interpolated Tamar episode focuses on a woman who successfully inserts herself into the sequence of generations that will eventually lead to
Shiloh, "the Prince of Peace, the Anointed One . . . the hero, who once would
be awakened out of the chosen seed, and the throne of whose kingdom would
be established for ever and ever" (1270).[60] In psychological terms, the process
of increasing individuation among the Hebrews represents the successful resolution of the Oedipus complex, as the faithful repress their incestuous and
parricidal desires to become civilized adults. "The bond of faith with God was
sexual . . . it had the civilizing effect of weakening the male of the human
species in the direction of the feminine" (59).[61] Joseph's brothers are guilty of
atavistic violence when they attack the father's favorite as an act of symbolic
parricide, just as Ruben commits symbolic incest by having sex with one of his
father's wives. Joseph, in contrast, resists the lure of Mut the mother and thus
demonstrates his greater capacity for personal and spiritual growth. This
shoring up of individual identity among people who originally "do not rightly
know who they are" (99)[62] goes hand in hand with the development of
monotheism. "The demands of the human ego are of central importance as a
precondition for the discovery of God" (1407).[63] God created man, true, but
Abraham also created God in the sense that he distilled multiple gods into a
single divine and omnipotent being: "Those mighty attributes that he ascribed
to Him were surely God's original property. . . . But by recognizing them,

teaching them, and realizing them in his own thought, was he not His father in a certain sense?" (346).[64]

In sum, two contrasting models of temporality inform *Joseph and His Brothers*, both based on the concept of repetition, but with diametrically opposed religious, psychological, and political implications. Figural history inscribes repetition into a spiral of progress leading to ever-greater psychological maturation and eventual spiritual salvation; mythic descents to the underworld promise only the eternal recurrence of the same. Here Apollo, there Dionysus; here individuation, rationality, the Enlightenment, and progress, there dissolution, undifferentiated sexual desire, atavistic violence, and death. We have returned to the tension central to *The Magic Mountain*, to the moment in the snow when Hans briefly realizes that he must break free of the horrible hags and their ritual violence, choose life over death, only to forget his promise to "be good" and drift back into the soporific routine of the sanatorium until he is cast out into the chaos of war.

The Magic Mountain looked back to the years leading up to the First World War; *Joseph and His Brothers* was conceived in the intellectual and political climate that eventually produced the Third Reich. In public, Mann urged caution against impending disaster, delivering a strongly worded "Appeal to Reason" in Berlin shortly after the National Socialist electoral victories of September 1930, and—after hesitating during the first years of exile—eventually becoming the conscience of the nation as the war wore on. But the creator of Thomas Buddenbrook and Gustav von Aschenbach had not forgotten the fragility of reason, nor how quickly the edifice of civilization can crumble: "It is the idea of visitation by drunken, ruinous, and destructive powers invading a life of composure that, with all its hopes for dignity and a modicum of happiness, is worn to that very composure" (882).[65] In *Joseph and His Brothers*, Mut-em-enet succumbs to destructive desires, while Joseph survives in a novel that leads to a resoundingly triumphant conclusion worthy of Wagner's *Meistersinger* and unmatched in Mann's fiction since *Royal Highness*. That triumph was short-lived, however, for immediately upon completing *The Tables of the Law* and thus the entire complex of biblical narratives, Mann began work on the tragic rise and fall of *Doctor Faustus*.

The Stories of Jacob: Pride and Prejudice

Like an overture to an opera, the prelude to *Joseph and His Brothers* introduces themes and conflicts central to the work as a whole: the theme of antiquity in

relation to the present and the fundamental tension between a forward-look-
ing faith in human progress and divine redemption versus the constant threat
of backsliding into barbarism. "Hell" refers in temporal terms to the distant
past; in mythic terms to the mysterious site of the god's death and resurrection
that is both tomb and womb; in cultural terms to a period of superstition and
violence; and in psychological terms, finally, to unbridled promiscuity and forbidden desires, including incest, homosexuality, bestiality, fratricide, and parricide. Each of these perspectives provides a partial answer to the question:
what is hell as Mann employs the term in *Joseph and His Brothers?* My interest
here as elsewhere centers on a slightly different question, however: *where* is
hell? Where do individual characters locate their personal experience of the
underworld, and onto which geographical areas do they project their fears and
prejudices?

For Jacob, hell is the realm of Laban, the underworld where he arrives pen-
niless and works for years for his crass and duplicitous uncle. Joseph experiences no less than three descents to the underworld in the novel: he is cast into
the well by his brothers, sold into slavery in Egypt, and condemned to prison
by the false accusations of Potiphar's wife. Each time he rises from the moment
of ritual death to a higher position than he had held before. For both father
and son, the underworld is a place of personal trial and misfortune. Of
broader implications for the cultural politics of the novel are the prejudices
projected onto entire landscapes and cultures. The most prominent of these is
Jacob's lifelong disdain for "apish Egypt" (73).[66]

Thomas Mann's Jacob is a man of strong religious faith and equally strong
prejudices against those who fail to conform to his point of view. In the opening scene he strongly disapproves of Joseph's nakedness and tendency toward
religious ecstasy, just as he rejects his visitor's polytheism and reverence for
clay idols. Jacob's distaste for the idol-worshipping, son-sacrificing Laban is
both immediate and long-lasting, and he barely conceals his disdain for his
stupidly cheerful brother Esau. Jacob avoids cities and temples and seeks out
instead the quiet solitude of open fields, where he can sit beneath sacred trees
and ponder the mysterious ways of his monotheistic God and steep himself in
the history of his family lineage. He has no tolerance for those who seek other
sorts of religious experience: "whenever God-given reason broke down and
lewd frenzy took its place, that was for him the beginning of what he called
'folly,' a very strong word in his mouth, strong enough to express utter disapproval" (337).[67]

From beginning to end, Jacob rejects anyone and anything associated with

Egypt. In his opinion, Egyptians are rich yet filthy and obscene. They wander around in transparent clothing, ready for sex at any time. They venerate animals and even celebrate religious rites in which virgins have public intercourse with goats. When Jacob curses Ruben for sporting with Bilhah, he calls him "a shameless hippopotamus—this last because of an Egyptian fable, according to which it was the hippopotamus's wicked practice to slay its father and then ravish its mother" (64–65).[68] On the eve of his wedding to what he thinks will be Rachel but in fact is Leah, Jacob dreams of the Egyptian god Anup, whose father Osiris had mistakenly slept with his sister Nephthys: "For one female body is like another, good for loving, good for conceiving" (233).[69] A realm of wealth, drudgery, and filthy immorality: this is Jacob's Egypt. "He called it Sheol, hell, the realm of death" (334).[70]

Jacob's prejudice against the Egyptians is matched by the Egyptian prejudice against the Hebrews, the Asiatic sand-dwellers to the East: "the Ebrews themselves were considered an abomination by the Egyptians, and to such an extent that they felt it beneath their dignity and offensive to pious scruples to break bread with such people" (678–79).[71] When Joseph refuses to be seduced by Mut, she denounces him as a dangerous foreigner, and on his way to prison Joseph's former subordinate taunts him as a barbarian who could not control his sexual urges. The tables turn when Joseph, risen to Pharaoh's right-hand man, tells his brothers through an interpreter that they "do not speak the language of human beings" (1307).[72] Even the benevolent Akhnaton cannot avoid condescension when he invites Jacob and his sons to come to Egypt, for as he dictates, "Pharaoh is well aware that your culture does not stand so high and that your requirements are easily met" (1386).[73]

To the mutual suspicion between the Hebrews and the Egyptians comes a common rejection of everything that lies to the south and everything black. "No Hamites were tolerated in Jacob's camp—because of the sin of their ancestor, who had been turned black all over for shaming his father" (12).[74] After Esau has been deceived out of his birthright by Jacob, he becomes "a man of the underworld" and moves south like the half-Egyptian Ishmael before him, "since the south lay within the conceptual aura of the underworld" (104).[75] Northern Egyptians in the former capital of Memphis look down their noses at the current rulers in Thebes, a city so far to the south that it was almost considered "part of wretched Kush and other Negro lands" (590).[76] They mock the pretensions of the god Amun, whom they strongly suspect was of lowly Nubian origins and yet has the audacity to consider himself the judge of what counts as authentically Egyptian.

Within Egyptian society, blacks function primarily as dehumanized slaves with exaggerated racial features. Upon entry into Egypt's capital, Joseph marvels at the Nubian "rubber-eaters" (744), "ebony-black Moors with incredible lips like padded cushions" (632), and when it is time to bring Jacob to the Land of Goshen, Joseph sends fancy Egyptian chariots decorated with hubcaps featuring "the heads of Moors" (1414).[77] Mut spends her days in luxury, "coddled by gently fawning eunuchs and naked Moorish maids of almost fierce servility" (822).[78] These "dark-skinned maids of honor" with "black, woolly hair" (889) and large earrings crouch like servile animals, and indeed, when requesting an audience with her husband, Mut sends as an emissary one of her "Moorish handmaids, a small naked animal" (834).[79] In characterizing Tabubu, Mann pulls out all the stops, heaping racial characteristics on this woolly-haired, black-skinned, leather-breasted rubber-eater, "who knew all sorts of wicked magic practiced in Negro lands" (907–8).[80] This "hag of the first water" (941)[81] indoctrinates Mut in the weird rites of a savage cult involving animal sacrifice under a full moon, and thus unleashes Mut's repressed sexuality with all the horror of the blackest magic from darkest Africa.

Taken at face value, *Joseph and His Brothers* is brimming with unchecked prejudice and racist stereotypes, and, as we have seen, Thomas Mann was prone to just this sort of attentiveness to racial difference—which at times was simply racism—throughout his life. The description of the incredibly thick lips of the Nubian rubber-eaters echoes his racist diatribes against the African troops stationed in Alsace-Lorraine shortly after the First World War, while his repeated references in his diaries to his black and yellow servants keep pace with the descriptions of dark-skinned, woolly-haired slaves that populate the fictional world of ancient Egypt. Mann's prediction shortly before his second journey to Egypt that he expects to find a land and a people "unchanged after three thousand five hundred years" corresponds to Orientalist stereotypes of an indolent and unchanging East.[82] In *Joseph and His Brothers*, however, Mann often signals ironic distance from the prejudices voiced by individual characters and ancient peoples. During the drunken festival on the day on which Mut makes her final attempt to seduce Joseph, "brightly costumed Negroes" entertain the crowds with grimaces and obscene pranks, "for they knew they were disdained and so played the fool, even if that was not their nature, in order to flatter the grotesque expectations the populace had of them" (1013).[83] Even as a boy, Joseph knows that his father's opinion of Egypt "contained grand generalizations, personal biases, and exaggerations" (74),[84] and many years later he assures Jacob that "the children of Egypt are like other children, not essentially better or worse" (1425).[85] Both Joseph and the black entertainers call attention to the distinction between prejudice and performance, between ideological projections onto people or places that declare that they are a certain way, and a more nuanced appreciation of what, for want of a better word, one might term reality. Rather than taking Jacob's perceptions of Egypt at face value, then, let us look more closely at the geopolitical realities of his fictional universe.

Jacob's repeated branding of the Egyptians as filthy, superstitious barbarians serves as a way to establish a group identity through negative identification: who are we? We are certainly *not* Egyptians. In 1936 Mann condemned just this sort of logic in his analysis of German anti-Semitism as the "aristocracy of the little—very little—man. 'I am nothing, to be sure—but I am not a Jew.'"[86] Jacob is reluctant to set foot on Egyptian soil and even the far more tolerant Joseph pulls back from Mut because "a proud tradition of laws of purity warned him against mixing his blood with hers" (925).[87] The narrator nevertheless repeatedly reminds us that the blood of the Hebrews is anything but pure: "not even in a dream could the people of El-Elyon attribute their interconnection to a unity and purity of blood" (100).[88] Joseph's brothers eventually marry women from the most disparate backgrounds, an awkward fact that "has been glossed over ... in a halfhearted effort to maintain the blood kinship of the entire spiritual tribe, though any real basis for it is rather weak" (1256).[89] If all else fails, you can always trace the common ancestry back to Adam, the narrator comments sarcastically: "One can always prove kinship by blood if one expands the perimeters wide enough" (1257).[90]

Despite Jacob's efforts to distance himself from Egyptians and other infidels and his concern for the spotlessness of a lineage that leads from Abraham to Shiloh, the Hebrews of *Joseph and His Brothers* are in fact a nomadic tribe in constant contact and exchange with the peoples of other cultures. Jacob first appears in an outfit that bespeaks "a very arbitrary, eclectic taste: elements of an Eastern cultural heritage were joined with those belonging more to the Ishmaelite or Bedouin traditions of the desert" (50).[91] We first meet Joseph babbling a mixture of prayers to Abraham and Hammurabi, just as he will later serve, albeit with a certain ironic detachment, as an Egyptian priest of the temple of Atum-Re. From the beginning, we are told "that there was something Egyptian about" the set of Joseph's shoulders (45).[92] He grows up in an area of Egyptian influence and learns the language easily as a boy, despite his father's disapproval, and thus it is not surprising that he all but becomes Egyptian "in appearance and demeanor" after decades in exile, for "there had always been something about him that tended to the Egyptian" (781).[93] Joseph refers to Rachel as Mami, "a name of Babylonian origin" (78),[94] while she wants to call Benjamin Ben-Oni in honor of the Egyptian god Osiris (84; IV: 111). Joseph marries an Egyptian and becomes the father of "Ephraim and Manasseh ... for better or worse half-Egyptian by blood" (1239);[95] his brothers marry women of Assyrian, Mesopotamian, Midianite, Moabite, and Ismaelite descent (1257; V: 1540–41); even Ham, "black of face" (1467) and ancestral father of the immoral Egyptians, was the father of Canaan and the son of Noah.[96] Nothing is "pure" about the Hebrews in *Joseph and His Brothers;* in terms of fashion, language, religion, and ethnicity, they represent an eclectic mixture of multiple cultures and traditions.

The prelude not only introduces abstract reflections on eternal recurrence and salvation history, but also situates the Hebrews in the political context of the time. The fourth paragraph consists of a single long sentence, in which the name of our hero, Joseph, is invoked not once but six times: "for there is a mystery about that name" (4).[97] The gist of the sentence is simple: absolute origins are impossible to find, but each group of people has a story about its own relative beginnings. "For example, for his part the young Joseph . . . was accustomed to seeing the beginning of all things or, better, of all things of personal importance in a southern Babylonian city called Uru" (3–4).[98] Between the beginning and end of this sentence, Mann inserts a telescoped glance at the world surrounding the young Joseph: Kurigalzu the Kassite rules in Babylon, Pharaoh reigns in Thebes, and a steady stream of trade and tribute passes between Egypt and the rising power of Assyria to the north.[99] Joseph and his people live in Canaan, near the city of Hebron, in an area also known by the Egyptian name of Upper Retenu. We soon learn that the story of the Hebrews began when Abraham left Babylon in search of God, traveled north to Haran, west to Canaan, and even south into Egypt before settling in "a country . . . whose national existence condemned it to hopeless political impotence and dependency," for Abraham wants to ponder his God and has "anything but a personal taste for imperial greatness or a gift for political vision" (7).[100]

Jacob shares the patriarch's disinterest in imperial politics, as we learn in the opening scene of the novel proper. He discovers young Joseph by the well after spending an evening with a visitor named Jebshe, who had brought along images of a female god and told stories of religious rites in which men and women exchanged clothing to celebrate a hermaphroditic deity. Such idolatry and lewdness are grist for Jacob's mill, and he is willing to argue at length about the distinction between clay images of pagan gods and the transcendent unity of his God. Jebshe eventually loses interest in this theological discussion, however, and turns his attention to "events out in the world and its empires, to commerce and intrigues" (56).[101] We learn among other things that Cyprians have been using a recent outbreak of the plague as an excuse to avoid paying tribute to Egypt, that another king related to the Egyptian rulers is under threat of attack by the Hittites, and that the flow of Syrian tribute into Egyptian coffers "would soon be a mere trickle" (57) as a result of Bedouin raids and rising Hittite power.[102] These details give us our first glimpse of the state of affairs in the Egyptian empire, which is old and vast, but currently under constant threat of losing control of its more distant territories and sources of income. We also witness Jacob's complete disinterest in political affairs, for "once God was no longer the subject of discourse his host's interest had diminished greatly" (57).[103] The same detachment from current events will have fatal consequences in the tragic tale of Jacob's daughter Dinah.

The story is interesting in part because of the view it affords us into the precarious state of the Egyptian empire. The nomad shepherd Jacob negotiates grazing rights for his flocks outside the city of Sichem or Shechem. The city is ruled by prince Hemor, a grouchy old man, and his son, Sichem, "a coddled young nobleman with his own harem, a layabout with a sweet tooth, an elegant drone" (121).[104] Shechem is not only a city of local importance, but also a distant colonial outpost of the Egyptian empire, occupied by a garrison of soldiers who feel sorry for themselves because they have been banished to the hinterlands. Their commander is the ridiculous young Weser-ke-Bastet or Beset, who wanders the town cloaked in garlands of flowers, offers weeping sacrifices to his mummified cats, and is best friends with the equally decadent Sichem. The Egyptian soldiers are distinguished only by their cowardice, and when they are eventually surprised and slaughtered by Joseph's brothers, Pharaoh is so preoccupied with his own poor health and the construction of his tomb that he ignores reports "concerning the 'loss of the king's cities' and 'the taking of Pharaoh's land by the Habiru'" (145).[105] The Egyptian courtiers find the faulty Babylonian of the dispatches more amusing than the news of a devastating defeat, and thus they are filed away and no action is taken against the Hebrews.

The episode introduces a recurring theme in *Joseph and His Brothers*, in which Egypt represents both the ancient past and modern decadence, a combination that Mann refers to paradoxically as "those late early times" (1231).[106] From our perspective, Egyptian civilization belongs to a remote era that predates even ancient Greece and Rome. In Jacob's eyes as well, Egyptians appear as primitive idolaters who have not yet progressed to the Hebrew belief in a single, spiritual God and are thus excluded from the salvation history that brings mutual refinement to both God and man. Within the context of their own civilization, however, the Egyptians portrayed in *Joseph and His Brothers* are latecomers: "This was the air of late autumn, the aura of a society of grandchildren and heirs already far removed from the foundations and patterns of their fathers, whose victories had left them in a position to regard as refined what had once been conquered" (683).[107] The cowardly Egyptian soldiers garrisoned in Shechem are heirs to an empire that they did not conquer themselves: "they were forever bragging, in phrases worthy of inscriptions, about the martial deeds of a previous king of their land, Thutmose the Third, who had led his Egyptian army in seventeen campaigns and conquered the region as far as the river Euphrates; but their own prowess lay chiefly in polishing off roast goose and beer" (122).[108] In time, it will fall to Joseph to restore order to the Egyptian nation and to reassert control over its vast empire.

During the sacking of Shechem, however, Joseph is only a toddler and the focus falls instead on his older brothers and their father. None of them appears in a particularly flattering light. The story begins when Hemor's son Sichem decides that he cannot live without Dinah, who is only thirteen but already as attractive as she will ever become. Hemor asks for her hand on behalf of his son, but the brothers refuse to give him a straight answer. Sichem then comes in person and is told that he must be circumcised before he can even consider marrying Dinah. He complies immediately and returns in a state of extreme discomfort a few days later, only to be told that the circumcision had not been performed in the proper manner or spirit. At this point Sichem simply abducts Dinah, who is not unwilling. Her outraged brothers demand that all the city's men must be circumcised with stone knives. Again they comply, joined by most of the occupation forces, and yet Joseph's brothers retaliate brutally, killing most of the men, selling the rest into slavery, and sacking the town. They leave Weser's mutilated corpse among broken flowers on the street and stuff the head of Sichem's battered body into a latrine.

The episode is generally read as an example of backsliding, of a criminal reversion to barbaric behavior of a sort that had become all too familiar among the SA thugs of Weimar Germany.[109] Jacob never forgives his sons for their actions, in particular the instigators Shimeon and Levi, whom he curses for their violence on his deathbed. But Jacob is not without guilt. He comes to Shechem after emerging from twenty-five years in the underworld of his uncle Laban, an experience that he characteristically ponders in terms of a mythic pattern: "the rise and fall of ascent into heaven, descent into hell, and rising yet again" (124).[110] Jacob's sense of self dissolves, and in his mind he becomes one with Abraham. "His soul was moved and exalted by thoughts of emulation, recurrence, the past made present" (127–28).[111] Time melts away: "the centuries did not exist" (128).[112] So absorbed is Jacob in such reflections that he fails to notice the growing tensions between the people of Shechem and the tribe of Israel, or, more precisely, he does notice, but represses the knowledge. "Jacob both knew and did not know this, which is to say: he looked the other way" (129–30).[113] Rather than responding directly to Hemor's request that his son be permitted to marry Dinah, Jacob turns to his sons for advice, and when they begin to make their duplicitous demands, he disappears. "Jacob was avoiding the encounter. He had left his sons in charge" (135).[114] As the brothers' demands on the people of Shechem escalate ominously, Jacob feels "dire misgivings" (141),[115] and yet the thought of how Abraham had once circumcised his entire family blinds him to the reality of the present moment. Once the damage is done, however, Jacob turns on his sons, cursing them bitterly for their savage deeds. But Jacob is also guilty of crimes of omission, a failure of leadership, and harsh punishment of others for events for which he is partially responsible. Dinah fares worst of all: she goes from being the object of barter between men to having her baby "exposed," that is, murdered by her own father. In a matter of months she is transformed from a budding teenager to a withered old woman. By the time that Jacob and his sons leave the smoldering ruins of Shechem, Dinah's life, which was just beginning, is essentially ended.

The events in Shechem cast a lasting pall on Jacob's otherwise admirable character. Mann portrays him as a man of blessing and profound thoughts who impresses even his enemies with his dignity, but he is also a trickster and a dissembler who beguiles Esau out of his birthright and does not hesitate to exaggerate his age and his limp in an effort to impress Pharaoh. His moral flaws do not disqualify him as the bearer of God's blessing and the leader of his people, just as the sinful Judah is astonished to learn that Jacob has chosen him to be his primary heir: "Well, well, in spite of everything, it seems. . . . This purity I thirsted for, was, it turns out, not essential for salvation" (1471).[116] Nevertheless, Jacob's self-absorbed detachment from current events and his culpable refusal to prevent his sons' violence suggest a critique of his character that brings him into surprising proximity to Akhnaton. On the surface, the carefully staged meeting of the two leaders toward the end of *Joseph the Provider* highlights the contrast between the two monotheists: Jacob appears as the heir to a proud tradition and patriarch of a tribe with a glorious future that will culminate in the coming of Shiloh, the Messiah. Akhnaton's monotheism arises out of an abrupt break with previous tradition and is destined to lead nowhere: soon after his death the Egyptians will revert to their old polytheistic traditions and religious rituals. And yet in their isolation from the common people, their proud persistence in cultural prejudice, and their aversion to realpolitik, Jacob and Akhnaton share similar shortcomings. It will fall to Joseph to show them a better way.

Joseph in Egypt: Romance and Racism

The first stages of Joseph's journey into Egypt reinforce the impression of an ancient land in a late stage of its history. After passing through the fortress of Zel and across the land of Goshen, Joseph and the Midianite traders come to the city of Per-Sopdu, which exudes a sense of slightly ridiculous fallen grandeur. Surrounded by carnations and the smell of cloves, weird priests with long fingernails complain bitterly about the new gods that have come to power in the southern city of Thebes. They stop next at the stinking city of cats, Per-Bastet, birthplace of the hapless commander of the garrison in Shechem. Here the atmosphere is more like what Jacob had led Joseph to expect in Egypt: ancient, orgiastic, and absurd. In the desert outside Memphis, Joseph ponders the pyramids and the Sphinx, which even at that time were crumbling ruins. In Memphis, the people "made fun of themselves because of what the city had once been and had long since ceased to be" (611).[117] The former capital still glitters with gold so bright that it causes its residents to suffer chronic eye inflammations, and yet it is a city that is down on its luck, "an erstwhile queen, the grave of its own greatness, a metropolis with an impertinently abbreviated name of death" (611).[118]

Already in Memphis, Joseph stays in a caravansary full of "a potpourri of the human race—Syrians, Libyans, Nubians, Mitannis, and even Cretans" (610),[119] and when he arrives at the current capital of Thebes, it is as if he had reached the center of the world. "No one looked at him and his party, for the foreign was ordinary here. . . . He saw skin of every shade, from obsidian black through all the stages of brown and yellow to cheesy white, he even saw yellow hair and azure-colored eyes, faces and garments of every cut—he saw humanity" (632–33).[120] Like postcolonial Paris or London today, ancient Thebes is full of people from all corners of the earth as a direct result of the colonial conquests of previous generations.[121] As Mut points out in a discussion with the priest Beknechons, Egypt was once "small and poor," but "now the Two Lands and Wase the Great teem with foreigners, overflow with treasures, and everything has become new" (775–76).[122]

The Egyptian response to the presence of foreign goods and people in their capital is marked by a fundamental ambivalence. On the one hand, as we have seen, the members of "this most arrogant of all created nations" (678)[123] regard other cultures with contempt. On the other hand, however, the Asiatic cultures that they disdain also exert an exotic appeal. Taking their cue from the fashion at Pharaoh's court, Egyptians "tried to intersperse their own conversations with foreign fragments, from Akkadia or Babylonia, as well as from the language of Joseph's world" (680).[124] Potiphar's house is decorated with what might best be termed *Kolonialwaren,* goods prized because of their exotic origins: "goods from the harbor—imports produced by foreigners" (681).[125] The source of the "illogical esteem" for the products of what Egyptians deemed to be inferior foreign cultures lay in the "liberal spirit of people who themselves had not defeated and subjugated those wretched foreign lands, but had let earlier generations do it for them and now permitted themselves to find refinement in their liberality" (681).[126] Joseph's position in Egypt is marked by the same ambivalence: although persecuted by some who resent the rise of the foreign interloper, he is promoted by others favorably inclined to the touch of the exotic that clings to him. Joseph is clever enough to capitalize on these sentiments, thus turning what could be his greatest liability into his greatest asset.

The cultural debates about the status of the foreign in Egypt play themselves out in the theological realm as well.[127] Those loyal to the god Amun-Re in Karnak cling to a xenophobic nationalism. Their god "was unbending and strict, a forbidding enemy of any speculation with a view to universality, ill disposed to all things foreign, rigid in the observation of national customs, locked in holy tradition" (763).[128] This group includes the high priest Beknechons, a reactionary zealot who condemns the current world and sees the incursion of foreign goods and peoples as a sign of weakness and loss of tradition; the evil dwarf Dudu, who makes it his goal in life to destroy the foreign slave Joseph; and Potiphar's wife Mut-em-enet, virgin priestess of the Order of Hathor and consort to the god Amun. Pharaoh and his court, on the other hand, incline toward the tolerant sun-god Atum-Re. This god is said to be filled with the "desire to expand and . . . to join in all-seeing concord with all the solar gods of other nations" (763).[129] Whereas Amun-Re is a relatively recent god marked by rigid intolerance, Atum-Re was "an ancient god, resourceful and open to the world" (763).[130]

The theological underpinnings of this tolerant religion stem from the ancient city of On, through which Joseph and the Midianites pass on their journey down to Wase or Thebes. There was a god of the living, Hor or Atum-Re, and Usir, a god of the dead; a god of light and a god of darkness. But since the sun that passes through the sky from east to west has to travel back through the underworld from west to east each night, they realize that "the two great gods were, strictly speaking, one and the same" (599).[131] The priests of On reconcile the apparent contradiction between polytheism and monotheism with recourse to the image of the triangle. At its base there are multiple gods, but the two sides rise ever closer toward one another until they join in a single point representing the one, transcendent god. Atum-Re in this larger sense is a generous god who can incorporate multiplicity within a larger unity: polytheism for the people, monotheism for the priests. The Theban god Amun had also recently been elevated to the position of sole god, but not "in the spirit of the triangle and of reconciliation, but rather as if in some way Amun had conquered and devoured Re" (600).[132] Violent conquest replaces tolerant coexistence; narrow-minded nationalism confronts liberal cosmopolitanism.

The theological debates lead to some of the more esoteric passages in *Joseph in Egypt*, whereas the subtle account of Mut's desire for Joseph has more of the immediate appeal of a traditional novel, and yet the novel's central plot and its excursions into political and religious theory are in fact intimately related. The story of Potiphar's wife occupies a mere fourteen verses in Genesis (39:7–20). She casts her eyes upon Joseph and demands that he lie with her; he refuses, she persists; when he finally flees her, leaving his robe in her hand, she accuses him falsely and Joseph is sent to prison. We never learn her name or anything about her person. The story is told for the sake of Joseph, showing how he resists temptation and—despite being punished for a crime he did not commit—manages to rise out of prison to become Pharaoh's right-hand man. In elaborating on the familiar story, Mann gives Potiphar's wife a name, a family history, and a psychological depth that goes far beyond the terse biblical narrative. Repeatedly resisting the traditional reading of Potiphar's wife as a calculating, evil seductress, Mann focuses instead on the psychological and physiological transformation of a woman who belatedly but all the more violently discovers forbidden sexual desires: the virginal wife of a castrated courtier falls in love with a foreign slave. Mann writes of self-deception and humiliation: the woman who consciously at least had never been particularly troubled by sexual desires and who took no human interest in the many slaves who attended her is gradually brought low by an irresistible obsession. At the same time, Mut's downfall also represents a defeat for the intolerant theology of Amun and the racist nationalism he represents.

As Mann tells the story, Mut would probably never have noticed Joseph had it not been for the dwarf Dudu, who is outraged that this foreigner should be granted preferential treatment. When his initial efforts to get Joseph assigned to some menial labor in the fields fail, he adopts subtler tactics. He calls Mut's attention to the remarkably handsome slave, ostensibly to provoke her outrage and enlist her support against the more tolerant position of her husband. Long before she admits it to herself, however, Dudu realizes that Mut is becoming attracted to Joseph. He encourages her desires by pretending to share her outrage at Joseph's advance, calculating that the best way to destroy the hated foreigner is to ensnare him in a love affair with the master's wife.

Mut's religious and political loyalties lie with Amun and Beknechons, but aspects of her family history and the god she worships call into question the demand for untrammeled national purity among her reactionary cohorts. Mut belongs to the aristocratic Order of Hathor together with a group of women known as "the harem." But "Amun-Re's great consort was named Mut, or 'the mother,' and Hathor of the fair countenance and cow eyes belonged instead to Re-Atum and was the wife of the lord of On" (766).[133] Why do the women worship the consort of the enemy god Atum-Re instead of the wife of their own god Amun? The answer lies in a double hostile takeover: just as the local god Amun has usurped the position of the more comprehensive and older god Atum-Re and declared himself the Egyptian national god Amun-Re, so, too, has his consort Mut had herself "equated with triumphant Hathor" (766).[134] Two points are noteworthy here: one is that Mann attributes the actions to the gods themselves and not the priests who interpret, or, from a more radically modern perspective, invent them. The effect is to create a certain ironic distance from the theological world he describes: we know that certain sects have attributed various powers to their gods for political purposes, but Mann presents the information to us as they would have presented it to their people. After this particularly convoluted bit of Egyptian theology, he adds only a brief, deadpan commentary: "Yes, these were the refinements of the land of Egypt, its politic way of counterbalancing forces" (766).[135] The other point is that the purity of the goddess that Mut and her fellow aristocrats worship is at best questionable, for one need only scratch the surface of the new god to discover the remnants of the old within.

Similar questions cling to Mut's family background. As the wife of a courtier who eventually rises to the position of "the king's Sole and True

Friends" (not to be confused with his real friends) (1011),[136] Mut belongs to the highest nobility. Her ancestors had been minor kings in Middle Egypt at a time when "a race of Asiatic nomads . . . had worn Re's double crown" (817).[137] After centuries of colonization, a group of powerful Egyptian princes rebelled, using the "foreign blood" (817)[138] of their Asiatic rulers as an effective rallying cry. Not all of the local Egyptians leaders recognized the successful rebels as their liberators, however; some actually preferred to remain vassals of their alien overlords. In time, these local kings rebelled against the new Theban kings in a mutiny that had to be violently suppressed. The victors appropriated the lands of the defeated rebels, but the rebels themselves were not exterminated. They remained powerful aristocrats, and, having sworn loyalty to Pharaoh, assumed important administrative posts in the new government.

From just such a family is Mut descended, for her ancestor Tetian was one of those "who had 'gathered malcontents' in his day and first had to be defeated before he acknowledged his liberation" (818).[139] The descendants of the mutinous warriors had become modern civil servants willing to marry their daughter to a eunuch for political advantage, "and by doing so had clearly proved that the virtue of fertility cherished by an old established family deeply rooted in the soil had been greatly qualified by modern notions" (818–19).[140] Mann's reference to the degeneration of a family once rooted in the national soil clearly draws on the register of Nazi ideology, particularly considering that the novel was first published in 1936, but Mann reverses the implications of this thought into its opposite: Mut's family had once proved its vitality by rebelling *against* indigenous Egyptian rulers in favor of Asian foreigners. The degeneracy of the later generation becomes defined in terms of its allegiance to a false homogeneity, a sham of *Gleichschaltung:* Mut marries a human capon who occupies positions of only ceremonial importance, and she worships a local god masquerading as a national hero.

Mut's seduction unfolds as a process of degradation in which the virgin priestess and Egyptian nationalist is defiled by sexual desires and corrupted by a taste for the foreign. The process is in its early stages when Mut takes the unusual step of requesting an audience with Potiphar to protest against Joseph's presence in the house. It takes some time before the long, stylized conversation gets to the main issue. Potiphar first announces his intention to throw a lavish party that will include as entertainment a troupe of Babylonian dancers. Mut reminds him that "Amun hates the freethinking that comes with things foreign" (845)[141] and predicts that his priest Beknechons will refuse to come. Indeed, Beknechons is outraged that Pharaoh "aids and abets freethinking and allows his inquisitive sages to flirt with things foreign and thus weaken the marrow of the nation's people" (845).[142] Potiphar reluctantly agrees not to invite the Babylonian dancers, but Mut wants more: he must also banish Joseph from the house. Potiphar responds with the highest praise for his Asian slave, which unconsciously thrills the smitten woman. As the narrator sardonically observes, the "human capacity for self-deception is astounding" (828).[143] At issue in the debate between Potiphar and Mut about Joseph, or Osarsiph, as he chooses to be called in Egypt, is whether you should judge a man by his talents or his place of birth. "Free or unfree, native or foreign" (858),[144] what does it matter if a man has a spark of genius, argues Potiphar, who with uncharacteristic boldness not only refuses to remove Joseph from the house, but promotes him to his chief servant and overseer of all the other slaves.

Mut has lost round 1, at least in the open battle, but her secret lust for the forbidden slave has jumped to a new level. As unconscious desires gradually become conscious, the former devotee of Amun and *völkisch* nationalism begins to change her religious beliefs. Dudu convinces her that Amun will not hold it against her if she begins worshiping Atum-Re, reminding her that during the religious ceremonies Hathor "is the sister and wife of Atum-Re, not of Amun" (870).[145] Seeking solace and divine sanction for her sacrilegious passion, Mut tries "to call religion to her aid by appealing to Atum-Re of On, the mild, inclusive god who was gracious to foreign nations, instead of to her former lord, the stern patriotic Amun" (885).[146] The transformation is complete by the time that she invites Joseph for an audience in her chambers, for he is astonished to discover that she now proudly displays a golden idol of Atum-Re on her private altar, "the brother and friend of foreign, Asian sun gods" (913)[147]—and this from an intimate of Beknechons and a formerly fanatical xenophobe!

Mut's change of religious sentiments is symptomatic of a transformation in which she outwardly accommodates herself to the Asiatic Hebrew and inwardly yields to black desires—the twin objects of Egyptian prejudice. She not only displays a shrine to the tolerant god, but also receives Joseph "in an Asiatic dress . . . [the] rich fabric for which she had ordered from a bearded Syrian in the bazaar of the City of the Living" (910).[148] Her newfound interest in the foreign extends to the point that she serves rare and expensive Chinese oranges when hosting a gathering of ladies and exposing them to Joseph's dangerous charms. These external changes in favor of the foreign correspond to an inner upwelling of sexual desire associated with blackness, bestiality, gender confusion, and incest. In Joseph's first conversation with Mut—long before she enlists the aid of Tabubu and her African black magic—he asks her advice about farming, wondering if they should plant more sorghum rather than barley. "I mean kaffir corn, the white sorghum grown by Negroes" (895),[149] he explains to her in the garden as she stands flanked by her "dark-skinned maids of honor" with their "black, woolly hair" (889) and oversized earrings.[150] Mut entertains Joseph in her room while sitting on a chair draped in the tail end of a lion skin, "while the head of the ravenous beast gaped its jaws at Joseph's feet" (915);[151] she wears a vulture's headdress when performing her religious rites, and she joins with Tabubu in sacrificing the dog. Her exchange of her normal Egyptian clothing for an Asiatic robe provides an uncomfortable reminder to Joseph of those religious ceremonies in which "men go about in the clothes of women and the woman in the garb of the man, and differences fall away" (911).[152] More dangerously still, Mut deliberately dresses in a robe that reminds Joseph of his mother, but Joseph refuses to follow in Oedipus's footsteps: "I will not sin against God . . . by disgracing and murdering the father and coupling with the mother like a shameless hippopotamus" (955).[153] When Joseph finally and definitively rejects Mut's advances, she abruptly reverts to her former ways, falsely accusing the "alien" of attempted rape, "which was not only untrue, but, sad to say, demagogic as well" (1028).[154] Mut's role in the story of Joseph is over. Her voluptuously engorged breasts shrivel up and her mind closes down. "Yes, henceforth Mut-em-enet was a cool nun of the moon . . . and—one must add—extremely bigoted" (1221).[155]

Mut-em-enet stands as a grandiose example of the sort of femme fatale that haunts Mann's work from its inception, but one that has been adapted in response to the political situation of the 1930s. Her transformation into a demonically destructive creature radiates fear of female sexuality and the blackness Mann associated with it, but there is more than misogyny and racism at work in *Joseph in Egypt*. By making Mut a hypocritical representative of a fanatically intolerant form of nationalism, Mann suggests that the politics of purity are based on a lie and that the primal desires they unleash can only lead to chaos and destruction. He does so by grafting the entire vocabulary of the forbidden that was present from the beginning of his career onto an indictment of his contemporary politics. Fascism is a woman; fascists whore after Baal, commit incest, dabble in black magic, and in general succumb to Dionysian intoxication; fascists live in the land down under, in the topsy-turvy underworld of apish Egypt.

Joseph the Provider: The Chosen One as *Realpolitiker*

Joseph plays with fire and almost succumbs to Mut's seduction, but in the end he resists. He is cast into prison, but senses correctly that the step down from Potiphar's top servant to Pharaoh's lowest slave is actually the beginning of a rise to even greater heights. Throughout the tetralogy, Joseph displays personal gifts and a capacity for growth unmatched by any of his contemporaries. Born as the first son of his father's greatest love, Joseph is blessed from birth with a cheerful disposition, great intelligence, and legendary good looks. After his jealous brothers cast him into the well, Joseph is smart enough to realize that he was wrong to think that the entire world must love him as much as his father, and in Egypt he is careful not to make enemies of those he bypasses on his way to the top. He retains a certain ironic distance from Egyptian customs and religion, but remains largely free of the mutual prejudices of the other Hebrews and Egyptians. Joseph is supremely confident of his own abilities without becoming arrogant or vindictive. Amenhotep, or Akhnaton, as he later calls himself, dies young and embittered, isolated from his people; Jacob spends his final hours cursing his sons; but Joseph triumphs as the most important man in Egypt who is willing to embrace and forgive the brothers who almost killed him and sold him into slavery. Associated with Adonis, Osiris, and Jesus Christ, Joseph occasionally seems too good to be true, more divine than human. But only at times. He is also a very shrewd politician, and it is in his role as Pharaoh's "supreme mouth" that he achieves his greatest success, strengthening the nation in a time of crisis and consolidating an empire on the brink of collapse.

Amenhotep comes to power as an adolescent prone to migraines, rapid mood swings, and a penchant for endless philosophical and theological speculation.[156] He is anxious to complete a temple for his God and to convert his people to the new belief, but lacks interest in the day-to-day affairs of state. "He suspected that not only was it one thing to found a world empire and quite another to help bring a universal god to life, but that also this second activity very possibly stood in some sort of contradiction to his royal responsibility to preserve and maintain the creation he had inherited" (1126).[157] Tradition required that a pharaoh newly ascended to the throne should "personally undertake a campaign of war and plunder against Asiatic or Negro lands" (1123),[158] but this sickly intellectual has no taste for war. His personal disinclination represents a danger for the empire, for his advisors correctly fear that if the subject territories discover that Pharaoh is more given to migraine headaches and religious trances than imperial conquest, they might well refuse to deliver the appropriate tribute. This is not to say that Mann portrays Pharaoh as evil or unaware of the world around him. He has traveled extensively throughout his empire, and ambassadors from all over the world routinely come to him: "the Lord of the Two Crowns simply sits in the beauty of his palace in the center of the world and, surrounded by the comfort due him, receives in tribute the thoughts of the inhabited earth" (1159).[159] He receives Joseph in a loggia decorated by a foreign artist from Crete and, like most of the upper-class Egyptians, mixes the occasional foreign word into his conversation. Even in his religious ecstasies, Pharaoh remains generous, praising his sole god for the diversity of his human creation: "Some are brown, others red, and others again are black, and still others like milk and blood—and in their many hues they reveal themselves in you and are your revelation" (1187).[160] When Joseph's brothers arrive, Pharaoh insists that they eat together with the Egyptian, although this goes against local custom, and he is viscerally opposed to the racism and xenophobia of those who worship Amun rather than his benevolent god Aton. His heart is in the right place, in other words; he lacks only the will to set his good intentions into action. As Joseph explains to his father, Pharaoh "tenderly strives to pursue the right path, even if he may not be the right man for it" (1431).[161]

Joseph is that man, as becomes evident in his first conversation with Pharaoh, an exchange that matches the discussion between Mut and Potiphar in its intricate artifice and psychological subtlety. The young pharaoh reminds the narrator of a slightly decadent British aristocrat, a representative of an empire in its late stages who has cultivated a taste for the people and products of areas colonized by former rulers, but one who lacks the political energy to maintain and extend his domains. Now troubled by seemingly portentous and yet mysterious dreams, he turns to Joseph for help. Joseph does not interpret Pharaoh's dreams directly, but rather guides him to discover their meaning for himself: the dreams can only mean that seven fat years will be followed by seven lean ones. Pharaoh is utterly delighted with the interpretation and willing to stop there, but his mother reminds him that the task has only just begun: he must prepare now for the events to come. By the end of the conversation, Pharaoh knows what he must do: appoint Joseph to do it for him.

Joseph begins by strengthening the power of the central government. Alluding to events that we have already encountered in the story of Mut's family background, Joseph reminds Pharaoh of how the local Egyptian kings who drove out the foreign rulers were incorporated into the nation and yet retained a good deal of their autonomy—so much so, in fact, that they represent a potential threat to Pharaoh's authority. Although, technically speaking, all property in Egypt belongs to Pharaoh, in practice, many of these local kings do not pay taxes on "inherited estates that stood out here and there like islands of an obsolete feudalism" (1224).[162] While Joseph allows certain temple lands to retain their tax-exempt status, "he rode roughshod over these stubborn barons, incorporating their properties from the very start and without further ado into his system of duties and reserves, and, over time, managing to expropriate them outright for the crown" (1225).[163] In time, Joseph also breaks up large estates ruled by "a previously intractable if not rebellious class of men" (1442),[164] distributing the land in smaller parcels to farmers more directly responsible to the state, and thus more motivated to adopt modern farming methods. Such lands belonged to the individuals and yet at the same time belonged to the state, and thus Joseph cast "a magic spell over the idea of property" (1441–42)[165] that prevented anyone from clinging to outmoded techniques or antiquated notions of feudal autonomy.

Joseph's foreign policy proceeds along similar lines. The news of Pharaoh's gentle nature soon makes its way to the colonies, where "a taste for impudence, defection, and betrayal began to spread" (1446).[166] The Syrians are breaking away to the north and Bedouins are raiding from the east, but Pharaoh lacks the strength or initiative to hold the crumbling empire together. Joseph realizes immediately that the foreign princes who might defy the Egyptian empire when they are in a position of power will come begging for help when they are starving, and Egypt has grain to sell—at top dollar, of course. They will come and they will pay, not only "in silver and wood for bread and seed" (1204),[167] but also with their children to be held as hostages—although Mann assures us that the children were treated well and actually received a better education in Egypt than they would have received at home.

Rulers of centralized nation-states or world empires do not fare well in Thomas Mann's earlier work. Hanno Buddenbrook suffers under the despotic Prussian teachers who subject citizens of the formerly independent city-state of Lübeck to the authority of the recently unified nation, and Mann repeatedly condemns the hypocrisy and violence of British and French imperialism in the *Reflections*. When Mann was writing *Joseph the Provider* in the early 1940s, German armies had conquered most of Europe, and the process of *Gleichschaltung* had forcibly silenced any dissent at home—developments that Mann roundly condemned in the monthly radio addresses that interrupted progress on his novel. Against these examples of foreign imperialism and domestic tyranny, Joseph suggests a different way. When he first arrives in prison, the bailiff Mai-

Sakhme quickly realizes that Joseph is not only born to lead, but that he will also treat all prisoners fairly, even if they are not Egyptian. Once uplifted to the role of Pharaoh's "supreme mouth," Joseph immediately appoints Mai-Sakhme as his second in command. While Joseph compels rich landowners to pay their fair share of taxes and demands prices that the market will bear when starving foreigners come seeking food, he does not confiscate property from obstreperous Egyptian aristocrats, nor does he practice violent conquest or enslave foreign enemies. While he serves an increasingly fanatical monotheist, he agrees with Amenhotep's mother, Tiy, that it is best to let the common people retain their familiar gods. Joseph works tirelessly for the Egyptian empire, but he never quite becomes Egyptian, maintaining an inner distance from his ceremonial religious duties that contrasts sharply with the bigoted zealotry of Beknechons and the other devotees of Amun's nationalist cult.

Joseph the Provider can be read as a transparent allegory in response to contemporary events, but it is also consistent with the political ideals of Mann's earlier career. The well-meaning but weak Amenhotep recalls Neville Chamberlain's policy of appeasement;[168] Beknechons awakens associations of Goebbels and his ilk, while the wise and strong Joseph stands in for Franklin Delano Roosevelt, providing for the poorest, taxing the richest, and asserting power when necessary on the world stage. Roosevelt was democratically elected, but Mann admired him more as a benevolent despot, a patriarchal figure who told the people what they should do, rather than one who followed the whims of the masses.[169] Mann's portrait of Joseph as a provider is not only in keeping with his image of FDR, but also in the spirit of his mildly ironic glorification of late feudalism in *Royal Highness* and his depiction of Consul Buddenbrook diffusing the anger of the revolutionary mob in 1848. In its celebration of Joseph as a Roosevelt figure, *Joseph the Provider* is Mann's most American novel, but it is a vision of America that is palatable to the senator's son from Lübeck. As soon as Roosevelt died and Senator McCarthy began to rouse the anti-Communist rabble, Thomas Mann recoiled with disgust and eventually retreated to the neutral ground of Switzerland.

Coda: *The Tables of the Law*

On January 18, 1943, just two weeks after completing *Joseph and His Brothers*, Mann began to write *The Tables of the Law*. It was a commissioned work, whose origins went back to the previous summer, when the Austrian exile Armin Robinson had asked Mann if he would be willing to collaborate on a film on the theme of the Ten Commandments. The work was to be polemical in nature, demonstrating the need for law and morality against the criminal regime of the Third Reich. When the MGM studio turned down the idea of a film, Robinson decided to publish a book with contributions from ten contemporary writers, each of whom was to focus on one of the commandments. Mann, as the most prominent of the invited authors, was to have pride of place at the beginning of the anthology; he also signed an advance contract in late December for the substantial sum of one thousand dollars. Work on the novella went quickly, and by March 17, 1943, Mann recorded in his diary that he had completed *The Tables of the Law* and thus the entire complex of biblical fiction that he had begun nearly two decades ago.[170]

In addition to the Pentateuch, one of Mann's primary sources was Freud's *Moses and Monotheism* (1939). With this late work, Freud made a bold and controversial statement about the origins of the Jewish religion. Bold, because he proposed that Moses was an Egyptian, even though the Bible states clearly that he was born a Hebrew, with both parents descendants of Levi (Exodus 2:1). Controversial, because Freud was suggesting that one of the most important Jewish patriarchs was in fact not a Jew, and also because—to the extent that Freud identified with Moses in his role as the founder and leader of the psychiatric movement—it suggested an element of Jewish self-hatred in Freud.[171] According to Freud, Moses became a monotheist at the court of Akhnaton, but when he realized that Akhnaton's ambition to establish monotheism in Egypt would fail, Moses decided to give the religion to the Hebrews and lead them out of Egypt to the land of Canaan. But why had monotheism arisen in Egypt in the first place? Because, speculates Freud, Egypt had become a vast empire, and if Egypt was to rule over the lands of Nubia, Palestine, Syria, and Mesopotamia, it would have to impose its God on them as well: "This imperialism was reflected in religion as universality and monotheism."[172] Egyptian monotheism was a direct result of Egyptian imperialism.

Mann's version of the story differs from both the Old Testament source and Freud's essay. In *The Tables of the Law,* Pharaoh's second daughter sees a handsome Hebrew slave working. She summons him to her, seduces him, and then has him slain before he gets thirty paces away from her pavilion. Nine months later she gives birth to a baby boy, who is raised by a Levite but educated as an Egyptian. After he murders one of Pharaoh's overlords and has to flee Egypt, Moses eventually marries a Midianite. Thus Mann's Moses is neither exclusively Hebrew nor Egyptian, but rather a mixture of the two, in terms of his biological parents and also his cultural influences. Mann explains his fa-

mous lack of eloquence from the fact that Moses was confused by the combination of Aramaic-Syrian-Chaldean that he learned among the Hebrews, the
Egyptian that he was taught at school, and the Midianite Arabic that he picked
up in the desert. Following a pattern in his works as old as Tonio Kröger and
Gustav von Aschenbach, Mann makes Moses a biological "half-breed" and a
cultural hybrid.[173]

What, then, did Mann learn from Freud's *Moses and Monotheism*, and,
more specifically, how did he respond to Freud's central thesis linking
monotheism to imperialism? At first glance, it would seem little or nothing:
Mann depicts the Egyptians in *Joseph and His Brothers* as the decadent heirs to
an empire they did not conquer themselves, and Akhnaton as a sickly dreamer
with no taste for violent conquest. Nor does Moses in *The Tables of the Law*
seek to extend a Hebrew empire by imposing monotheism on others. Quite the
contrary, in fact: his goal is to transform the "ill-mannered horde" of the Jews
into "a set apart and sanctified people, a purified community with its eyes fixed
upon the Invisible and addressed to Him alone.[174] Monotheism is to be the
defining feature of the Chosen People, not a weapon in the struggle for world
conquest. In contrast to the enervated Egyptians in *Joseph and His Brothers*,
however, the Hebrews of *The Tables of the Law* are a militant people intent on
conquering lands for themselves. Moses is happy to delegate military matters
to Joshua and his lieutenant Caleb, who led the Hebrews to victory in the battle over the Amalekites; afterwards, the Hebrews swell their ranks by adopting
the orphaned children and marrying the widowed wives of their enemies.
Meanwhile, Moses is engaged in a different kind of moral imperialism: "For
Moses too, Jahwe meant, of course, the exodus; but not so much as a campaign
to conquer land" (11)[175] as the effort to impose monotheism and morality on
the dissolute Hebrew people. Moses' task is to instigate the "process of civilization" among his people by serving as judge in individual disputes and giving
them general laws or commandments to govern their conduct. His monotheistic religion is what Freud terms "a religion of instinctual renunciation."[176] In
the process, Moses must also learn to control himself. "His birth was irregular,
hence it was he passionately loved order, the absolute, the shalt and shalt not,"
writes Mann in the opening sentence of the novella. "His senses were hot, so he
craved the spiritual, the pure, the holy" (1).[177]

The Tables of the Law culminates in a heartfelt peroration against those
who break God's laws and revert from civilization back to barbarism, a transparent reference to the Germans under National Socialism. In fact, Mann incorporated the final paragraph of the novella into his radio address to the Ger-

man people on April 25, 1943. Mann's decision to write a novella about Mosaic Law at a time when Jews were being imprisoned and murdered by the millions was an act of solidarity with the Jewish people and a defense of the civilizing power of their religion, and yet it met with mixed reviews, particularly among Jewish readers.[178] To some, the flippant tone of the story seemed irreverent. Orthodox readers reacted against Mann's tendency here, as in *Joseph and His Brothers*, to downplay divine intervention and provide plausible explanations for miraculous events. For example, it is not the finger of God that inscribes the Ten Commandments onto the tablets, but Moses who invents Hebrew script and painstakingly chisels the text onto the stone slab. The very suggestion that Moses was the illegitimate son of a Hebrew slave and an Egyptian princess was also offensive to those who revered him as one of the founding fathers of Judaism, as was Mann's portrait of him as an alternately dictatorial and duplicitous leader. Mann's characterization of the Jewish people, finally, as riffraff or an unruly mob (*Gehudel, Pöbelvolk*) hardly seemed appropriate in a work that was supposed to be defending Jewish civilization against Nazi barbarism. Once again, as Jacques Darmaun has argued, Mann was displaying an astonishing lack of tact in a delicate situation.[179] Or, as Ritchie Robertson summarizes, Mann bases his depiction of Moses and the Jews on two anti-Semitic stereotypes: in Moses we find the image of the rational Jew, "originally propagated by Mendelssohn but reinterpreted by anti-Semites like Chamberlain as an iron will to calculate and dominate," while in the Jewish mob we find "the natural Jew, who is an entirely sensual being, as indifferent to civilized taboos as the incestuous pair in *Wälsungenblut.*"[180]

Mann's primary target in *The Tables of the Law* is not the Jews but the Germans. What makes the text questionable to some is that he mounts his critique on the back of what can be seen as anti-Semitic clichés: the Jewish rabble stands in for the German masses, while Moses imposes his law on them with an authoritarian violence that seems uncomfortably close to the dictators Mann would resist.[181] Critics sensitive to the subtle undercurrent of anti-Semitism in Mann's text have nevertheless turned a blind eye to its more blatant racism and misogyny, for in *The Tables of the Law* as well as in *Joseph and His Brothers*, Mann links barbarism to blackness, female sexuality, and the south. In one of the most significant deviations from the biblical source, Mann's Moses takes a black woman from the land of Kush to be his mistress.[182] As in the case of Tabubu in *Joseph in Egypt*, Mann dips deeply into the well of undiluted prejudice in describing the unnamed "moor"[183] as a racial type rather than an individual. "In her way she was a splendid piece of flesh, with towering breasts and rolling whites to her eyes; she had pouting lips, wherein to sink in a kiss might be an adventure to any man, and her skin smelled of spicery" (44).[184] Unlike Joseph, who manages to resist Mut, even though she is under the spell of Tabubu's black magic, Moses not only succumbs to the Moor's charms, but hypocritically defends his actions as a permissible exception to the rules of sexual restraint that he imposes on others.

In the end, Moses brings his newly chiseled tablets to his people, replacing the ones that he had shattered in self-righteous rage, and they all say "Amen!" to the curse on those who sin against civilization and pay homage to false idols. *The Tables of the Law* nevertheless underscores the fragility of the balance that Joseph establishes in Egypt in a story that again combines elements of anti-Semitism in its seeming celebration of the Jews, and that formulates its condemnation of fascist idolatry and moral duplicity in the language of Orientalism.

CHAPTER SEVEN

Doctor Faustus: From Sonderweg to Universal Catastrophe

Thomas Mann's *Doctor Faustus* is a book of the end in multiple senses of the term.[1] Mann was convinced that this would be his final work, his *Parsifal*, a summa of the themes that had been present from the beginning of his career and had evolved in response to changing times.[2] The book is also about the potential end of the German nation, tracing a path of history that leads from Luther and the Reformation to the smoking ruins of the German cities and the gates of the concentration camps opened for the eyes of a horrified world. Where could Germany possibly go from here? Mann's narrator, Serenus Zeitblom, leaves us with an apocalyptic image of Germany surrounded by demons and plunging ever deeper into an abyss; he offers only the most tenuous hope that perhaps some day Germany will find forgiveness for its sins. Still other passages extend the sense of an ending to a five-hundred-year phase in the history of Western civilization: "The feeling that an epoch was coming to an end, an epoch that embraced not just the nineteenth century, but also reached back to the end of the Middle Ages, to the shattering of scholastic ties, to the emancipation of the individual and the birth of freedom . . . in short, the epoch of bourgeois humanism."[3]

The expansion of a specifically German catastrophe of the twentieth century to the collapse of bourgeois humanism since the Renaissance introduces an ambivalence of central importance to *Doctor Faustus,* in which National Socialism is portrayed alternately as a result of the peculiarities of German history and as a symptom of larger forces in the process of Western civilization. The same ambivalence haunts Mann's major essay of the period, "Germany and the Germans" (1945), which seeks to explain why the land of Schiller, Goethe, and Beethoven could have started two world wars and committed some of the most shocking crimes against humanity that the world has ever known. I will begin with a brief look at the arguments that Mann sets out in this essay before turning to the interrelated themes of National Socialism, artistic genius, exoticism, and the Jewish question in *Doctor Faustus.*

Germany and the Germans

Mann's primary answer to the question of why the Germans turned to National Socialism lies in a version of the *Sonderweg* thesis, the argument that German political history and the German national character were significantly different from those of other European nations and thus particularly susceptible to an authoritarian government and irrational violence.[4] The Germans had never entirely entered the modern age, Mann contends. At the time of the Reformation there was still a strong tendency toward the "hysteria of the dying Middle Ages, something of latent spiritual epidemic" that remained present in the Lübeck of Thomas Mann's childhood: "an anciently neurotic substratum ... an arcane spiritual state."[5] The Germans have retained a dangerous inclination toward the "chthonian, irrational, and demonic forces of life," a Romantic tendency that pulls them away from "the philosophical intellectualism and rationalism of enlightenment—a revolt of music against literature, of mysticism against clarity" (315).[6] The introspective character of the Germans has led to a fatal divorce of poetry and philosophy from the political realm. Luther liberated the individual from the theological authority of the church, but reacted violently against the peasants who tried to free themselves from their feudal lords. There was no tradition of political freedom in Germany and thus the Germans could not participate in the liberal nationalism inspired by the French Revolution: "It might be said that the very concept of the 'nation' in its historical affinity with that of liberty is foreign to Germany" (311).[7] As a result, "the customary European, national-democratic road to unity was not the German road" (315–16).[8] The Germans remained mystical and musical, but also politically servile, psychologically unstable, and fatally inclined to sign a pact with the devil.

Mann's image of the Germans is not entirely negative in "Germany and the Germans." While most Germans reacted violently against Napoleon, Goethe was repulsed by "the barbaric-racial element in this uprising" and retained his faith in "the super-national world of Germanism, world literature" (312).[9] At the end of the essay Mann speculates that the better qualities of the Germans might reemerge in a postnational era, "in which the national individualism of the nineteenth century will dissolve and finally vanish" (318).[10] The German "seclusiveness" (*Weltscheu*) had always contained a significant "longing for companionship" (*Weltverlangen*) (319; XI: 1148), he maintains, and perhaps in an era of loosened political and economic borders, the Germans could become exemplary citizens of the world, rather than militant members of a barbaric nation-state. In fact, Mann presents himself as just such a model of liberal cosmopolitanism in the introduction to the essay. Here he begins by remarking on how strange it is that he, a seventy-year-old German man, should be delivering his lecture in English, in the capital of the United States, as an American citizen. And yet, he continues, there is a certain logic to this unexpected turn of events: "As things stand today, my type of Germanism is most suitably at home in the hospitable Panopolis, the racial and national universe called America. . . . As an American I am a citizen of the world (*Weltbürger*)—and that is in keeping with the original nature of the German" (304).[11] The best way to be German in 1945 was to be an American.

In both cases, the Germans are different from other Europeans: their excessive inwardness either predisposes them to irrationalism and renders them susceptible to authoritarian government, or inoculates them against nationalist zeal and opens at least select individuals—Goethe, Mann, and the hypothetical citizens of a postwar global community—to a cosmopolitan receptivity to foreign influence. Mann's argument does not stop here, however, for he introduces other ideas that complicate the *Sonderweg* thesis and qualify the virtues of cosmopolitanism. Toward the end of the essay, Mann writes of the "universalism and cosmopolitanism" of the Holy Roman Empire that underwent a dialectical reversal in modern Germany: "The Germans yielded to the temptation of basing upon their innate cosmopolitanism a claim to European hegemony, even to world domination, whereby this trait became its exact opposite, namely the most presumptive and menacing nationalism and imperialism" (314).[12] In 1939 Mann had already argued that the Germans had stopped acting like Germans because they wanted to be like the English. Under the Nazis, Germany had become a degraded and distorted image of itself, "all for the sake of finally and thoroughly getting their power into shape, all for the sake of 'world domination' (*Weltherrschaft*), all stemming from an inappropriate envy of England."[13] A year later, Mann repeated this point in a speech in English titled "War and Democracy" at the Los Angeles Club: "The German hatred of England is the product of an admiration which does not see that England had as much reason to admire Germany—for entirely different reasons than those which arouse Germany's envy of England's role. The Germans saw the English as a 'master race'—and they wanted to be the same."[14]

On one hand, then, Mann views National Socialism as a disastrous consequence of the German *Sonderweg*, as Germans turned their backs on rationalism and democracy and submitted themselves to despotic authorities. On the other hand, however, he maintains that the Germans who seized control were only doing what other countries had already done; in fact, National Socialism represents an abandonment of Germany's peculiar nature out of a misguided desire to emulate other European nations. Germany differs from Britain and France only in the belatedness with which it embraced militant nationalism and in the ferociousness of its imperial aggression.

Aesthetic Totalitarianism: Leverkühn, Mann, and Adorno

Of central importance in *Doctor Faustus* is the special but oblique link between the protagonist, Adrian Leverkühn, and the German nation. In the novel's long subtitle, Zeitblom refers to Leverkühn as a *Tonsetzer* (composer), using the Germanic term rather than the Latinate *Komponist*, and Mann stressed in his correspondence the connection between Leverkühn and Germany: "the theme of evil inspiration and genialization (*Genialisierung*), which ends by being taken by the devil, that is, with paralysis" on the part of the artist and "the idea of intoxication in general and anti-rationality . . . and thus also the political, fascist, and with that, the sad fate of Germany."[15] But Adrian Leverkühn is not a Nazi, not a Nazi sympathizer or "fellow traveler," and there is nothing overtly fascist about his art.[16] He is rather a reclusive intellectual and avant-garde composer with decidedly cosmopolitan taste. His uncle's musical instrument business sets the tone, for he not only has ties with clients in all the major German cities, "but also with foreign firms in London, Lyons, Bologna, even New York" (44).[17] Many of Leverkühn's closest acquaintances are not properly German, certainly not in any *völkisch* sense: Wendell Kretschmar is a German-American; Rüdiger Schildknapp is an Anglophile who avoids Germans whenever possible; Jeanette Scheurl remains suspended between the German and French languages; Kunigunde Rosenstiel is Jewish; Marie Godeau is French-Swiss, and Frau von Tolna is Hungarian. Although Leverkühn admires Beethoven and the German *Volkslied* and is inspired by authors such as Klopstock and Kleist, he also incorporates Italian, Slavic, English, French, and American musical and literary influences into his works. While the German armies are trying to conquer the world, Leverkühn retreats from Munich to an isolated farm in the country. His "wish for alien air" (224) drives him to Italy, but once there he has no interest in tourism—Adrian "'wanted to see nothing'" (226).[18] He is ambitious in the sense that he wants to "break through" to a new, radical, and more authentic sort of music, but avoids or actively resists conducting or publishing his own works, or any sort of behavior that would place him or his work in the public eye. While his fellow students pontificate about the German essence and mission in the world, Leverkühn maintains an ironic distance; when almost all Germans are swept up in enthusiasm at the beginning of the First World War, Leverkühn again remains untouched by the commotion. Like Hans Castorp, he does not read newspapers and has no contact with the events that affect most Germans during the tumultuous years of the early twentieth century. If he had a patron saint, it would be Kaiser Otto the Third, who is buried in Kaisersaschern and "called himself both Emperor of the Romans and Saxonicus, not because he wanted to be a Saxon," but "because he had defeated the Saxons" (39).[19] "It was not for nothing that he was a son of the town in which Otto III lay buried," for he is filled with "distaste for the Germanness that he embodied" (175).[20]

If Leverkühn is "typically German," it is in the old-fashioned sense of being a provincial cosmopolitan and not because he has anything to do with the militarist, imperialist ambitions of modern Germany: "It was a baroque idea, but one deeply rooted in his nature—composed of arrogance, a recluse's shyness, the old-fashioned German provincialism of Kaisersaschern, and an explicit cosmopolitanism" (175).[21] The language used to describe his musical breakthrough nevertheless parallels the political ideology of the protofascist intellectuals that surround him. With them, Leverkühn shares a desire to break the bonds of mere reason and tap into something more primitive, elemental, and passionate. He speaks of a new era when art will have a quasi-religious cultic function in ways that recall the Nazis' appropriation of Christian and pagan symbolism in their public rituals. The description of Leverkühn's final works, with their combination of absolute, rigid order with wild glissandi and frenetic drumming, summon up images of the carefully choreographed Nuremberg rallies, where thousands stood in precise geometrical formations to listen in rapture to the rantings of Adolf Hitler, or to those tightly wrapped "soldier males" of the German *Freikorps*, enmeshed in their emotional armor and finding release only in moments of ecstatic violence.[22] Once again, this is not to say that there is anything overtly fascist about Leverkühn's music; he is not said to have composed the "Horst Wessel Lied" or anything remotely like it. His works nevertheless are described as structural parallels of protofascist ideology and National Socialist political practice.

The logic that allows Mann to link the avant-garde creations of a reclusive cosmopolitan to a fervently nationalistic mass political movement lies at least in part in the work of Theodor W. Adorno, who has at times been called the "coauthor" of *Doctor Faustus*.[23] As is well known, Mann was most at home in the world of Wagner's music, or, as he put it with a self-deprecating reference to Marlene Dietrich's song in *The Blue Angel*, "I am attuned to Romantic kitsch from head to toe" (*Ich bin da im Grunde von Kopf bis Fuß auf romantischen Kitsch eingestellt*).[24] Leverkühn, in contrast, was to compose radically modern works, and thus Mann turned to Adorno for help. "What I need are a few characterizing, realizing *details* (you only need a few) that give the reader a plausible, indeed, convincing image."[25] Adorno was understandably flattered by the attention of the Nobel Prize laureate twenty-eight years his senior, particularly because he was a longtime admirer of Thomas Mann's work. In his response to Mann's request, Adorno tells the touching story of how as a teenager he had once recognized Mann walking on a beach and had fantasized about what it would have been like if the master had actually spoken to him, so that Mann's invitation to help with the new novel was better than his wildest dreams, "a bit of realized utopia that almost never happens."[26] Adorno was delighted to share with Mann his unpublished manuscript on the *Philosophy of Modern Music* and to ghost-write Leverkühn's music. As Mann recalled in *The Story of a Novel,* he realized immediately that he had found the right person at the right time: "this was my man" (43).[27]

Further comments in *The Story of a Novel* make clear that Mann was drawn to Adorno for reasons that went far deeper than the need for some technical advice on how to produce plausible descriptions of imaginary music. Mann readily concedes that Kretzschmar's lecture on the late Beethoven and the description of serial music in chapter 22 of his novel are based entirely on Adorno's work, and yet he goes on to claim that the ideas were so familiar to him that it was as if they were his own: "I discovered in myself, or, rather, re-discovered as a long familiar element in myself, a mental alacrity for appropriating what I felt to be my own, what belonged to me, that is to say, to the 'subject'" (45–46).[28] In proclaiming his affinity for Adorno's thought, Mann is also deflecting potential objections to his montage technique: appropriating Adorno's ideas for the novel is not intellectual property theft because they were really Mann's ideas first: "after prolonged activity of the mind it frequently happens that things which we once upon a time threw upon the waters return to us recast by another's hand and put into different relationships but still reminding us of what was once our own" (46).[29]

What was it about Adorno's work that made it seem so familiar to Thomas Mann? The answer lies in their mutual understanding of the artist as a seismograph and a shared cultural pessimism. As Adorno argues in the *Philosophy of Modern Music,* the autonomous, harmoniously self-contained work of art is no longer possible: "Under the coercion of its own objective consequences music has critically invalidated the idea of the polished work and disrupted the collective continuity of its effect."[30] The impossibility stems from two different sources: one lies in the history of music and the other in the contemporary culture industry. In ideas that Mann will echo in *Doctor Faustus*, Adorno argues that the development of art progresses according to its own internal logic. A chord sequence or combination of notes that had been innovative in the past can no longer be used today: "It is not simply that these sounds are antiquated and untimely, but that they are false. They no longer fulfill their function."[31] If they are to ring true today, the tonal harmonies of a previous generation must be replaced by the dissonance of serial music. Complementing the notion that modern music emerges out of an irreversible historical process intrinsic to the logic of its own development is the understanding of high modernism as the dialectical counterpart to the debased products of the culture industry: "Radical music, from its inception, reacted similarly to the commercial depravity of the traditional idiom. It formulated an antithesis against the extension of the culture industry into its own domain."[32] In a world where everyone else is humming along to the mindless ditties of the advertising agencies, the purveyors of authentic music refuse to join the chorus. Such music cannot promise transcendence or escape from a debased world, as Adorno stresses in *Minima Moralia*. "Each statement, each piece of news, each thought has been preformed by the centres of the culture industry."[33] Radical music can only attempt to express "the untransfigured suffering of man,"[34] but even the most resolutely dissonant music turns into an image of the "worthless totality"[35] it would like to resist: "That certain freedom, into which it undertook to transform its anarchistic condition, was converted in the very hands of this music into a metaphor of the world against which it raises its protest. It flees forward into order."[36] In the end, there can be no positive alternative to a debased reality that is all-pervasive and thoroughly corrupt: "Wrong life cannot be lived rightly" (*Es gibt kein richtiges Leben im falschen*).[37]

Such ideas stand in close proximity to some of Mann's deepest convictions. In the early years of his career, Mann had championed the notion of a nonpolitical artist whose works nevertheless captured the spirit of the age more accurately than the overtly political novels of writers like his brother Heinrich. In Adorno, Mann found a kindred spirit: "The seismographic registration of traumatic shock becomes, at the same time, the technical structural law of music," writes Adorno in the *Philosophy of Modern Music*.[38] "The forms of art reflect the history of man more truthfully than do documents themselves."[39] The more sensitive the artist, the more precisely his art will register the shocks of the modern world; the more detached the artist remains from the hustle and bustle of daily life, the more engaged his work will be with the spirit of the age. Of course, engaged art in the sense of political activism would be pointless in Adorno's bleak world: "There is no way out of entanglement. The only responsible course is to deny oneself the ideological misuse of one's own existence, and for the rest to conduct oneself in private as modestly, unobtrusively and unpretentiously as is required, no longer by good upbringing, but by the shame of still having air to breathe, in hell."[40] In effect, Leverkühn follows Adorno's advice, retreating from a world that inspires only disdain and derision to concentrate his energies on his esoteric art.

But Thomas Mann did not. While Adorno and Max Horkheimer were developing a theory of the culture industry that saw little difference between fascist propaganda and the American advertising industry, between Hitler and Hollywood, Mann was speaking out about his admiration of Franklin Delano Roosevelt and delivering a series of impassioned radio addresses urging the Germans to turn away from fascism.[41] Why, then, did Mann seek out Adorno as an intellectual ally and revert to the cultural pessimism of his early career when writing *Doctor Faustus*? To put it another way, why is there no public intellectual in the novel of the sort that Thomas Mann had become? Why does his artistic representation of the Third Reich focus on an apolitical artist who produces politically suspect art and an impotent intellectual who has retreated into the privacy of his room to write with trembling hand the biography of his deceased friend?

The simple answer is that Mann was a complex individual who never entirely abandoned his deep-seated pessimism, even when the demands of the day required him to defend reason and democracy. As Hermann Kurzke has described it, Mann always suspected that there was something ludicrous about the artist as politician, but he was willing in extreme circumstances to subordinate his philosophical pessimism to ethical pragmatism: "Schopenhauer's pessimism may be closer to the truth, but it is more useful to believe in optimism. . . . As a philosophy, optimism is not tenable, but as ethics it is. It is useful."[42] Under duress, Mann could and did profess a belief in progress, Kurzke continues, but this faith was only "a life-sustaining illusion. Aesthetically it is therefore ridiculous, now as ever."[43] In writing *Doctor Faustus*, Mann cast aside the veil of reason aside to stare without flinching into the heart of darkness. The result was an indictment of Germany that extended to Western civilization as a whole and included himself as well.

Hetaera Esmeralda

The central premise of *Doctor Faustus* is that a gifted composer voluntarily contracts syphilis to heighten his genius by having sex with an infected prostitute. Mann's earliest plans for a reworking of the Faust theme date back to approximately 1904, a period marked by personal crisis, as Mann renounced his love for Paul Ehrenberg in favor of the "austere happiness" of his marriage to Katia Pringsheim.[44] The sketch of his plans for a reworking of the Faust theme reads as follows: "The syphilitic artist, driven by longing, approaches a pure, sweet, young girl. He gets engaged to the unsuspecting girl and shoots himself right before the wedding."[45] The outline fits into the pattern of several of Mann's early works, in which a man is stigmatized and yet distinguished by something that makes him different from the originary *Bürger:* an illness, a withered hand, a drop of foreign blood, or illicit sexual desires. When Mann returned to the Faust theme nearly forty years later, he faced a new challenge: how to relate the private preoccupations of his youth to an analysis of National Socialism. In the process, his initial conception underwent a fundamental change: the "pure, sweet young girl" became a diseased prostitute.

Leverkühn refers to her with the name of a mysterious and dangerous butterfly that his father had shown him as a boy. In symbolic terms, Leverkühn's entry into the brothel and embrace of Esmeralda is a descent to the underworld of the sort that Joseph undergoes on three different occasions, although with opposite results. Joseph is cast into the well, thrown into slavery, and locked up in prison, but each time he rises to greater glory than before; Adrian Leverkühn's taste of the forbidden fruit grants him sporadic moments of hectic genius before leading him inevitably to paralysis, madness, and death. As Zeitblom tells us in his first sentence, he will recount the provisional biography of "a revered man sorely tried by fate, which both raised him up and cast him down" (5).[46] Here again, we begin with simple questions: what and where is the underworld in *Doctor Faustus*? That is, how does Mann flesh out the abstract categories of the irrational and the demonic in his novel? Where does he locate them on the map? And for an answer we turn to the figure of Hetaera Esmeralda.

Although Esmeralda appears only briefly in the novel, she has an overdetermined symbolic weight that is striking even in a work notorious for its density of reference and cross-reference. Who is she and what does she represent? She is most obviously a woman, a woman who is both highly sexualized and sick. As the devilish theologian Eberhard Schleppfuss will stress, "whenever the topic was the power of demons over human life, sexual matters always played a conspicuous role" (113).[47] Temptation ultimately comes from the devil, he concedes, but the devil's curse lay upon the source of temptation: "The object, the *instrumentum* of the tempter, was the female" (114).[48] Marriage serves the purpose of the "domestication of what is naturally evil, of sex" (200),[49] but the prostitute is sexuality unchained, Blake's sick rose, Brentano's "dear girl" (*lieb Mädel*): "When you once gave me / the cool drink at night / you poisoned my life / my soul was so sick, so sick / Oh dear girl, how bad you are!"[50]

Hetaera Esmeralda is also foreign, or is at least associated with certain places that resonate with meaning in Mann's fiction. The first is Hungary. As Oskar Seidlin demonstrated in a classic case of literary detective work, the prostitute stands at the center of a network of references to the eastern European nation:[51] Leverkühn first meets her in Leipzig, but he contracts the illness during "his visit to Pressburg, or Poszony as the Hungarians call it" (164).[52] In one of his lectures, Schleppfuss tells the story of the otherwise virile Heinz Klöpfgeissel, who becomes impotent when he tries to have sex with a prostitute, "a Hungarian female" (116).[53] Then there is Madame von Tolna, a mysterious Hungarian noblewoman and Adrian's benefactress. Leverkühn travels to her estate with Rudi Schwerdtfeger, "his former Hungarian traveling companion" (455),[54] where it is strongly hinted that they have a homosexual love affair. Finally, the Hungarian music critic Desiderius Fehér writes one of the few perceptive analyses of Leverkühn's demanding compositions.

The encounter with the infected prostitute in Hungary thus follows the pattern established by such figures as Tadzio, Hippe, and Clavdia Chauchat, linking Eastern Europe to illicit passion. Other details point to Spain, or "Spane," as Mann referred to it in one of his more creative misspellings in his diaries,[55] that realm of rigid discipline and sexualized violence that Hans Castorp had already described to Joachim Ziemssen's mother as the mirror image of Eastern Europe. Leverkühn describes Esmeralda as wearing a little Spanish jacket, and Zeitblom imagines "the stubbed-nose girl beside him—*Hetaera esmeralda*—her powdered demiglobes in a Spanish bodice" (158).[56] Arabian Spain is also the realm of Klingsohr and the enchantress Kundry in Wagner's *Parsifal*, who nearly succeeds in seducing Parsifal from his service to the Holy Grail. And here we come full circle, for Kundry's palace stands at the gateway to the Orient, where Moorish Spain leads to northern Africa—hence the reference to Esmeralda's fellow prostitutes as "daughters of the desert" (158)[57]—and from there on to the "Asiatic" realm of Eastern Europe.

The reference to Esmeralda's "almond eyes" (152) (*Mandelaugen*, 192) adds

Jewishness to the symbolic field that surrounds her. This is not to say that she is or is not "really" Jewish; what matters is not so much definite proof as imaginative association. Saul Fitelberg, who most definitely is Jewish, has the same "almond eyes" (419),[58] as did Baronessa Ada, the Jewish femme fatale in the early novella *Der Wille zum Glück*.[59] The Hungarian critic who appreciates Leverkühn's work has the same last name as one of Mann's Jewish friends as a boy,[60] and Leo Naphta and in all likelihood Edhin Krokowski are also eastern European Jews associated with religious fanaticism and the irrational, subconscious mind.

Finally, Esmeralda has associations with the New World, more specifically, Brazil. Mann found the description of the butterfly in a book called *Falterschönheit* (The Beauty of Butterflies) by Adolf Portmann, who had in turn relied on a work by H. W. Bates, *The Naturalist on the River Amazon*. As Gunilla Bergsten summarizes, "Hetaera Esmeralda first appears in *Doctor Faustus* as a real, South American butterfly."[61] Brazil is of course the birthplace of Julia Mann, and the appealing figure of Imma Spoelmann in *Royal Highness* has a South American mother as well, but the New World was also considered the source of syphilis, which made its first appearance in Europe immediately after Columbus returned from the West Indies.[62]

In sum, the prostitute Hetaera Esmeralda is a walking catalog of every binary opposition central to Thomas Mann's literary imagination: male versus female, heterosexual versus homosexual, health versus sickness, Christian versus Jewish, formless Eastern Europe and overly rigid Spain in opposition to the German "Land of the Center," Occident versus Orient, Old Europe versus the New World. By introducing Esmeralda's disease into his body, Leverkühn becomes a little "Hungarian," "Spanish," "Brazilian," and "Jewish." The element of foreignness, in turn, infects his music. Zeitblom notes with concern that even Leverkühn's most radiant works have a disquieting element of "the demonic and irrational" (6).[63] Such elements include not only the "magical, fanatical, Negro-like drumming and booming gongs" (393)[64] in Leverkühn's *Apocalypse*, but also the references to Esmeralda in the "he a e es" sequence of notes encrypted into his works. To these we could add the coded reference to Adorno in the three-tone sequence of "Wie-sengrund."[65] In context, the association of an idyllic musical theme with "sky of blue" or "meadow-land" (58) seems innocuous enough, but readers familiar with *The Story of a Novel* will note the subliminal link to Theodor Wiesengrund Adorno, whose "father was a German Jew" (43).[66] By introducing the name Wiesengrund into the novel, Mann reveals the Jewishness that Adorno repressed by adopting his mother's maiden name for his publications. Leverkühn not only has the illness of the almond-eyed prostitute in his blood, but also inscribes that infection into his music: in symbolic terms, both Leverkühn and his music are "Jewish"—and Jacques Darmaun has cleverly suggested that his name could be read as "der kühne Levy" (bold Levy) or "LevyCohn."[67]

Germanic Evil as Civilization's Other

Before pursing the implications of Leverkühn's "Jewishness" further, let us pause for a few preliminary conclusions. One is that the overdetermined figure of Hetaera Esmeralda reminds us once again that Jewishness in Mann's fiction is typically embedded in a network of related categories of sexual, racial, and national difference. A second is that we need to view individual characters in *Doctor Faustus* in the larger context of the novel's reflections on the origins of National Socialism and the history of Western civilization. In both cases, the general principles invoked at the outset of this study apply: that of osmosis, that is, the tendency of one stigmatized category to bleed into others; and that of reversal, as seemingly distinct categories or characters flip without notice into their opposites. For instance, in Leverkühn's conversation with the devil in his guise as a pimp, we are reminded that the arrival in Germany at the time of Luther of the infectious bacteria that cause syphilis—"the small delicate folk, living corkscrews, our dear guests from the Indies" (247)[68]—coincided with crusades against the Turks, thus establishing an associative link between Orient and Occident, between a sexually transmitted disease from the New World and a threatening incursion of infidels from the East.

Another intriguing set of associations surrounds the mysterious figure of Madame von Tolna. As early as 1948, Victor Oswald speculated that she might actually be the woman who had once infected Leverkühn: she is the widow of a dissipated Hungarian nobleman who could conceivably have married a former prostitute, although Madame von Tolna's fluency in several European languages and her familiarity with the European intellectual and artistic avant-garde seem unlikely for a woman who spent her formative years in dimly lit brothels.[69] What matters here, as so often in Mann's fiction, is not positive identification but imaginative association, and in this regard there is in fact a close link between Hetaera Esmeralda and Madame von Tolna: the prostitute is linked to the Mediterranean through her Spanish jacket, her almond eyes, and her association with other "daughters of the desert"; Tolna has Turkish servants and her travels take her to Naples and Egypt. Both are tied to Hungary, and the ring with the emerald from the Ural Mountains on the Eurasian border also awakens memories of the South American butterfly or "Esmeralda" that infected Leverkühn with its poison.

With these examples of overlapping categories of exoticism in mind, let us turn to the relationship between Germany and Europe as it appears in *Doctor Faustus*. In this regard, the novel offers mixed messages, or perhaps, to use Leverkühn's description of music, presents "ambiguity as a system" (51).[70] On the one hand, Mann's novel adopts ideas expressed elsewhere about National Socialism as an upwelling of latent hysteria, as a specifically German illness, often using identical language to "Germany and the Germans." Thus Kaisersaschern is given the attributes of Lübeck, where time stands still and at any moment late medieval hysteria can burst out in the otherwise "sensibly practical, modern town" (39).[71] The Winfried group of students drones on about the metaphysical gift that is the distinguishing feature of German youthfulness, its reckless willingness to "plunge back into what is elemental" (127).[72] "Yes, we are a completely different nation, one that is a contradiction to sobriety and common sense," writes Zeitblom in the midst of the Second World War; although the situation keeps getting worse, the German "tragically heroic state of mind" (185) will not permit them to stop fighting until inconceivable disaster strikes.[73] In the novel as well as the essay, we are told that Germany is to music as France is to literature and that, for the Germans, "the psychological element is always primary, the essential motivating factor" and not the political (323).[74] What is true for the German *Volk* as a whole is true for the individual German as well: "I am speaking of the *volk*, but that same ancient collective layer exists in each of us," an "archaic apprehension," a tendency toward "regressive evil" (40–41).[75] Even when Leverkühn leaves Kaisersaschern, it never leaves him, or, as Mann has the devil put it in a moment of self-parody, "Where I am, there is Kaisersaschern" (242).[76]

On the other hand, the supposedly German tendency toward demonic, chthonic irrationalism is repeatedly linked to everything foreign in Leverkühn's pact with the devil: African drumming, Amazonian butterflies, Spanish seductresses, and homosexual encounters in Hungary. The tendency carries over to other parts of the novel, where elements of the foreign crop up just when things seem most typically German. In "Germany and the Germans," Mann credits Luther with single-handedly creating the modern German language in his translation of the Bible, and yet the Leverkühn family Bible with preface and commentary by Luther is said to have been owned by a German princess who married the son of the Russian Peter the Great, only to fake her death and marry a Frenchman in Martinique—thus linking this quintessentially German book to both Eastern Europe and the West Indies. Leverkühn adopts a pseudo-Lutheran style of old-fashioned German to describe his first visit to old German city of Leipzig, but he arrives "during one of its fairs" when the streets are full of people "from all parts of Europe, besides Persia, Armenia, and other Asiatic lands" (148–49).[77] Just before Leverkühn's first meeting with Hetaera Esmeralda inside the brothel, he has a similar encounter with the foreign outside on the streets of Leipzig: people "gaze upon you with exotic eyes and speak in tongues of which you ne'er have heard a sound before. Right stirring it was, and you feel the world's pulse within your own body" (151).[78] When Leverkühn travels to Hungary for his rendezvous with the infected prostitute, he uses as a pretense for the journey a desire to attend the Austrian premiere of Richard Strauss's *Salome*—a premier quite possibly attended by Adolf Hitler as well, thus linking the associative complex of foreign exoticism surrounding Hetaera Esmeralda to the origins of German fascism.[79] Leverkühn then seeks a cure for his illness from Dr. Zimbalist, who sports "a tag of a moustache beneath his nostrils" in a style "which would later become a hallmark of a face in world history" (168). The same doctor decorates his waiting room "with potted plants—palms and African hemp" (167).[80]

Clarissa Rodde commits suicide with a vial of poison that she hides in a hollow book beneath a paperweight in the shape of a skull, while her seemingly proper sister, Ines Rodde, takes overdoses of morphine with a coterie of friends that includes "a divorced Romanian authoress from Transylvania" (406)[81] and Natalia Knöterich, "a brunette who wore earrings and long black curls that dangled down over her cheeks, with an exotic Spanish look about her" (212).[82] When Leverkühn dramatizes scenes from the *Gesta Romanorum* using puppets rather than people, he not only consults Kleist's essay on the marionette theater, but also studies "the very ingenious hand puppets and shadow plays of the Javanese" (337).[83] The interest in Asian art recurs in the figure of Sixtus Kridwiss, "a graphic artist, an ornamenter of books, and a collector of East Asian color woodcuts and ceramics" (381).[84] His guests ridicule reason, the Enlightenment, and the Weimar Republic, and speak of the need for violence and myth to exert dictatorial control over the masses while they sit in an apartment decorated "from the Sung dynasty!" (382).[85]

The propensity toward evil that lurks in the depths of the German soul rises to the surface in the guise of foreign exoticism; the Germanic genius of Adrian Leverkühn cannot unleash its full creative power until he contracts the sexually transmitted disease of a Spanish-Hungarian-Jewish-Brazilian prostitute. The paradoxical fusion of opposites is in keeping with the double explanation of the origins of German fascism in *Doctor Faustus:* on the one hand, the Germans' *Sonderweg,* their fatal attraction to music and the irrational, their aversion to reason and democracy, is responsible for their destruction. On the other hand, the Germans are merely imitating the imperialism of other European nations. They come later and compensate by trying harder, but their methods and goals are typically European rather than specifically German. As Zeitblom recalls, the German soldiers who set off to fight in the First World War were convinced that it would be "the breakthrough that would make us a dominant world power . . . [they were] filled with the certainty that the hour of Germany's era had come . . . that after Spain, France, and England it was now our turn to put our stamp upon the world" (318).[86] Their defeat in this war made them all the more sensitive to the "feeling that an epoch was coming to an end. . . . No wonder . . . that in an overthrown nation like Germany it occupied people's minds more than it did those of the victors, whose average emotional state was, as the result of victory, far more conservative" (372).[87] The Germans become the canaries in the coal mines of Western civilization, the first to sense the impending doom that is about to engulf them all. From this perspective, German fascism is not specifically German at all, but rather the radical avant-garde of a European movement representing the culmination and the end of the five-hundred-year history of European humanism, which is also the era of exploration, nationalism, and imperialism.

Already in the *Reflections* Mann had argued that the "process of civilization" is intrinsically imperialistic when exported from Europe to the rest of the world. Civilization by definition needs its opposite; it must have barbarians to conquer, colonize, and convert. As Mann suggested as early as *Buddenbrooks,* however, there is always the danger of reversal: civilization can become infected by the foreign; figures like Christian Buddenbrook can go native. In the apocalyptic and totalitarian world of *Doctor Faustus,* Western civilization as a whole turns into its opposite. Enlightenment brings darkness, progress becomes reaction, the enemy without becomes the enemy within. German fascism is presented as a specifically German evil in the guise of a foreign infection; that which makes Germany different from the rest of Europe becomes aligned with everything in the rest of the world against which Europe defines itself. German fascism is the return of the repressed of Western civilization: the barbarian in the metropolis, the Jew among Christians.

Doctor Faustus and the Jewish Question

On the evening of December 25, 1933, Mann asked his children "what was the nicest thing about Christmas." "When Papa imitated a Jew at dinner!"[88] Mann's shtick as a Jew was a kind of "ethnic drag," a performance of ethnicity primarily for comic effect—although one in questionable taste, given the circumstances.[89] Never one to be deterred by concerns of political correctness, however, Mann was happy to repeat his private performance in public as the garrulous eastern European Jew, Saul Fitelberg. On at least several different occasions, Mann selected chapter 37 of *Doctor Faustus* for his public readings, which consists primarily of a monologue in a mixture of German and French by the agent who seeks to pry Adrian Leverkühn out of rural Bavaria and to introduce him to the glittering world of Parisian high society and European fame. While the diaries often present Mann as a brooding hypochondriac, he was also an actor and entertainer who thrived on the rapport that he could establish with an appreciative audience; the Fitelberg episode is a linguistic tour de force of an appropriate length that could no doubt be milked for knee-slapping laughter. "The greatest success with the Fitelberg chapter; multiple curtain calls," noted Mann after a reading on September 24, 1951; his audience in Zurich had followed him "with utmost attention and hilarity."[90]

From the beginning, however, some listeners and readers have been concerned about the representation of Saul Fitelberg and other Jewish characters in *Doctor Faustus*. Klaus Mann was already uneasy when his father read aloud his new chapter about the Jewish music agent Fitelberg to an intimate circle of family and friends. "Concerns of anti-Semitism that I cannot share," noted Mann later that evening in his diary.[91] Two years later Alfred Werner published an article titled "Thomas Mann's Failure" in which he questioned why an artist of Mann's stature and moral authority would repeatedly introduce Jewish characters into his novels that are either ridiculous or downright evil.[92] Mann dismissed Werner's accusations as "dumb and harmless,"[93] yet questions about his representation of the Jews in *Doctor Faustus* have only grown sharper in recent years. In a widely influential article, Egon Schwarz noted that Mann continues to employ the sorts of negative Jewish stereotypes present in his earliest fiction.[94] While Thomas Mann had cordial relations with Albert Schweitzer and a close friendship with Bruno Walter, Jews of similar status and accomplishment find no place in his fiction. *Doctor Faustus* evinces great sympathy and concern for the Germans, but it does not dwell on the sufferings of the Jews. In a novel that lays the blame for National Socialism largely on the irresponsible flirtation of German intellectuals with antidemocratic philosophies of irrationalism and violence, anti-Semitism is striking by its absence from their protofascist discussions.[95] Even worse: Chaim Breisacher, the Jew whom Serenus Zeitblom finds the most repulsive individual among Leverkühn's circle of acquaintances, advocates killing "the feeble-minded and those incapable of survival" (389) in the name of racial hygiene,[96] thus placing an argument for genocide in the mouth of a Jew. "At the very least this is a case of almost perversely bad taste," comments Ruth Angress-Klüger; "at worst it is a whitewash of German intellectuals."[97]

Against these accusations one could mount a very limited defense. Anti-Semitism is in fact not entirely absent from the novel: Rüdiger Schildknapp is happy to accept diner invitations from rich Jewish families in Leipzig, "although he had been heard to make anti-Semitic remarks" (181).[98] The subsequent description of the Jewish hosts to their parasitic dinner guest seems hardly calculated to refute charges of anti-Semitism, however: "these wives of Jewish publishers and bankers looked up to him with that profound admiration their race has for German master blood and long legs, and took great pleasure in giving him presents" (181).[99] Here again, Zeitblom is not Thomas Mann, and the reference to the impecunious, probably homosexual Anglophile as an example of "German master blood" certainly has an element of irony. Against the charge that the Holocaust finds no place in *Doctor Faustus* we could point out that the forty-sixth chapter describes how an American general ordered the citizens of Weimar to file past the crematories of the nearby Buchenwald concentration camp, challenging the notion that they were just going about their daily business in town and had no idea what was happening just a few miles away, "though at times the wind blew the stench of burned human flesh up their noses" (505).[100] True, the victims are not explicitly identified as Jewish, but at a time when images and firsthand accounts of the horrors of the concentration camps were widely disseminated in the news media, it could be argued that the implicit reference to the primarily Jewish victims would have been obvious enough. Even so, Mann's persistent representation of caricatured Jews in *Doctor Faustus,* the absence of anti-Semitism from the discussions in the novel that lay the foundation for German National Socialism, and the discrepancy between Zeitblom's infinite sympathy for the plight of the Germans and his silence about the suffering of the Jews have left many readers disturbed and have compromised the reputation of Mann's magnum opus about Germany and the Germans.

My goal here is neither to condemn the representation of Jews in *Doctor*

Faustus—there is no need to repeat what has already been said—nor to exonerate Thomas Mann—for this one would need to look beyond the novel to his many public denunciations of Nazi Germany and anti-Semitism before, during, and after writing *Doctor Faustus*. I seek rather to reintegrate isolated Jewish figures into the larger symbolic network of *Doctor Faustus* and into the logic that informs Mann's analysis of German National Socialism and Western civilization. With this in mind, let us look more closely at the figures of Saul Fitelberg and Chaim Breisacher.

Fitelberg makes his most important statements at the end of his unsuccessful attempt to draw Leverkühn out of his self-imposed isolation. Jews are like Germans, he maintains, in the arrogant belief that they are a Chosen People, destined for greatness, "both equally hated, despised, feared, envied. . . . One speaks of the age of nationalism. But in reality there are only two nationalisms, the German and the Jewish, and all the rest is child's play" (428).[101] The Jews are therefore drawn to the Germans as kindred spirits, and yet they realize that it is a fatal attraction: they will never be considered "popular, national, *volkstümlich*" in a way that is typically German, and they also know that "the German character . . . *est essentiellement anti-sémitique*" (427).[102] Fitelberg lives the life of a diasporic Jew: although he has the almond-shaped eyes of the Mediterranean, he moves restlessly between Poland, Germany, and France; he is also socially mobile, insinuating himself into Parisian high society despite his humble origins; linguistically hybrid in his constant mixture of German and French, and by profession a mediator between artists and their public. Making a virtue out of necessity, Fitelberg warns Leverkühn that he and the rest of the Germans should do by choice what the Jews have been forced to do by circumstance: give up their arrogant sense of exclusivity and get out into the world; otherwise "the Germans will bring about their own misfortune, a truly Jewish misfortune, *je vous le jure*" (428).[103]

Leverkühn does not follow Fitelberg out into the world, but Thomas Mann did. Against the charge that Fitelberg debases art by putting it up for sale, one could point out that Thomas Mann was never shy or apologetic about demanding appropriate compensation for his work; he had a large family to support and needed the money. Nor did Mann avoid the limelight; on the contrary, he aggressively sought fame and representational status from the beginning of his career, traveled thousands of miles on lecture tours throughout Europe and across North America, and thrived on his public performances—including his performance of Saul Fitelberg. Mann also agreed with Fitelberg in his assessment of the German people as dangerously nationalistic and in need of either absorbing more cosmopolitan influences or being scattered into the world, rather than trying to take it over. Mann's choice of the Fitelberg chapter for public readings thus cuts two ways: on the one hand, it allowed him to entertain the audience by slipping into an improbable role with the chameleon-like facility of a Felix Krull: Germany's *poeta doctus* and Nobel laureate does a stand-up comedy routine as a caricatured eastern European Jew. On the other hand, there is a strong element of self-parody in the role that arises from Mann's long-term unease with himself in the role of "civilization's literary man," the (Jewish) *Litterat*, the public intellectual and advocate of democracy and the Enlightenment.

While Leverkühn remains in rural Pfeiffering, he, too, is in touch with the world, although in different and more sinister ways. As noted, Leverkühn has always been cosmopolitan in his intellectual taste and artistic influences, which effectively prevent him from being either a SA thug or a reactionary ideologue of the sort that haunt the Kridwiss circle. Leverkühn's breakthrough to a new cultic-barbaric post-autonomous music nevertheless parallels Germany's political breakthrough to the choreographed madness of the National Socialists, a process that Walter Benjamin famously described as the effort to "render politics aesthetic."[104] Once again, Adrian Leverkühn is neither a torchbearer in the fascist parades nor a composer of political anthems, but he shares the infection in the form of artistic genius heightened by a sexually transmitted disease. The syphilis in his blood releases the latent Germanic madness that is always ready to break out like a medieval Saint Vitus' dance on the streets of Kaisersaschern, but it is a madness that is simultaneously linked to the foreign, the anti-German, through the overdetermined figure of Hetaera Esmeralda.

The foreign bodies that infect Leverkühn in the form of his illness suggest a surprising parallel to another figure in *Doctor Faustus*: Dr. Chaim Breisacher, a Jew "of fascinating ugliness—who here [in the Schlaginhaufens' salon] played the role, apparently with a certain malicious delight, of the foreign leaven in the bread" (294).[105] Zeitblom portrays Breisacher as the worst of the reactionary intellectuals in the Schaginhaufen salon. Breisacher is "a philosopher of culture, whose opinions, however, were directed against culture insofar as he affected to see all of history as nothing but a process of decline" (295).[106] Voicing ideas that Mann found in Oskar Goldberg's *Die Wirklichkeit der Hebräer* (The Reality of the Hebrews), Breisacher laments the replacement of a race- and *Volk*-specific god with a universal deity, the degradation of blood sacrifice into mere symbolism, the replacement of magic with prayer, and the emergence of ethical concepts of sin and punishment as symptoms of decline from the amoral vitalism of an ancient, cultic religion.[107] Most ominously and most controversially, Breisacher foresees a time in the near future when society will choose to eliminate its undesirables in the name of racial hygiene. If irresponsible irrationalism on the part of German intellectuals is an indirect cause of German National Socialism, as Mann suggests in this novel, then Breisacher's ideology is worse than ironic. By avoiding the topic of anti-Semitism in the protofascist discussions among Christian intellectuals in the novel, and by placing an argument for genocide in the mouth of a repulsively ugly Jew, Thomas Mann suggests that the Jews are indirectly responsible for their own misfortune, that German fascism arises from a Jewish conspiracy.[108]

Does Breisacher actively cause the rise of the Third Reich, or does he merely intuit and express what was going to happen anyway? Zeitblom's interpretation suggests the latter, noting Breisacher's "keen sensitivity for the intellectual commotion of the time, his nose for each new expression of its will" (294),[109] an awareness that Zeitblom contends is typical of "Jewish sagacity," with its "keen-eared sensitivity for what is new and yet to come" (300).[110] The Jews become the seismographs of German society in a way that directly parallels Leverkühn's role as a nonpolitical artist who is nevertheless in synch with the spirit of the age. Mann's transfer of his old understanding of the artist as a seismograph onto his analysis of German fascism and the Jewish question yields some surprising results. As we have seen, Mann identifies German fascism in *Doctor Faustus* simultaneously and paradoxically as a specifically German malady and as an infection of the foreign. By a reversal of the same logic, the Jew becomes not only the foreign body in the German *Volk*, that is, that which is most alien and must be expelled, but also that which is most intrinsically German, the latent illness that can break out at any time. The artist, in turn, is another foreign body in the German people, an outsider marked by illness, sexual deviance, and racial difference—recall Leverkühn's infection by the almond-eyed prostitute—but also an intrinsically German medium that senses and records in avant-garde art the darkest impulses of the German soul.

In *Doctor Faustus*, Mann creates an Adornoesque world of totalitarian logic and negative dialectics: Zeitblom oscillates between laments about the course of events that he is powerless to prevent and occasional lapses into an identification with the fascist mentality that that he would like to resist. Leverkühn's cosmopolitanism is both benign and malignant: benign in the sense that it is evidence of an openness to the world that brings his art into the vanguard of European music and would have made it impossible to perform in Nazi Germany, malignant in that it feeds on the disease that links the specifically German propensity toward madness and violence with the peoples who live on the dark continents surrounding Fortress Europe. The equation of fascism with both atavistic passions peculiar to the German nation and with an incursion of foreign primitivism into the heart of European civilization leads to a series of homologies from which there is no escape: the Germans are at once unique, following their *Sonderweg* against the grain of European history, and at the vanguard of European imperialism, pressing the process of civilization forward until it inverts into its opposite, where progress becomes reaction and civilization reverts to a new barbarism. The artist is both insider and outsider, the voice of dissonance against the forced harmony of a totalitarian *Gleichschaltung*, and yet the creator of an art form that expresses the suffering of the system it cannot escape. Even the Jews, the prime scapegoats and victims of National Socialism, become complicit in their own demise, for the Jew, like the artist, is a "foreign body" in society, outcast from it and yet for precisely that reason in touch with its innermost impulses.

Thus Mann's indictment of German fascism is also an indictment of European imperialism. What from one perspective is an aberration from the norms of Western civilization inverts dialectically into critique of the same civilization as intrinsically racist and imperialist, following the logic that was behind Mann's critique of the "imperium of civilization" in the *Reflections of a Nonpolitical Man*. By the same token, the implicit association of artists with Jews as social outcasts who are nevertheless attuned to the spirit of the society that surrounds them reflects Mann's lifelong conception of the artist as seismograph. In this case, however, the old logic yields disturbing, even outrageous results, for it portrays the Jews as avant-garde intellectuals who are the first to formulate the barbaric logic that will lead to their own annihilation. In his political speeches and essays of the time, Mann unequivocally condemned German fascism and the persecution of the Jews. *Doctor Faustus* was also conceived as a coming to terms with Nazi Germany, but in its consistency with the logic that informs Mann's artistic production, it not only transforms the German *Sonderweg* into an apocalyptic indictment of Western civilization, but also portrays the Jews as the agents of their own destruction.

CHAPTER EIGHT

Confessions of Felix Krull: The Final Journey

In the spring of 1952 Thomas Mann toyed briefly with the idea of taking a trip around the world. As he made plans for what would turn out to be his final return to Europe, he contemplated continuing from Europe back to California via India and Japan, with an additional stopover in Hawaii.[1] He even went so far as to consult his doctor about the possibility of the journey, who discouraged the idea because of the inoculations that would have been required and perhaps also because he considered the stress ill-advised for a seventy-six-year-old man who had survived a major operation for lung cancer a few years earlier.[2] Erika had been skeptical about the plan from the start, and even before he spoke with his doctor, Mann was also beginning to have cold feet: "The world journey seems like madness to me after all."[3]

In the end, Mann chose to live vicariously, sending a fictional character off on an adventure that he could not experience himself. When casting about for a new project after completing *The Holy Sinner* in the fall of 1950, Mann latched on to the idea of continuing the *Confessions of Felix Krull*, which he had left as a fragment decades earlier.[4] "The homosexual novel interests me not the least because of the experiences of the world and travel that it offers."[5] The reference to the work as a "homosexual novel" underscores its thematic proximity to *Death in Venice*, to which Mann had turned when he found it impossible to complete *Felix Krull* in 1911, but the travel motif links it to Goethe's *Faust*. "The Faustian quality of the material. Schiller's insistence to Goethe that Faust must be led out into the world. Extension of the setting to America."[6] We last see Felix Krull in Lisbon, Portugal, about to set sail to Argentina.[7] From there he was to have journeyed on to North America, "the islands of the South Seas and Japan, followed by an interesting voyage to Egypt, Constantinople, Greece, Italy, and so forth."[8] By the time part 1 of the novel was published in September 1954, however, Mann knew that he would never complete the work. He was too old and tired, as he explained to his friend Emil Preetorius, and he would rather devote his remaining energy to a more appropriate and dignified topic than the erotic adventures of a young man.[9]

In several senses, however, the novel as we have it can be seen as a self-contained whole as well as a fragment, a homecoming as well as an unfinished journey. At a time when Mann struggled to find new ideas for his fiction, the *Confessions of Felix Krull* allowed him to circle back to an abandoned project from his early career and to bring it to a provisional conclusion; he was justifiably proud of his ability to pick up where he had left off nearly four decades ago. Krull's journey to Portugal with the further goal of South America can also be seen as a return in fictional form to Julia Mann's Portuguese-Brazilian origins, thus complementing the "thoughts of 'Papa' and the feeling for rounding-off my biography" that Mann noted when preparing for his final trip to Lübeck in the spring of 1955.[10] Like Thomas Mann, Krull is born "only a few years after the glorious founding of the German Empire" (2).[11] He arrives in Lisbon in 1895, at a time when King Carlos I is "depressed by political cares which had begun immediately after his coronation six years before, through the conflict of Portuguese and British interests in Central Africa" (321),[12] but Professor Kuckuck has already told Krull of happier times when Lisbon was "the richest city in the world, thanks to the voyages of discovery" that were launched from its port (255).[13] While the power of the Portuguese empire has faded into the past, the Lisbon that Krull visits bears witness to its history in the polyglot racial mixture of its present-day inhabitants: "in the course of two thousand years Venetians, Carthaginians, Romans, Vandals, Suevians, West Goths, and especially the Arabs, the Moors, have co-operated to produce the type that awaits you," explains Professor Kuckuck to Krull, "not to forget a sizable admixture of Negro blood from the many dark-skinned slaves that were brought in when Portugal owned the whole African coast" (256).[14] Lisbon is thus both the city from which Europe launched its first expeditions of exploration and the city to which the peoples of the world have returned, a modern colonizing power of Africa and South America, and itself a colony of multiple empires from antiquity to the Middle Ages. Felix Krull's journey to Lisbon thus marks a fitting conclusion to Mann's lifelong interest in questions of racial difference in the Age of Empire.

Felix Krull and the Primordial Race

Unlike the many tormented characters that haunt Mann's fiction, Felix Krull is blissfully unproblematic, serenely confident of his innate superiority. As a result, he has no ambition to occupy any particular place in society; he feels no need to improve himself through education or to accomplish great deeds. He also has no desire to right social wrongs or to foment revolution; he likes himself and he likes the world just as it is. The very certainty of his sense of self gives him the freedom to live his life as a masquerade, to slip into new identities that fit as well as the clothing that he buys off the rack. From his early days as Schimmelpreester's "natural costume boy" (20),[15] Krull can wear any outfit and play any role, from liftboy to aristocrat. He changes names like some men change their neckties; he can alter his handwriting and is even willing to substitute the Marquis de Venosta's childhood memories for his own. He gladly exchanges his native Germany for Paris, and he cheerfully leaves Paris for his journey around the world. The one thing that he does not want is to get stuck in any particular place or in any given identity. As Krull explains, he wants the freedom "to live like a soldier but not as a soldier, figuratively but not literally, to be allowed in short to live symbolically" (101).[16]

One of the keys to Krull's talent for mimicry lies in his power of observation. Krull delights in the multitude of visual pleasures that the world has to offer, beginning, of course, with "the appealing face Nature granted me and the altogether winning appearance that my miserable clothing could not conceal" (103).[17] As an impoverished youth, Krull spends his evenings appreciating the finer things in life in shop windows, lingering for hours outside displays of fine furniture, elegant clothing, jewelry, flowers, perfumes, and fancy foods. "O scenes of the beautiful world! Never have you presented yourselves to more appreciative eyes" (75).[18]

Not surprisingly, Krull casts his discerning eyes on people as well as things, and—like Thomas Mann—is quick to assign them to national, ethnic, and racial categories. These include characters either explicitly identified as Jews or those given attributes suggesting possible Jewishness. Among the former is a Jewish banker, "one of the most hardhearted cutthroats who ever lured a harried and unwary businessman into his net" (49–50),[19] and his amply endowed wife, "who awesomely overflowed her jet-embroidered dress in every direction" (13).[20] Other questionable characters include Krull's hook-nosed godfather Schimmelpreester, a self-styled artist who designs the label for the family's rotgut champagne and allows himself to be called "'Herr Professor' though it is doubtful whether he was officially entitled to this distinction" (1).[21] Schimmelpreester gets Krull a job in a Parisian hotel run by his intimate friend Isaak Stürzli, who is known as the Rhinoceros because of the hideous wart on the end of his nose.[22] To these possibly Jewish characters one could add the clockmaker Jean-Pierre, a worn-out man of dubious morality whose eyes glitter and face quivers when he stares at Krull's stolen jewelry.

To identify such characters as negative Jewish stereotypes would be to be-labor the obvious; they take their place in the long lineup that extends from the Hagenströms to Chaim Breisacher, from Leo Naphta to Siegfried Aarenhold. Schimmelpreester, Stürzli, Jean-Pierre, the Jewish banker and his wife are not the only characters in *Felix Krull* who are either reduced to or associated with a particular ethnic or racial type, however. Krull receives early instruction in the "naughty school of love" from Rozsa, a "wild Eastern blossom ... born in Hungary, but of the most doubtful antecedents" (111–13).[23] He is befriended in Paris by Stanko, a Croat with "eyes of a Slavic cast" (128)[24] whose loud outfits give him an "ambiguously exotic appearance" (182).[25] Together with Stanko, Krull attends circus performances that feature the androgynous trapeze artist Andromache and the lion tamer Monsieur Mustafa, who "had gold rings in his ears, was naked to the waist, and wore wide red trousers and a red hat" (188).[26] Young Eleanor Twentyman develops a crush on Felix Krull, who enjoys the attention, as he explains, because "I have always had a weakness for the Anglo-Saxon type, of which she was a very notable example" (202).[27] During his nightly wanderings through Frankfurt, young Felix Krull passes by the brightly lit entryways to "music halls and vaudeville houses, in front of which, perhaps, some gigantic Negro ... towers fabulously" (72),[28] and upon arrival in Lisbon, Krull is taken to his hotel by a coachman with "pointed moustaches and slightly Negroid lips" (274).[29]

Two figures stand out among this catalog of exotic characters. One evening in Frankfurt, Krull sees a young man and woman step out onto a balcony, "obviously a brother and sister, possibly twins—they looked very much alike." They capture Krull's attention because they are extraordinarily good-looking and somewhat "foreign in appearance, dark-haired, they might have been Spanish, Portuguese, South American, Argentinian, Brazilian," speculates Krull, "but perhaps, on the other hand, they were Jews—I could not swear they were not and I would not on that account be shaken in my enthusiasm, for gently reared children of that race can be most attractive" (76).[30] In the uncompleted continuation of the novel, Krull was to have met up with this brother-sister pair in Argentina. Although he does not yet realize that they are the same individuals that he once saw in Frankfurt, he is told in Lisbon that they are the children of a Venezuelan woman married to an Argentinian who was killed in the revolution of 1890. She subsequently married the wealthy Consul Meyer, but her children bear the name of her first husband, Novaro. They now divide their time between Buenos Aires and a country estate, and it is there that Felix Krull, in his guise as the Marquis de Venosta, was to have met them again.[31]

Felix Krull unfortunately remained a fragment and we can only speculate on what might have happened. What matters in the novel that we do have is the ambiguous appeal of the exotic couple—appealing in part because of their physical beauty, but also appealing in their very ambiguity. They may be brother and sister, they may be lovers, they might even be both, given Mann's predilection for incestuous siblings that includes Siegfried and Sieglinde Aarenhold, Potiphar's parents Huya and Tuya, and Pope Gregorius of *The Holy Sinner*, who is not only the product of forbidden love between brother and sister, but also goes on to marry his mother. In these cases, incestuous sex is linked to the desire for exclusivity on the part of the partners: the Aarenhold twins enjoy each other before Sieglinde is to be defiled by the base goy; the Egyptian nobles keep sex in the family in a misguided attempt to elevate the status of their offspring, whom they also castrate; Sibylla rejects all suitors as inadequate and sleeps instead with her brother Wiligis. The couple in *Felix Krull* is distinguished because they are strikingly handsome and framed in a stagelike setting, but not because they represent a particular social class or easily identifiable ethnic type. They are not "white," as Viktor Mann would say, but exactly who they are and where they come from is left uncertain.

The indeterminate origin of the exotic couple in Frankfurt anticipates the racial mixture that Felix Krull encounters among the Portuguese. Professor Kuckuck has already informed Krull in the train about the various national and racial elements that have been absorbed into the Portuguese blood, and Krull sets off on his first morning in Lisbon brimming with "a vibrant curiosity about as yet unknown human types" (279).[32] What appeals to Krull about the Portuguese is not that they conform to a single, "pure" ethnic or racial type, but that their distinguishing feature is their very diversity. It is as if the human race, having begun with a common ancestor and then evolved into a series of diverse cultures and racial types around the world, has come back together in the polyglot Portuguese. As Krull notes, Professor Kuckuck's lessons in the train and his subsequent guided tour of the natural history museum have prepared him to receive "new impressions, racial impressions, for example, such as the experience of seeing the primordial race to which such interesting admixtures have been added at various periods, and which offers eye and heart a majestic image of racial dignity" (314).[33]

Felix Krull finds the distilled essence of the Portuguese racial type in Professor Kuckuck's wife and daughter. Kuckuck is a German who has been in Portugal for twenty-five years. He married Senhora Maria Pia, "a child of the country—*née* da Cruz . . . of ancient Portuguese stock" (259),[34] and together they have one daughter, Susanna or Zouzou. Krull encounters them for the first time by chance as he stops for tea at an outdoor café in Lisbon and is immediately drawn to the strikingly attractive pair. Zouzou bears an uncanny similarity to the Marquis de Venosta's Parisian girlfriend Zaza, although "transmuted from the Parisian to the exotic and Iberian" (282),[35] while Krull describes the mother as he might have labeled a striking animal species in Kuckuck's natural history museum: "'Ancient Iberian stock, presumably,' I thought to myself, 'therefore with a Celtic admixture. And every sort of Phoenician, Carthaginian, Roman, and Arabic strain may be involved'" (283).[36] Subsequent references to Senhor Maria Pia invariably describe her as an "august representative of her race" (345),[37] which has "some property of blood in it, a racial arrogance that had an animal quality about it, and was for that very reason exciting" (304).[38]

The Lisbon episode—and the novel as we have it—culminates in a visit to a bullfight. The mother appears in national costume for the event, an "ethnic masquerade" that startles and yet deeply impresses Krull, and although Zouzou wears no *mantilha,* Krull finds that "the charming cluster of dark curls at her temples was ethnic mark enough" (365).[39] As the excitement builds in the crowd and the ritual slaughter takes place in the bullring, Krull glances from Maria Pia's "surging breast to the living statue of man and animal" below, and finds that the distinction between the two is "rapidly dissolving, for more and more the stern and elemental person of this woman seemed to me one with the game of blood below" (371).[40] On the following morning, Krull pays one of his last visits to Professor Kuckuck and his family on the eve of his departure to Argentina. After lunch, Krull sneaks back to rendezvous with Zouzou in the garden and is in the midst of a passionate embrace when surprised by a sternly disapproving Maria Pia. The rebuke apparently masks an element of jealousy, for we suddenly jump to a rapturous scene in which Maria Pia and Krull are swept up in a "whirlwind of primordial forces" and born "into the realm of ecstasy . . . stormier than at the Iberian game of blood" (378).[41] This was the last paragraph of fiction that Mann ever published.

Far from diminishing in his final years, Mann's interest in racial distinctions remained as strong as it had been at the beginning of his career. While Professor Kuckuck's perorations about "the emergence of Being out of Nothingness, the awakening of Life out of Being, and the birth of Man" (265) add philosophical depth to what had begun as a comic picaresque novel, they also add geographical and historical specificity to the "ephemeral episode" of being, the "interlude between Nothingness and Nothingness" that constitutes

our world (266).[42] As Kuckuck describes it, Portugal is the site of ancient conquests, the hub of early modern exploration and colonization, and the current
home to postcolonial diversity. Within this setting, Felix Krull can admire the
racial diversity of the general Portuguese population and yield to the lure of
two women who embody the distilled essence of the racial type. Such women
have always been a source of both fear and fascination in Mann's fiction, although usually the negative predominates in a pattern that extends from the
voluptuous, dark-skinned Amra in *Little Louise,* who humiliates and destroys
her husband Jacoby, to the multiply marked prostitute who infects Adrian Leverkühn with her deadly disease. In a few cases, strong-willed individuals are
able to discipline their desires, resulting in the "austere happiness" of Klaus
Heinrich's marriage and the creative energy of Tonio Kröger and Gustav von
Aschenbach. In his final work, however, Mann allows his unproblematic protagonist unproblematic bliss in the arms of more than one racially marked
woman, from Rosza's "naughty school of love" to Maria Pia's cries of ecstasy.
These and other scenes—most notably Krull's night of debauchery as Madame
Diane Houplflé's "petit esclave stupide" (169; VII: 442)—can be read as homosexual fantasies displaced into fiction and transposed into heterosexual encounters; Mann did, after all, refer to *Felix Krull* as his homosexual novel.[43]
Homosexuality is, however, only one manifestation of a nether world that exists in opposition to bourgeois norms and includes other individuals and peoples marked by racial, religious, or geographical difference. Those who succumb to this world are usually destroyed; those who escape, like Joseph from
Mut-em-enet, do so at the cost of bitter renunciation. In the *Confessions of Felix Krull,* however, Mann for once granted his protagonist a dispensation from
suffering, unchaining the dogs in the basement and letting them howl with
pleasure.

Conclusion

As Thomas Mann neared the end of his life, he became increasingly convinced
that it was the end of an era as well. The sense of finality that had haunted him
while writing *Doctor Faustus* became more acute when it was complete. Unable
to conceive of a life without regular work, and yet plagued by minor ailments
and flagging energy that made it difficult to write, Mann struggled with de-
pression in his final years and at times felt that he was merely marking time
until death. As always, Mann felt that his personal sufferings were sympto-

matic of a larger historical change. Hitler was dead, Germany had been reduced to rubble, and a new world order had emerged, with the United States and the Soviet Union as the new superpowers and the fault lines of the Cold War running through the center of Germany and the heart of Berlin.

In 1941 Mann had already argued that the era of German nationalism, with its attendant tendency toward imperialism, would soon be a thing of the past. "Germany will be Europe, just as everything superior about Germany always was Europe," declares Mann, and, indeed, "even 'Europe' today is already a provincialism."[44] Mann's comments seem particularly prescient when viewed from the twenty-first-century perspective of Germany's integration into the European Union and its participation in a global network of commerce and communication. As the world becomes increasingly interconnected, boundaries between discrete nation-states become more porous, while at the same time, local communities struggle to assert their identity against the homogenizing trends of global culture. While nations and nationalism have by no means disappeared in the twenty-first century, they are pulled between local allegiances and global alliances in new ways. These recent developments highlight the fact that modern nation-states have not existed forever, and that even at the height of the nationalist era they had to negotiate their authority between local traditions and global concerns.

Thomas Mann's life coincided with the rise of the German nation-state to imperial grandeur and its fall to humiliating defeat and lasting shame. He reflected on the trajectory of German history in novels that stretched from *Buddenbrooks* to *Doctor Faustus* and in essays that ranged from the defiant nationalism of the *Reflections of a Nonpolitical Man* to the mea culpa of "Brother Hitler" and "Germany and the Germans." Not surprisingly, then, Mann has been viewed as the representative German writer of the twentieth century, an identification between the individual and the nation that Mann encouraged throughout his career. My effort in this book, in contrast, has been to place Mann in global context, while reminding readers as well of his rootedness in a particular local culture. Thomas Mann was born as a citizen of the recently united German Reich, but his father was a prominent member of an independent city-state at the hub of a northern European commercial network with roots stretching back to the late Middle Ages; his mother was born in Brazil as the result of new transatlantic trade routes. Mann married into a prominent family of assimilated German Jews, spent nearly two decades in exile, and died as an American citizen in Switzerland; his descendants are scattered around the globe.[45] As a result of his family origins and personal experiences, Mann was acutely attuned throughout his life to national, religious, and what he always described as racial difference, both at home and abroad. One of my main goals has been to place his relationship to Judaism and the Jews in the larger context of his attitude toward racial distinctions in general—a relationship complicated by his conflicted self-understanding as a bourgeois artist of mixed race and respectable pater familias with predominantly homosexual desires.

Mann does not always emerge as an appealing figure in the pages of this book. Mann's biographers must weigh his periodic racism and occasional anti-Semitic remarks—frequently but not always in the privacy of his diaries—against his role as a public intellectual tireless in his opposition to German fascism and other reactionary ideas and individuals. No one is perfect, and Mann's personal flaws have been exposed more than most by his life in the public eye and the posthumous revelations of his diaries, but I see no reason not to acknowledge his willingness to change with changing times and to admire his denunciation of nationalist bigotry and advocacy of cosmopolitan tolerance. As a literary critic, however, my focus has been somewhat different. Rather than looking for isolated incidents in Mann's life that place him either in flattering or unflattering light, I have been interested in pervasive patterns within his literary works. These patterns reveal, on the one hand, a dark pool of tempting poison that seeps by osmosis from one stigmatized category to the next—from homosexuals to blacks to Jews to Nazis, from Eastern Europe to South America, from Egypt to Portugal—and on the other, a fluctuation between self-aggrandizement and self-abasement that can, in the blink of an eye, turn stigmatized others into signs of self-hatred, the land of the center into a cesspool of evil.

Mann thinks dialectically but without synthesis, both within particular works and over the course of time: Settembrini advances an argument and Naphta not only opposes it, but undermines it from within; Mann claims that he is *Litterat* in 1910, condemns "civilization's literary man" in 1915, and concedes in 1918 that he is a literary man after all, waging a futile war with words against literature. Mann embeds the negative dialectics of his intellectual arguments in fictional texts with fully realized characters and a wealth of imaginative detail. As a result, philosophical approaches to his fiction are frustrated in two distinct ways: first, the very instability of the dialectical arguments make it difficult or impossible to pin Mann down to a particular point of view—the perennial controversy regarding the status of the italicized lesson that Hans Castorp learns in the snowstorm in relation to *The Magic Mountain*'s inconclusive conclusion is a case in point. Second, the identification of the threatening underworld with Schopenhauer's Will or Nietzsche's Dionysus blanches figurative richness into philosophical abstraction. The lasting appeal of Mann's fiction lies in its subtlety of detail, its rich web of allusions, and the shimmering instability of its surface; in what it reveals and conceals about the intimate desires and fears of its author; and in its seismographic sensitivity to the preoccupations and prejudices of the German nation in the Age of Empire.

Notes

Chapter One

1. Reich-Ranicki, "Was halten Sie von Thomas Mann?" in Reich-Ranicki, *Thomas Mann und die Seinen*, 264–70. Results of the original survey appeared in *Text + Kritik*, ed. Arnold, "Deutsche Schriftsteller über Thomas Mann."

2. *Die Manns: Ein Jahrhundertroman*, directed by Heinrich Breloer, 2002.

3. Krüll, *Im Netz der Zauberer*. See also Roggenkamp, *Erika Mann*, for a relentlessly critical assault on Mann.

4. Harpprecht, *Thomas Mann*.

5. Sene, "Johann Ludwig Hermann Bruhns." See also Krüll, *Im Netz der Zauberer*, 22–42.

6. "Im Urwalde, nahe dem Atlantischen Ozean, südlich des Äquators, war es, wo Dodo das Licht der Welt erblickte" (Julia Mann, "Aus Dodos Kindheit," 7).

7. "am 14. August 1851, als das Ehepaar von einer seiner Besitzungen zur anderen in der Gegend von Angra durch Tropenwald reiste—die Herrin im Tragstuhl, der Herr zu Pferde, Sklaven voran und im Nachtrab—, gab es einen plötzlichen Halt. Die Herrin mußte schnell unter die Bäume gebettet werden. Schwarze Frauen stürzten herzu, und bald darauf hielten sie dem Herren ein Töchterchen entgegen, indes droben Papageien kreischten, neugierige Affen lugten und winzige Kolibris wie bunte Strahlen durch den Schatten zuckten. Die Eltern nannten die Kleine zärtlich "Dodo," und man taufte sie Julia. Julia da Silva Bruhns, das war unsere Mutter" (Viktor Mann, *Wir waren fünf*, 17).

8. "die kontinentale Hegemonie Deutschlands unter Bismarck und die Hochblüte des britischen Imperiums unter Viktoria" ("Meine Zeit," *Gesammelte Werke* XI: 304). Wherever possible I quote from the *Große kommentierte Frankfurter Ausgabe* of Thomas Mann's works, giving the volume number in Arabic numerals followed by the page number. In cases where the new edition is not yet available, I quote from Mann's thirteen-volume *Gesammelte Werke*, giving the volume number as here in Roman numerals followed by the page number. Unless otherwise noted, all translations are my own.

9. Sene, "Johann Ludwig Hermann Bruhns," 102.

10. Ibid., 102.

11. Jens and Jens, *Auf der Suche*, 66–87. Klaus Mann imagines the news of his uncle's death reaching Munich in a dramatic scene in his autobiography (*Der Wendepunkt*, 52; *The Turning Point*, 20). Mann's children were told that Erik Pringsheim had fallen off his horse; Hedwig Pringsheim (Mann's mother-in-law) suspected that he had been murdered by his wife (*Auf der Suche*, 84).

12. Mann, *Tagebücher,* March 19, 1955; see commentary to this entry in *Tagebücher 1953–55,* 737–38. Subsequent references to Mann's diary entries are listed with the abbreviation "Tb" followed by the date.

13. Anna accompanied the children to Lübeck after their mother died, but was then sent back to Brazil by Bruhns and given her freedom. Julia describes the heart-rending departure of Anna from her wards in Lübeck in her memoires (Julia Mann, "Aus Dodos Kindheit," 17–18).

14. "rein nordischer Abkunft . . . eine alte Kolonialfamilie . . . streng katholisch und allesamt 'Weiße' und 'Freie' " (Viktor Mann, *Wir waren fünf,* 16).

15. Sene, "Johann Ludwig Hermann Bruhns," 105–6.

16. Julia Mann, "Aus Dodos Kindheit," 10.

17. "von der paradiesischen Schönheit der Bucht von Rio, von Giftschlangen, die sich auf der Pflanzung ihres Vaters zeigten und von Negersklaven mit Stöcken erschlagen wurden." "Das Bild der Mutter," *Gesammlte Werke,* XI: 421.

18. "Wann kamen denn nu Ludwig sin lütten Swatten?" Julia Mann, "Aus Dodos Kindheit," 17.

19. "der Anblick der bunt gekleideten Negerin mit den fünf tiefbraun gebrannten Kindern in gelbem Nanking und weißen Panamahüten [brachte] die ganze Straßenjugend auf die Beine" (ibid., 19).

20. "drüben" (Viktor Mann, *Wir waren fünf,* 15).

21. Klaus Mann, *The Turning Point,* x.

22. Ibid., xi.

23. Frido Mann, *Brasa;* he recounts his visits to Brazil and efforts to establish a cultural center in Paraty in his autobiography, *Achterbahn,* 308–47.

24. Heinrich Mann, *In einer Familie* (1894).

25. Thomas to Heinrich Mann, Dec. 5, 1905: "Mama tells me that you are working on a new novel whose beginning is based on Mama's memoires" (Ich höre von Mama, daß Dich ein neuer Roman beschäftigt, dessen Anfang aus Mama's Memoiren gemacht ist) (21: 336).

26. "was wir im Leben sein werden, entscheidet das Blut, welches wir bei unserer Geburt mitbekommen" (Heinrich Mann, *Zwischen den Rassen,* 47).

27. "Rassen . . . die germanische und die lateinische" (ibid., 141).

28. *Death in Venice,* 200 ("die Merkmale fremder Rasse" 2.1: 508). Mann noted in a letter to Heinrich that he found it difficult to judge *Zwischen den Rassen* by distanced aesthetic criteria because it entranced him "primarily as a personal document and confession" ("vorwiegend als persönliches Dokument und Bekenntnis") (June 7, 1907, 21: 375).

29. Klaus Mann, *The Turning Point,* xi.

30. "ganz unten auf der Landkarte" (2.1: 247).

31. On the link between Freudian psychoanalysis and colonialism see Khanna, *Dark Continents.*

32. On these and other German writers who wrote about life in the colonies, see Friedrichsmeyer, Lennox, and Zantop, *The Imperialist Imagination.*

33. "Pfeilspitze" (Viktor Mann, *Wir waren fünf,* 89).

34. "Indianergeschichten" ("On Myself," XIII: 129).

35. "Wüstenpoesie" ("Zur jüdischen Frage," 15.1: 428).

36. "der Typus des durchaus vergnügten Juden" ("Zur jüdischen Frage," 15.1: 430).

37. "Leugnet die Juden als 'Volk.' 'Rasse' ist vollends kompromittiert. Wie soll man sie nennen? Denn irgend etwas anderes ist es mit ihnen und nicht nur Mediterranes. Ist dies Erlebnis Anti-Semitismus? Heine, Kerr, Harden, Kraus bis zu dem fascistischen Typ Goldberg—es ist doch *ein* Geblüt" (Tb, Oct. 27, 1945). Mann refers to the poet Heinrich Heine, the critic Alfred Kerr, the editor Maximilian Harden, the satirist Karl Kraus, and the Orientalist Oskar Goldberg.

38. Debates about Mann and the Jews began during his lifetime and have continued ever since. Stern offers a succinct overview in "Thomas Mann und die jüdische Welt" with references for further reading. Noteworthy among older criticism is Loewenstein's balanced essay "Thomas Mann zur jüdischen Frage" and Schwarz's important study "Die jüdischen Gestalten in *Doktor Faustus.*" Darmaun explores Mann's attitude toward Jews and his depiction of them in all phases of his career from an evenhanded perspective (*Thomas Mann*); see also the contributions to the more recent volume *Thomas Mann und das Judentum* (ed. Dierks and Wimmer). Angress-Klüger's critique "Jewish Characters in Thomas Mann's Fiction" takes a more aggressive stance and has had a lasting impact on the field. Similarly critical assessments of Mann can be found in Brenner, "Beyond Naphta"; Harpprecht, *Thomas Mann;* Roggenkamp, *Erika Mann;* and Elsaghe, *Die imaginäre Nation* and *Thomas Mann und die kleinen Unterschiede,* 141–258. Mann's strongest defenders against the charge of anti-Semitism include Vaget, "*Sang réservé* in Deutschland" and "Von hoffnungslos anderer Art," and Kurzke, *Thomas Mann: Life,* 187–214.

39. See Reich-Ranicki, "Die ungeschminkte Wahrheit" (The Unvarnished Truth), in *Thomas Mann,* 29–50.

40. Mendelssohn, "Vorbemerkungen," xiii–xiv; the original quotation is in English. On Mann's furtiveness while writing in his diary, see ibid., ix.

41. "Heitere Entdeckungen dann, in Gottes Namen. Es kenne mich die Welt, aber erst, wenn alles tot ist" (Tb, Oct. 13, 1950).

42. "Es ist gar zu unglaubwürdig albern und verrückt" (Tb, Apr. 1, 1933).

43. "schauderhaft, höchst schauderhaft" (Tb, Sept. 15, 1935).

44. "grotesk und blödsinnig" (Tb, Nov. 15, 1935).

45. "Ankündigung riesiger Propaganda Aktion gegen die Juden in ganz Deutschland!" "Idiotismus. Sicher hat das Volk genug" (Tb, Nov. 22, 1938).

46. "entsetzliche Zunahme der Juden-Massacres in Europa" (Tb, July 9, 1944).

47. "die ungeheure Schande" (Tb, Apr. 27, 1945).

48. "Die deutschen KZ," *Essays,* 6: 11–13.

49. On Mann's friendship with Bruno Walter—one of the very few individuals outside his immediate family that Mann addressed with the familiar "du"—see Vaget, *Seelenzauber,* 241–69.

50. Tb, Jan. 21, 1942.

51. For instance, Mann notes receiving a letter from a Jewish couple on January 24, 1945, that reads in part: "After all the horrors that have befallen the German Jews by the German people, it seems to me unspeakably mysterious and meaningful that this book was written by a non-Jewish German. . . . There are no words to thank you for it—it is overwhelming" (Nach allem Grauenhaften, was den deutschen Juden vom deutschen Volk widerfuhr, scheint es mir unsagbar geheimnisvoll und vieldeutig, daß dieses Buch von einem deutschen Nichtjuden geschrieben wurde . . . Es gibt gar keine Worte dafür zu danken—es ist überwältigend) (Cited from the commentary to the *Tagebücher 1944–46*, 562–63).

52. See for instance his "Statement zum Palestine White Paper" (in *Tagebücher 1944–46*, 798–801); "Zum Problem des Antisemitismus" (XIII: 479–90); "An Enduring People" (XIII: 502–12).

53. "Amerikaner von Geburt, hat deutsches, brasilianisches, jüdisches und schweizerisches Blut" (Tb, Aug. 31, 1940).

54. "Herkunft und Blutzusammensetzung" (Tb, Apr. 6, 1953).

55. "Hübscher junger Schuhputzer mexikanischen Typs" (Tb, Feb. 22, 1940).

56. "junger Eskimo-Jäger von kindlicher Schönheit" (Tb, Dec. 17, 1934).

57. "Der Junge, wahrscheinlich Philippino-Race, reizend" (Tb, Jan. 3, 1941).

58. "Jüngling . . . jüdisch, recht feinen Typs . . . zart und anziehend" (Tb, Apr. 16, 1933).

59. "Im Speisewagen junger Negro-Waiter . . . von ausnehmend angenehmen Gesichtszügen, intelligenten Manieren, schlanker Figur. Die Rasse hat sonst nie Anziehung für mich" (Tb, Aug. 29, 1950).

60. "Olympia-Reportagen aus Berlin . . . vom Verlauf des sensationellen 100 m-Laufs, in dem zwei amerikanische *Neger* siegten. Hübsch!" (Tb, Aug. 3, 1936).

61. Tb, June 23, 1938.

62. "Dann hatten wir—damals konnte man das immerhin haben—ein schwarzes *couple*" (Katia Mann, *Meine ungeschriebenen Memoiren,* 131).

63. Klaus Mann, *The Turning Point,* 46–52; *Der Wendepunkt,* 93–101.

64. Jens and Jens, *Frau Thomas Mann,* 229.

65. "Eintritt des neuen Neger-Couples aus Texas" (Tb, Aug. 16, 1942).

66. "Eintritt der neuen Negresse" (Tb, July 12, 1943).

67. "Day off der Schwarzen" (Tb, Oct. 24, 1948).

68. "Rückkehr der Joe. Ihr nigger wird das hospital zu ernstlicher Kur aufsuchen" (Tb, Aug. 14, 1948).

69. "Beschluß der Gelben, noch zu bleiben" (Tb, July 1, 1946).

70. "Verabschiedung von den Gelben, die das Haus hüten" (Tb, Apr. 22, 1947).

71. Harpprecht, *Thomas Mann,* 1029.

72. "Erheiterung über die Radio-Nummer des Mannes mit dem Neger-Diener Rochester" (Tb, Jan. 11, 1948).

73. "Die Negerin Leona krank" (Tb, Mar. 20, 1945).

74. "Die Negerin Jo besucht ihren Mann im Gefängnis" (Tb, Feb. 9, 1947).

75. "Die schwarze Joe . . . kehrt zurück" (Tb, Aug. 28, 1948).

76. See Heinrich Mann's autobiographical novella *Die beiden Gesichter*, in which he recalls the great respect with which his father was regarded in Lübeck (in *Das Kind*, 14–18; esp. 15).

77. "Begegnung am Lift mit dem jüdischen jungen Mädchen" (Tb, Mar. 2, 1934).

78. "Der Hausherr feminine, ein junger Köllner offenbar sein Geliebter" (Tb, Apr. 5, 1941).

79. "Netter junger Mann, den Erika als 'schwul' rekogniszierte" (Tb, Nov. 5, 1950).

80. "Ins Schauspielhaus, Matinee des Mimiker-Tänzers Marceau. . . . Selbstverständlich homosexuell" (Tb, Jan. 17, 1954).

81. Tb, Jan. 4, 1949.

82. "Zum Abendessen Dr. Valentiener . . . wahrscheinlich homosexuell" (Tb, Sept. 25, 1948).

83. "Zum Thee Herr *Brandt* aus Berlin . . . etwas jüdisch" (Tb, Nov. 20, 1935).

84. "Unten Begrüßung mit dem Hausherrn, ursprünglich Mediziner, jetzt Geschäftsmann . . . wohl Jude" (Tb, Jan. 10, 1936).

85. "Er scheint kein Jude zu sein" (Tb, Feb. 10, 1950).

86. "Tragikomischer Brief eines Juden Mayer in New York; jüdisches Familienschicksal, typisch" (Tb, July 7, 1940).

87. "Unerschöpfliches, nicht abzuschließendes Gespräch über den verbrecherischen und ekelhaften Wahnsinn, die sadistischen Krankheitstypen der Machthaber" (Tb, Mar. 27, 1933).

88. "Fuldas Klagen und jüdische Verzweiflung tragikomisch" (Tb, Apr. 1, 1933). See also commentary to *Tagebücher 1951–52*, 495.

89. "höchst widerwärtigen Fall Auerbach . . . Andererseits jüdische Über-Empfindlichkeit und Deckung der Talentlosigkeit durch Judentum. Nicht jede schlechte Kritik erklärt sich aus Antisemitismus" (Tb, Sept. 4, 1952). See also commentary to *Tagebücher 1951–52*, 694.

90. "An Jakob Wassermann," 15.1: 354–57; esp. 357. See also Darmaun on this exchange (*Thomas Mann*, 123–24).

91. "die mir wie eh' und je widerstehen" (Tb, Apr. 30, 1934).

92. "Allzu ausschließlich jüdischer Kreis" (Tb, Jan. 22, 1943).

93. "Jüdische Buffet Dinner Party bei Singers, gräßlich" (Tb, Nov. 15, 1947).

94. "Über das witzelnde Judentum à la Schlamm, brilliant, bereits in amerikanischem Slang" (Tb, June 17, 1942).

95. "übermütige und vergiftende Nietzsche-Vermauschelung" (Tb, Apr. 10, 1933; see also commentary to *Tagebücher 1944–46*, 383–84). According to Katia Mann, Mann's lifelong hatred of Alfred Kerr stemmed from the fact that Kerr had proposed to her before Mann did (*Meine ungeschriebenen Memoiren*, 20). See also Kurzke, *Thomas Mann: Life*, 198–205.

96. "Scheußliche Schmähkarte unter der Post, jüdelnd" (Tb, Sept. 6, 1940).

97. "Schrieb vormittags energischen Brief an Frank über das infame jüdische Cliquen-Wesen beim 'Tagebuch' (Kestner—Döblin)" (Tb, May 23, 1937). On the background for Mann's outburst, see commentary to *Tagebücher 1937–39*, 590–91.

98. "indem sie einen Bluts- und Cliquen-Genossen mit unverschämter Ostentation gegen mich, den dummen Goi, auf den Schild erhebt" (cited from *Tagebücher 1937–39*, notes, 590–91).

99. "Die Juden haben eben mehr Wahrheitssinn, ihr Gehirn ist unverkleistert von Mythus" (Tb, Aug. 5, 1934).

100. "Wahrhaftig, die deutsche Literatur braucht die Juden!" (Tb, Jan. 22, 1938).

101. "der seine halbwahren, amüsanten Reden über die unerträgliche Hegemonie führte, die vor Hitler die Juden in Deutschland ausgeübt haben" (Tb, Mar. 19, 1936).

102. "Die Revolte gegen das Jüdische hätte gewissermaßen mein Verständnis, wenn nicht der Wegfall der Kontrolle des Deutschen durch den jüdischen Geist für jenes so bedenklich und das Deutschtum nicht so dumm ware, meinen Typus mit in den selben Topf zu werfen und mich mit auszutreiben" (Tb, Apr. 20, 1933).

103. "der Haß von Vereinfachten gegen die Nüance" (ibid.).

104. "Diese Revolution rühmt sich ihrer Unblutigkeit, ist aber dabei die Haßerfüllteste und mordlustigste, die je da war. Ihr ganzes Wesen ist . . . Haß, Ressentiment, Rache, Gemeinheit" (ibid.).

105. Goldhagen, *Hitler's Willing Executioners*, 81. In his sensational and controversial study, Goldhagen argues that the Holocaust occurred because vast majority of Germans were eliminationist anti-Semites, that is, people who hated the Jews so much that they wanted to kill them. Browning argues instead that most of the German perpetrators were ordinary Germans in extraordinary circumstances, and reminds us that not all anti-Semites were the same (*Ordinary Men*). Browning's argument is in some ways more disturbing, because it suggests that virtually anyone, and not just a rabid ideologue, can be coerced into committing atrocities under the right conditions.

106. "Bruder Hitler" was written in the spring and summer of 1938. It was published in English as "That man is my brother" in March 1939 (*Essays* 4: 432–34).

107. "Als Philo- oder Antisemit also präsentiert sich der Schriftsteller Thomas Mann . . . genau so weit, wie er sich brüstet oder schämt, wie er sich selbst liebt oder verachtet" (Detering, *"Juden,"* 100).

108. Angress-Klüger could still make this claim with some justification in 1990 ("Jewish Characters," 169), but Elsaghe's repeated invocations of a conspiracy theory do not ring true (*Die imaginäre Nation*, 13; *Thomas Mann*, 2–3).

109. Angress-Klüger, "Jewish Characters," 169.

110. "dies an äußerer Dramatik recht reichlich ist für ein Menschenleben" ("Meine Zeit," XI: 305).

111. Thomas Mann, *Über mich selbst*.

112. "weil ihr einziger Reiz darin besteht, mein Leben, wie in den Faustus hineinzulegen" (Tb, Oct. 9, 1951).

113. "das wunderliche und äußerst persönliche Werk" (Tb, Sept. 13, 1943).

114. "ein radikales Bekenntnis" (Tb, Jan. 1, 1946).

115. "Im Ganzen hege ich große Scheu vor dem direkt Autobiographischen, das mir als schwierigste, fast unlösbar schwierige Aufgabe für den literarischen Takt erscheint" (Mann to Alexander M. Frey, Jan. 19, 1952, *Briefe* 3: 240).

116. "geringe Neigung oder gar keine, Ihnen einen autobiographischen Vortrag zu halten" (XI: 302).

117. Mann, "Goethe und Tolstoi," 15.1: 382–83.

118. Mann, "Dem Dichter zu Ehren." See commentary to this essay in *Essays* 5: 345–46.

119. According to Katia Mann, Thomas Mann received a review copy of Adorno and Horkheimer's *Dialectic of Enlightenment* from the *New York Times*. "Du, davon verstehe ich gar nichts" (I can't understand a word), Mann allegedly said to Golo, who dutifully wrote the review that was published under his father's name (*Meine ungeschriebenen Memoiren*, 160–61).

120. "bedenklich anmutende Montage-Technik . . . im Aufmontieren von faktischen, historischen, persönlichen, ja literarischen Gegebenheiten" (Entstehung, XI: 165). Translation substantially modified from *Story of a Novel*, 32.

121. "in einer Art von höherem Abschreiben" (Mann to Adorno, Dec. 30, 1945, *Briefe* 2: 470).

122. "Bruchstücke einer groen Konfession" (Goethe, *Dichtung und Wahrheit*, book 7; in *Werke* 9: 283). "Alles, was tief ist, liebt die Maske" (Nietzsche, *Jenseits von Gut und Böse*, section 40; in *Werke* 3: 49).

123. "gerade als ob ich es je mit einem andern 'Stoff' zu tun gehabt hätte, als mit meinem eigenen Leben. Wer ist ein Dichter? Der, dessen Leben symbolish ist" (Mann, "Über Königliche Hoheit II," 14.1: 242).

124. "In mir lebt der Glaube, daß ich nur von mir zu erzählen brauche, um auch der Zeit, der Allgemeinheit die Zunge zu lösen" (ibid., 14.1: 242).

125. "über das Wesen einer freilich unagitatorischen und nur seismographischanzeigenden Empfindlichkeit, die mir als eine andere, stillere und indirektere Form politischen Wissens erscheinen wollte" (Mann, "Lebensabriss," *Essays* 3: 210).

126. *Death in Venice*, 202. "eine geheime Verwandtschaft, ja Übereinstimmung zwischen dem persönlichen Schicksal seines Urhebers und dem allgemeinen des mitlebenden Geschlechtes" (Mann, *Der Tod in Venedig*, 2.1: 510).

127. Mann, *The Story of a Novel*, 143. "Der Dichter (und auch der Philosoph) als Melde-Instrument, Seismograph, Medium der Empfindlichkeit, ohne klares Wissen von dieser seiner organischen Funktion und darum verkehrter Urteile nebenher durchaus fähig,—es scheint mir die einzig richtige Perspektive" ("Entstehung," XI: 240).

128. "Schriftstellertum ist Sensitivität und ein Voransein um 5 bis 10 Jahre" (Tb, Sept. 5, 1933).

129. For an authoritative survey of Nietzsche's influence on early twentieth-century German thought, see Aschheim, *The Nietzsche Legacy*.

130. "im Vergleich mit uns [ist] eigentlich alles Übrige minderwerthig" (Mann to Heinrich Mann, Jan. 8, 1904; 21: 262; italics in original).

131. "das Verhängnis Deutschlands. . . . Es ist nicht Größenwahn, sondern nur Bedürfnis und Gewohnheit intimer Anschauung, wenn ich dies Verhängnis längst in meinem Bruder und mir symbolisiert und personifiziert sehe" (Mann to Ernst Bertram, Nov. 25, 1916; 22: 163).

132. "Wo ich bin, ist Deutschland." Quoted from the commentary to "Bruder Hitler," in *Essays* 4: 440.

133. Habermas, *Structural Transformation*, 1–26.

134. Landes, *Women and the Public Sphere*.

135. "Ich erwachte z. B. eines Morgens mit dem Entschluß, heute ein achtzehn-jähriger Prinz namens Karl zu sein. Ich kleidete mich in eine gewisse liebenswürdige Hoheit und ging umher, stolz und glücklich mit dem Geheimnis meiner Würde" (Mann, "Kinderspiele," 14.1: 80). Mann incorporated the same passage almost verbatim into *Felix Krull* (book 1, chap. 2).

136. On the ideological origins of fascist ideology out of a certain strain of German romanticism see Mosse, *The Crisis of German Ideology*.

137. On these three thinkers see Stern, *Politics of Cultural Despair;* on the ideological abuse of the Faust myth by German nationalists, see Schwerte, *Faust und das Faustische.*

138. "Das Volk spricht gar nicht, wann die einzelnen Individuen sprechen, aus denen das Volk besteht. Das Volk spricht nur dann, wann die Volkheit … in den Individuen zu Worte kommt, wann das Bewußtsein der allen Einzelnen gemeinsamen Grund- und Stammnatur wach [wird]" (Lagarde, *Deutsche Schriften,* 118).

139. Norton, *Secret Germany,* 527.

140. On this work see ibid., 671–74.

141. Fest, *Hitler,* 3–9.

142. "eine unsäglich inferiore, aber massenwirksame Beredsamkeit" ("Bruder Hitler," *Essays* 4: 306).

143. Mosse, *Nationalization of the Masses.*

144. Anderson, *Imagined Communities.*

145. Geary, *The Myth of Nations;* Peterson, *History, Fiction, and Germany.*

146. Hobsbawm, "Introduction."

147. Applegate, *A Nation of Provincials,* 13.

148. Confino, *Nation as Local Metaphor,* 188, 184–85.

149. Cited in Gossman, *Basel,* 411.

150. Gossman, *Basel,* 244.

151. "die antisemitischen Schreihälse des Landes zu verweisen" (Nietzsche, *Werke* 3: 164).

152. See Holub, "Nietzsche's Colonialist Imagination," for a nuanced account of Nietzsche's attitudes toward German imperialism and colonialism.

153. See Mohler (*Die konservative Revolution*) and Breuer (*Anatomie*) on Germany's "Conservative Revolution." Gossman notes parallels between the cities of the Rhine basin and the Hanseatic cities on the North and Baltic Seas (*Basel,* 7–8).

154. *Reflections of a Nonpolitical Man,* 98; "von dem Niedergange eines dortigen Handelshauses inmitten der deutschen Siegesprosperität" (13.1: 152). References to the English translation hereafter cited in the text.

155. "das Zeitalter der Hansa, das Zeitalter der Städte, es war ein reines Kulturzeital-ter, kein politisches" (13.1: 125).

156. "deutsche Menschlichkeit, Freiheit und Bildung" (13.1: 150).

157. "der Triumph der 'Realpolitik,' die Härtung und Verhärtung Deutschlands zum 'Reich' . . . Emanzipation und Ausbeutung; Macht, Macht, Macht!" (13.1: 151).

158. Zantop, *Colonial Fantasies,* 17–30.

159. On Germany's colonial ambitions in the First World War see Fischer, *Germany's Aims;* the original German title of the book was *Griff nach der Weltmacht* (The Grasp for World Power). On German imperialism see Wehler, *Bismarck und der Imperialismus;* Graichen and Gründer, *Deutsche Kolonien;* and Honold and Scherpe, *Mit Deutschland.*

160. Belgum, *Popularizing the Nation,* 142–82; Lindtke, *Die Stadt der Buddenbrooks,* 21.

161. Honold and Scherpe, *Mit Deutschland;* Penny and Bunzl, *Worldly Provincialism.*

162. Badenberg, "Spiel um Kamerun" and "Usambara-Kaffee."

163. Forster, *Reise um die Welt.* On early German racial theory see Zantop, *Colonial Fantasies,* 66–80; Eze, *Race and the Enlightenment;* Eigen Figal, *Heredity;* and Eigen and Larrimore, *German Invention of Race.*

164. Poliakov, *The Aryan Myth.*

165. Said, *Orientalism,* 204.

166. Although the term "Jewish question" (Judenfrage) had already been used in eighteenth-century Britain, it began to play a central role in cultural and religious debates in Germany with Karl Marx's *Zur Judenfrage* (1844), written in response to Bruno Bauer's *Die Judenfrage* (1843) (Auerbach, *The "Jewish Question,"* ix–xi). The term is often placed in quotation marks because of its close link with anti-Semitism, presenting as it does the Jews as a "question" or "problem" that must be solved rather than as an integral component of German or European society (see Goldhagen, *Hitler's Willing Executioners,* 63–64). Elon offers a highly readable account of the changing fortunes of Jews in Germany from the eighteenth century to 1933 (*Pity of It All*). Robertson provides an excellent survey in *The "Jewish Question."*

167. See Elon for a general overview of Jewish assimilation from the late eighteenth to the early twentieth century (*Pity of It All*). See also Robertson, *The "Jewish Question,"* 233–378.

168. Goldhagen, *Hitler's Willing Executioners,* 80–81.

169. On the influx of eastern European Jews into Western Europe and the prejudice they inspired see Aschheim, *Brothers and Strangers;* Elon, *Pity of It All,* 270–73.

170. Hitler, *Mein Kampf,* 52, 56.

171. Elon, *Pity of It All,* 149–83, 205; Robertson, *The "Jewish Question,"* 53–54.

172. Van Rahden, *Jews and Other Germans.*

173. Weininger, *Sex and Character,* 329–30. See Gilman, *Jewish Self-Hatred;* and Luft, *Eros and Inwardness,* 45–88.

174. On Jews as effeminate see Sombart, *Die deutschen Männer,* 229; Le Rider, *Modernity,* 165–83; Robertson, *The "Jewish Question,"* 296–302; and Boyarin, *Unheroic Conduct,* 1–29. On Jews as blacks see Poliakov, *The Aryan Myth,* 7–8; Gilman, *Franz Kafka,* 108; Gilman, *Difference and Pathology,* 30–35.

175. Gilman, *Franz Kafka,* 198.

176. Wehler, *The German Empire*, 90–94.

177. McClintock, *Imperial Leather*, 5, 61.

178. On Jewish assimilation in relation to colonial mimicry see Boyarin, *Unheroic Conduct*, 226.

179. Joch, "Koloniales in der Karikatur," 72–73.

180. In this my work differs from Elsaghe's studies of Thomas Mann. Both of his books (*Die imaginäre Nation* and *Thomas Mann*) are arranged thematically rather than chronologically.

Chapter Two

1. Said makes the shift in *Culture and Imperialism* from a discussion of Orientalism more narrowly defined in his book of that name to the broader opposition between the imperial powers and their colonies. See also Zantop on "Occidentalisms-Orientalisms" in *Colonial Fantasies*, 14–16.

2. Girard, *Deceit, Desire, and the Novel*, 14.

3. Freud, *Civilization and Its Discontents*, 72. Elsaghe bases his study *Thomas Mann und die kleinen Unterschiede* on Freud's concept. He focuses on four stigmatized groups in Mann's fiction: the Swiss, Catholics, Jews, and women writers.

4. Mann, *Buddenbrooks*, trans. John E. Woods, 563. Subsequent references to this edition given parenthetically in the text, with the original German in footnotes. " 'Ich bin geworden wie ich bin . . . weil ich nicht werden wollte wie du. Wenn ich dich innerlich gemieden habe, so geschah es, weil ich mich vor dir hüten muß, weil dein Sein und Wesen eine Gefahr für mich ist' " (1.1: 638).

5. Mann based the family history of the Buddenbrooks closely on his own, although with minor differences. See the "Materialien und Dokumente" in 1.2: 571–683, as well as the "Stellenkommentar" for comments on specific passages (1.2: 229–417). See Boa for a brief discussion of the cultural geography of *Buddenbrooks* in relation to contemporary *Heimatkunst* ("Global Intimations," 22–24).

6. "Laden" (1.1: 52).

7. "man befindet sich eben in einem fremden Lande" (1.1: 337).

8. "in einem ungebildeten Bierdialekt" (1.1: 423).

9. "etwas Besonderes, etwas Ausländisches" (1.1: 141).

10. "so blond wie möglich" (1.1: 132).

11. "Es ist gar nicht der Mann. Es ist die Stadt" (1.1: 423).

12. "Preußenerfindung. . . . Und unsere Selbständigkeit? Und unsere Unabhängigkeit?" (1.1: 44).

13. Lindtke, *Die Stadt der Buddenbrooks*, 24. On the historical setting of the novel see also Vogt, *Thomas Mann*, 29–39; Swales, *Buddenbrooks*, 89–103; and Sagave, "Zur Geschichtlichkeit."

14. "Die treue Preußin" (1.1: 369).

15. "Was geht Sie das eigentlich an? Sie sind ja gar kein Preuße" (1.1: 151).

16. "Schranken, Abstand, Aristokratie—hier wie dort!" (1.1: 151).

17. "Je, Herr Kunsel, denn wull wi noch een" (1.1: 209).

18. "nicht ohne Genugtuung auf das reiche Frankfurt, das seinen Glauben an Oesterreich bezahlen mußte, indem es aufhörte, eine freie Stadt zu sein" (1.1: 480).

19. "Erschütterungen und Umwälzungen des kaum beendeten Krieges" (1.1: 614).

20. "eine große Stadt des geeinten Vaterlandes" (1.1: 705).

21. "Herangewachsen in der Luft eines kriegerisch siegreichen und verjüngten Vaterlands, huldigte man Sitten von rauher Männlichkeit" (1.1: 793).

22. "als outlaws und fremdartige Sonderlinge" (1.1: 793).

23. "Staat im Staate . . . preußische Dienststrammheit . . . Autorität, Pflicht, Macht, Dienst, Carrière" (1.1: 796).

24. Bloch refers to Germany as "the classic land of dissimultaneity" (*das klassische Land der Ungleichzeitigkeit*) in his efforts to trace the origins of German fascism (*Erbschaft dieser Zeit*, 113) and Vogt borrows the term in his discussion of *Buddenbrooks* (*Thomas Mann*, 38). Swales also provides insightful comments about conflict between the contrasting worlds of Lübeck and Berlin (*Buddenbrooks*, 89–103).

25. "Thränen-Trieschke aus Berlin" (1.1: 309).

26. "Er hielt von allen Lehrern am meisten auf Disziplin, musterte die Front der strammstehenden Schüler mit kritischem Blick und verlangte kurze und scharfe Antworten" (1.1: 810).

27. "'Wir müssen zusammenhalten!' pflegte er zu schlechten Schülern zu sagen, indem er sie am Arme packte. 'Die Sozialdemokratie steht vor der Thür!'" (1.1: 822).

28. "einen ölig-sprituösen Geruch, wo er ging und stand, und Einige sagten, er tränke Petroleum" (1.1: 822).

29. Lindke lists the population of the inner city of Lübeck as 24,000 in 1835 and 30,500 in 1867, while noting that Hamburg nearly doubled during the same period (*Die Stadt der Buddenbrooks*, 9). Pinson lists the population of Hamburg as 127,985 in 1820, 308,446 in 1870, and 953,103 in 1910 (*Modern Germany*, 221).

30. Sombart, *Die deutschen Männer*, 249, 296–97.

31. Tobin, "Making Way," 320; also Heilbut, *Thomas Mann*, 158.

32. Weisinger, "Distant Oil Rigs," 186–87.

33. See Vaget's suggestive comments on the association of Hamburg in *Buddenbrooks* with economic misfortune, immorality, social and psychological humiliation, and the threatening world to the south ("Discreet Charm," 197–203).

34. "ein paar Zimmer im Gasthause Stadt Hamburg" (1.1: 107).

35. "aus durablem und elegantem englischen Stoff" (1.1: 486).

36. "ganze Erscheinung [hatte] etwas Englisches angenommen, was nicht übel zu ihr paßte" (1.1: 285).

37. "in einem gelben und großkarierten Anzug, der durchaus etwas Tropisches an sich hatte" (1.1: 282).

38. "exotischen Gewaltthätigkeit" (1.1: 296).

39. "er redete in Zungen. Er sprach englisch, spanisch, plattdeutsch und hamburgisch, er schilderte chilenische Messerabenteuer und Diebsaffären aus Whitechapel" (1.1: 492).

40. Elias, *The Civilizing Process*, 41.

41. Mann to Otto Grautoff, February 17, 1906 (21: 72).

42. See Besser on the "Tropenkoller" (tropical rage) that supposedly afflicted those who remained too long in the colonies, and Noyes on the fear that black women could seduce white men ("Wo sind die Mütter?" 370). On the fear of degeneration due to racial mixtures see Schwarz, "Bastards"; Graichen and Gründer, *Deutsche Kolonien*, 277.

43. "'N Aap is hei!'" = Er ist ein Affe (1.1: 17).

44. "'Äußerlich, mein gutes Kind, äußerlich bist du glatt und geleckt, ja, aber innerlich, mein gutes Kind, da bist du schwarz ...'" (1.1: 18).

45. "einem vor Bosheit tollen Affen" (1.1: 249)

46. "innerlich Schwarz ... wie Herr Stengel seinerzeit immer gesagt haben soll" (1.1: 373).

47. "etwas Fremdes und Ausländisches" (1.1: 95).

48. "pompöse Duos" "[er] spielte die Geige wie ein Zigeuner, mit einer Wildheit, einer Leidenschaft" (1.1: 324–25).

49. René Maria von Throta comes from the Catholic Rhine region, and his middle name is also typically Catholic (Elsaghe, *Thomas Mann*, 103–5). Among the many things that Tony hates about Bavaria is its Catholicism, whereas Tom has a secret sympathy for the religion.

50. 1.1: 527; see commentary, 1.2: 354. The English translation omits the historical reference: "a light silk short-waisted jacket" (471).

51. See Kurzke on the central theme of *Heimsuchung* (the visitation of destructive forces) in Mann's work (*Mondwanderungen*, 117).

52. Wolf, "Hagenströms."

53. Although Elsaghe is correct to note that many critics miss or ignore the partial Jewishness of the Hagenström family (*Die imaginäre Nation*, 178), the topic has hardly gone unnoticed. Sagave links Mann's depiction of the Hagenströms to the sort of anti-Semitic caricatures published in "Das Zwanzigste Jahrhundert" ("Zur Geschichtlichkeit," 447). See also Wolf, "Hagenströms," 38; Darmaun, *Thomas Mann*, 27; and Elsaghe, *Die imaginäre Nation*, 188–205.

54. "der eine Jüdin, eine geborene Oppenheimer, heiratete" (1.2: 645).

55. "Familie Kohn (Fehling)" (1.2: 462). See also 1.2: 256–57.

56. 1.1: 127. Wolf, "Hagenströms," 48.

57. Elsaghe, *Die imaginäre Nation*, 194. Roggenkamp notes that while Alfred Pringsheim, Thomas Mann's father-in-law, was forced to change his name to "Israel" in 1939, his mother-in-law Hedwig Pringsheim was for unknown reasons able to avoid being named "Sara" or "Sarah" (*Erika Mann*, 52, 164).

58. Breuer, "Das 'Zwanzigste Jahrhundert.'"

59. "'Thränen-Trieschke!' rief sie. 'Grünlich! Permaneder! Tiburtius! Weinschenk! Hagenströms!'" (1.1: 739).

60. "Assez, meine Liebe! So undelikate Worte" (1.1: 260).

61. "Gegen einen Haufen Mist kann man nicht anstinken" (1.1: 737).

62. The inscription still stands on the door to today's Buddenbrook house (1.2: 249).

63. "keineswegs die Heimstätte makelloser Moralität. . . . Man entschädigte sich hier für seine auf dem Comptoirbock seßhaft verbrachten Tage nicht nur mit schweren Weinen und schweren Gerichten" (1.1: 343).

64. "die übrigens Semlinger hieß" (1.1: 66).

65. Elsaghe, *Thomas Mann*, 205; on the association of Frankfurt with Jewishness, Elsaghe, 203–4.

66. With a nod to Wolfgang Iser, Elsaghe refers to Mann's "Leerstellentechnik" (gap or empty space technique) (*Thomas Mann*, 171; cf. also 172, 194).

67. The question as to whether or not the Hagenströms are fundamentally different from the Buddenbrooks has a long history. Lukács started the debate by claiming that they were members of the modern capitalist bourgeoisie (*Thomas Mann*, 18), whereas the Buddenbrooks remained rooted in an older tradition of the German burgher (18; see also Diersen, *Thomas Mann*, 37). More recent critics have argued convincingly that both families are part of the same social class and share the same ethos (Wolf, "Hagenströms," 51; Swales, *Buddenbrooks*, 92; Zeller, *Bürger oder Bourgeois?* 26).

68. "wo ein nicht kleiner Teil der Landleute in den Händen von Juden ist" (1.1: 499).

69. "Halsabscheider" "einen Wucherprofit" (1.1: 499–500).

70. "den hausierenden Juden" (1.1: 503).

71. "Juden? Halsabscheider? . . . Aber es ist von *dir* die Rede, Tom, von *dir!*" (1.1: 499).

72. "Doktor Breslauer, einen rechten Teufelsbraten, einen geriebenen Redner, einen raffinierten Rechtsvirtuosen, dem der Ruhm vorangeht, so und so vielen betrügerischen Bankerottiers am Zuchthaus vorbeigeholfen zu haben" (1.1: 579).

73. Darmaun assumes that he is Jewish (*Thomas Mann*, 33), as does Elsaghe (*Die imaginäre Nation*, 190).

74. "war aus Schlesien gebürtig, woselbst sein alter Vater noch lebte" (1.1: 483).

75. 1.2: 289. As Zeller notes, the patrician leaders of Lübeck were de facto aristocrats (*Bürger oder Bourgeois*, 15).

76. "auch auf Nichtchristen" (1.1: 193).

77. "die Revolution ist in Berlin an ästhetischen Teetischen vorbereitet worden" (1.1: 212).

78. "an den aesthetischen Theetischen einiger geistreicher jüdischer Damen" (1.2: 296).

79. "durablen englischen Winteranzug" (1.1: 662).

80. "mit butterfarbenem Haar und übermäig leidenschaftslosen, augenscheinlich anglisierenden . . . Gesichtszügen" (1.1: 382).

81. "wie ein schwarzes Teufelchen" (1.1: 69).

82. "die aussah wie eine Negerin und ungeheure goldene Ohrringen trug" (1.1: 94).

83. "Du bist ein Auswuchs, eine ungesunde Stelle am Körper unserer Familie!" (1.1: 352).

84. On this optical phenomenon see Gombrich, *Art and Illusion*, 5–6.

85. "der ehrlichste und gutmütigste Mensch von der Welt" (1.1: 197).

86. "die Wut der entfesselten Sklaven" (1.1: 207).

87. "ein Nabob aus Indien" (1.1: 653). The English translation omits "from India."

Ryan notes the detail of the nabob from India and comments that the "exotic overseas world" was "in fact an intimate part of nineteenth-century business and political life" (*"Buddenbrooks,"* 128). I am in agreement with her call for a cultural studies approach to *Buddenbrooks* that shows "how the novel registers nineteenth-century cultural realities while at the same time understanding them as imagined and constructed" (134).

88. "von einem Deutschen . . . nur von einem *Lübecker"* ("Ansprache in Lübeck," XI: 534).

89. "das Nationale, ja Regionale" ("On Myself," XIII: 141).

90. Chakrabarty, *Provincializing Europe,* 239.

Chapter Three

1. Böhm, *Zwischen Selbstzucht und Verlangen,* 197–233; Kurzke, *Thomas Mann: Life,* 120–33.

2. *Tonio Kröger,* 82. "Zigeuner im grünen Wagen" (2.1: 252).

3. *Death in Venice,* 257. "Unzucht und Raserei des Unterganges" (2.1: 584).

4. *Buddenbrooks,* 11. "glatt und geleckt . . . aber innerlich . . . schwarz" (1.1: 18).

5. "Die entscheidende Erwägung und Sicherheit bleibt mir, daß ich mich meiner Natur nach im Bürgerlichen bergen darf, ohne eigentlich zu verbürgerlichen" (Tb, May 22, 1919).

6. Jens and Jens, *Frau Thomas Mann,* 32.

7. "daß ich keine Jüdin bin, das weiss ich einmal ganz gewiß" (ibid., 33). Jüngling and Rossbeck cover much of the same ground in their retelling of Katia Pringsheim's relation to Judaism in her childhood and her marriage to Thomas Mann (*Katia Mann*). As Roggenkamp stresses repeatedly, both mother and daughter always vehemently denied their Jewishness (*Erika Mann*).

8. "Ich finde, wenn Pringsheims Protestanten sind, sollten sie bei einem solchen Wendepunkt in Katias Leben es auch beweisen" (Jens and Jens, *Frau Thomas Mann,* 96).

9. "Kein Gedanke an Judenthum kommt auf, diesen Leuten gegenüber . . . man spürt nichts als Kultur" (Mann to Heinrich Mann, Feb. 27, 1904, 21: 271).

10. "Die Lösung der Judenfrage," 14.1: 174–78. See also Dr. Sammet in *Royal Highness,* a positively portrayed assimilated Jew.

11. "Ich bin Christ, aus guter Familie, habe Verdienste, die gerade diese Leute zu würdigen wissen" (Mann to Heinrich Mann, Feb. 27, 1904, 21: 272).

12. "Moses-Körbchen . . . wie nordisch Eis . . . hansischen Vätern . . . das arabische Näschen" (VIII: 1086–87).

13. "Momentweise glaube ich, ein klein bischen Judenthum durchblicken zu sehen, was mich jedesmal sehr heiter stimmt" (Mann to Heinrich Mann, Nov. 20, 1905, 21: 333).

14. "schlank und etwas chinesenhaft" (Mann to Heinrich Mann, Apr. 1, 1909, 21: 412).

15. Elsaghe has written about the combination of anti-Semitism and Orientalism in Mann's work (see in particular his reading of *Death in Venice* in *Die imaginäre Nation,* 27–60). On the intrinsic link between the two concepts see Said, *Orientalism,* 27–28.

16. "unser Blut [ist] mit lateinamerikanischem gemischt" ("Das Bild der Mutter," XI: 420).

17. Derrida, *Dissemination*, 95–117.

18. "der heulende Triumph der unterdrückten Triebwelt" ("On Myself," XIII: 136).

19. Lowe-Porter translated Mann's novella as *The Blood of the Walsungs*, but I prefer the German title with its clear reference to Wagner's heroes in *Die Walküre*.

20. Mann had previously published a poem in the same journal, *Die Gesellschaft*, in October 1893 (2.2: 15), and a brief sketch titled "Vision" in a school newspaper.

21. "Wenn eine Frau heute aus *Liebe* fällt, so fällt sie morgen um *Geld*" (2.1: 49).

22. "Da stürzte er sich auf sie und bedeckte sie mit wahnsinnigen, grausamen, geißelnden Küssen" (2.1: 47).

23. "verbitterten, traurigen Brutalität" (2.1: 49).

24. "eine häßliche kleine Jüdin in einem geschmacklosen grauen Kleid" (2.1: 56–57).

25. "nicht den geringsten Zweifel . . . über ihre wenigstens zum Teil semitische Abstammung" (2.1: 55).

26. "jenes junge Mädchen mit der lautlosen, vulkanischen, glühend sinnlichen Leidenschaft" (2.1: 61).

27. "am Morgen nach der Hochzeitsnacht,—beinahe in der Hochzeitsnacht" (2.1: 70).

28. "Ich fühle mich im Süden zu Hause" (2.1: 62).

29. 2.2: 45.

30. "entbehrt sie jedes weiblichen Reizes" (2.1: 95).

31. "Sie will mich quälen und verhöhnen!" (2.1: 107).

32. "jene ohnmächtige, süßlich peinigende Wut (2.1: 109).

33. "Wie ein Hund . . . irrsinnige Wut . . . wollüstige Haß" (2.1: 118).

34. "ein Weib mit vollkommen männlich gebildetem Hirn . . . die körperlichen Reize . . . eines Besens" (2.1: 205).

35. Hatfield, *Thomas Mann*, 19.

36. "ebenfalls von einer südlichen Sonne gereift erschienen und mit ihrer vegetativen und indolenten Üppigkeit an diejenigen einer Sultanin gemahnten" (2.1: 160).

37. "Spatzenhirn . . . sinnlicher Bosheit . . . grausamen Lüsternheit . . . lüsternen Verschlagenheit . . . Unheil zu stiften" (2.1: 180, 164, 161).

38. "eine Anzahl scheußlicher Neger, in schreienden Kostümen und mit blutroten Lippen, welche die Zähne fletschten und ein barbarisches Geheul begannen" (2.1: 176).

39. Le Rider, *Modernity*; Izenberg, *Modernism and Masculinity*.

40. "und in die doch der warme Wind die schwüle Trägheit des Orients hinüberträgt" ("The Will to Happiness," 2.1: 64). See Boa on Venice as a feminized space in *Death in Venice*, where boundaries between Occident and Orient crumble, undermining Aschenbach's carefully maintained identity as an upper-class European man ("Global Intimations," 27–33).

41. "Die Verlobung—auch kein Spaß, Du wirst es glauben . . . mich in die neue Familie einzuleben, einzupassen (so gut es geht)" (Mann to Heinrich Mann, Dec. 23, 1904, 21: 312).

42. "wieder einmal . . . fremd, grässlich, demüthigend, entnervend, entkräftend" (Mann to Heinrich Mann, June 11, 1906, 21: 367).

43. "ein bischen mehr Klosterfrieden" (Mann to Heinrich Mann, Nov. 18, 1905, 21: 315).

44. "Mich quält der Gedanke, daß ich mich nicht hätte menschlich attachiren und binden dürfen" (Mann to Heinrich Mann, June 8, 1906, 21: 365).

45. On the history of the novella's composition, publication, and reception see Vaget, *Thomas Mann-Kommentar*, 155–69 and 2.2: 314–29. Essential reading for the frequently told story of the novella's complicated history includes Pringsheim, "Ein Nachtrag," and Vaget, *"Sang réservé* in Deutschland."

46. Darmaun, *Thomas Mann*, 40–53; Harpprecht, *Thomas Mann*, 261.

47. Viktor Mann, *Wir waren fünf*, 326.

48. Pringsheim, "Ein Nachtrag," 268.

49. "ein Wurm . . . eine Laus, jawohl . . . Machenschaften" (2.1: 434). English quoted from Lowe-Porter's translation of *The Blood of the Walsungs* in Mann, *Death in Venice*, 293; trans. modified.

50. "unmöglich . . . klein, häßlich, früh gealtert" (2.1: 429).

51. "aschblond, ein strenges Mädchen von achtundzwanzig mit Hakennase, grauen Raubvogelaugen und einem bittern Munde" (2.1: 430).

52. Anderson notes the link between assimilation and "animal mimicry," and traces the "figurative bestialisation of the Jewish protagonists" of *Wälsungenblut* ("'Jewish' Mimesis?" 195, 201); see also Elsaghe, *Die imaginäre Nation*, 143–44.

53. Elsaghe, *Thomas Mann*, 189. He also notes that the oscillation between culture and nature was a typical feature of Mann's contemporary anti-Semitic discourse (*Die imaginäre Nation*, 101).

54. "Tenni, Lion und Therese, das ist zuviel, und, offen gesagt, auch zu jüdisch" (in Jens and Jens, *Frau Thomas Mann*, 198). She refers to Richard Tennenbaum, Ferdinand Lion, and Therese Giehse.

55. Goldhagen, *Hitler's Willing Executioners*.

56. "von fremder, von hoffnungslos anderer Art" (2.1: 451; trans. modified).

57. Anderson, "Mann's Early Novellas," 94; Roggenkamp, *Erika Mann*, 103.

58. "der erzene Lärm, wild, kannibalisch" (2.1: 429).

59. "wilden Akzent" (2.1: 448).

60. "im Osten an entlegener Stätte" (2.1: 434).

61. "wie unter einer fremden, heißeren Sonne verdorrt" (2.1: 429).

62. "ein ragender Sklave . . . den beiden zierlichen und warm vermummten, dunklen, seltsamen Geschöpfen" (2.1: 457).

63. 4.2: 466–67.

64. Spinell is from Lemberg (today Lvov in Ukraine), a city in Eastern Europe with a high percentage of Jews, and he is named after "some sort of mineral or gem" (*den Namen irgendeinen Minerals oder Edelsteines*), suggesting typically Jewish names ending in "Stein," "Gold," or "Silber." According to Elsaghe, his elaborately artificial handwriting

that is "painted" (*gemalt*) onto the page also suggests an inauthenticity associated with the Jews (*Thomas Mann*, 170–74); cf. also Barker, "Bloss aus Lemberg."

65. *Death in Venice*, 200; "die Merkmale fremder Rasse" (2.1: 508).

66. On Mann's prejudice against women writers see Elsaghe, *Thomas Mann*, 261–308. Mann's artist is not the hypermasculine Renaissance man in vogue in fin de siècle Germany, however (Ruehl, "Death in Florence"), but one who could appropriate "'feminine' transcendence" into his art (Izenberg, *Modernism and Masculinity*; also Detering, "*Juden*," 25–64). See Härle, *Männerweiblichkeit*.

67. Kurzke, *Thomas Mann: Epoche*, 87–92; Lämmert, "Doppelte Optik."

68. Levesque, "The Double-Edged Sword."

69. Mann began to assemble materials for what he thought would be a short *Fürsten-Novella* (novella about a prince) in 1903 and did not complete what turned out to be his second novel until 1909. See 4.2: 9–81 for a detailed account of the novel's genesis.

70. "Biographical models can be identified for all major characters in the novel" (*Für alle Hauptfiguren des Romans lassen sich biographische Modelle ausmachen*) (4.2: 96). See also Mendelssohn, *Der Zauberer*, 2: 1155–1253, and Weigand, "Die symbolisch-autobiographische Gehalt."

71. "I remember well that I often glanced up at the *Meistersinger* as I worked" (*Ich erinnere mich wohl, daß ich während der Arbeit öfters zu den Meistersingern emporblinzelte*) (Mann to Bertram, Jan. 28, 1910, 21: 441).

72. *Royal Highness*, 8. "die Fürsten [sind] Bauern; ihre Vermögen bestehen aus Grund und Boden, ihre Einkünfte aus landwirtschaftlichen Erträgnissen" (4.1: 20). References to the English translation are included hereafter in the text.

73. "Industrielle und Finanzleute" (4.1: 20).

74. "Das Volk war fromm und treu, es liebte seine Fürsten wie sich selbst, es war von der Erhabenheit der monarchischen Idee durchdrungen, es sah einen Gottesgedanken darin" (4.1: 45).

75. "Hokuspokus der Hoheit" (4.1: 162) trans. modified from "flummery of Highness" (134).

76. "die berühmte Blockhead-Farm . . . jenes Landgütchen, das mit seiner Steinölquelle binnen kurzem das Hundert- und Aberhundertfache seines Kaufpreises wert war" (4.1: 205–6).

77. "als die fürchterlichen Dividenden einzustreichen und noch immer reicher und reicher zu werden, bis es kaum noch zu sagen war" (4.1: 168).

78. On the ambivalent status of the novel as either political apology or political critique, see Dedner, "Über die Grenzen," 255; also 4.2: 159.

79. "Aber für politische Freiheit habe ich gar kein Interesse. . . . Ich habe im Grunde ein gewisses fürstliches Talent zum Repräsentieren" (Mann to Heinrich Mann, Feb. 27, 1904, 21: 269, 271).

80. "Dein Jammerbild ist mir keine schreckende und beschämende Mahnung aus einer fremden Welt. Wir sind ja Brüder!" ("Die Hungernden," 2.1: 379).

81. *Tonio Kröger*, 191; "die Stolzen und Kalten, die auf den Pfaden der großen, der dämonischen Schönheit abenteuern und den 'Menschen' verachten" (2.1: 318).

82. "Davis' Eltern waren Deutsche (eigentlich Davidsohn oder Davids) sind nach Amerika ausgewandert als kleine Händlersleute. Samuel D. wird in Milwaukee geboren . . . heirathet eine in der Nähe von Bahia geborene Plantagenbesitzerstochter mit deutschem Vater und portugiesischer Mutter." Mann's note 36e (4.2: 431); see also note 35a (4.2: 421).

83. "Die Eltern des Millionärs Samuel Davis waren also arme jüdische Auswanderer aus Deutschland namens Davidson, und Imma wäre eine amerikanische 'Vierteljüdin' mit deutschen und portugiesischen Vorfahren gewesen" (Mendelssohn, *Der Zauberer*, 1: 725). See also Detering's commentary to the critical edition, which identifies Imma and her father as originally the offspring of "deutsch-*jüdischer* Auswanderer" (4.2: 48).

84. "Er ist Prostestant" (note 35a, 4.2: 421).

85. Katia Mann, *Meine ungeschriebenen Memoiren*, 66–67; also quoted in 4.2: 49–50.

86. 4.2: 96.

87. "Frau aus dem Süden,—kreolisches Blut, eine Person mit deutschem Vater und eingeborener Mutter" (4.1: 168; English translation modified).

88. "*Kreole* in den ehemal. französ., spanischen u. portugiesischen Kolonien Amerikas oder Afrikas die *Eingeborenen* von rein europäischem Blute . . . *Mestize* (wörtlich Mischling) dem Sprachgebrauch nach Mischlinge von Weißen und Indianern . . . *Farbige* im allgem. im Gegensatz zu (eingeb.) Europäern und Kreolen die eingeborenen Indianer, (Neger) ~~etc.~~ u. die durch Vermischung dieser untereinander *oder mit den Weißen* entstandenen Mischlinge; im besonderen nur diese *Mischlinge* im Gegensatz zu den Weißen, Negern, Indianern *pur sang*" (Note 56a, 4.2: 466–67).

89. "eine Dame mit indianischem Blut . . . eine Quinterone . . . eine Farbige" (4.1: 291–92; English translation modified). In this exchange, Imma says that her grandfather married "in Bolivia or thereabouts" (245) (*in Bolivia . . . oder in dieser Gegend* [4.1: 291]); later she is said to have Portuguese ancestors, among others. Bolivia was a Spanish, not Portuguese, colony. In an earlier draft of the novel, the elder Spoelmann was to have met his wife in San Francisco, not Bolivia, and she was to have been from Bahia, Brazil, which would have identified her more closely with Mann's mother (4.2: 431). Mann may have introduced Bolivia to blur the more obvious autobiographical reference, only to create new confusion between Spanish and Portuguese. But the precise location is perhaps of less significance than the fact that it is from "ganz unten auf der Landkarte," as Tonio Kröger puts it, or, as Imma states, "in Bolivia, or thereabouts."

90. "eine Deutsch-Amerikanerin mit halbenglischem Blut, und deren Tochter ist nun Miß Spoelmann" (4.1: 16).

91. "Er erwähnte der vierfachen Blutzusammensetzung Imma Spoelmanns—denn außer dem deutschen, portugiesischen und englischen fließe ja, wie man vernähme, auch ein wenig von dem uradligen Blut der Indianer in ihren Adern" (4.1: 374).

92. *Joseph and His Brothers*, 954; "Mit der Mutter schläft jeder—weißt du das nicht?" (V: 1175).

93. "war etwas Kindliches in ihrer Sprechweise" (4.1: 240).

94. "'Kleine Schwester' . . . ein Sonderfall von Verlobungsgespräch" (4.1: 370).

95. "Feenkind aus Fabelland" (4.1: 324); "Königin von Saba" (4.1: 363).

96. "ein strenges Glück" (4.1: 399).

97. *"Er wird leben, und man wird ihm vom Golde aus Reich Arabien geben"* (4.1: 397; italics in original).

98. Detering, *"Juden,"* 148.

99. Marc Weiner, *Richard Wagner,* 118–19, 121–24, 184–86, 298–305. After enjoying an otherwise "splendid" performance of *Die Meistersinger,* Mann commented that he found "die Beckmesser-Szene unleidlich" (*the Beckmesser scene hard to take*). "Immer wieder muß man doch bei Beckmesser an den 'Juden im Dorn' denken" (*Again and again Beckmesser reminds you of the "Jew in the Thorn Bush"* [an anti-Semitic Grimm fairy tale]). Tb, May 29, 1954. See also Mann to Emil Preetorius, Dec. 6, 1949, *Briefe* 3: 114.

100. Böhm, *Zwischen Selbstzucht und Verlangen,* 296–301.

101. "Malheur von Geburt" (4.1: 91; English translation modified).

102. "ein geborener Zigeuner" (4.1: 95).

103. In response to gentle criticism from Hermann Hesse, Mann confessed that he had been thinking of Wagner's *Meistersinger* when writing the novel and that he shared Wagner's ambition to appeal to both the common crowd and the discerning critic: *"I want [to appeal to] the stupid ones too"* (*"Mich verlangt auch nach den Dummen"*) (italics in original; Mann to Hesse, Apr. 1, 1910, 21: 448). See also Lämmert, "Doppelte Optik."

Chapter Four

1. For this reason, *Reflections* is often simply ignored or condemned rather than discussed in detail. Increasingly, however, critics have begun to regard the work as a central document in the history of Mann's political thought and even his "most precise self-portrait" (*die genaueste . . . Selbstporträt*) and thus "the indispensable key" (*der unentbehrliche Schlüssel*) to understanding Mann's life and works (Fest, *Die unwissenden Magier,* 66). Still-useful older studies include Sontheimer, *Thomas Mann,* and Keller, *Der unpolitische Deutsche.* Hermann Kurzke has been particularly important in reevaluating the *Reflections* (*Auf der Suche;* "Die Quellen"; *Thomas Mann: Epoche,* 139–70; *Thomas Mann Handbuch,* 678–95). The insights of these articles are now gathered together in Kurzke's commentary to the new critical edition, vol. 13.2. Other good studies include Reed, *Thomas Mann,* 179–225; Gökberk, "War as Mentor"; and Gut, *Thomas Manns Idee,* 76–115.

2. As Hatfield put it, Mann's work "is a repetitious, confused, wordy book, marked by . . . pseudo profundity . . . Mann argues . . . with the enthusiastic looseness of the autodidact" (*Thomas Mann,* 65–66).

3. Mann's biographer Harpprecht is particularly harsh in his assessment of *Reflections* and what it reveals about the self-absorbed author's detachment from the realities of war (*Thomas Mann,* 389, 398, 413, 416, 420, 428).

4. *Reflections*, 1; 13.1: 11. Subsequent references to the *Reflections* will be to Walter D. Morris's translation with page numbers in the body of the text and to the German original from volume 13.1 of the *Große kommentierte Frankfurter Ausgabe* in footnotes.

5. 350; 13.1: 517. By contrast, Mann responded sympathetically to *The Best Years of Our Lives*, the controversial post–Second World War film about physically disabled and psychologically traumatized war veterans struggling to fit back into civilian life (Mann to Agnes Meyer, Oct. 10, 1947, *Briefe* 2: 556–57).

6. Precisely because of its origins in the turmoil of war and its internal complexity, *Reflections* has invited debate about its place in intellectual history. Kurzke views it as a major work of the postwar "Conservative Revolution" (*Thomas Mann: Epoche*, 152), for example, whereas Kroll argues that *Reflections* is "profoundly anti-revolutionary" and thus "not suitable for appropriation" by the movement ("Conservative at the Crossroads," 226).

7. "Zur jüdischen Frage," *Essays*, 2: 93.

8. Borchmeyer argues that Mann is conservative in the sense of the late eighteenth century, not the early twentieth, viewing *Reflections* as a respectable continuation of classical Weimar's antirevolutionary thought ("Politische Betrachtungen").

9. "man könnte das Buch die *intellektuellen Buddenbrooks* nennen" (cited from *Thomas Mann an Ernst Bertram*, 234; commentary to Mann's postcard of Apr. 13, 1918).

10. "das Imperium der Zivilisation" (13.1: 43).

11. "der *Imperialismus der Zivilisation*" (italics in original; 13.1: 57).

12. "diese spezifisch französischen Ideengehalte der 'Menschenrechte' und des historischen Stabilismus . . . sie hinaus in die Welt zu tragen, die Welt und *alle* anderen Nationen damit zu erfüllen" (13.1: 201).

13. "ein paar Riesenweltreiche . . . welche—gehöre Deutschland nun dazu oder nicht—die Verwaltung des Erdballs unter sich verteilt haben werden" (13.1: 386).

14. "des Weltimperiums der Zivilisation . . . eine alle Nationalkultur nivellierende Entwicklung im Sinn einer homogenen Zivilisation" (13.1: 264).

15. "eine[] völlige[] Nivellierung, journalistisch-rhetorischen Verdummung und Verpöbelung" (13.1: 283).

16. Barbar, *Jihad vs. McWorld*.

17. "hat nichts als Entschuldigungen. . . . Schließlich handelt es sich da um Asien, um 'dunkle Massen,' um niggers" (13.1: 388, 389).

18. Kontje, *German Orientalisms*, 73–74.

19. For instance, Chakrabarty exposes the contradiction between the European rhetoric of universal rights and the colonial practice of exploitation and racism, while seeking a way to preserve local cultural diversity in the face of increasing global homogeneity (*Provincializing Europe*).

20. As Gut observes, the ideological positions represented in the *Reflections* and *Der Untertan* could hardly be more different (*Thomas Manns Idee*, 86–88).

21. Although Mann's critical remarks about expressionism in the *Reflections* are frequently cited (cf. Donahue, "Introduction," 2–4), he actually knew almost nothing of

the movement and used the term mainly to disparage his brother's satirical fiction (Kurzke, "Die Quellen," 303).

22. "Die Korporation, der Waffendienst und die Luft des Imperialismus hatten ihn erzogen und tauglich gemacht" (Heinrich Mann, Der Untertan, 100).

23. "Man mußte konkurrenzfähig werden. Der Platz an der Sonne!" (ibid., 107).

24. "Wollt ihr, daß euer Kaiser euch Kolonien schenkt? . . . Dann schärft ihm gefälligst das Schwert!" (ibid., 379).

25. "Der Ozean ist unentbehrlich für Deutschlands Größe . . . denn das Weltgeschäft ist heute das Hauptgeschäft!" (ibid., 466).

26. Graichen and Gründer, Deutsche Kolonien, 88–89.

27. Ibid., 77; see also Scherpe, "Massaker und Maskerade," 83–84.

28. Graichen and Gründer, Deutsche Kolonien, 147. On the Herero massacre see Hull, Absolute Destruction, 7–90.

29. In Lotte in Weimar, Thomas Mann would portray Goethe as a character who refused to join in the popular anti-French German nationalism at the time of the Napoleonic Wars.

30. Paul de Lagarde, for instance, called for the systematic colonization of Hungary, Silesia, and Bohemia, while renouncing interest in distant lands (Deutsche Schriften, 25–27). Julius Langbehn made passing reference to discoveries in Africa in Rembrandt als Erzieher, while insisting that it was more important now for Germans to discover themselves at home (46). On Lagarde, Langbehn, and Moeller van den Bruck as anti-rational anti-Semites who helped lay the ideological foundation for National Socialism, see Stern, Politics of Cultural Despair. Hitler repeatedly and emphatically rejected Germany's quest for overseas colonies in favor of expansion into Eastern Europe in Mein Kampf (137, 140, 664; cf. also Fest, Hitler, 214, 540). On German colonial policy under Hitler, see Graichen and Gründer, Deutsche Kolonien, 399–451.

31. See Fischer on the German sense of victimization and their hostility to European imperialism from the early modern period to the "Age of Goethe" (Das Eigene). As Zantop argued, nineteenth-century Germans often voiced criticism of other European colonial powers while stressing that when given the chance, they would not be guilty of similar abuses (Colonial Fantasies, 29).

32. "die geistige Invasion, die möglicherweise bei weitem stärkste und überwältigendste politische Invasion des Westens, die je deutsches Schicksal geworden" (13.1: 38).

33. "Militarismus, Herrentum und Macht" (13.1: 260).

34. "einer neuen Epoche der deutschen Zivilisation und des Imperialismus . . . die Entwicklung Deutschlands zur Demokratie" (13.1: 263).

35. "Amerikanisierung des deutschen Lebensstils . . . der scharfen Luft der preußisch-amerikanischen Weltstadt" (13.1: 154–55).

36. "Was das Luthertum war, ist jetzt das Franztum in diesen / Letzten Tagen, es drängt ruhige Bildung zurück" (In recent days the French have become what Lutheranism was: they repress quiet personal development) (Goethe, Werke, 1: 211). See also Humboldt, Ideen.

37. *Deutsche Schriften,* 126–27.

38. "von seinen Juden gesäubert" (*Deutsche Schriften,* 406).

39. "die Gesamtheit aller deutsch empfindenden, deutsch denkenden, deutsch wollenden Deutschen" (*Deutsche Schriften,* 167).

40. "Es ist wahr . . . die Völker als mythische Individuen anzuschauen, ist eine primitive-volkstümliche Anschauungsweise, und Patriotismus selbst möchte eine Ergriffenheit von eher mythisch-primitiver, als politisch-geistiger Natur bedeuten" (13.1: 165–66).

41. "so ist er Künstler und Dichter vielleicht nur eben so weit, als er *Volk* ist und volkhaft primitiv zu schauen und zu empfinden nie ganz verlernte" (13.1: 166).

42. "Volk spricht nur dann, wann die Volkheit . . . in den Individuen zu Worte kommt" (13.1: 166; in Lagarde, *Deutsche Schriften,* 118).

43. "weil ich nur der eigenen inneren Stimme zu lauschen brauchte, um auch die Stimme der Zeit zu vernehmen" (13.1: 31).

44. "It is no longer the general public that is speaking, but rather an isolated remnant of a declining social class" *(Nicht mehr die Allgemeinheit spricht, sondern ein vereinsamter Spätling einer absteigenden Klasse).* Kurzke, *Auf der Suche,* 147.

45. "aus der organischen Tiefe des nationalen Lebens" (13.1: 271).

46. "'Volksstaat' . . . unter einem Führer, der Züge des Großen Mannes von deutschem Schlage trägt" (13.1: 399).

47. "Aber um Gottes Willen, ganz herein mit ihnen, oder ganz hinaus" (*Deutsche Schriften,* 35).

48. "Abstammung vom selben Stammvater" (*Deutsche Schriften,* 124).

49. "die Juden bleiben Juden" (*Deutsche Schriften,* 322).

50. "Bei allem, was man Kritisches über die *Betrachtungen* sagen kann: antisemitisch sind sie nicht" (Kurzke, *Thomas Mann: Epoche,* 153; see also Keller, *Der unpolitische Deutsche,* 98–101).

51. Darmaun places the Jewish question in the *Reflections* into the larger context of Mann's essays, letters, and diaries of the period. While he acknowledges Mann's effort to avoid open anti-Semitism in the *Reflections,* he demonstrates convincingly the associative "overlap of Jewishness with the Latin-Roman-Catholic West" (*Überlappung von Jüdischem mit dem lateinisch-romanisch-katholischen Westen*) in Mann's works (*Thomas Mann,* 93). Mann's tendency toward polemical generalizations often leaves "no further difference between Jews, Freemasons, alleged democrats, demagogic manipulators, representatives of the Enlightenment" (*kein Unterschied mehr zwischen Juden, Freimaurern, angeblichen Demokraten, demagogischen Drahtziehern, Aufklärern*) (97).

52. Kurzke, "Die Quellen," 303.

53. Wysling published the entire fragmentary essay, with a detailed introduction and extensive notes ("Geist und Kunst"). See also Reed, *Thomas Mann,* 119–43; Kurzke, *Thomas Mann: Epoche,* 86–96; Darmaun, *Thomas Mann,* 65–80; Detering, *"Juden,"* 85–96; Gut, *Thomas Manns Idee,* 31–51.

54. See Kurzke for a succinct summary of the intellectual-historical origins of au-

tonomy aesthetics and the theory of genius (*Thomas Mann: Epoche*, 92–96). Steinecke provides the best summary of nineteenth-century German debates about the status of the modern novel (*Romantheorie*).

55. "Die chauvinistische Mode in der Dichtung" ("Geist," 204).

56. "Das ursprüngliche Genie ohne Lektüre ein Aberglaube" ("Geist," 153).

57. "Schreiben können gilt nichts, aber was lallend aus orphischen Tiefen kommt oder zu kommen vorgiebt, wird sehr geschätzt" ("Geist," 158).

58. "Die Litteraturfeindschaft den Deutschen gewissermaßen eingeboren . . . Berlin besser dran, weil Helligkeit, Witz. . . . Außerdem jüdischer Geist. Volk des Buches" ("Geist," 157).

59. "Gott Lob, daß ich kein Jude bin. Man würde sonst sofort sagen: Natürlich, drum auch!—Ich habe dafür ein wenig romanisches Blut, das in mir gegen die antiliterarische Simpelei protestiert" ("Geist," 158).

60. "wesentlich jüdisch" ("Geist," 197). Bartels had also attacked *Buddenbrooks* because Mann seemed unconcerned at the rise of the Jewish Hagenström family at the expense of the Buddenbrooks (1.2: 191–92).

61. "Juden-Nähe- und Juden-Abhängigkeit . . . die Tochter des jüdischen Mathematikprofessors Pringsheim . . . Portugiesin, also möglicherweise nicht ohne Juden- und Negerblut" (1.2: 190, 192).

62. "Nein, man kann Wagnern nicht verehren!" ("Geist," 203).

63. "Der Litterat im üblen Sinne scheint mir ein Schriftsteller zu sein, sich gefallend in einem . . . Geschmack, der nicht zu ihm gehört. . . . Gewisse jüdische Romantiker" ("Geist," 186).

64. "eine sublime Perversität. . . . Man soll wissen, wer man ist [. . . sonst wird man nicht überzeugen. . . . Was man hervorbringt, ist 'Litteratur'" ("Geist," 186).

65. "ein kluger Jude . . . der innerlich den Teufel an den Vorzug nationaler Beschränktheit glaubt, sich seiner bedient, um anzuzeigen, da hier dem Publikum etwas Kernig-Gemütvolles und treuherzig Bodenständiges eingehändigt werde . . . ein abschreckendes Beispiel . . . für das, was im niedrigsten Sinne 'litterarisch' ist" ("Geist," 205).

66. "unser gesamtes Zivilisationsliteratentum [hat] bei ihm schreiben gelernt" (13.1: 95).

67. "der des in Paris akklimatisierten Juden Heinrich Heine" (13.1: 96).

68. "Er ist in voller Aktion, in politischer Rage . . . er steckt die Daumen in die Weste und ahmt gassenhumoristisch einen Juden nach" (13.1: 123–24).

69. "wilde Rhetorik . . . er zeichnet sich obendrein Lévy" (13.1: 491).

70. Detering identifies this "constitutive ambivalence" (*konstitutive Ambivalenz*) as the key to Mann's early work (*"Juden,"* 95).

71. "so schien mir vielmehr, daß ich das eigenste Mittel der anderen usurpiert und gegen sie gewandt hätte" (13.1: 178).

72. "Ich war witzig, ich war antithetisch, wo es sich um das Leben—ich war *französisch*, wo es sich um Deutschland handelte" (13.1: 190).

73. "ein halber Westler" (13.1: 103).

74. "Solchen Einflüssen, solchen Bedürfnissen und Empfänglichkeiten entsprach denn auch nur zu sehr meine eigene schriftstellerische Haltung: sie war der Art, daß Leute . . . einen Juden aus mir machen wollten" (13.1: 97).

75. The fundamental irony of Mann's highly rhetorical rejection of rhetoric has not gone unnoticed among his critics (see Kurzke, "Die Quellen," 304; Borchmeyer, "Politische Betrachtung," 87; Gökberk, "War as Mentor," 63; Kroll, "Conservative at the Crossroads," 237).

76. "daß man seine Deutschheit möglicherweise verlieren muß, um sie zu finden" (13.1: 78).

77. "inneren Feinden" (13.1: 51).

78. "*Exotismus,* bestehend in einem schon physischen Ekel vor dem Nahen, Heimatlich-Wirklichen" (13.1: 602).

79. "da ohne einen Zusatz von Fremdem vielleicht kein höheres Deutschtum möglich ist; da gerade die exemplarischen Deutschen Europäer waren und jede Einschränkung ins Nichts-als-Deutsche als barbarisch empfunden hätten" (13.1: 78). On the self-contradictory nature of Mann's argument in the *Reflections* see Gökberk, "War as Mentor," 63–71. Gut also notes that *Reflections* contains a surprising defense of German cosmopolitanism (*Thomas Manns Idee,* 114).

80. "Entfaltung, Entwicklung, Besonderheit, Mannigfaltigkeit, Reichtum an Individualität war immer das Grundgesetz deutschen Lebens. Dies Leben widerstrebte immer der Zentralisierung, bezog niemals Konvenienzen von einem kapitalen Mittelpunkt" (13.1: 304–5).

81. "Nur deutsch, das ist klein-deutsch, das ist nicht welt-deutsch, das ist Deutschtum geringer und verkümmerter Art" ("Vom Beruf des deutschen Schriftstellers," *Essays* 3: 291).

82. "Deutschtum als völkischem Reinpräparat . . . Rückfall ins Barbarische . . . dunkel und fremd . . . ohne die Deutschtum nicht Deutschtum ware" ("Zum Problem," XIII: 483–84).

83. "kosmopolitisch und international" (13.1: 35).

84. "nicht international, sondern übernational" (13.1: 227).

85. "Waren meine Ahnen nicht Nürnberger Handwerker von jenem Schlage, den Deutschland in alle Welt und bis in den fernen Osten entsandte, zum Zeichen, es sei das Land der Städte?" (13.1: 126–27).

86. "On Myself," XIII: 141.

87. "er war ja nicht nur übernational, sondern auch übereuropäisch, ein Asiat, der erste große Verehrer Asiens in Europa . . . Überdeutschtum . . . als eine Steigerung, nicht als eine Verwischung und Aufhebung des Deutschtums" (13.1: 148).

88. Izenberg, *Modernism and Masculinity,* 145–55; also Harpprecht, *Thomas Mann,* 380–86, 408, 481; Heilbut, *Thomas Mann,* 293–97; and Kurzke, *Thomas Mann: Life,* 217.

89. Belgum, *Popularizing the Nation.* For good broad overviews of the history of gender roles in general and masculinity in particular, see Mosse, *Nationalism and Sexuality* and *The Image of Man.*

90. Tobin, *Warm Brothers,* 194–210.

91. Aschheim, *The Nietzsche Legacy*.

92. "Diese neue Tafel, o meine Brüder, stelle ich über euch: *werdet hart!*" Nietzsche, *Werke*, 2: 460.

93. McAleer, *Dueling;* cf. also Harpprecht, *Thomas Mann*, 334.

94. Aschheim, *The Nietzsche Legacy*, 82.

95. Ibid., 128–63.

96. Theweleit, *Male Fantasies*, 2: 176–91.

97. Herf, *Reactionary Modernism*, 74. Jünger, *Der Kampf.*

98. Hesse, *Demian*, 135.

99. "Krieg! Es war Reinigung, Befreiung, was wir empfanden, und eine ungeheuere Hoffnung" ("Gedanken im Krieg," 15.1: 32).

100. "Zivilisation und Kultur sind nicht nur nicht ein und dasselbe, sondern sie sind Gegensätze . . . eine stilvolle Wildheit. . . . Zivilisation aber ist Vernunft, Aufklärung, Sänftigung" ("Gedanken im Krieg," 15.1: 27).

101. "Geist ist zivil . . . er ist der geschworene Feind der Triebe, der Leidenschaften, er ist antidämonisch, antiheroisch. . . . Das Genie [ist] Ausströmung einer tieferen, dunkleren und heißeren Welt, deren Verklärung und stilistische Bändigung wir Kultur nennen" ("Gedanken im Krieg," 15.1: 27–28).

102. "Diese Nation nimmt Damenrechte in Anspruch, es ist kein Zweifel" ("Gedanken im Krieg," 15.1: 42).

103. Heilbut, *Thomas Mann*, 278.

104. "einem rechten Weibsjahrhundert, welches von dem 'Parfüm des Ewig-Weiblichen' ganz erfüllt und durchtränkt war" ("Frederick," 15.1: 72).

105. Mann, "Frederick," 15.1: 73. In deference to Wilhelminian decorum, Mann did not actually write the word *Scheide* (meaning both "sheath" and "vagina" in German), leaving only a suggestive hyphen in its place. See Harpprecht, *Thomas Mann*, 385.

106. "*Männer fehlten;* und er argwöhnte zu seinem bitteren Verdrusse, da sein eigner Sohn nicht Manns genug sei" (Nietzsche, *Werke* 3: 119).

107. As Sontheimer documents, Mann's essay was controversial in right-wing circles because some felt that it was too critical of Frederick's character (*Thomas Mann*, 19–20).

108. "hat etwas Wildes, Radikales, Bösartiges, Unbedingtes, Gefährliches" ("Frederick," 15.1: 66).

109. "boshafter Troll" ("Frederick," 15.1: 120).

110. "damit eines großen Volkes Erdensendung sich erfülle" ("Frederick," 15.1: 122).

111. "große Herrschaftsrechte, gültigen Anspruch auf die Teilhaberschaft an der Verwaltung der Erde, kurz, auf politische Macht . . . zu mindesten Stunden, wo dieser Glaube schwankt und beinahe am Boden liegt" (13.1: 224).

112. "aber ein *Herrscher*volk? Ich zweifle. Ich *ver*zweifle alle paar Tage daran" (13.1: 226).

113. "in einer, wie er genau weiß, aussichtslosen Verteidigung" (13.1: 75).

114. "Machtjunker, noch ein Schwer-Industrieller, noch auch nur ein kapitalverbundener Sozialimperialist . . . Deutschlands Berufenheit zur Großen Politik und imperialen Existenz . . . machtpolitischer Konkurrent, sondern . . . sein geistiger Gegner" (13.1: 37).

115. "feminine und verlogen" (13.1: 25).

116. "Die ungeheure Männlichkeit seiner Seele, sein Antifeminismus, Anti-demokratismus,—was wäre deutscher?" (13.1: 91).

117. "In Deutschlands Seele werden die geistigen Gegensätze *Europas* ausgetragen,— im mütterlichen und im kämpferischen Sinne 'ausgetragen' " (13.1: 60).

118. "*Verfalls*psychologen . . . der Prophet irgend eines unanschaulichen 'Übermenschen' " (13.1: 87).

119. "die wir unter dem Hohnlächeln der Renaissance-Männer ein weibliches Kultur- und Kunstideal verehren" ("Das Ewig-Weibliche," 14.1: 59).

120. Kurzke, *Thomas Mann: Life,* 230–31. See also Kurzke, *Thomas Mann: Epoche,* 165–70.

121. " 'Rückfall'[ ] ins Primitive" (13.1: 166).

122. "dem geilen Ästhetizismus und Exotismus . . . Anthropophagenplastik . . . negerhafte Genußsucht" (13.1: 531–32).

123. "ein Tier mit Lippen so dick wie Kissen" ("An die Redaktion des 'Svenska Dagbladet,' " 15.1: 123).

124. "das Abendland . . . vor den Greueln der Völkerwanderung von unten" (Tb, May 5, 1919).

125. "die Darstellung eines innerpersönlichen Zwiespalts und Widerstreites. Daß sie es sind, das macht dies Buch, welches kein Buch und kein Kunstwerk ist, beinahe zu etwas anderem: beinahe zu einer Dichtung" (13.1: 45). Translation modified.

Chapter Five

1. "*vor* einer gewissen, Leben und Bewußtsein tief zerklüftenden Wende und Grenze" (5.1: 9).

2. For a detailed summary of the novel's origins see 5.2: 9–46. Reed places particular stress on the evolving process of composition in his interpretation of the novel (*Thomas Mann,* 226–74); see also Vaget, "Making of *Magic Mountain.*"

3. Fischer, *Germany's Aims,* 23.

4. Ibid., 607–8.

5. "Jedenfalls muß das Ganze als 'Geschichte aus der alten Zeit' stark gekennzeichnet werden" (Tb, Apr. 12, 1919).

6. "Bewaffnete Arbeiter. Automobile mit Soldaten" (Tb, Apr. 14, 1919).

7. "*Ich begann nach 4jähriger Unterbrechung wieder am 'Zauberberg' zu schreiben*" (italics in original; Tb, Apr. 20, 1919).

8. "Und somit fangen wir an" (5.1: 10).

9. Mann, "Der Entwicklungsroman," 15.1: 173–76; "Einführung in den Zauberberg," XI: 616–17. Following Mann's lead, older criticism frequently discusses *The Magic Mountain* as an example of an unconventional German *Bildungsroman.* See for example Weigand, *Thomas Mann's Novel,* 4; Scharfschwerdt, *Thomas Mann,* 114–74; Jacobs, *Wilhelm Meister,* 233–38; Reed, *Thomas Mann,* 226–74; and Minden, *The German Bildungsroman,* 205–44.

10. While Vaget stresses the opposition between Lübeck and Hamburg in *Buddenbrooks*, he claims that both cities become part of the larger Hanseatic realm in *The Magic Mountain* ("The Discreet Charm," 197). I stress here rather Hamburg's double role as it is linked both to the Hanseatic past and to the modern industrial and imperial age.

11. "die scharfen Gerüche gehäufter Kolonialwaren in der Nase . . . die Mammutleiber gedockter Asien- und Afrikafahrer" (5.1: 51).

12. See Weisinger, "Distant Oil Rigs," 186–87.

13. "Tomato Ketchup zum Roastbeef" (5.1: 49).

14. "Epochal für die Entwicklung unserer Schiffahrt . . . die geplante Elbregulierung" (5.1: 28).

15. "qui retournera bientôt dans les plaines . . . à rendre son pays grand et puissant par son travail honnête sur le chantier" (5.1: 517). John E. Woods italicizes sentences in his English translation that are in French in the German original.

16. "ein angehender Schiffbaumeister, ein Mann des Weltverkehrs und der Technik . . . ein Draufgänger . . . ein profaner Zerstörer alter Gebäude und landschaftlicher Schönheiten, ungebunden wie ein Jude und pietätlos wie ein Amerikaner" (5.1: 58–59).

17. "Ur-Ur-Ur-Ur,—diesen dunklen Laut der Gruft und der Zeitverschüttung" (5.1: 38).

18. "modrig-kühle Luft der Katharinenkirche oder der Michaeliskrypte" (5.1: 39).

19. "eines wechselnden Bleibens, das Wiederkehr und schwindelige Einerleiheit war" (5.1: 40).

20. "als lebte er im vierzehnten Jahrhundert" (5.1: 41).

21. "eigentlich sah er ganz so aus, wie man nicht aussah, wenn die Demokraten aus einen rechnen konnten . . . ein Hemmschuh werden, ein konservatives Element?" (5.1: 58).

22. "Geradezu mittelalterlich mutet es an" (5.1: 96).

23. "Namen aus allen Winden und Welten, sie lauteten englisch, russisch oder doch allgemein slawisch, auch deutsch, portugiesisch und anderswie" (5.1: 487).

24. "schöne lackierte Kistchen mit einem Globus, vielen Medaillen und einem von Fahnen umflatterten Ausstellungsgebäude in Gold geschmückt" (5.1: 383).

25. On "commodity racism and imperial advertising," see McClintock, *Imperial Leather*, 207–31; also Badenberg, "Usambara-Kaffee" and "Zwischen Kairo."

26. "abenteuerliche Welt . . . eine gewisse Schwäche" (5.1: 478).

27. On Chauchat's association with women's emancipation, sexuality, anarchy, and homosexuality, see Böhm, "Die homosexuellen Elemente."

28. Weisinger, "Distant Oil Rigs," 185.

29. "weichen, gleichsam knochenlosen Sprache" (5.1: 177).

30. "Orgasmus des Gehirns" (5.1: 454).

31. "Die sehr interessante Einleitung . . . über die slawische Rasse" (Tb, Oct. 15, 1918).

32. See the summary of Moeller van den Bruck's argument in 5.2: 78–79.

33. "das Produkt einer alten Rassenmischung, einer Versetzung germanischen Blutes mit wendisch-slawischem—oder auch umgekehrt" (5.1: 184).

34. Said famously referred to "the passive, seminal, feminine, even silent and supine East" (*Orientalism*, 138). On interracial romance see Pratt, *Imperial Eyes*, 86–107; and Zantop, *Colonial Fantasies*, 121–61.

35. Pratt, *Imperial Eyes*, 97; see also Zantop, *Colonial Fantasies*, 121–40.

36. Lubich, "Thomas Manns *Der Zauberberg*."

37. Böhm writes of Castorp's doubly ambivalent response to Chauchat, consisting of both attraction to and repulsion from her antibourgeois behavior and the combination of hetero- and homosexual desire that she arouses ("Die Homosexuellen Elemente," 151).

38. Vaget argues that Castorp's international taste in music marks him as what Nietzsche termed a "good European" as opposed to a German nationalist ("'Politically Suspect,'" 131). Both *Aida* and *Carmen* portray interracial or cross-cultural romances, thus touching on typically European themes with less unambiguously positive connotations.

39. Weisinger, "Distant Oil Rigs," 191.

40. Sedgwick, *Between Men*. Manet's *Dejeuner sur l'herbe* illustrates the cover of the paperback edition of *Between Men*.

41. "Kolonial-Holländer, ein Mann von Java, ein Kaffeepflanzer" (5.1: 827).

42. "Ich bin gar nicht männlich auf die Art, daß ich im Manne nur das nebenbuhlende Mitmännchen erblicke,—ich bin es vielleicht überhaupt nicht, aber bestimmt nicht auf diese Art, die ich unwillkürlich 'gesellschaftlich' nenne, ich weiß nicht, warum" (5.1: 885–86).

43. "*Der Mensch soll um der Güte und Liebe willen dem Tode keine Herrschaft einräumen über seine Gedanken*" (5.1: 748).

44. "Granatapfel" (5.1: 536).

45. "die Vereinigung der befreiten Völker zur Errichtung des allgemeinen Glückes … mit leidenschaftlich diktatorischem Schwung" (5.1: 234–35).

46. "Denn immer neue Völker raffte die Menschlichkeit auf ihrem glänzenden Wege mit fort, immer mehr Erde eroberte sie in Europa selbst und begann, nach Asien vorzudringen" (5.1: 240).

47. "der Anblick und Geruch sprudelnden Blutes mit der Idee des Heiligen und Geistigen" (5.1: 664).

48. "junge Exoten, portugiesische Südamerikaner, die 'jüdischer' aussahen als er … der … sogar ein wolliger Mohrentyp [war], dabei aber sehr vornehm" (5.1: 671).

49. "etwas innig Schreckhaftes . . . eine im Größenverhältnis primitive verfehlte Figur mit kraß herausgearbeiteter Anatomie" (5.1: 592).

50. "dem geilen Ästhetizismus und Exotismus . . . Anthropophagenplastik . . . negerhafte Genußsucht" (13.1: 531–32).

51. "die ebenfalls Krieg geführt und Babylonien erobert hätten, obgleich sie Semiten und also beinahe Juden gewesen seien" (5.1: 561).

52. "den Charakter des Herrenzimmers eigentlich nicht wahrte" (5.1: 592).

53. "zierlich" (5.1: 88).

54. "miekrig" (5.1: 582).

55. "ich [habe] noch nicht einmal eine Zeitung in der Hand gehabt" (5.1: 573).

56. "Liberalisierung des Islams . . . Der aufgeklärte Fanatismus" (5.1: 573–74).

57. On the political background of this discussion see 5.2: 273–75; also Nunes, *Die Freimauerei*, 112–13. Mann's source for this passage may have been Wichtl, *Weltfreimauerei* (1919), 100–103.

58. Fukuyama, *End of History.*

59. "den absoluten Befehl, die eiserne Bindung . . . Disziplin, Opfer, Verleugnung des Ich, Vergewaltigung der Persönlichkeit" (5.1: 603).

60. For broader studies of the sexual politics of masculinity and male bonding in relation to the state among intellectuals associated with the conservative revolution, see Theweleit, *Male Fantasies;* Sombart, *Die deutschen Männer;* Izenberg, *Modernism and Masculinity;* Hewitt, *Political Inversions;* and Breuer, *Anatomie,* 41–48.

61. Harpprecht, *Thomas Mann,* 409.

62. "als wärs ein Stück von mir" (Tb, Sept. 18, 1918). See also Mann to Bertram, March 18, 1918 (*Mann Bertram Briefwechsel,* 61), and again September 21, 1918 (22: 249–53).

63. Tb, September 15, 1918.

64. Aschheim, *The Nietzsche Legacy,* 77.

65. "Härte, Verwegenheit, Mut und Entdeckerlust" (Bertram, *Nietzsche,* 50).

66. "Auch Nietzsches Ideal war ein reformatorisch männisches: männlichere Wertschätzungen, männlichere Tugenden, männlichere Leitbilder—auch Nietzsche hat, gleich Dürer, nur in männlichen Typen sein Höchstes sehen und geben können" (ibid., 58).

67. For Mann's praise of Spengler's works, see Tb, July 24, 1919, and December 24, 1919. For an overview of Mann's changing response to Spengler see Koopmann, "Der Untergang"; Nicholls, "Thomas Mann and Spengler"; and Gut, *Thomas Manns Idee,* 125–31; 162–70.

68. Spengler, *Preussentum und Sozialismus,* 72, 74. On this work see Gay, *Weimar Culture,* 85–86.

69. "mit diktatorischer Machtvollkommenheit" (56).

70. "Werdet Männer . . . Wir brauchen Härte, wir brauchen eine tapfre Skepsis, wir brauchen eine Klasse von sozialistischen Herrennaturen" (98).

71. Heilbut, *Thomas Mann,* 313. For a succinct overview of Mann's relationship to these and other thinkers of Germany's "Conservative Revolution," see Kurzke, *Thomas Mann: Epoche,* 171–82.

72. Blüher, *Die Rolle der Erotik.*

73. "jüdisches Denkprodukt" (Blüher, *Deutsches Reich,* 22).

74. "Ein ausgezeichneter Vortrag, mir fast Wort für Wort aus der Seele geredet" (Tb, Feb. 11, 1919).

75. Theweleit, *Male Fantasies.*

76. Hunt, *The Family Romance.*

77. "'Ich singe den Leib, den elektrischen' . . . ein erotisch-allumarmender Demokratismus" ("Von deutscher Republik," 15.1: 551–52). On Mann's unconventional Novalis interpretation see Uerlings, *Friedrich von Hardenberg,* 528.

78. "Von deutscher Republik," 15.1: 554.

79. On the contemporary reaction to Mann's lecture see the commentary to "Von deutscher Republik," *Essays* 2: 345–46 and 15.2: 348–49. Whether or not Mann's political views changed substantially in 1922 is one of the perennially debated topics of Mann scholarship, with opinions ranging from Seidlin's insistence that Mann's postwar embrace of democracy marked a genuine transformation in his political thought ("Thomas Mann und die Demokratie," 121) to Fest's claim that Mann and his brother Heinrich remained the same: ignorant, nonpolitical "magicians" with their heads in the clouds (*Die unwissenden Magier*). For more nuanced discussions of the topic see Reed, *Thomas Mann*, 275–316; Kurzke, *Thomas Mann: Epoche*, 170–81; Fechner, *Thomas Mann*, 291–97; and Gut, *Thomas Manns Idee*, 159–61.

80. See for instance the late essay "Meine Zeit," XI: 313–14.

81. "eine Angelegenheit scharfer Judenjungen" ("Von deutscher Republik," 15.1: 530; repeated 544).

82. "die von der politischen Mystik des Slaventums gleich weit entfernt ist wie vom anarchischen Radikal-Individualismus eines gewissen Westens" (15.1: 540).

83. Habermas, *Structural Transformation*, 31–43; see also Koselleck, *Kritik*, 61–81.

84. "Ich spüre da geradezu was Militärisch-Jesuitisches in der Freimauerei" (5.1: 766).

85. Nunes, *Die Freimauerei*, 126.

86. "zu indischer und arabischer Weisheit und magischer Naturerkenntnis" (5.1: 768).

87. "morgenländischen Mystik" (5.1: 768).

88. "lapis philosophorum, das mann-weibliche Produkt aus Sulfur und Merkur, die res bina, die zweigeschlechtige prima material" (5.1: 770).

89. "Elemente orgiastischer Urreligiosität, gelöste und nächtliche Opferdienste zu Ehren von Sterben und Werden, Tod, Verwandlung und Aufstehung" (5.1: 772).

90. Abbott, "Der Zauberberg," 140; Nunes, *Die Freimauerei*, 122–27.

91. Abbott was the first to recognize the importance of Thalmann's work for *The Magic Mountain* ("Der Zauberberg"). See also Nunes, *Die Freimaueri*.

92. Wichtl, *Weltfreimauerei*, ed. Schneider, 7.

93. "eine Art Gegenstück zu dem, welches später der preußische Friederich für seine Infanterie erlassen" (5.1: 674).

94. "Hm. Spanien, das liege andererseits ebenso weit von der humanistischen Mitte ab,—nicht nach der weichen, sondern nach der harten Seite; es sei nicht Formlosigkeit, sondern Überform, der Tod als Form, sozusagen" (5.1: 760).

95. "Es könne aber auch etwas recht boshaft Terroristisches zustande kommen, wenn der Osten nach Spanien gehe" (5.1: 761).

96. Vaget, "Making of *Magic Mountain*," 24–25.

97. "Ein gräßliches Volk, gräßlich, gräßlich ... alle überpersönliche, mythische Antipathie, deren ich fähig bin, ein wirklich schüttelnder Abscheu, gilt der Mischung infamer, ohne Zweifel sexuell betonten Grausamkeit und humanitär-sentimentalen

Phrasenschmisses, den sie Europa vor Augen führen" (Mann to Bertram, June 10, 1923, 22: 484).

98. "Ja, er ist verloren!" (5.1: 804).

99. Cf. Darmaun, *Thomas Mann*, 141–43; Elsaghe, "Naphta," 176–77.

100. "die männliche Heiterkeit vorurteilsloser Forschung!" (5.1: 1017).

101. "Nordische Kühle . . . eine gläsern-keusche, kindlich-jungfräuliche Atmosphäre" (5.1: 993).

102. "mit exotisch schleppenden Akzenten" (5.1: 991).

103. "seine braunen exotischen Augen in die hellblauen" (5.1: 996).

104. "Die Magnetisierung, wenn es denn eine solche war, stärkete sie zu weiterem Ringen" (5.1: 1030).

105. For a succinct summary of Mesmer's ideas in historical context, see Safranski, *E. T. A. Hoffmann*, 294–310.

106. On the Romantic interest in mining as "the image of the soul" see Ziolkowski, *German Romanticism*, 18–63.

107. "Es geht um die Macht. . . . Für die Opfer ist der Magnetismus die Erfahrung des Ich-Verlustes unter der psychodynamischen Gewalt einer totalitären Macht" (Safranski, *E. T. A. Hoffmann*, 303, 305).

108. "in einer Art Sitzungskostüm . . . ihre jungfräuliche Brust . . . dass sie unter diesem Gewande wenig trage" (5.1: 1019).

109. Koc, "Magical Enactments," 112–13.

110. "zum Zeichen einer Schamhaftigkeit, die nach Lage der Dinge wohl begreiflich war" (5.1: 1020).

111. "ein heißes 'Ja!'" (5.1: 1023).

112. Koc, "Magical Enactments," 113–15.

113. "plaudern" (5.1: 996).

114. "hat in seinem Kopf nur einen Gedanken, und der ist schmutzig" (5.1: 99).

115. See Theweleit, *Male Fantasies*, 1: 94, for an example of racist propaganda against French black colonial troops (further examples are on display in the permanent exhibit at the Deutsches Historisches Museum in Berlin). The original poster for *King Kong* (1933) featured the scantily clad, blond Fay Wray in the grasp of a ferocious ape in a film that clearly played on racial tensions in America.

116. "es möchten Verbindungen und Zusammenhänge zwischen den untersten und lichtlosen Gegenden der Einzelseele und einer durchaus wissenden Allseele bestehen" (5.1: 992).

117. "Man träumt anonym und gemeinsam, wenn auch auf eigene Art. Die große Seele, von der du nur ein Teilchen, träumt wohl mal durch dich, auf deine Art" (5.1: 746).

118. "Orakel, Magie, Päderastie, Vitzliputzli, Menschenopfer, orgiastische Kultformen, Inquisition, Autodafés, Veitstanz, Hexenprozesse, Blüte des Giftmordes und die buntesten Greuel" ("Gedanken im Krieg," 15.1: 27). On Mann's use of primitive imagery in this essay see Scherpe, "Die Mobilmachung."

119. Lehnert, "Langemarck," 286–89; Vaget, " 'Politically Suspect,' " 133.

120. Sie werden getroffen, sie fallen, mit den Armen fechtend, in die Stirn, in das Herz, ins Gedärm geschossen" (5.1: 1083).

121. "sollte jedoch kein Grund sein, es in die Lage zu bringen" (5.1: 1083).

122. "Es war der Tod" (5.1: 988).

123. "Sympathie mit dem Tode" (5.1: 988).

124. "Ergebnisse der Finsternis. Finstere Ergebnisse. Folterknechtssinn und Menschenfeindlichkeit in spanischem Schwarz mit der Tellerkrause und Lust statt Liebe" (5.1: 989).

125. *Reflections,* 33; 13.1: 57.

126. "um als Seelenzauberkünstler dem Liede Riesenmaße zu geben und die Welt damit zu unterwerfen. Man mochte wahrscheinlich sogar Reiche darauf gründen, irdisch-allzu irdische Reiche, sehr derb und fortschrittsfroh und eigentlich gar nicht heimwehkrank" (5.1: 990).

127. "Ja, Selbstüberwindung, das mochte wohl das Wesen der Überwindung dieser Liebe sein,—dieses Seelenzaubers mit finsteren Konsequenzen!" (5.1: 989–90).

128. Vaget, " 'Politically Suspect,' " 135–37.

129. "auf den Lippen das *neue* Wort der Liebe, das er noch nicht zu sprechen wußte" (5.1: 990).

130. "Wird auch . . . einmal die Liebe steigen?" (5.1: 1085).

131. "der still und freundlich spähend auf Hans Castorp, auf diesen allein, gerichtet war" (5.1: 1032).

Chapter Six

1. See Grimm, *Joseph und Echnaton,* 9–68, for a detailed account of Mann's two trips to Egypt (the second in 1930).

2. "soziale Provokation . . . als beifällige Schilderung einer Orgie des nachkriegerischen Kapitalismus mit Neureichen in den strahlenden Luxuskabinen" ("Unterwegs," 15.1: 953).

3. "es ist auch wieder ein deutsches Fahrzeug, das unsere Flagge auf hoher See und in den fremden Häfen zeigt . . . die sehr wohltut nach den exotischen Bizarrerien, in die es einen getragen" (15.1: 953).

4. "auf afrikanische Art . . . wie ich sie nie im Leben gesehen . . . einem Gelichter, gegen das die Soldojäger Süditaliens der reine britische Hochadel sind" (15.1: 956, 955).

5. "aber sie sind schlimmer als die wirklichen" (15.1: 955).

6. "Wir taten den schwülen Orient ab, unsere Seele ward licht und heiter. . . . Man wünscht dort inbrünstig, immer möchten die Perser, in welcher Gestalt sie auch kommen, wieder geschlagen werden" (15.1: 961).

7. "das kann bestimmten, wenn auch noch etwas schattenhaften Plänen, die ich im Geheimen hege, nützlich sein" (Mann to Betram, Feb. 4, 1925, *Mann an Ernest Bertram,* 136).

8. "Das alte Lied!" ("Lebensabriss," XI: 138).

9. "die letzten Zeilen von *Joseph der Ernährer* und damit von *Joseph und seine Brüder*" (Tb, Jan. 4, 1943).

10. "Erst jetzt realisiere ich, was es heißt, ohne das Joseph-Werk zu sein, die Aufgabe, die in dem ganzen Jahrzehnt immer neben mir, vor mir stand" (Tb, Mar. 17, 1943).

11. "Ich sehe darin weit mehr ein Monument meines Lebens, als ein solches der Kunst und des Gedankens, ein Monument der *Beharrlichkeit*" (Tb, Jan. 4, 1943).

12. "Manns eigentliches Hauptwerk" (Kurzke, *Mondwanderungen*, 174). See also Heftrich, "Potiphars Weib," 58.

13. Lowe-Porter's English translation appeared in four volumes between the years 1934 and 1944. See Wagener, "Thomas Mann in der amerikanischen Literaturkritik," 933–35. Even then, not all readers were equally entranced. Writing for the *New York Times*, Orville Prescott declared *Joseph the Provider* "aggressively dull, soporifically dull," while in *The New Yorker* Hamilton Basso proclaimed Thomas Mann "one of the greatest living bores" (cited in Wagener, 934–35).

14. Angress-Klüger, "Jewish Characters," 170.

15. Ibid., 170.

16. Elsaghe, *Thomas Mann*, 6. In both this book and in *Die imaginäre Nation*, Elsaghe makes only brief passing references to Mann's longest novel. Schwarz's seminal article on "Die jüdischen Gestalten" also brackets out the *Joseph* novels (87).

17. Of course, not all critics have looked the other way; my point is only that some of those critics most interested in Mann's response to the Jewish question have not focused as much attention on the novel as one might have expected.

18. Thus Kurzke refers to *Joseph* as Mann's "Zuflucht, Trost, Heimat" (refuge, comfort, home) (*Mondwanderungen*, 140).

19. "Der Mythos wurde in diesem Buch dem Fascismus aus den Händen genommen . . . die Geburt des Ich aus dem mythischen Kollektiv" ("Joseph und seine Brüder," *Essays* 5: 189, 196). On the Romantic revival of myth and its appropriation by right-wing ideologues, see Williamson, *The Longing for Myth*, and Lincoln, *Theorizing Myth*.

20. The term *Rechenschaft* has the sense of an account as a coming to terms with something, giving a justification for something—in this case, Mann's journey into what had been enemy territory less than a decade ago.

21. On the much-researched topic of Thomas Mann's Bachofen reception, see (in chronological order): Lehnert, "Thomas Manns Vorstudien," 486–96; Dierks, *Studien zu Mythos*, 169–82; Koopmann, *Der schwierige Deutsche*, 65–78; Heftrich, "Matriarchat und Patriarchat"; and Galvan, *Zur Bachofen-Rezeption*.

22. "Die deutsch-romantische Revolution vom Anfang des 19. Jahrhunderts gegen die Aufklärung, den Idealismus und die Klassik des 18." ("Pariser Rechenschaft," 15.1: 1159).

23. "diesen ganzen Joseph-Görres-Komplex von Erde, Volk, Natur, Vergangenheit und Tod, einen revolutionären Obskurantismus, derb charakterisiert" (ibid., 15.1: 1159).

24. "Rede über Lessing" (1929); "Die Stellung Freuds in der modernen Geistesgeschichte" (1929); "Goethe als Repräsentant des bürgerlichen Zeitalters" (1932).

25. "Massenopiat des Dritten Reiches . . . epileptische Ekstase" ("Deutsche Ansprache: ein Appell an die Vernunft," *Essays* 3: 269).

26. The stress on Mann's universal humanism in *Joseph* begins with Käte Hamburger (*Thomas Manns biblisches Werk*) and continues through Kurzke's *Mondwanderungen*, an indispensable, concise introduction to *Joseph and His Brothers*. Assmann's *Thomas Mann und Ägypten* provides a subtle reading of the novel from the perspective of an Egyptologist. Heftrich's monumental *Geträumte Taten* shows how Mann reworked aspects of Goethe's *Faust II*, Wagner's operas, and Bachofen's philosophy, but is marred by excessive quotation and a narrow focus on intrinsic textual and intertextual analysis.

27. Darmaun, *Thomas Mann*, 190–93. See also Marquardt, *Erzählte Juden*, 188–245.

28. Robertson, *The "Jewish Question,"* 228–29.

29. Cited from Vaget, *Thomas Mann-Kommentar*, 277.

30. Marquardt, *Erzählte Juden*, 42–44, 132, 137, 149.

31. "Im Zeichen des Orientalismus" ("Pariser Rechenschaft," 15.1: 1181).

32. On the popular enthusiasm for Egypt in the wake of Howard Carter's discoveries see Hornung, "Thomas Mann."

33. "monumentaler Kindlichkeit und Fröhlichkeit, an sieghafter Rassenfrische" (15.1: 1154); "das klassische und unwandelbare asiatische Lächeln" (15.1: 1181); the reference to male prostitutes is on 15.1: 1164.

34. On Mann's reception of Freud and Jung, see Dierks, *Studien zu Mythos*, and "Kultursymbolik."

35. "seine Sammlung archäologischer Merkwürdigkeiten . . . indische Schnitzereien, Frühfunde aus ägyptischen Gräbern, griechische Kleinplastiken sehr merkwürdiger Art" ("Meine Goethereise," XIII: 69).

36. "in das Wissen vom Primitiven, vom Urmenschen" (XIII: 400).

37. For further elaboration of this idea, see also "Die Stellung Freuds," *Essays* 3: 122–23.

38. "der in vollkommener Trance und schrecklichen Zuckungen der erschöpften Jünglinge endete" ("Bruder Hitler," *Essays* 4: 309).

39. "des gutmütigen Gelächters der SS-Hottentotten" ("Der Judenterror," *Essays* 5: 203).

40. "die unsinnige Idee der Rasse-Reinheit des deutschen Volkes" ("Das Problem der Freiheit," *Essays* 5: 70).

41. "Zum Problem," XIII: 483.

42. "Man spricht heute viel von 'Totalität,' und sofern dieser Begriff auf den Staat angewandt wird, ist er etwas Fürchterliches, Monströses und Unmenschliches" ("Zur Gründung einer Dokumenten-Sammlung," XI: 466).

43. "Die Juden aber stellen in deutscher Sphäre dies geistige Element körperlich, blut- und rassenmäßig . . . dar" ("Zum Problem des Antisemitismus," GW XIII: 483–84).

44. Tb, April 20, 1933 (see introduction). A right-wing newspaper columnist referred to Thomas Mann in 1928 derisively as a "Portugiesensproß" (offspring of Portugal). In commentary to *Essays* 3: 396.

45. "Die Erlösung des rationalen europäischen Geistes vom dumpfen orientalischen

Mutterboden wird in Joseph personalisiert und in seiner Geschichte thematisiert" (The redemption of European rationality from the dull Oriental mother-ground is personalized in Joseph and thematized in his story) (Junge, "Thomas Manns fiktionale Welt Ägypten," 49). See also Dierks on Egypt in *Joseph* as "europäische Projektionen, Projektionen Europas" over the Orient ("Kultursymbolik," 131). Both Junge and Dierks are too quick to equate Jacob's prejudices with Mann's opinion. While Mann does reveal his reservations about modern Egypt in "Unterwegs," he undermines the absolute distinction between the Hebrews and the Egyptians in his novel.

46. Mann, "Joseph und seine Brüder," *Essays* 5: 194.

47. "nur ein bedingter, besonderer Anfang der Dinge" (IV: 18).

48. "Tief ist der Brunnen der Vergangenheit" (IV: 9).

49. "Ewigkeit gewinnen und Allgegenwart, also erst recht das Leben" (IV: 53).

50. "Denn das Wesen des Lebens ist Gegenwart, und nur mythischer Weise stellt sein Geheimnis sich in den Zeitformen der Vergangenheit und der Zukunft dar" (IV: 53).

51. "Gestaltung, Umgestaltung . . . die Mütter" (Goethe, *Faust*, part 2, lines 6287, 6285).

52. "Die Idee der Sichtbarmachung des zu den Müttern Gegangenen im Dreifußrauch stark einschlägig im *Joseph*" (Tb, Dec. 13, 1935).

53. Jeremias, *Das Alte Testament*. See also Kurzke, *Mondwanderungen*, 93–110; Assmann, *Thomas Mann und Ägypten*, 55.

54. Frye, *The Secular Scripture*, "Themes of Descent," 97–126.

55. As has often been noted, Hans Castorp's "anonymous and collective" vision in the snow in *The Magic Mountain* is more Jungian than Freudian, and Dierks notes with astonishment that Mann continued to employ Jungian concepts in the early 1930s, even though he was aware that Jung had severely compromised himself and his work by lending support to National Socialism (Dierks, "Thomas Mann und die 'jüdische Psychoanalyse'"). In 1941, Mann gently but firmly chided Joseph Campbell for recommending political indifference to youth at a time when the reading or publishing of Thomas Mann's books in Germany—of which Campbell professed to be an admirer—was forbidden and could result in imprisonment and beatings in concentration camps (Mann to Campbell, Jan. 6, 1941, *Briefe*, 2: 173–74).

56. On Mann's effort to combine the stasis of a worldview based on mythic repetition with the promise of Christian salvation history, see Kurzke, *Mondwanderungen*, 23–27; Assmann, *Thomas Mann und Ägypten*, 74; and Lehnert, "Ägypten," 96–97.

57. On the interpretation of the Old Testament as a prefiguration of the New, see Auerbach, "Figura."

58. "weil man einem Gotte diente, dessen Wesen nicht Ruhe und wohnendes Behagen war, einem Gotte der Zukunftspläne" (IV: 52).

59. "dessen zeitlicher Standort am Quellpunkt weitläufigsten Werdens war" (V: 1755).

60. "der Friedensfürst und der Gesalbte . . . der einst erweckt werden sollte aus erwähltem Samen, und dem der Stuhl seines Königsreiches sollte bestätigt sein ewiglich" (V: 1557). In Genesis 49:10, Jacob blesses Judah and promises that his people will rule

"until Shiloh come," a reference from the Christian perspective to Jesus Christ as prophesized in Isaiah 9:6: "For unto us a child is born . . . and his name shall be . . . The Prince of Peace."

61. "Der Treubund mit Gott war geschlechtlich . . . dem menschlich Männlichen sittigenderweise eine Abschwächung ins Weibliche zu" (IV: 80).

62. "die nicht recht wissen, wer sie sind" (IV: 128).

63. "Der Anspruch des menschlichen Ich auf zentrale Wichtigkeit war die Voraussetzung für die Entdeckung Gottes" (V: 1721).

64. "die mächtigen Eigenschaften, die er ihm zuschrieb, waren wohl Gottes ursprüngliches Eigentum. . . . Aber war er es nicht dennoch in einem gewissen Sinne, indem er sie erkannte, sie lehrte und denkend verwirklichte?" (IV: 428).

65. "Es ist die Idee der Heimsuchung, des Einbruchs trunken zerstörender und vernichtender Mächte in ein Gefaßtes und mit allen seinen Hoffnungen auf Würde und ein bedingtes Glück der Fassung verschworenes Leben" (V: 1085–86). On the central importance of this quotation for Mann's worldview, see Kurzke, *Mondwanderungen*, 117.

66. "Vom äffischen Ägypterland" (IV: 96). John E. Woods translates "äffisch" as "monkey-faced"; I have changed this to the more literal "apish."

67. "Wo aber der Gottesverstand in die Brüche ging und geiler Taumel an seine Stelle trat, da begann das für ihn, was er 'eine Narrheit' nannte, ein sehr starkes Wort in seinem Munde, stark genug, das äußerste an Mißbilligung auszusagen" (IV: 417).

68. "schamloses Flußpferd, dies letztere unter dem Einfluß eines ägyptischen Gerüchtes, das Flußpferd habe die wüste Gewohnheit, seinen Vater zu töten und sich gewaltsam mit seiner Mutter zu paaren" (IV: 86).

69. "Denn es ist ein Frauenleib wie der andere, gut zum Lieben, zum Zeugen gut" (IV: 291).

70. "er nannte es 'Scheol,' die Hölle, das Totenreich" (IV: 414).

71. "die Ebräer [waren] selber ein solcher [Greuel], und zwar in dem Grade, daß es ihnen gegen Würde und frommen Anstand ging, mit solchen Leuten das Brot zu essen" (IV: 830). On the Egyptian prejudice toward the Hebrews in *Joseph* see Assmann, *Thomas Mann und Ägypten*, 100, 158.

72. "[Ihr redet] die Sprache der Menschen nicht" (V: 1601).

73. "Weiß doch Pharao, daß eure Kultur nicht gar so hoch steht und eure Ansprüche leicht zu befriedigen sind" (V: 1695).

74. "auf Jaakobs Hof [wurden] keine Chamiten geduldet, ihres Ahnen wegen, des Vaterschänders, der über und über schwarz geworden war" (IV: 20–21).

75. "Mann der Unterwelt . . . denn der Süden lag im Denklichte des Unterweltlichen" (IV: 143–35).

76. "beinahe dem elenden Kusch und den negerländern beigerechnet" (IV: 724).

77. "Gummiessern" (V: 918); "ebenholzschwarzer Mohren mit unglaublich gepolsterten Lippenbergen" (IV: 774); "Mohrenköpfe" (V: 1729).

78. "auf Händen getragen von der wilden Unterwürfigkeit nackter Mohrenmädchen und zärtlich katzbuckelnder Verschnittener" (V: 1012).

79. "dunkelhäutigen Ehrenmädchen . . . schwarzem und wolligem . . . Haar" (V: 1095); "eines von Muts nackten Mohrenmädchen, ein Tierchen" (V: 1028).

80. "die sich auf allerlei arge Künste der Negerländer . . . verstand" (V: 1117).

81. "Vettel reinsten Wassers" (V: 1159).

82. "Den Himmel und viel Menschliches meine ich nach dreitausendfünfhundert Jahren dort unverändert zu finden" ("Lebensabriss," XI: 144). See also "Unterwegs": "Das Morgenland . . . Doch, doch, ich habe es aufgenommen. Ich trage zeitlose Bilder mit fort, die unverändert sind seit den Tagen der Isis und sperberköpfiger Götter" (15.1: 958).

83. "bunt aufgeputzte Neger . . . denn sie wußten sich verachtet und benahmen sich närrischer, als es in ihrer Natur lag, um den grotesken Vorstellungen zu schmeicheln, die das Volk von ihnen hegte" (V: 1245).

84. "starke Verallgemeinerungen, Einseitigkeiten und Übertreibungen enthielt" (IV: 98).

85. "die Kinder Ägyptens sind wie andere Kinder, nicht wesentlich besser und schlechter" (V: 1742–43).

86. "der Not-Aristokratismus kleiner, sehr kleiner Leute. 'Ich bin zwar nichts— aber ich bin kein Jude'" ("Die Juden warden dauern!" Essays 4: 177).

87. "sein Blut zu vermischen ein erbstolzes Reinheitsgebot ihn warnte" (V: 1139).

88. "Nicht einmal im Traum aber konnten die Leute El eljons ihrem Zusammenhange Einheit und Reinheit des Blutes zuschreiben" (IV: 129).

89. "manche Beschönigungen . . . an denen zugunsten der Bluteinheit des geistlichen Stammes halb und halb festgehalten wurde, obgleich sie auf schwachen Füßen standen" (V: 1540).

90. "Bluteinheit ist immer nachzuweisen, wenn man den Rahmen weit genug zieht" (V: 1541).

91. "recht willkürlich im Geschmack und zusammengesetzt: Elemente östlicher Kulturübereinkunft begegneten sich darin mit solchen, die eher dem Ismaelitisch-Beduinischen und der Wüstenwelt zugehörten" (IV: 69).

92. "mit Schultern, deren . . . Sitz ägyptisch anmutete" (IV: 62).

93. "nach Physiognomie und Gebärde . . . sein Habitus [hatte] immer schon eine gewisse verwandte Annäherung an den ägyptischen gezeigt" (V: 963).

94. "der babylonischer Herkunft war" (IV: 103).

95. "schlecht und recht ägyptisches Halbblut" (V: 1519).

96. "schwarz von Angesicht" (V: 1793); Genesis 9:18–27; Jeremias, Das Alte Testament, 147.

97. "denn um den Namen steht es geheimnisvoll" (IV: 10).

98. "Der junge Joseph zum Beispiel . . . erblickte in einer südbabylonischen Stadt namens Uru . . . den Anfang aller, das heißt: seiner persönlichen Dinge" (IV: 10–11).

99. Mann found many of these details in Jeremias, Das Alte Testament.

100. "ein Land, dessen zersplittertes Staatsleben es zu politischer Ohnmacht und Abhängigkeit hoffnungslos bestimmte . . . nichts weniger als für seinen Geschmack an imperialer Größe und seine Anlage zur politischen Vision" (IV: 14).

101. "Vorkommnisse der Welt und ihrer Reiche . . . auf Händel und Umtriebe" (IV: 76).

102. "bald genug spärlicher fließen würden" (IV: 77).

103. "doch war des Wirtes Teilnahme an der Unterhaltung stark herabgesetzt, seit nicht länger von Gott die Rede war" (IV: 77).

104. "ein verhätscheltes Herrensöhnchen mit eigenem Harem, ein Teppichlieger und Süßigkeitenschlecker, eine elegante Drohne" (IV: 155).

105. "'verlorengingen die Städte des Königs' und 'abgefallen sei das Land Pharao's zu den Chabiren'" (IV: 184).

106. "jener späten Frühe" (V: 1509).

107. "Es war Spätherbst, das Schon-fernab-Sein einer Gesellschaft von Enkeln und Erben von den Gründungen und Mustern der Väter, deren Siege sie in den Stand gesetzt hatten, das Besiegte fein zu finden" (IV: 835).

108. "so führten sie zwar die Kriegstaten eines früheren Königs ihres Landes, Thutmose's des Dritten, und des ägyptischen Heeres, das unter ihm in siebzehn Feldzügen die Lande bis zum Strome Euphrat erobert hatte, mit inschriftenhafter Prahlerei im Munde, stellten aber selber ihren Mann hauptsächlich beim Vertilgen von Gänsebraten und Bier" (IV: 156).

109. Mann, "Gegen Dickfelligkeit," in *Essays* 3: 75–77; see also the commentary to this passage *Essays*, 3: 394; and Gut, *Thomas Manns Idee*, 289–91.

110. "ein Auf und Ab von Himmelfahrt, Höllenfahrt und Wiedererstehen" (IV: 159).

111. "Seine Seele war bewegt und erhoben von Nachahmung, Wiederkehr, Vergegenwärtigung" (IV: 163).

112. "es gab die Jahrhunderte nicht" (IV: 163).

113. "Jaakob wußte es und wußte es nicht, das heißt: er sah davon ab" (IV: 165).

114. "Jaakob vermied die Begegnung. Er ließ seine Söhne walten" (IV: 172).

115. "grasse Ahnungen" (IV: 178).

116. "Nun denn, trotzdem offenbar . . . die Reinheit, nach der ich lechzte, war, wie sich zeigt, nicht unerläßlich zum Heil" (V: 1798).

117. "die Leute von Menfe [machten] sich lustig um dessentwillen, was ihre Stadt einst gewesen und was sie längst nicht mehr war" (IV: 748–49).

118. "eine gewesene Königin, das Grab seiner Größe, eine Weltstadt mit schnoddrig abgekürztem Todesnamen" (IV: 749).

119. "eine von allerlei Menschengeblüt, syrischem, libyschem, nubischem, mitannischem und sogar kretischem, vollgestopfte Karawanserei" (IV: 747).

120. "Ihn selbst und die Seinen sah niemand an, da Fremdheit hier alltäglich . . . war . . . er sah Häute in allen Abschattungen vom Obsidian-Schwarz über viele Stufen von Braun und Gelb bis zum Käseweiß, er sah sogar gelbes Haar und azurfarbene Augen, Gesichter und Kleider von jedem Schnitt, er sah die Menschheit" (IV: 774–75).

121. Mann found references to Egypt's cosmopolitan diversity in the German translation of Weigall, *The Life and Times of Akhnaton;* see for example pages 7 and 30 in the English edition; also Hornung, *Echnaton*, 31–32.

122. "klein und arm. . . . Nun wimmeln die Länder und Wêse, die Große, von Fremden, die Schätze strömen, und alles ist neu worden" (V: 957).

123. "in diesem dünkelhaftesten aller erschaffenen Länder" (IV: 829).

124. "sie versuchten selber, ausländische Brocken, akkadisch-babylonische sowohl wie solche aus Josephs Sprachsphäre, in ihre Rede zu mischen" (IV: 832).

125. "Hafengüter, das heißt: eingeführte Fremderzeugnisse" (IV: 833).

126. "unfolgerichtige Schätzung . . . die Freigeisterei von Leuten, die das elende Ausland nicht selbst besiegt und unterworfen hatten, sondern das durch Frühere hatten besorgen lassen und sich nun erlaubten, es fein zu finden" (IV: 833).

127. Mann's primary source on Egyptian religion and the rise of monotheism was Weigall, *Life and Times;* see also Hornung, *Echnaton;* and Assmann, *Thomas Mann und Ägypten,* 102–8.

128. "war starr und streng, ein verbietender Feind jeder ins Allgemeine ausschauenden Spekulation, unhold dem Ausland und unbeweglich beim nicht zu erörternden Völkerbrauch, beim heilig Angestammten verharrend" (V: 942).

129. "Ausdehnungslust . . . sich in Beziehung und in ein weltläufiges Einvernehmen zu setzen mit allen möglichen Sonnengöttern der Völker" (V: 941).

130. "das Uralte . . . beweglich und weltfroh" (V: 942).

131. "diese beiden großen Götter waren genau genommen ein und derselbe" (IV: 735).

132. "nicht im Geiste des Dreiecks und der Versöhnung . . . vielmehr in dem Sinn, als ob Amun den Rê besiegt und verzehrt und sich einverleibt habe" (IV: 736).

133. "Amun-Rê's große Gemahlin [war] Mut oder 'Mutter' genannt und Hathor, die Kuhäugige, schön von Antlitz, vielmehr zu Rê-Atum, dem Herrn von On, als seine Herrin gehörte" (V: 945).

134. "so setzte auch Mut . . . sich der bezwingenden Hathor gleich" (V: 945).

135. "Ja, das waren die Feinheiten und staatsklugen Gleichsetzungen Ägyptenlandes!" (V: 945).

136. "einzigen und wirklichen Freunden sowie Freunden schlechthin des Königs" (V: 1243).

137. "fremde Herrscher, von asiatischem Hirtengeblüt . . . Rê's Doppelkrone getragen [hatten]" (V: 1007).

138. "fremdes Geblüt" (V: 1007).

139. "der seinerzeit 'die Rebellen gesammelt' und in der Schlacht hatte besiegt werden müssen, ehe er sich als befreit bekannte" (V: 1008).

140. "bewiesen sie klärlich, daß in ihnen der Fruchtbarkeitssinn ihrer bodensässigerdverbundenen Vorfahren schon viel neuzeitliche Abschwächung erfahren hatte" (V: 1008–9).

141. "Amun haßt die Lockerung durch das Fremde" (V: 1041).

142. "der Lockerkeit Vorschub leistet und seinen versuchenden Denkern gestattet, des Reiches Volksmark zu weichen durch tändeldes Fremdtum" (V: 1042).

143. "Die Fähigkeit des Menschen zum Selbstbetrug ist erstaunlich" (V: 1020).

144. "frei oder unfrei, einheimisch oder fremd" (V: 1057).

145. "die das ist Atum-Rê's heilige Eheschwester . . . und nicht des Amun" (V: 1071).

146. "mit der Religion zu helfen, indem sie sich . . . gegen des volksstrengen Amun, ihren bisherigen Herrn, auf Atum-Rê von On, den milde-ausdehnungsfreundlichen und den Fremdländern holden, berief" (V: 1090).

147. "dem . . . fremdfreundlichen Bruder asiatischer Sonnenherren" (V: 1024).

148. "in asiatischer Tracht, einem reichen Gewande zu dem sie sich die Stoffe in der Stadt der Lebenden im Handelsgewölbe eines bärtigen Syrers hatte erstehen lassen" (V: 1121).

149. "ich meine die Mohrenhirse, das Negerkorn, ich meine das weiße" (V: 1101).

150. "die dunkelhäutigen Ehrenmädchen . . . deren schwarzem und wolligem . . . Haar" (V: 1095).

151. "während der Kopf des Beutetieres dem Joseph mit klaffendem Rachen zu Füßen lag" (V: 1126).

152. "wenn sich in Weibertracht ergehen die Männer und im Kleide des Mannes das Weib und die Unterschiede dahinfallen" (V: 1122).

153. "ich will nicht dergestalt sündigen wider Gott . . . daß ich den Vater schände und morde und mit der Mutter ein Paar mache als schamloses Flußpferd" (V: 1176).

154. "So Muts nicht nur unwahre, sondern leider auch hetzerische Rede" (V: 1263–64).

155. "Ja, eine kühle Mond-Nonne . . . war Mut-em-enet von nun an . . . und—so muß man hinzufügen—außerordentlich bigott" (V: 1497).

156. Mann based his portrait of Akhnaton largely on the German translation of Weigall's *The Life and Times of Akhnaton*. For an excellent introduction to the man and his religion from a more recent perspective, see Hornung, *Echnaton*. Grimm's *Joseph und Echnaton* parallels extensive source material with specific passages of Mann's text.

157. "Er vermutete, daß es nicht nur ein anderes war, ein Weltreich zu gründen, und ein anderes, einem Weltgott ins Leben zu helfen, sondern daß diese zweite Beschäftigung möglicherweise auch in einem irgendwie gearteten Widerspruch stand zu der königlichen Aufgabe, die ererbte Schöpfung zu bewahren und aufrechtzuerhalten" (V: 1383).

158. "persönlich einen Kriegs- und Plünderzug, sei es ins Asiatische oder in die Negerländer" (V: 1379).

159. "der Herr der Kronen [sitzt] nur da in der Schönheit seines Palastes inmitten der Welt und empfängt in gebührender Bequemlichkeit den Gedankentribut der bewohnten Erde" (V: 1424).

160. "Einige sind braun, andere rot, wieder andere Schwarz und noch andere wie Milch und Blut—so abgetönt offenbaren sie sich in dir und sind deine Offenbarung" (V: 1457).

161. "den zart Bemühten, der recht wohl auf dem Wege ist, wenn auch der Rechte nicht für den Weg" (V: 1749).

162. "Erbgüter, die wie Inseln eines überalterten Feudalismus hie und da über das Reich sich hin hervortaten" (V: 1501).

163. "ging er gegen die verstockten Barone sehr scharf vor, indem er von Anfang an ihren Bodenbesitz ohne Federlesens in sein Abgaben- und Rücklage-System einbezog und mit der Zeit zu ihrer schlichten Enteignung zugunsten der Krone gelangte" (V: 1501).

164. "einer bisher sehr unfügsamen, ja aufsässigen Menschenklasse" (V: 1763).

165. "den Eigentumsbegriff zu verzaubern" (V: 1762).

166. "Die Neigung zur Frechheit, zum Abfall und zum Verrat griff um sich" (V: 1767).

167. "Silber und Holz . . . für Brot und Saat" (V: 1476).

168. Assmann, *Thomas Mann und Ägypten*, 164.

169. Kristiansen, "Ägypten als symbolischer Raum," 32–34.

170. We can follow the evolution of the project precisely in Mann's diaries from the summer of 1942 through the spring of 1943. Vaget provides a succinct summary of the novella's composition and reception (*Thomas Mann-Kommentar*, 271–88).

171. Robertson, The "Jewish Question," 142–50.

172. Freud, *Moses and Monotheism*, 22.

173. Vaget, *Thomas Mann Kommentar*, 271.

174. Mann, *The Tables of the Law*, 36. The English translation cited hereafter in the text. "ungebärdigen Horden . . . ein außergewöhnliches und abgesondertes [Volk], eine reine Gestalt, aufgerichtet dem Unsichtbaren und ihm geheiligt" (VIII: 846).

175. "Für ihn bedeutete Jahwe zwar ebenfalls den Auszug, aber nicht sowohl den Kriegszug zur Landgewinnung" (VIII: 819).

176. Freud, *Moses and Monotheism*, 152.

177. "Seine Geburt war unordentlich, darum liebte er leidenschaftlich Ordnung, das Unverbrüchliche, Gebot und Verbot. . . . Er war sinnenheiß, darum verlangte es ihn nach dem Geistigen, Reinen und Heiligen" (VIII: 808).

178. Vaget, *Thomas Mann-Kommentar*, 277–81.

179. Darmaun, *Thomas Mann*, 220.

180. Robertson, The "Jewish Question," 229.

181. Gut, *Thomas Manns Idee*, 317–19; Darmaun, *Thomas Mann*, 225.

182. In Numbers 12:1–2 Miriam and Aaron criticize Moses for having taken a Cushite wife; in Mann's text she is identified as a mistress and her racial features are emphasized.

183. The "Mohrin" in German (VIII: 855), translated as "Ethiopian" (44).

184. "In ihrer Art war sie ein prachtvolles Stück, mit Bergesbrüsten, rollendem Augenweiß, Wulstlippen, in die sich im Kuß zu versenken ein Abenteuer sein mochte, und einer Haut voller Würze" (VIII: 855).

Chapter Seven

1. See Hans Mayer's important early discussion of Thomas Mann's "Buch des Endes" (esp. 270, 302–3). Also Heftrich, "*Doktor Faustus*," 139; and Görner, *Thomas Mann*, 139–59. A detailed account of the novel's origins is available in 10.2: 9–59.

2. "Es wird mein *Parsifal*" (It will be my *Parsifal*). Mann to Klaus Mann, April 27, 1943, *Briefe* 2: 309. See also Tb, March 21, 1943, and *Die Entstehung des Doktor Faustus*, XI: 157 (*The Story of a Novel*, 19).

3. *Doctor Faustus*, trans. John E. Woods, 371–72. References to the English translation hereafter cited in the text. "Das Gefühl, daß eine Epoche sich endigte, die nicht nur das neunzehnte Jahrhundert umfaßte, sondern zurückreichte bis zum Ausgang des Mittelalters, bis zur Sprengung scholastischer Bindungen, zur Emanzipation des Individuums, der Geburt der Freiheit . . . kurzum, die Epoche des bürgerlichen Humanismus" (10.1: 512).

4. Plessner presented an influential version of the *Sonderweg* thesis in *Die verspätete Nation*. Plessner contributed to Mann's journal *Mass und Wert*, and Mann was probably familiar with Plessner's work (10.2: 376). On the proximity of Mann's argument to Plessner's see Gut, *Thomas Manns Idee*, 334. Blackbourn and Eley challenge the *Sonderweg* thesis in *The Peculiarities of German History*.

5. Mann, "Germany and the Germans," 306. "Hysterie des ausgehenden Mittelalters, etwas von latenter seelischer Epidemie . . . ein altertümlich-neurotischer Untergrund . . . eine seelische Geheimdisposition" ("Deutschland und die Deutschen," XI: 1130)'. Subsequent references to the English translation are included in the text.

6. "chthonischen, irrationalen und dämonischen Kräften des Lebens . . . philosophischen Intellektualismus und Rationalismus der Aufklärung—eines Aufstandes der Musik gegen die Literatur, der Mystik gegen die Klarheit" ("Deutschland," XI: 1143).

7. "Man kann sagen, daß der Begriff der 'Nation' selbst, in seiner geschichtlichen Verbundenheit mit dem der Freiheit, in Deutschland landfremd ist" ("Deutschland," XI: 1137).

8. "der europa-übliche national-demokratische Weg zur Einigung [war] der deutsche Weg nicht" ("Deutschland," XI: 1143).

9. "das barbarisch-völkische Element in dieser Erhebung . . . das Übernationale, das Weltdeutschtum, die Weltliteratur" ("Deutschland," XI: 1138).

10. "in dem der nationale Individualismus des neunzehnten Jahrhunderts sich lösen, ja schließlich vergehen wird" ("Deutschland," XI: 1147).

11. "Wie heute alles liegt, ist meine Art von Deutschtum in der gastfreien Kosmopolis, dem rassischen und nationalen Universum, das Amerika heißt, am passendsten aufgehoben. . . . Als Amerikaner bin ich Weltbürger,—was von Natur der Deutsche ist" ("Deutschland," XI: 1127).

12. "Universalismus und Kosmopolitismus. . . . Die Deutschen ließen sich verführen, auf ihren eingeborenen Kosmopolitismus den Anspruch auf europäische Hegemonie, ja auf Weltherrschaft zu gründen, wodurch er zu seinem strikten Gegenteil, zum anmaßlichsten und bedrohlichsten Nationalismus und Imperialismus wurde" ("Deutschland," XI: 1141).

13. "alles um sich endlich und gründlich für die Macht in Form zu bringen, alles um der 'Weltherrschaft' willen, alles aus unangebrachtem Neide auf England" ("Dieser Krieg," *Essays* 4: 101).

14. Mann refers to his lecture in a diary entry of October 3, 1943. "War and Democracy" is reprinted in the *Tagebücher 1940–1943*, 1036–49; the passage quoted here is from page 1043.

15. "das Thema der schlimmen Inspiration und Genialisierung, die mit dem Vom Teufel geholt Werden, d.h. mit der Paralyse endet . . . die Idee des Rausches überhaupt und der Anti-Vernunft . . . dadurch aus das Politische, Faschistische, und damit das traurige Schicksal Deutschlands" (Mann to Klaus Mann, Apr. 27, 1943, *Briefe* 2: 309).

16. Reed, *Thomas Mann*, 374; Vaget, *Seelenzauber*, 34.

17. "sondern auch zu Firmen des Auslandes, nach London, Lyon, Bologna, sogar nach New York" (10.1: 63).

18. "Wunsch nach Fernluft . . . der ja 'nichts sehen wollte' " (10.1: 307–8).

19. "Imperator Romanorum und Saxonicus . . . aber nicht, weil er ein Sachse sein wollte, sondern . . . weil er die Sachsen besiegt hatte" (10.1: 56–57).

20. "Nicht umsonst war er [Leverkühn] der Sohn der Stadt, in der Otto III. begraben lag. . . . Abneigung gegen das Deutschtum, das er verkörperte" (10.1: 240).

21. "Es war eine barocke Idee, die aber tief in seinem aus hochmütiger Weltscheu, dem altdeutschen Provinzialismus von Kaisersaschern und einem ausgesprochenen Gesinnungskosmopolitismus sich zusammensetzenden Wesen wurzelte" (10.1: 240).

22. Theweleit, *Male Fantasies*, vol. 2: 112–13; 127; see also Sontag, "Fascinating Fascism," 102.

23. See Dörr, "Thomas Mann und Adorno," 288; also Kurzke, *Thomas Mann: Life*, 474. Readers interested in the frequently discussed relationship between Thomas Mann and Adorno should begin with Mann's *Entstehung des Doktor Faustus*, the Mann-Adorno *Briefwechsel*, Adorno's essay on Mann in *Noten zur Literatur* 3: 19–29, and Katia Mann's *Meine ungeschriebenen Memoiren*, 157–61. In addition to Dörr, useful secondary literature includes Heimann, "Thomas Manns *Doktor Faustus*"; Sauerland, " 'Er wußte noch mehr' "; Neumann, "Zwölftontechnik?"; and Vaget, *Seelenzauber*.

24. Mann to Bruno Walter, March 1, 1945; *Briefe* 2: 416. In the filmed version of Heinrich Mann's *Professor Unrat*, Marlene Dietrich sings "Ich bin von Kopf bis Fuß auf Liebe eingestellt," rendered in English as "Falling in love again."

25. "Was ich brauche, sind ein paar charakterisierende, realisierende *Exaktheiten* (man kommt mit wenigen aus), die dem Leser ein plausibles, ja überzeugendes Bild geben" (Mann to Adorno, Dec. 30, 1945, *Briefe* 2: 472).

26. "ein Stück verwirklichter Utopie, wie es einem kaum je zuteil wird" (Adorno to Mann, June 3, 1945; *Thomas Mann/Adorno Briefwechsel*, 17).

27. "Das ist mein Mann" (*Entstehung*, XI: 172).

28. "Ich entdeckte in mir, oder fand in mir wieder als etwas längst Vertrautes eine unbedenkliche Bereitschaft zur Aneignung dessen, was ich als mein eigen empfinde, was zu mir, das heißt zur 'Sache' gehört" (*Entstehung*, XI: 174).

29. "Nach einem langen geistigen Wirken geschieht es sehr häufig, daß Dinge, die man voreinst in den Wind gesät, von neuerer Hand umgeprägt und in andere Zusammenhänge gestellt, zu einem zurückkehren und einen an sich selbst und das Eigene erinnern" (*Entstehung*, XI: 174).

30. Adorno, *Philosophy of Modern Music,* 29.

31. Ibid., 34.

32. Ibid., 5.

33. Adorno, *Minima Moralia,* 108 (aphorism 71).

34. Adorno, *Philosophy of Modern Music,* 41–42.

35. Adorno and Horkheimer, *Dialectic of Enlightenment,* 141.

36. Adorno, *Philosophy of Modern Music,* 112.

37. Adorno, *Minima Moralia,* 39; in the original German: *Minima Moralia,* 42 (aphorism 18).

38. Adorno, *Philosophy of Modern Music,* 42.

39. Ibid., 43.

40. Adorno, *Minima Moralia,* 27–28.

41. As Hohendahl rather blandly notes, Adorno "did not participate in the war effort" (*Prismatic Thought,* 28).

42. "Mag der Pessimismus Schopenhauers der Wahrheit näherkommen, nützlicher ist es, an den Optimismus zu glauben. . . . Als Philosophie ist der Optimismus nicht haltbar, aber als Ethik. Er ist nützlich" (Kurzke, *Thomas Mann: Epoche,* 272). See also Kristiansen, "Geschichtsfatalist."

43. "eine lebensnützliche Illusion. Ästhetisch ist [der Glaube] deshalb nach wie vor lächerlich" (Kurzke, *Thomas Mann: Epoche,* 272).

44. Mann's thoughts on the Faust theme are in a notebook dated 1901, but the entry itself dates from around 1904 (10.2: 12–13).

45. "Der syphilitische Künstler nähert sich von Sehnsucht getrieben einem reinen, süßen jungen Mädchen, betreibt die Verlobung mit der Ahnungslosen und erschießt sich dicht vor der Hochzeit" (10.2: 13).

46. "des teuren, vom Schicksal so furchtbar heimgesuchten, erhobenen und gestürzten Mannes und genialen Musikers" (10.1: 11).

47. "wann nur immer von der Macht der Dämonen über das Menschenleben darin die Rede war, [spielte] das Geschlechtliche eine hervorstechende Rolle" (10.1: 154).

48. "Der Gegenstand, das instrumentum des Versuchers, war das Weib" (10.1: 156).

49. "Domestizierung des Naturbösen, des Geschlechts" (10.1: 273).

50. "Als du mir einst gegeben / zur Nacht den kühlen Trank, / vergiftetest du mein Leben, / da war meine Seele so krank, so krank. / O lieb Mädel, wie schlecht bist du!" Clemens Brentano's poem "O lieb Mädel, wie schlecht bist du," is cited from 10.2: 1059.

51. Seidlin, "Doctor Faustus."

52. "auf den Besuch von Preßburg, ungarisch Pozsony genannt" (10.1: 225).

53. "einem ungrischen Weibe" (10.1: 158).

54. "seinen ungarischen Reisegefährten" (10.1: 629).

55. Tb, March 31, 1948. Mann routinely refers to the "oak meal" that he eats for breakfast (Jan. 1, 1941; Jan. 24, 1941; Mar. 20, 1941), an amusing reminder that his English was never as fluent as that of Erika or Klaus.

56. "die Stumpfnäsige neben ihm—Hetaera Esmeralda—gepuderte Halbkugeln im spanischen Mieder" (10.1: 217).

57. Trans. modified. "Wüstentöchter" (10.1: 217). The phrase suggests a link to Nietzsche's poem "Unter Töchtern der Wüste" in *Zarathustra;* Leverkühn's experience in the bordello in Leipzig is modeled on Nietzsche's biography (10.2: 410).

58. "Mandelaugen" (10.1: 578).

59. "The face with the black almond eyes" ("Das Gesicht . . . mit . . . den mandelförmigen, schwarzen Augen") (*Der Wille zum Glück,* 2.1: 55).

60. In the unpublished essay, "Zur jüdischen Frage," Mann recalled a Jewish boy among his classmates "named Fehér, Hungarian by birth, with exaggerated racial features to the point of ugliness" (*namens Fehér, Ungar von Geburt, einem Typus, prononciert bis zur Häßlichkeit*) (15.1: 428).

61. "beim ersten Auftauchen der Hetaera esmeralda im *Doktor Faustus* handelt es sich um einen wirklichen, südamerikanischen Schmetterling" (Bergsten, *Thomas Manns Doktor Faustus,* 63).

62. In preparation for writing *Doctor Faustus,* Mann consulted a series of articles by Dr. Martin Gumpert on the origins of syphilis. In a passage that Mann underlined in his copy of the text, Gumpert argues that syphilis was brought to Europe by sailors of Columbus returning from the New World. "Zum Streit um den Ursprung der Syphilis," in the Thomas Mann Archive, Signatur 4981; cited also in 10.2: 431.

63. "das Dämonische und Widervernünftige" (10.1: 13).

64. Translation modified; "magisch-fanatisch-negerhaftes Trommeln" (10.1: 542).

65. The reference to Adorno "Wie-sengrund" (10.1: 83) is lost in the literal English translation of "Wiesengrund" as "meadow-land" (58).

66. "Sein Vater war deutscher Jude" (XI: 172).

67. Darmaun, *Thomas Mann,* 288.

68. "die zarten Kleinen, das Volk der Lebeschräubchen, die lieben Gäste aus Westindien" (10.1: 338).

69. Oswald was the first to claim that Hetaera Esmeralda and Madame von Tolna are in fact the same character ("Thomas Mann's *Doktor Faustus,*" 252), a conclusion accepted by both Seidlin (*Doctor Faustus,* 600–601) and Reed (*Thomas Mann,* 391–92). One might protest that the evidence is at best circumstantial, but definitive proof is less important in Mann's symbolic universe than guilt by association. Whether or not Madame von Tolna really is Hetaera Esmeralda or not remains uncertain, but a suggestion has been made, a hint has been given, and that is enough.

70. "Zweideutigkeit als System" (10.1: 74).

71. "verständig-nüchternen modernen Stadt" (10.1: 58).

72. "unterzutauchen im Elementaren" (10.1: 175).

73. "Ja, wir sind ein gänzlich verschiedenes, dem Nüchtern-Üblichen widerspreches Volk . . . tragisch-heroische Seelenlage" (10.1: 254).

74. "das Seelische [ist] immer das Primäre und eigentlich Motivierende" (10.1: 447).

75. "Ich spreche vom Volk, aber die altertümlich-volkstümliche Schicht gibt es in uns allen . . . etwas Archaisch-Apprehensives . . . Rückständig-Bösen" (10.1: 59–60).

76. "Wo ich bin, da ist Kaisersaschern" (10.1: 330).

77. "in den Messe-Zeiten . . . aus allen Teilen Europas, dazu aus Persien, Armenien

und anderen asiatischen Ländern" (10.1: 204–5).

78. "sehen dich wohl mit exotischen Augen an und reden in Zungen, von denen du nie einen Laut gehört. War recht aufregend, und du fühltest den Puls der Welt dir im eigenen Leibe schlagen" (10.1: 208).

79. 10.2: 426–27. See also Vaget, *Seelenzauber*, 197, 226.

80. "einem nur unter den Nasenlöchern stehen gelassenen Schnurrbärtchen . . . später zum Attribut einer welthistorischen Maske werden sollte . . . mit Topfpflanzen, Zimmerlinden und Palmen" (10.1: 229–30).

81. "eine von ihrem Manne geschiedene rumänisch-siebenbürgische Schriftstellerin" (10.1: 559). In Mann's first draft she was identified as a "Schriftstellerin aus Budapest" (writer from Budapest) (10.2: 741).

82. "brünett, mit Ohrringen und schwarzen, in die Wangen sich biegenden Ringellöckchen, von spanisch-exotischem Einschlag" (10.1: 289).

83. "die sehr kunstreichen Handpuppen- und Schattenfiguren-Spiele der Javanen" (10.1: 466).

84. "Graphiker, Buchschmuck-Künstler und Sammler ostasiatischer Farbenholzschnitte und Keramik" (10.1: 525).

85. "mit reizenden chinesischen Malereien in Tusche und Farbe (aus der Sung-Zeit!)" (10.1: 526).

86. "ein neuer Durchbruch: derjenige zur dominierenden Weltmacht . . . erfüllt von der Gewißheit, daß Deutschlands säkulare Stunde geschlagen habe . . . daß nach Spanien, Frankreich, England wir an der Reihe seien, der Welt unseren Stempel aufzudrücken" (10.1: 439).

87. "Das Gefühl, daß eine Epoche sich endigte. . . . Kein Wunder . . . daß es in einem gestürzten Lande, wie Deutschland, entschiedener die Gemüter beherrschte, als bei den Siegervölkern, deren durchschnittlicher Seelenzusand, eben vermöge des Sieges, weit konservativer war" (10.1: 512–13).

88. "was von Weihnachten das Schönste gewesen sei . . . als Herr Papale bei Tisch einen Juden nachmachte!'" (Tb, Dec. 25, 1933).

89. On this concept see Sieg, *Ethnic Drag*.

90. "Größter Vortragserfolg seit dem Fitelberg-Kapitel, zahlreiche 'Vorhänge' . . . bei größter Aufmerksamkeit und Heiterkeit" (Tb, Sept. 24, 1951). See also Tb, July 2, 1947: "Die tief befriedigende Matinee im Schauspielhaus, wo ich Fitelberg . . . las. Beifallsdonner" (The deeply satisfying matinee at the Schauspielhaus [Zurich]. Thundering applause).

91. "Bedenken des Antisemitismus, / das ich nicht teilen kann" (Tb, Aug. 18, 1946).

92. Cited in *Tagebücher 1946–48*, 854.

93. "Dumm und harmlos" (Tb, Dec. 31, 1948).

94. Schwarz, "Die judischen Gestalten." See also Angress, "Jewish Characters," and Darmaun, *Thomas Mann*, 233–91.

95. Schwarz, "Die jüdischen Gestalten," 99; "Jews, yes, anti-Semites hardly or not at all" (Angress-Klüger, "Jewish Characters," 164). See also Wimmer, "*Doktor Faustus.*"

96. "die Tötung Lebensunfähiger und Schwachsinniger" (10.1: 537).

97. Angress-Klüger, "Jewish Characters," 162.

98. "obgleich man antisemitische Äußerungen von ihm hören konnte" (10.1: 248).

99. "die jüdischen Verlegersfrauen und Bankiersdamen, blickten mit der tiefge-fühlten Bewunderung ihrer Rasse für deutsches Herrenblut und lange Beine zu ihm auf und genossen es sehr, ihn zu beschenken" (10.1: 249).

100. "obgleich der Wind ihnen den Stank verbrannten Menschenfleisches von dorther in die Nasen blies" (10.1: 696).

101. "Gleicherweise sind sie verhaßt, verachtet, gefürchtet, beneidet. . . . Man spricht vom Zeitalter des Nationalismus. Aber in Wirklichkeit gibt es nur zwei Nationalismen, den deutschen und den jüdischen, und der aller anderen ist Kinderspiel dagegen" (10.1: 591).

102. "Deutsch, das heißt ja vor allem: volkstümlich . . . deutschen Charakter, qui est essentiellement anti-sémitique" (10.1: 589–90).

103. "sie werden sich . . . ins Unglück bringen, in ein wahrhaft jüdischen Unglück, je vous le jure" (10.1: 592).

104. Benjamin, *Illuminations*, 241; the original German phrase is "Ästhetisierung der Politik."

105. "von faszinierender Häßlichkeit, der hier, offenbar mit einem gewissen boshaften Vergnügen, die Rolle des fermentösen Fremdkörpers spielte" (10.1: 405).

106. "ein Kulturphilosoph, dessen Gesinnung aber insofern *gegen* die Kultur gerichtet war, als er in ihrer ganzen Geschichte nichts als einen Verfallsprozeß zu sehen vorgab" (10.1: 406).

107. Goldberg, *Die Wirklichkeit der Hebräer*, 15–16.

108. In his diary entry of July 15, 1934, Mann notes that Oskar Goldberg—together with several members of Stefan George's inner circle—was Jewish, and yet expressed ideas compatible with the state that persecuted him. Mann goes on to speculate that in their heart of hearts (*in tiefster Seele*) many Jews are in agreement "mit ihrer neuen Rolle als geduldete Gäste" (with their new role as tolerated guests) in Germany.

109. "seine witternde Fühlung mit der geistigen Bewegung der Zeit, seine Nase für ihre neuesten Willensmeinungen" (10.1: 406).

110. "jüdischen Geist . . . seine hellhörige Empfänglichkeit für das Kommende, Neue" (10.1: 414).

Chapter Eight

1. Tb, April 23 and 25, 1952.

2. Tb, May 12, 1952.

3. "Die Weltreise kommt mir doch wie Wahnsinn vor" (Tb, Apr. 30, 1952; Erika voiced her reservations on Apr. 25, 1952).

4. On the history of the novel's composition see Wysling, "Archivalisches Gewühle."

5. "Der homosexuelle Roman interessiert mich nicht zuletzt wegen der Welt- und Reise-Erfahrungen, die er bietet" (Tb, Nov. 25, 1950).

6. "Das Faustische des Stoffes. Das Insistieren Schillers bei Goethe, Faust müsse in die Welt geführt werden. Erweiterung des Schauplatzes nach Amerika" (Tb, Nov. 25, 1950).

7. Mann planned to model Krull's adventures in South America closely on the diaries of Hedwig Pringsheim, who traveled to Argentina in 1907–8 to visit her banished son Erik (Jens and Jens, *Auf der Suche*).

8. Mann, *Confessions of Felix Krull*, 242. Subsequent references to the English translation are included in the text; "die Südsee-Inseln und Japan, gefolgt von einer interessanten Seefahrt nach Ägypten, Konstantinopel, Griechenland, Italien und so weiter" (VII: 517). On Mann's plans for the continuation of the novel, see Wysling, "Thomas Manns Pläne."

9. Mann to Preetorius, 6 September 1954; *Briefe* 3: 356–57.

10. "der Gedanke an 'Papa' u. ein Gefühl für biographische Rundung" (Tb, Mar. 3, 1955).

11. "wenige Jahre nur nach der glorreichen Gründung des Deutschen Reiches" (VII: 266). In his notes for the novel, Mann identified Felix Krull's birth year as his own: 1875 (Wysling, "Thomas Manns Pläne," 150).

12. "bedrückt . . . von politischen Sorgen, die schon gleich nach seiner Thronbesteigung, vor sechs Jahren, durch den Konflikt der portugiesischen und englischen Interessen in Zentral-Afrika" (VII: 601).

13. "die reichste Stadt der Welt, dank jenen Entdeckungsfahrten" (VII: 531).

14. "im Lauf von zweitausend Jahren haben Phönizier, Karthager, Römer, Vandalen, Sueven und Westgoten, dazu besonders die Araber, die Mauren, mitgearbeitet, den Typ zu schaffen, der Sie erwartet—einen netten Zuschuß von Negerblut nicht zu vergessen" (VII: 532).

15. "Er hat einen Kostümkopf" (VII: 284).

16. "soldatisch, aber nicht als Soldat, figürlich, aber nicht wörtlich, daß im Gleichnis leben zu dürfen eigentlich Freiheit bedeute" (VII: 372).

17. "bei dem anziehenden Lärvchen, das die Natur mir vermacht, und einer allgemein gewinnenden Kondition, die durch armselige Kleidung . . . nicht unkenntlich gemacht werden konnte" (VII: 373).

18. "O Szenen der schönen Welt! Nie habt ihr euch empfänglicheren Augen dargeboten" (VII: 344).

19. "einer der verhärtesten Halsabschneider war, welche jemals bedrängte und unbedachte Geschäftsleute in ihre Netze gelockt haben" (VII: 319).

20. "die auf eindrucksvolle Weise überall aus ihrem mit Jett übersäten Kleide quoll" (VII: 277).

21. "obgleich ihm dieser schöne, begehrenswerte Titel von Amts wegen vielleicht nicht einmal zukam" (VII: 265).

22. On the unusual combination of a typically Jewish first name with a typically Swiss family name, see Elsaghe, *Thomas Mann*, 13–19.

23. "schlimme Liebesschule … wilde Blüte des Ostens … aus Ungarn gebürtig, doch ungewissester Herkunft" (VII: 382–85).

24. "slavisch geschnittenen Augen" (VII: 401).

25. "zweideutig exotisch" (VII: 454).

26. "mit goldenen Ringen in den Ohren, nackt bis zum Gürtel, in roten Pluderhosen und roter Mütze" (VII: 461).

27. "Da ich von je eine Schwäche für den angelsächsischen Typ gehegt habe und sie diesen sehr ausgeprägt darstellte" (VII: 475).

28. "die Musikhallen, die Spezialitätentheater … worin etwa ein riesiger Mohr … märchenhaft aufragt" (VII: 341).

29. "leicht aufgeworfenen Lippen unter einem gezwirbelten Schnurrbärtchen" (VII: 551).

30. "Geschwister offenbar, möglicherweise ein Zwillingspaar—sie sahen einander sehr ähnlich . . . Leicht überseeischen Ansehens, dunkelhäuptig, mochten sie spanisch-portugiesische Südamerikaner, Argentinier, Brasilianer—ich rate nur— sein; vielleicht aber auch Juden,—ich möchte mich nicht verbürgen und ließe mich nicht beirren, den luxuriös erzogene Kinder dieses Stammes können höchst anziehend sein" (VII: 345).

31. Wysling, "Thomas Manns Pläne," 151–55. Mann modeled the details about the Novaro family background on Hedwig Pringsheim's travel diary (Jens and Jens, Auf der Suche, 126).

32. "die vibrierende Neugier nach nie erfahrener Menschlichkeit" (VII: 557).

33. "diese Eindrücke, rassische Eindrücke etwa, die Erfahrung von Ur-Rasse, der die interessantesten Zuflüsse aus verschiedenen Zeitaltern beschieden waren und die dem Auge, dem Herzen das Bild majestätischer Blutswürde bietet . . ." (VII: 594).

34. "ein Landeskind … eine geborene da Cruz … erzportugiesisches Blut" (VII: 535).

35. "aus dem Pariserischen ins Iberisch-Exotische hinüberchrakterisiert" (VIII: 560).

36. "'Alt-iberisches Blut, mutmaßlich,' dachte ich bei mir selbst, 'also mit keltischem Einschlag. Und allerlei Phönizisches, Karthagisches, Römisches und Arabisches mag auch im Spiele sein'" (VII: 561).

37. "hehr vor Rasse" (VII: 627).

38. "etwas rein Blutmäßiges, ein Rassedünkel mit, der etwas Animalisches und gerade dadurch Erregendes hatte" (VII: 583).

39. "genügten ja auch die reizenden Schläfensträhnen ihres schwarzen Haares als ethnische Kennzeichnung" (VII: 648).

40. "die Rassekönigin mit dem wogenden Busen … abwechselnd mit der rasch sich auflösenden tier-menschlichen Schaugruppe, da die gestrenge und elementare Person dieser Frau mir mehr und mehr eins wurde mit dem Blutspiel dort unten" (VII: 654).

41. "Ein Wirbelsturm urtümlicher Kräfte … ins Reich der Wonne … stürmischer als beim iberischen Blutspiel" (VII: 661).

42. "Das Entspringen des Seins aus dem Nichts, die Erweckung des Lebens aus dem Sein und die Geburt des Menschen . . . rasch vorübergehende Episode . . . zwischen Nichts und Nichts" (VII: 542).

43. On the scene with Madame Houpflé as displaced homoeroticism see Reed, *Thomas Mann*, 429–30; also Lubich, *"The Confessions,"* 209–10.

44. "Deutschland wird Europa sein, wie alles höhere Deutschland immer Europa war. . . . Auch ist 'Europa' heute schon ein Provinzialismus" ("Deutschlands Weg nach Hitlers Sturz," *Essays* 5: 159).

45. Frido Mann has been particularly interested in underscoring the global connections of the extended Mann family ("Eine Familie zwischen den Kontinenten" and *Achterbahn*).

Works Cited

Thomas Mann: Primary Sources

Mann, Thomas. *Große kommentierte Frankfurter Ausgabe: Werke, Briefe, Tagebücher.* Ed. Heinrich Detering, Eckhard Heftrich, Hermann Kurzke, Terence J. Reed, Thomas Sprecher, Hans R. Vaget, and Ruprecht Wimmer. Frankfurt am Main: Fischer, 2002–.

1.1 *Buddenbrooks.*

1.2 *Buddenbrooks Kommentarband.* Ed. *Eckhard Heftrich and Stephan Stachorski with Herbert Lehnert.*

2.1 *Frühe Erzählungen 1893–1912.*

2.2 *Frühe Erzählungen Kommentarband.* Ed. Terence J. Reed with Malte Herwig.

4.1 *Königliche Hoheit.*

4.2 *Königliche Hoheit Kommentarband.* Ed. Heinrich Detering with Stephan Stachorski.

5.1 *Der Zauberberg.*

5.2 *Der Zauberberg Kommentarband.* Ed. Michael Neumann.

10.1 *Doktor Faustus.*

10.2 *Doktor Faustus Kommentarband.* Ed. Ruprecht Wimmer with Stephan Stachorski.

13.1 *Betrachtungen eines Unpolitischen.*

13.2 *Betrachtungen enes Unpolitischen Kommentarband.* Ed. Hermann Kurzke.

14.1 *Essays I: 1893–1914.*

14.2 *Essays I Kommentarband.* Ed. Heinrich Detering with Stephan Stachorski.

15.1 *Essays II: 1914–1926.*

15.2 *Essays II 1914–1926.* Ed. Hermann Kurzke with Jöelle Stoupy, Jörn Bender, and Stephan Stachorski.

21 *Briefe I: 1889–1913.* Ed. Thomas Sprecher, Hans R. Vaget, and Cornelia Bernini.

22 *Briefe II: 1914–1923.* Ed. Thomas Sprecher, Hans R. Vaget, and Cornelia Bernini.

Briefe. Ed. Erika Mann. 3 vols. Frankfurt am Main: Fischer, 1979.

Essays. Ed. Hermann Kurzke and Stephan Stachorski. 6 vols. Frankfurt am Main: Fischer, 1993–97.

Gesammelte Werke. 13 vols. Frankfurt am Main: Fischer, 1960–74.

Tagebücher. Ed. Peter de Mendelssohn and Inge Jens. 10 vols. Frankfurt am Main: Fischer, 1977–95.

Thomas Mann an Ernst Bertram: Briefe aus den Jahren 1910–1955. Pfullingen: Neske, 1960.

Thomas Mann Heinrich Mann Briefwechsel 1900–1949. Ed. Hans Wysling. Frankfurt am Main: Fischer, 1995.
Thomas Mann Theodor W. Adorno Briefwechsel 1943–1955. Ed. Christoph Göde. Frankfurt am Main: Fischer, 2003.

Translations

Buddenbrooks: The Decline of a Family. Trans. John E. Woods. New York: Knopf, 1993.
Confessions of Felix Krull, Confidence Man: The Early Years. Trans. Denver Lindley. New York: Knopf, 1955.
Death in Venice and Other Stories. Trans. David Luke. New York: Bantam, 1988.
Death in Venice and Seven Other Stories. Trans. H. T. Lowe-Porter. New York: Knopf, 1963.
Doctor Faustus: The Life of the German Composer Adrian Leverkühn as Told by a Friend. Trans. John E. Woods. New York: Knopf, 1997.
"Germany and the Germans." Trans. Frederick A. Lubich. *Thomas Mann: Death in Venice, Tonio Kröger, and Other Writers.* Ed. Frederick A. Lubich. New York: Continuum, 1999. 303–19.
Joseph and His Brothers. Trans. John E. Woods. New York: Knopf, 2005.
The Magic Mountain: A Novel. Trans. John E. Woods. New York: Knopf, 1995.
Reflections of a Nonpolitical Man. Trans. Walter D. Morris. New York: Ungar, 1983.
Royal Highness. Trans A. Cecil Curtis. Berkeley: University of California Press, 1992.
The Story of a Novel: The Genesis of Doctor Faustus. Trans. Richard and Clara Winston. New York: Knopf, 1961.

Secondary Literature

Abbott, Scott H. "*Der Zauberberg* and the German Romantic Novel." *Germanic Review* 55 (1980): 139–45.
Adorno, Theodor W. *Minima Moralia: Reflexionen aus dem beschädigten Leben.* Frankfurt am Main: Suhrkamp, 1951.
Adorno, Theodor W. *Minima Moralia: Reflections from Damaged Life.* Trans. E. F. N. Jephcott. London: NLB, 1974.
Adorno, Theodor W. *Philosophy of Modern Music.* Trans. Anne G. Mitchell and Wesley V. Blomster. New York: Seabury, 1973.
Adorno, Theodor W. "Zu einem Porträt Thomas Manns." *Noten zur Literatur,* vol. 3. Frankfurt am Main: Suhrkamp, 1965. 19–29.
Adorno, Theodor W., and Max Horkheimer. *Dialectic of Enlightenment.* Trans. John Cumming. New York: Continuum, 1972.
Anderson, Benedict. *Imagined Communities: Reflections on the Origin and Spread of Nationalism.* 2nd ed. London: Verso, 1991.
Anderson, Mark M. "'Jewish' Mimesis? Imitation and Assimilation in Thomas Mann's

'Wälsungenblut' and Ludwig Jacobowski's *Werther, der Jude.*" *German Life and Letters* 49 (1996): 193–204.

Anderson, Mark M. "Mann's Early Novellas." *The Cambridge Companion to Thomas Mann.* Ed. Ritchie Robertson. Cambridge: Cambridge University Press, 2002. 84–94.

Angress-Klüger, Ruth. "Jewish Characters in Thomas Mann's Fiction." *Horizonte: Festschrift für Herbert Lehnert zum 65. Geburtstag.* Ed. Hannelore Mundt, Egon Schwarz, and William J. Lillymann. Tübingen: Niemeyer, 1990. 161–72.

Arnold, Heinz Ludwig, ed. "Deutsche Schriftsteller über Thomas Mann." In *Text + Kritik: Sonderband Thomas Mann.* 1976; revised and expanded edition 1982. 195–237.

Applegate, Celia. *A Nation of Provincials: The German Idea of Heimat.* Berkeley: University of California Press, 1990.

Aschheim, Steven E. *Brothers and Strangers: The East European Jew in German and German Jewish Consciousness.* Madison: University of Wisconsin Press, 1982.

Aschheim, Steven E. *The Nietzsche Legacy in Germany 1890–1900.* Berkeley: University of California Press, 1992.

Assmann, Jan. *Thomas Mann und Ägypten: Mythos und Monotheismus in den Josephsromanen.* Munich: Beck, 2006.

Auerbach, Erich. "Figura." *Scenes from the Drama of European Literature: Six Essays.* Gloucester, MA: Meridian, 1973. 11–76.

Auerbach, Rena R., ed. *The "Jewish Question" in German-Speaking Countries, 1848–1914: A Bibliography.* New York: Garland, 1994.

Badenberg, Nana. "Spiel um Kamerun." *Mit Deutschland um die Welt: Eine Kulturgeschichte des Fremden in der Kolonialzeit.* Ed. Alexander Honold and Klaus R. Scherpe. Stuttgart: Metzler, 2004. 86–94.

Badenberg, Nana. "Usambara-Kaffee und Kamerun-Kakao im Kolonialwarenhandel." *Mit Deutschland um die Welt: Eine Kulturgeschichte des Fremden in der Kolonialzeit.* Ed. Alexander Honold and Klaus R. Scherpe. Stuttgart: Metzler, 2004. 94–105.

Badenberg, Nana. "Zwischen Kairo und Alt-Berlin." *Mit Deutschland um die Welt: Eine Kulturgeschichte des Fremden in der Kolonialzeit.* Ed. Alexander Honold and Klaus R. Scherpe. Stuttgart: Metzler, 2004. 190–99.

Barber, Benjamin R. *Jihad vs. McWorld: How Globalism and Tribalism Are Reshaping the World.* New York: Random House, 1995.

Barker, Andrew. "'Bloss aus Lemberg gebürtig': Detlev Spinell, The Austrian Jewish Aesthete in Thomas Mann's *Tristan.*" *Modern Language Review* 102 (2007): 440–50.

Belgum, Kirsten. *Popularizing the Nation: Audience, Representation, and the Production of Identity in Die Gartenlaube 1853–1900.* Lincoln: University of Nebraska Press, 1998.

Benjamin, Walter. *Illuminations: Essays and Reflections.* Ed. Hannah Arendt. Trans. Harry Zohn. New York: Schocken, 1968.

Bergsten, Gunilla. *Thomas Manns Doktor Faustus: Untersuchungen zu den Quellen und zur Struktur des Romans.* 2nd ed. Tübingen: Niemeyer, 1974.

Bertram, Ernst. *Nietzsche: Versuch einer Mythologie.* Berlin: Bondi, 1920.

Besser, Stephan. "Tropenkoller." *Mit Deutschland um die Welt: Eine Kulturgeschichte des Fremden in der Kolonialzeit.* Ed. Alexander Honold and Klaus R. Scherpe. Stuttgart: Metzler, 2004. 300–309.

Blackbourn, David, and Geoff Eley. *The Peculiarities of German History: Bourgeois Society and Politics in Nineteenth-Century Germany.* New York: Oxford University Press, 1984.

Bloch, Ernst. *Erbschaft dieser Zeit.* Rpt. Frankfurt am Main: Suhrkamp, 1962.

Blüher, Hans. *Deutsches Reich, Judentum und Sozialismus: Eine Rede an die Freideutsche Jugend.* Prien: Anthropos, 1920.

Blüher, Hans. *Die Rolle der Erotik in der männlichen Gesellschaft: Eine Theorie der menschlichen Staatsbildung nach Wesen und Wert.* Jena: Diedrichs, 1917–19.

Boa, Elizabeth. "Global Intimations: Cultural Geography in *Buddenbrooks, Tonio Kröger,* and *Der Tod in Venedig.*" *Oxford German Studies* 36 (2006): 21–33.

Böhm, Karl Werner. "Die homosexuellen Elemente in Thomas Manns *Zauberberg.*" *Stationen der Thomas-Mann-Forschung: Aufsätze seit 1970.* Ed. Hermann Kurzke. Würzburg: Königshausen and Neumann, 1985. 145–65.

Böhm, Karl Werner. *Zwischen Selbstzucht und Verlangen: Thomas Mann und das Stigma Homosexualität. Untersuchungen zu Frühwerk und Jugend.* Würzburg: Königshausen, 1991.

Borchmeyer, Dieter. "Politische Betrachtungen eines angeblich Unpolitischen: Thomas Mann, Edmund Burke und die Tradition des Konservatismus." *Thomas Mann Jahrbuch* 10 (1997): 83–104.

Boyarin, Daniel. *Unheroic Conduct: The Rise of Heterosexuality and the Invention of the Jewish Man.* Berkeley: University of California Press, 1997.

Breloer, Heinrich, director. *Die Manns: Ein Jahrhundertroman.* Film. 2001.

Brenner, Michael. "Beyond Naphta: Thomas Mann's Jews and German-Jewish Writing." *A Companion to Thomas Mann's* The Magic Mountain. Ed. Stephen D. Dowden. Columbia, SC: Camden, 1999. 141–57.

Breuer, Stefan. *Anatomie der konservativen Revolution.* Darmstadt: Wissenschaftliche Buchgesellschaft, 1993.

Breuer, Stefan. "Das 'Zwanzigste Jahrhundert' und die Brüder Mann." *Thomas Mann und das Judentum.* Ed. Manfred Dierks and Ruprecht Wimmer. Thomas Mann Studien 30. Frankfurt am Main: Klostermann, 2004. 75–95.

Browning, Christopher R. *Ordinary Men: Reserve Police Battalion 101 and the Final Solution in Poland.* New York: Harper, 1992.

Chakrabarty, Dipesh. *Provincializing Europe: Postcolonial Thought and Historical Difference.* Princeton: Princeton University Press, 2000.

Confino, Alon. *The Nation as a Local Metaphor: Württemberg, Imperial Germany, and National Memory, 1871–1918.* Chapel Hill: University of North Carolina Press, 1997.

Darmaun, Jacques. *Thomas Mann, Deutschland und die Juden.* Tübingen: Niemeyer, 2003.

Dedner, Burghard. "Über die Grenzen humoristischer Liberalität: Zu Thomas Manns Roman *Königliche Hoheit.*" *Wirkendes Wort* 24 (1974): 250–67.

Derrida, Jacques. *Dissemination.* Trans. Barbara Johnson. Chicago: University of Chicago Press, 1981.

Detering, Heinrich. *"Juden, Frauen und Litteraten": Zu einer Denkfigur beim jungen Thomas Mann.* Frankfurt am Main: Fischer, 2005.

Dierks, Manfred. "Kultursymbolik und Seelenlandschaft: 'Ägypten' als Projektion." *Thomas Mann Jahrbuch* 6 (1993): 113–31.

Dierks, Manfred. *Studien zu Mythos und Psychologie bei Thomas Mann: Am seinem Nachlaß orientierte Untersuchungen zum "Tod in Venedig", zum "Zauberberg" und zur "Joseph"-Tetralogie.* Bern: Francke, 1972.

Dierks, Manfred. "Thomas Mann und die 'jüdische' Psychoanalyse: Über Freud, C. G. Jung, das 'jüdische Unbewußte' und Manns Ambivalenz." *Thomas Mann und das Judentum.* Ed. Manfred Dierks and Ruprecht Wimmer. Thomas Mann Studien 30. Frankfurt am Main: Klostermann, 2004: 97–126.

Dierks, Manfred, and Ruprecht Wimmer, eds. *Thomas Mann und das Judentum.* Thomas Mann Studien 30. Frankfurt am Main: Klostermann, 2004.

Diersen, Inge. *Thomas Mann: Episches Werk, Weltanschauung, Leben.* Berlin: Aufbau, 1975.

Donahue, Neil H. "Introduction." *A Companion to the Literature of German Expressionism.* Ed. Neil H. Donahue. Rochester, NY: Camden, 2005.

Dörr, Hansjörg. "Thomas Mann and Adorno: Ein Beitrag zur Entstehung des *Doktor Faustus.*" *Literaturwissenschaftliches Jahrbuch,* n.s. 11 (1970): 285–322.

Eigen, Sara, and Mark Larrimore, eds. *The German Invention of Race.* Albany: State University of New York Press, 2006.

Eigen Figal, Sara. *Heredity, Race, and the Birth of the Modern.* New York: Routledge, 2008.

Elias, Norbert. *The Civilizing Process: The History of Manners and State Formation and Civilization.* Trans. Edmund Jephcott. 1939. Reprint, Oxford: Blackwell, 1994.

Elon, Amos. *The Pity of It All: A History of Jews in Germany, 1743–1933.* New York: Henry Holt, 2002.

Elsaghe, Yahya. *Die imaginäre Nation: Thomas Mann und das "Deutsche".* Munich: Fink, 2000.

Elsaghe, Yahya. "Naphta and His Ilk: Jewish Characters in Mann's *The Magic Mountain.*" *Thomas Mann's The Magic Mountain: A Casebook.* Ed. Hans Rudolf Vaget. New York: Oxford University Press, 2008. 171–199.

Elsaghe, Yahya. *Thomas Mann und die kleinen Unterschiede: Zur erzählerischen Imagination des Anderen.* Cologne: Böhlau, 2004.

Eze, Emmanuel Chukwudi, ed. *Race and the Enlightenment: A Reader.* Cambridge, MA: Blackwell, 1997.

Fechner, Frank. *Thomas Mann und die Demokratie: Wandel und Kontinuität der demokratierelevanten Äußerungen des Schriftstellers.* Berlin: Duncker and Humblot, 1990.

Fest, Joachim C. *Die unwissenden Magier: Über Thomas und Heinrich Mann.* Berlin: Siedler, 1985.

Fest, Joachim C. *Hitler.* Trans. Richard Winston and Clara Winston. San Diego: Harcourt Brace, 1974.

Fischer, Bernd. *Das Eigene und das Eigentliche: Klopstock, Herder, Fichte, Kleist. Episoden aus der Konstruktionsgeschichte nationaler Intentionalitäten.* Berlin: Schmidt, 1995.

Fischer, Fritz. *Germany's Aims in the First World War.* New York: Norton, 1967.

Forster, Georg. *Reise um die Welt.* Ed. Gerhard Steiner. Frankfurt am Main: Insel, 1967.

Freud, Sigmund. *Civilization and Its Discontents.* Trans. and ed. James Strachey. New York: Norton, 1961.

Freud, Sigmund. *Moses and Monotheism.* New York: Vintage, 1939.

Friedrichsmeyer, Sara, Sara Lennox, and Susanne Zantop, eds. *The Imperialist Imagination: German Colonialism and Its Legacy.* Ann Arbor: University of Michigan Press, 1998.

Frye, Northrop. *The Secular Scripture: A Study of the Structure of Romance.* Cambridge: Harvard University Press, 1976.

Fukuyama, Francis. *The End of History and the Last Man.* New York: Free Press, 1992.

Galvan, Elisabeth. *Zur Bachofen-Rezeption in Thomas Manns "Joseph"-Roman.* Frankfurt am Main: Klostermann, 1996.

Gay, Peter. *Weimar Culture: The Outsider as Insider.* New York: Harper & Row, 1970.

Geary, Patrick J. *The Myth of Nations: The Medieval Origins of Europe.* Princeton: Princeton University Press, 2002.

Gilman, Sander L. *Difference and Pathology: Stereotypes of Sexuality, Race, and Madness.* Ithaca: Cornell University Press, 1985.

Gilman, Sander L. *Franz Kafka: The Jewish Patient.* New York: Routledge, 1995.

Gilman, Sander L. *Jewish Self-Hatred: Anti-Semitism and the Hidden Language of the Jews.* Baltimore: Johns Hopkins University Press, 1986.

Girard, René. *Deceit, Desire, and the Novel: Self and Other in Literary Structure.* Trans. Yvonne Freccero. Baltimore: Johns Hopkins University Press, 1976.

Goethe, Johann Wolfgang. *Werke.* 14 vols. Hamburg: Wegner, 1953.

Gökberk, Ülker. "War as Mentor: Thomas Mann and Germanness." *A Companion to Thomas Mann's Magic Mountain.* Ed. Stephen D. Dowden. Rochester, NY: Camden House, 1999. 53–79.

Goldberg, Oskar. *Die Wirklichkeit der Hebräer: Einleitung in das System des Pentateuch.* Berlin: David, 1925.

Goldhagen, Daniel Jonah. *Hitler's Willing Executioners: Ordinary Germans and the Holocaust.* New York: Vintage, 1997.

Gombrich, Ernst Hans. *Art and Illusion: A Study in the Psychology of Pictorial Representation.* Princeton: Princeton University Press, 1969.

Görner, Rüdiger. *Thomas Mann: Der Zauber des Letzten.* Düsseldorf: Artemis & Winkler, 2005.

Gossman, Lionel. *Basel in the Age of Burckhardt: A Study in Unseasonable Ideas.* Chicago: University of Chicago Press, 2000.

Graichen, Gisela, and Horst Gründer. *Deutsche Kolonien: Traum und Trauma*. Berlin: Ullstein, 2005.

Grimm, Alfred. *Joseph und Echnaton: Thomas Mann und Ägypten*. Mainz am Rhein: Zabern, 1992.

Gut, Philipp. *Thomas Manns Idee einer deutschen Kultur*. Frankfurt am Main: Fischer, 2008.

Habermas, Jürgen. *The Structural Transformation of the Public Sphere: An Inquiry into a Category of Bourgeois Society*. Trans. Thomas Burger. Cambridge: MIT Press, 1991.

Hamburger, Käte. *Thomas Manns biblisches Werk: Der Joseph-Roman, die Moses-Erzählung "Das Gesetz"*. Munich: Nymphenburger, 1981.

Härle, Gerhard. *Männerweiblichkeit: Zur Homosexualität bei Klaus und Thomas Mann*. 2nd ed. Frankfurt am Main: Hain, 1993.

Harpprecht, Klaus. *Thomas Mann: Eine Biographie*. Reinbek bei Hamburg: Rowohlt, 1995.

Hatfield, Henry. *Thomas Mann*. Rev. ed. New York: New Directions, 1962.

Heftrich, Eckhard. *"Doktor Faustus:* Die radikale Autobiographie." *Thomas Mann 1875–1975*. Ed. Beatrix Bludau, Eckhard Heftrich, and Helmut Koopmann. Frankfurt am Main: Fischer, 1977. 135–54.

Heftrich, Eckhard. *Geträumte Taten: Joseph und seine Brüder*. Frankfurt am Main: Klostermann, 1993.

Heftrich, Eckhard. "Matriarchat und Patriarchat: Bachofen im Joseph-Roman." *Thomas Mann Jahrbuch* 6 (1993): 205–21.

Heftrich, Eckhard. "Potiphars Weib im Lichte von Wagner und Freud: Zu Mythos und Psychologie im *Josephs*roman." *Thomas Mann Jahrbuch* 4 (1991): 58–74.

Heilbut, Anthony. *Thomas Mann: Eros and Literature*. Berkeley: University of California Press, 1995.

Heimann, Bodo. "Thomas Manns *Doktor Faustus* und die Musikphilosophie Adornos." *Deutsche Vierteljahrsschrift* 38 (1964): 248–66.

Herf, Jeffrey. *Reactionary Modernism: Technology, Culture, and Politics in Weimar and the Third Reich*. Cambridge: Cambridge University Press, 1984.

Hesse, Hermann. *Demian*. Trans. Michael Roloff and Michael Lebeck. New York: Harper and Row, 1968.

Hewitt, Andrew. *Political Inversions: Homosexuality, Fascism, and the Modernist Imaginary*. Stanford: Stanford University Press, 1996.

Hitler, Adolf. *Mein Kampf*. Trans. Ralph Manheim. Boston: Houghton Mifflin, 1971.

Hobsbawm, E. J. "Introduction: Inventing Traditions." *The Invention of Tradition*. Ed. E. J. Hobsbawm and Terence Ranger. Cambridge: Cambridge University Press, 1983. 1–14.

Hohendahl, Peter Uwe. *Prismatic Thought: Theodor W. Adorno*. Lincoln: University of Nebraska Press, 1995.

Holub, Robert C. "Nietzsche's Colonialist Imagination: Nueva Germania, Good Europeanism, and Great Politics." *The Imperialist Imagination: German Colonialism and Its Legacy*. Ed. Sara Friedrichsmeyer, Sara Lennox, and Susanne Zantop. Ann Arbor: University of Michigan Press, 1998. 33–49.

Honold, Alexander, and Klaus R. Scherpe, eds. *Mit Deutschland um die Welt: Eine Kulturgeschichte des Fremden in der Kolonialzeit.* Stuttgart: Metzler, 2004.

Hornung, Erik. *Echnaton: Die Religion des Lichts.* Düsseldorf: Patmos, 2005.

Hornung, Erik. "Thomas Mann, Echnaton, und die Ägyptologen." *Thomas Mann Jahrbuch* 6 (1993): 59–70.

Hull, Isabel V. *Absolute Destruction: Military Culture and the Practices of War in Imperial Germany.* Ithaca: Cornell University Press, 2005.

Humboldt, Wilhelm von. *Ideen zu einem Versuch, die Grenzen der Wirksamkeit des Staates zu Bestimmen.* Stuttgart: Verlag Freies Geistesleben, 1962.

Hunt, Lynn. *The Family Romance of the French Revolution.* Berkeley: University of California Press, 1992.

Izenberg, Gerald N. *Modernism and Masculinity: Mann, Wedekind, Kandinsky through World War I.* Chicago: University of Chicago Press, 2000.

Jacobs, Jürgen. *Wilhelm Meister und seine Brüder: Untersuchungen zum deutschen Bildungsroman.* Munich: Fink, 1972.

Jens, Inge, and Walter Jens. *Auf der Suche nach dem verlorenen Sohn: Die Südamerika-Reise der Hedwig Pringsheim 1907/08.* Reinbek bei Hamburg: Rowohlt, 2006.

Jens, Inge, and Walter Jens. *Frau Thomas Mann: Das Leben der Katharina Pringsheim.* Reinbek bei Hamburg: Rowohlt, 2003.

Jeremias, Alfred. *Das Alte Testament im Lichte des Alten Orients.* Leipzig: Hinrichs, 1916.

Joch, Markus. "Koloniales in der Karikatur." *Mit Deutschland um die Welt: Eine Kulturgeschichte des Fremden in der Kolonialzeit.* Ed. Alexander Honold and Klaus R. Scherpe. Stuttgart: Metzler, 2004. 66–76.

Junge, Friedrich. "Thomas Manns fiktionale Welt Ägypten." *Thomas Mann Jahrbuch* 6 (1993): 37–57.

Jünger, Ernst. *Der Kampf als inneres Erlebnis.* 5th ed. Berlin: Mittler, 1936.

Jüngling, Kirsten, and Brigitte Rossbeck. *Katia Mann: Die Frau des Zauberers.* Berlin: Ullstein, 2004.

Khanna, Ranjana. *Dark Continents: Psychoanalysis and Colonialism.* Durham: Duke University Press, 2003.

Keller, Ernst. *Der unpolitische Deutsche: Eine Studie zu den* Betrachtungen eines Unpolitischen *von Thomas Mann.* Bern: Francke, 1965.

Koc, Richard. "Magical Enactments: Reflections on 'Highly Questionable' Matters in *Der Zauberberg.*" *Germanic Review* 68 (1993): 108–17.

Kontje, Todd. *German Orientalisms.* Ann Arbor: University of Michigan Press, 2004.

Koopmann, Helmut. "Der Untergang des Abendlandes und der Aufgang des Morgenlandes: Thomas Mann, die Josephsromane und Spengler." *Jahrbuch der deutschen Schillergesellschaft* 24 (1980): 300–31.

Koopmann, Helmut. *Der schwierige Deutsche: Studien zum Werk Thomas Manns.* Tübingen: Niemeyer, 1988.

Koopmann, Helmut, ed. *Thomas Mann Handbuch.* 3rd ed. Frankfurt am Main: Fischer, 2005.

Koselleck, Reinhart. *Kritik und Krise: Eine Studie zur Pathogenese der bürgerlichen Welt.* Frankfurt am Main: Suhrkamp, 1976.

Kristiansen, Børge. "Ägypten als symbolischer Raum der geistigen Problematik Thomas Manns: Überlegungen zur Dimension der Selbstkritik in *Joseph und seine Brüder.*" *Thomas Mann Jahrbuch* 6 (1993): 8–36.

Kristiansen, Børge. "Geschichtsfatalist mit schlechtem Gewissen: Thomas Mann und der Nationalsozialismus." *Thomas Mann Jahrbuch* 3 (1990): 95–117.

Kroll, Joe Paul. "Conservative at the Crossroads: 'Ironic' vs. 'Revolutionary' Conservatism in Thomas Mann's *Reflections of a Non-Political Man.*" *Journal of European Studies* 34 (2002): 225–46.

Krüll, Marianne. *Im Netz der Zauberer: Eine andere Geschichte der Familie Mann.* Frankfurt am Main: Fischer, 1993.

Kurzke, Hermann. *Auf der Suche nach der verlorenen Irrationalität: Thomas Mann und der Konservatismus.* Würzburg: Königshausen & Neumann, 1980.

Kurzke, Hermann. "Betrachtungen eines Unpolitischen." *Thomas Mann Handbuch.* Ed. Helmut Koopmann. 3rd ed. Frankfurt am Main: Fischer, 2005. 678–95.

Kurzke, Hermann. *Mondwanderungen: Wegweiser durch Thomas Manns Joseph-Roman.* Frankfurt am Main: Fischer, 1993.

Kurzke, Hermann. "Die Quellen der *Betrachtungen eines Unpolitischen:* Ein Zwischenbericht." *Thomas Mann Studien* 7 (1986): 291–310.

Kurzke, Hermann. *Thomas Mann: Epoche, Werk, Wirkung.* 3rd ed. Munich: Beck, 1997.

Kurzke, Hermann. *Thomas Mann: Life as a Work of Art: A Biography.* Trans. Leslie Willson. Princeton: Princeton University Press, 2002.

Lagarde, Paul de. *Deutsche Schriften.* 3rd ed. Göttingen: Dietrich, 1892.

Lämmert, Eberhard. "Doppelte Optik: über die Erzählkunst des frühen Thomas Mann." *Literatur Sprache Gesellschaft.* Ed. Karl Rüdinger. Deutsche Sprache und Literatur 111. Munich: Bayerischer Schulbuch, 1970. 50–72.

Landes, Joan B. *Women and the Public Sphere in the Age of the French Revolution.* Ithaca: Cornell University Press, 1988.

Langbehn, Julius. *Rembrandt als Erzieher: Von einem Deutschen.* 72–76th ed. Leipzig: Hirschfeld, 1922.

Lehnert, Herbert. "Ägypten im Bedeutungssystem des Josephromans." *Thomas Mann Jahrbuch* 6 (1993): 93–111.

Lehnert, Herbert. "Langemarck—historisch und symbolisch." *Orbis Litterarum* 42 (1987): 271–90.

Lehnert, Herbert. "Leo Naphta und sein Autor." *Orbis Litterarum* 37 (1982): 47–69.

Lehnert, Herbert. "Thomas Manns Josephstudien: 1927–1939." *Jahrbuch der deutschen Schillergesellschaft* 10 (1966): 378–406.

Lehnert, Herbert. "Thomas Manns Vorstudien zur Josephstetralogie." *Jahrbuch der deutschen Schillergesellschaft* 7 (1963): 458–520.

Le Rider, Jacques. *Modernity and the Crises of Identity: Culture and Society in Fin-de-Siècle Vienna.* Trans. Rosemary Morris. New York: Continuum, 1993.

Levesque, Paul. "The Double-Edged Sword: Anti-Semitism and Anti-Wagnerianism in Thomas Mann's *Wälsungenblut*." *German Studies Review* 20 (1997): 9–21.

Lincoln, Bruce. *Theorizing Myth: Narrative, Ideology, and Scholarship*. Chicago: University of Chicago Press, 1999.

Lindtke, Gustav. *Die Stadt der Buddenbrooks: Lübecker Bürgerkultur im 19. Jahrhundert*. Lübeck: Schmidt-Römhild, 1965.

Loewenstein, Kurt. "Thomas Mann zur jüdischen Frage." *Bulletin des Leo Baeck Instituts* 37 (1967): 1–59.

Lubich, Frederick A. "*The Confessions of Felix Krull, Confidence Man*." *The Cambridge Companion to Thomas Mann*. Ed. Ritchie Robertson. Cambridge: Cambridge University Press, 2002. 199–212.

Lubich, Frederick A. "Thomas Manns *Der Zauberberg*: Spukschloß der Großen Mutter oder Die Männerdämmerung des Abendlandes." *Deutsche Vierteljahrsschrift für Literaturwissenschaft und Geistesgeschichte* 67 (1993): 729–63.

Luft, David S. *Eros and Inwardness in Vienna: Weininger, Musil, Doderer*. Chicago: University of Chicago Press, 2003.

Lukács, Georg. *Thomas Mann*. Berlin: Aufbau, 1949.

Mann, Frido. *Achterbahn: Ein Lebensweg*. Reinbek bei Hamburg: Rowohlt, 2008.

Mann, Frido. *Brasa: Roman*. Munich: Nymphenburger, 1999.

Mann, Frido. "Eine Familie zwischen den Kontinenten: Entscheidung oder Schicksal?" *Julia Mann: Brasilien-Lübeck-München. Das Leben der Mutter der Brüder Mann*. Ed. Dieter Strauss and Maria A. Sene. Lübeck: Dräger, 1999. 135–41.

Mann, Heinrich. *Das Kind: Geschichten aus der Familie*. Ed. Kerstin Schneider. Frankfurt am Main: Fischer, 2001.

Mann, Heinrich. *Der Untertan*. Afterword by Wilfried F. Schoeller. Frankfurt am Main: Fischer, 2000.

Mann, Heinrich. *In einer Familie: Roman*. Afterword by Klaus Schröter. Frankfurt am Main: Fischer, 2000.

Mann, Heinrich. *Zwischen den Rassen: Roman*. Afterword by Elke Emrich. Frankfurt am Main: Fischer, 1987.

Mann, Julia. "Erinnerungen aus Dodos Kindheit." *Julia Mann: Ich spreche so gern mit meinen Kindern: Erinnerungen, Skizzen, Briefwechsel mit Heinrich Mann*. Ed. Rosemarie Eggert. Berlin: Aufbau, 1991. 7–49.

Mann, Katia. *Meine ungeschriebenen Memoiren*. Ed. Elisabeth Plessen and Michael Mann. Frankfurt am Main: Fischer, 2000.

Mann, Klaus. *Der Wendepunkt: Ein Lebensbericht*. Reinbek bei Hamburg: Rowohlt, 1984.

Mann, Klaus. *The Turning Point: Thirty-five Years of This Century*. Introduction by Shelley L. Frisch. New York: Wiener, 1984.

Mann, Viktor. *Wir waren fünf: Bildnis der Familie Mann*. Frankfurt am Main: Fischer, 1994.

Marquardt, Franka. *Erzählte Juden: Untersuchungen zu Thomas Manns Joseph und seine Brüder und Robert Musils Mann ohne Eigenschaften*. Münster: Lit, 2003.

Mayer, Hans. "Buch des Endes: Doktor Faustus." Hans Mayer. *Thomas Mann.* Frankfurt am Main: Suhrkamp, 1980. 270–327.

McAleer, Kevin. *Dueling: The Cult of Honor in Fin-de-Siècle Germany.* Princeton: Princeton University Press, 1994.

McClintock, Anne. *Imperial Leather: Race, Gender, and Sexuality in the Colonial Contest.* New York: Routledge, 1995.

Mendelssohn, Peter de. *Der Zauberer: Das Leben des deutschen Schriftstellers Thomas Mann.* 3 vols. Frankfurt am Main: Fischer, 1975–92.

Mendelssohn, Peter de. "Vorbemerkungen des Herausgebers," in Thomas Mann, *Tagebücher 1933–34.* Ed. Peter de Mendelssohn. Frankfurt am Main: Fischer, 1977. v–xxii.

Minden, Michael. *The German Bildungsroman: Incest and Inheritance.* Cambridge University Press, 1997.

Mohler, Armin. *Die konservative Revolution in Deutschland 1918–1932: Ein Handbuch.* 2nd ed. Darmstadt: Wissenschaftliche Buchgesellschaft, 1972.

Mosse, George L. *The Crisis of German Ideology: Intellectual Origins of the Third Reich.* New York: Schocken, 1964.

Mosse, George L. *The Image of Man: The Creation of Modern Masculinity.* New York: Oxford University Press, 1996.

Mosse, George L. *Nationalism and Sexuality: Respectability and Abnormal Sexuality in Modern Europe.* New York: H. Fertig, 1985.

Mosse, George L. *The Nationalization of the Masses: Political Symbolism and Mass Movements in Germany from the Napoleonic Wars through the Third Reich.* New York: Fertig, 1975.

Neumann, Michael. "Zwölftontechnik? Adrian Leverkühn zwischen Schönberg und Wagner." *Literaturwissenschaftliches Jahrbuch,* n.s. 43 (2002): 193–211.

Nicholls, Roger A. "Thomas Mann and Spengler." *German Quarterly* 58 (1985): 361–74.

Nietzsche, Friedrich. *Werke.* 3 vols. Ed. Karl Schlechta. Frankfurt am Main: Ullstein, 1976.

Norton, Robert E. *Secret Germany: Stefan George and His Circle.* Ithaca: Cornell University Press, 2002.

Noyes, John K. "Wo sind die Mütter?" *Mit Deutschland um die Welt: Eine Kulturgeschichte des Fremden in der Kolonialzeit.* Ed. Alexander Honold and Klaus R. Scherpe. Stuttgart: Metzler, 2004. 367–72.

Nunes, Maria Manuela. *Die Freimauerei: Untersuchungen zu einem literarischen Motiv bei Heinrich und Thomas Mann.* Bonn: Bouvier, 1992.

Oswald, Victor A., Jr. "Thomas Mann's *Doktor Faustus:* The Enigma of Frau von Tolna." *Germanic Review* 23 (1948): 249–53.

Penny, Glenn, and Matti Bunzl, eds. *Worldly Provincialism: German Anthropology in the Age of Empire.* Ann Arbor: University of Michigan Press, 2003.

Peterson, Brent O. *History, Fiction, and Germany: Writing the Nineteenth-Century Nation.* Detroit: Wayne State University Press, 2005.

Pinson, Koppel S. *Modern Germany: Its History and Civilization.* 2nd ed. New York: Macmillan, 1966.

Plessner, Helmuth. *Die verspaetete Nation: Über die politische Verführbarkeit bürgerlichen Geistes.* Stuttgart: Kohlhammer, 1962.

Poliakov, Léon. *The Aryan Myth: A History of Racist and Nationalist Ideas in Europe.* Trans. Edmund Howard. London: Chatto, 1974.

Pratt, Mary Louise. *Imperial Eyes: Travel Writing and Transculturation.* Routledge: London, 1992.

Pringsheim, Klaus. "Ein Nachtrag zu 'Wälsungenblut.'" *Betrachtungen und Überblicke: Zum Werk Thomas Manns.* Ed. Georg Wenzel. Berlin: Aufbau, 1966. 253–68.

Rahden, Till van. *Jews and Other Germans: Civil Society, Religious Diversity, and Urban Politics in Breslau 1860–1925.* Trans. Marcus Brainard. Madison: University of Wisconsin Press, 2008.

Reed, T. J. *Thomas Mann: The Uses of Tradition.* 2nd ed. Oxford: Clarendon, 1996.

Reich-Ranicki, Marcel. *Thomas Mann und die Seinen.* Stuttgart: Deutsche Verlags-Anstalt, 1987.

Robertson, Ritchie. *The "Jewish Question" in German Literature, 1749–1939: Emancipation and Its Discontents.* Oxford: Oxford University Press, 1999.

Roggenkamp, Viola. *Erika Mann: Eine jüdische Tochter: Über Erlesenes und Verleugnetes in der Familie Mann-Pringsheim.* Zurich: Arche, 2005.

Ruehl, Martin A. "Death in Florence: Thomas Mann and the Ideologies of *Renaissancismus* at the Fin de Siècle." *Germany at the Fin de Siècle: Culture, Politics, and Ideas.* Ed. Suzanne Marchand and David Lindenfeld. Baton Rouge: Louisiana State University Press, 2004. 186–223.

Ryan, Judith. "*Buddenbrooks:* Between Realism and Aestheticism." *The Cambridge Companion to Thomas Mann.* Ed. Ritchie Robertson. Cambridge: Cambridge University Press, 2002. 119–36.

Safranski, Rüdiger. *E. T. A. Hoffmann: Das Leben eines skeptischen Phantasten.* Munich: Hanser, 1984.

Said, Edward W. *Culture and Imperialism.* New York: Knopf, 1993.

Said, Edward W. *Orientalism.* New York: Vintage, 1979.

Sauerland, Karol. "'Er wußte noch mehr . . .'. Zum Konzeptionsbruch in Thomas Manns *Doktor Faustus* unter dem Einfluß Adornos." *Orbis Litterarum* 34 (1979): 130–45.

Scharfschwerdt, Jürgen. *Thomas Mann und der deutsche Bildungsroman: Eine Untersuchung zu den Problemen einer literarischen Tradition.* Stuttgart: Kohlhammer, 1967.

Scherpe, Klaus R. "Die Mobilmachung des Fremden." *Mit Deutschland um die Welt: Eine Kulturgeschichte des Fremden in der Kolonialzeit.* Ed. Alexander Honold and Klaus R. Scherpe. Stuttgart: Metzler, 2004. 449–56.

Scherpe, Klaus R. "Massaker und Maskerade." *Mit Deutschland um die Welt: Eine Kulturgeschichte des Fremden in der Kolonialzeit.* Ed. Alexander Honold and Klaus R. Scherpe. Stuttgart: Metzler, 2004. 77–85.

Schwarz, Egon. "Die jüdischen Gestalten in *Doktor Faustus.*" *Zur Modernität von Thomas Manns Doktor Faustus.* Ed. Herbert Lehnert and Peter Pfeiffer. Frankfurt am Main: Klostermann, 1989. 79–101.

Schwarz, Thomas. "Bastards." *Mit Deutschland um die Welt: Eine Kulturgeschichte des Fremden in der Kolonialzeit.* Ed. Alexander Honold and Klaus R. Scherpe. Stuttgart: Metzler, 2004. 373–380.

Schwerte, Hans. *Faust und das Faustische: Ein Kapitel deutscher Ideologie.* Stuttgart: Klett, 1962.

Sedgwick, Eve Kosofsky. *Between Men: English Literature and Male Homosocial Desire.* New York: Columbia University Press, 1985.

Seidlin, Oskar. "*Doctor Faustus:* The Hungarian Connection." *German Quarterly* 56 (1983): 594–607.

Seidlin, Oskar. "Thomas Mann und die Demokratie." *German Quarterly* 16 (1943): 117–23.

Sene, Maria A. "Johann Ludwig Hermann Bruhns." *Julia Mann: Brasilien-Lübeck-München. Das Leben der Mutter der Brüder Mann.* Ed. Dieter Strauss and Maria A. Sene. Lübeck: Dräger, 1999. 101–11.

Sieg, Katrin. *Ethnic Drag: Performing Race, Nation, Sexuality in West Germany.* Ann Arbor: University of Michigan Press, 2002.

Sombart, Nicolaus. *Die deutschen Männer und ihre Feinde: Carl Schmitt—ein deutsches Schicksal zwischen Männerbund und Matriarchatsmythos.* Frankfurt am Main: Fischer, 1997.

Sontag, Susan. "Fascinating Fascism." *Under the Sign of Saturn.* New York: Farrar, Straus Giroux, 1972. 71–105.

Sontheimer, Kurt. *Thomas Mann und die Deutschen.* Frankfurt am Main: Fischer, 1961.

Spengler, Oswald. *Preußentum und Sozialismus.* Munich: Beck, 1920.

Steinecke, Hartmut. *Romantheorie und Romankritik in Deutschland: Die Entwicklung des Gattungsverständnisses von der Scott-Rezeption bis zum programmatischen Realismus.* 2 vols. Stuttgart: Metzler, 1975–76.

Stern, Fritz. *The Politics of Cultural Despair: A Study in the Rise of the Germanic Ideology.* Berkeley: University of California Press, 1961.

Stern, Guy. "Thomas Mann und die jüdische Welt." *Thomas Mann Handbuch.* Ed. Helmut Koopmann. 3rd ed. Frankfurt am Main: Fischer, 2001. 54–67.

Swales, Martin. *Buddenbrooks: Family Life as the Mirror of Social Change.* Boston: Twayne, 1991.

Thalmann, Marianne. *Der Trivialroman des 18. Jahrhunderts und der romantische Roman: Ein Beitrag zur Entwicklungsgeschichte der Geheimbundmystik.* Rpt. Nendeln, Liechtenstein: Kraus, 1978.

Theweleit, Klaus. *Male Fantasies.* 1977–78. Trans. Erica Carter, Stephen Conway, and Chris Turner. 2 vols. Minneapolis: University of Minnesota Press, 1987–89.

Tobin, Robert D. "Making Way for the Third Sex: Liberal and Antiliberal Impulses in Mann's Portrayal of Male-Male Desire in His Early Short Fiction." *A Companion to German Realism.* Ed. Todd Kontje. Rochester, NY: Camden House, 2002. 307–38.

Tobin, Robert D. *Warm Brothers: Queer Theory in the Age of Goethe.* Philadelphia: University of Pennsylvania Press, 2000.

Uerlings, Herbert. *Friedrich von Hardenberg, genannt Novalis: Werk und Forschung.* Stuttgart: Metzler, 1991.

Vaget, Hans Rudolf. "The Discreet Charm of the Hanseatic Bourgeoisie: Geography, History, and Psychology in Thomas Mann's Representations of Hamburg." *Patriotism, Cosmopolitanism, and National Culture: Public Culture in Hamburg 1700–1933.* Ed. Peter Uwe Hohendahl. Amsterdam: Rodopi, 2003. 193–205.

Vaget, Hans Rudolf. "The Making of *The Magic Mountain.*" *Thomas Mann's The Magic Mountain: A Casebook.* Ed. Hans Rudolf Vaget. New York: Oxford University Press, 2008. 13–30.

Vaget, Hans Rudolf. "'Politically Suspect': Music on the Magic Mountain." *Thomas Mann's The Magic Mountain: A Casebook.* Ed. Hans Rudolft Vaget. New York: Oxford University Press, 2008. 123–41.

Vaget, Hans Rudolf. "*Sang réservé* in Deutschland: Zur Rezeption von Thomas Manns *Wälsungenblut.*" *German Quarterly* 57 (1984): 367–76.

Vaget, Hans Rudolf. *Seelenzauber: Thomas Mann und die Musik.* Frankfurt am Main: Fischer, 2006.

Vaget, Hans Rudolf. "Thomas Mann, Schiller, and the Politics of Literary Self-Fashioning." *Monatshefte* 97 (2005): 494–510.

Vaget, Hans Rudolf. *Thomas Mann-Kommentar zu sämtlichen Erzählungen.* Munich: Winkler, 1984.

Vaget, Hans Rudolf. "'Von hoffnungslos anderer Art.' Thomas Manns *Wälsungenblut* im Lichte unserer Erfahrung." *Thomas Mann und das Judentum.* Ed. Manfred Dierks and Ruprecht Wimmer. *Thomas Mann Studien* 30. Frankfurt am Main: Klostermann, 2004: 35–57.

Vogt, Jochen. *Thomas Mann: Buddenbrooks.* Munich: Fink, 1983.

Wahrig, Gerhard. *Deutsches Wörterbuch.* 7th ed. Ed. Renate Wahrig-Burfeind. Munich: Wissen Media Verlag, 2005.

Wagener, Hans. "Thomas Mann in der amerikanischen Literaturkritik." *Thomas Mann Handbuch.* 3rd ed. Ed. Helmut Koopmann. Frankfurt am Main: Fischer, 2005. 925–40.

Wehler, Hans-Ulrich. *Bismarck und der Imperialismus.* Cologne: Kiepenhauer & Witsch, 1969.

Wehler, Hans-Ulrich. *The German Empire, 1871–1918.* 1973. Trans. Kim Traynor. Oxford: Berg, 1985.

Weigall, Arthur. *The Life and Times of Akhnaton: Pharaoh of Egypt.* 2nd ed. London: Thornton Butterworth, 1922.

Weigand, Hermann J. "Die symbolisch-autobiographische Gehalt von Thomas Manns Romandichtung *Königliche Hoheit.*" *PMLA* 46 (1931): 867–79.

Weigand, Hermann J. *Thomas Mann's Novel "Der Zauberberg": A Study.* New York: Appleton-Century, 1933.

Weiner, Marc A. *Richard Wagner and the Anti-Semitic Imagination.* Lincoln: University of Nebraska Press, 1995.

Weininger, Otto. *Sex and Character.* Trans. Anon. New York: Fertig, 2003.

Weisinger, Kenneth. "Distant Oil Rigs and Other Erections." *A Companion to Thomas Mann's The Magic Mountain,* ed. Stephen D. Dowden, 177–220. Columbia, SC: Camden House, 1999.

Wichtl, Friedrich. *Weltfreimaurerei Weltrevolution Weltrepublik: Eine Untersuchung über Ursprung und Endziele des Weltkrieges.* Munich: Lehmann, 1919.

Wichtl, Friedrich. *Weltfreimaurerei Weltrevolution Weltrepublik: Eine Untersuchung über Ursprung, Verlauf und Fortsetzung des Weltkrieges und über das Wirken des Freimaurerbundes in der Gegenwart.* 13th ed. Ed. Robert Schneider. Munich: Lehmann, 1936.

Williamson, George S. *The Longing for Myth in Germany: Religion and Aesthetic Culture from Romanticism to Nietzsche.* Chicago: University of Chicago Press, 2004.

Wimmer, Ruprecht. "*Doktor Faustus* und die Juden." *Thomas Mann Studies* 30 (2004): 149–62.

Wolf, Ernest M. "Hagenströms: The Rival Family in Thomas Mann's *Buddenbrooks.*" *German Studies Review* 5 (1982): 35–55.

Wysling, Hans. "Archivalisches Gewühle: Zur Entstehungsgeschichte der *Bekenntnisse des Hochstaplers Felix Krull.*" Thomas-Mann-Studien 1. Munich: Francke, 1967. 234–57.

Wysling, Hans. "'Geist und Kunst.' Thomas Manns Notizen zu einem 'Literatur-Essay': Ediert und kommentiert von Hans Wysling." *Thomas Mann Studien* 1 (1967): 123–233.

Wysling, Hans. "Thomas Manns Pläne zur Fortsetzung des *Krull.*" *Thomas-Mann-Studien* 3. Munich: Francke, 1974. 149–66.

Zantop, Susanne. *Colonial Fantasies: Conquest, Family, and Nation in Precolonial Germany, 1770–1870.* Durham: Duke University Press, 1997.

Zeller, Michael. *Bürger oder Bourgeois? Eine literatursoziologische Studie zu Thomas Manns* Buddenbrooks *and Heinrich Manns* Im Schlaraffenland. Stuttgart: Klett, 1976.

Ziolkowski, Theodore. *German Romanticism and Its Institutions.* Princeton: Princeton University Press, 1990.

Index

Abbott, Scott H., 214n91
Adorno, Theodor, 16, 97, 157–60, 163–64, 172, 191n111, 227n23, 229n65
    Minima Moralia, 159
    Philosophy of Modern Music, The, 158–60
Anderson, Mark M., 200n52
Angress-Klüger, Ruth, 120, 169, 187n38, 190n108
Applegate, Celia, 20
Arndt, Ernst Moritz, 121
Aschheim, Steven E., 101, 191n129
Assmann, Jan, 218n26
Auerbach, Philipp, 11–12

Bachofen, Johann Jacob, 20–21, 79, 121, 123
Baeumler, Alfred, 121, 123
Bartels, Adolf, 73, 207n60
Bates, Henry Walter, 163
Bauer, Bruno, 193n166
Bebel, August, 68
Beethoven, Ludwig van, 153, 156, 158
Benjamin, Walter, 171
Benn, Gottfried, 8
Berger, Elmer, 6
Bergsten, Gunilla, 163
Bertram, Ernst, 8, 17, 65–66, 83, 109, 119
    Nietzsche: Attempt at a Mythology, 101
Besser, Stephan, 196n42
Bismarck, Otto von, 3, 21, 24, 31, 69, 78
Bizet, Georges
    Carmen, 95, 212n38
Blake, William, 162
Bloch, Ernst, 195n24
Blüher, Hans, 103, 106
    "The German Reich, Jewry, and Socialism," 102
    Role of Eroticism in Male Society, The, 102
Boa, Elizabeth, 194n5, 199n40
Böhm, Karl Werner, 211n27, 212n37
Borchmeyer, Dieter, 204n8
Boyarin, Daniel, 194n178

Brentano, Bernard von, 12
Brentano, Clemens, 162
Brod, Max, 16
Browning, Christopher R., 190n105
Bruhns, Johann Ludwig Hermann (maternal grandfather), 2–5, 186n13
Bruhns, Maria, née da Silva (maternal grandmother), 2–4
Bülow, Frieda von, 6
Burckhardt, Jacob, 20–21, 68

Campbell, Joseph, 219n55
    Hero with a Thousand Faces, 127
Carlebach, Ephraim, 6
Chakrabarty, Dipesh, 44, 204n19
Chamberlain, Houston Stewart, 22, 71, 75, 151
Chamberlain, Neville, 148
Columbus, Christopher, 163
Confino, Alon, 20
Conrad, Joseph, 6
Cook, James, 22

Dahn, Felix, 19
Dante, 86
Darmaun, Jacques, 122, 151, 164, 187n38, 206n51
Darwin, Charles, 23
Dedner, Burghard, 201n78
Derrida, Jacques, 47
Detering, Heinrich, 14, 64, 202n83, 207n70
Dierks, Manfred, 218n34, 219n45, 219n55
Dietrich, Marlene, 158, 227n24
Döblin, Alfred, 12
Dohm, Hedwig, 46
Donahue, Neil H., 204n21
Dostoyevsky, Fyodor, 71, 93
Droysen, Johann Gustav, 20
Dürer, Albrecht, 101

Ehrenberg, Paul, 45, 161
Einstein, Albert, 8